Fushigi Yûgi
BYAKKO SENKI

D0802884

[THE UNIVERSE OF THE FOUR GODS]

In Chinese tradition, Seiryu, Byakko, Suzaku and Genbu are the four gods who guard the four cardinal points: east, west, south and north, respectively. They divide the 28 heavenly constellations into four houses, with each god ruling over seven constellations.

1

STORY + ART *Yuu Watase*

CONTENTS

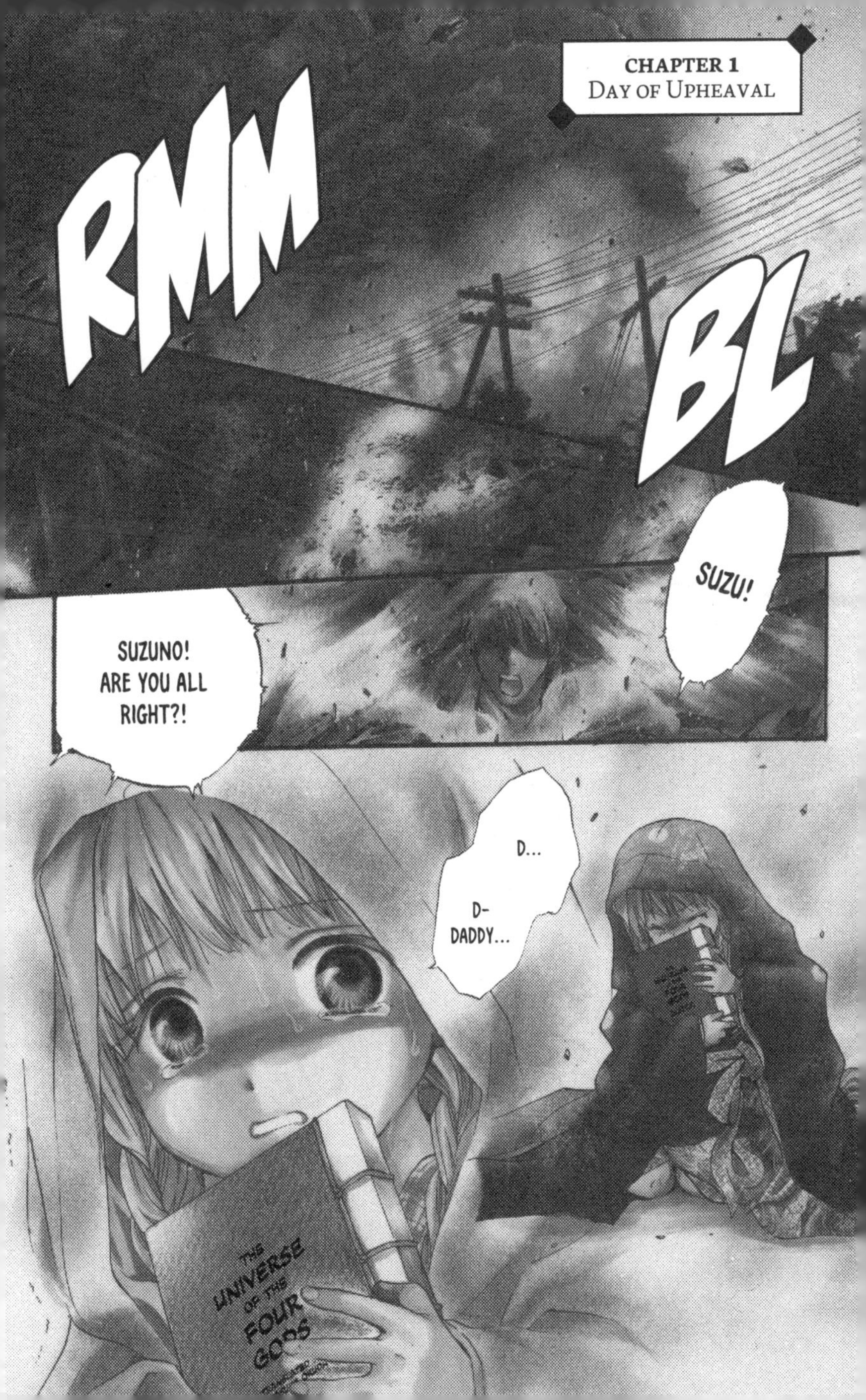
CHAPTER 1
DAY OF UPHEAVAL
RMM
BL
SUZU!
SUZUNO! ARE YOU ALL RIGHT?!
D...
D- DADDY...
THE UNIVERSE OF THE FOUR GODS

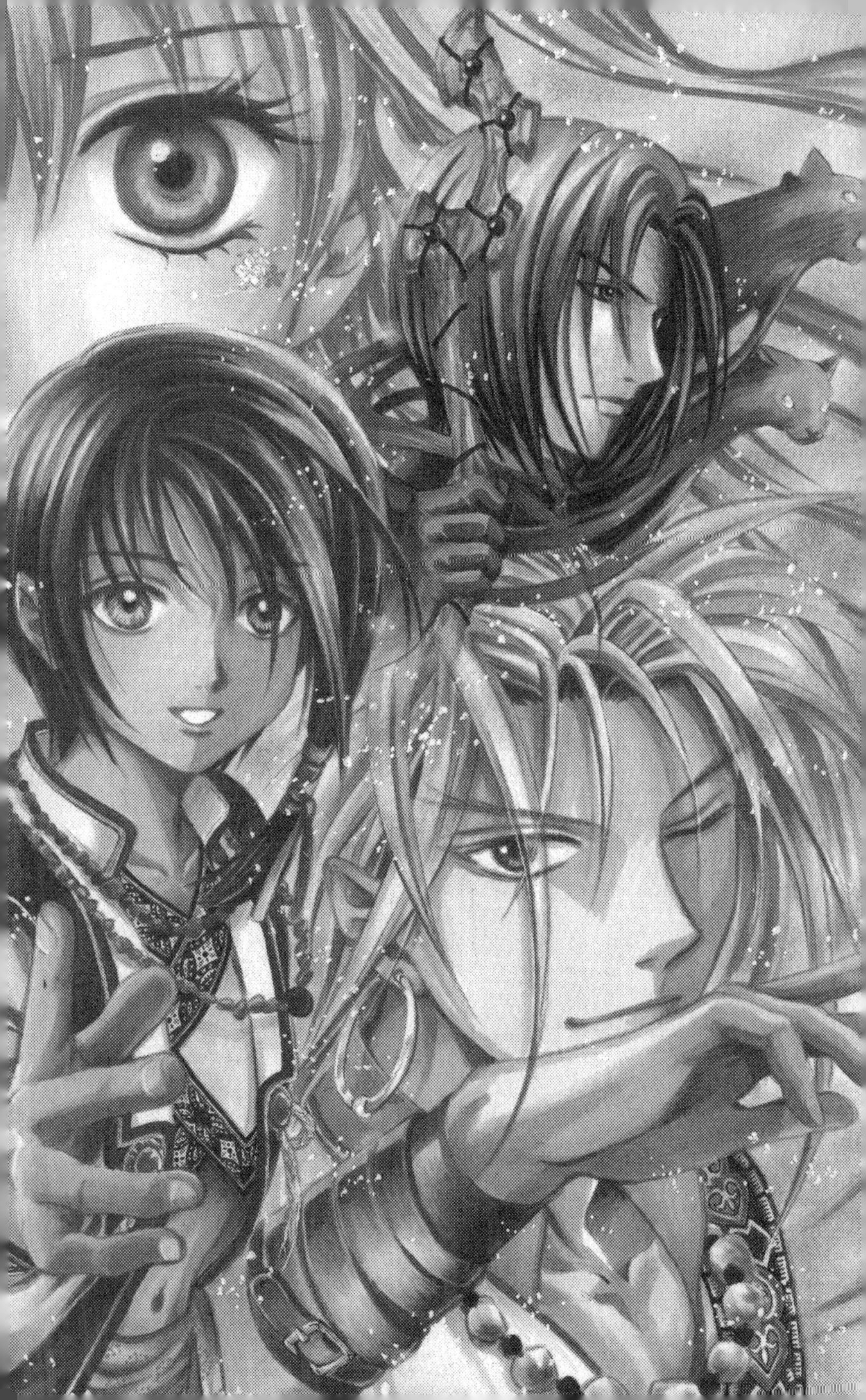

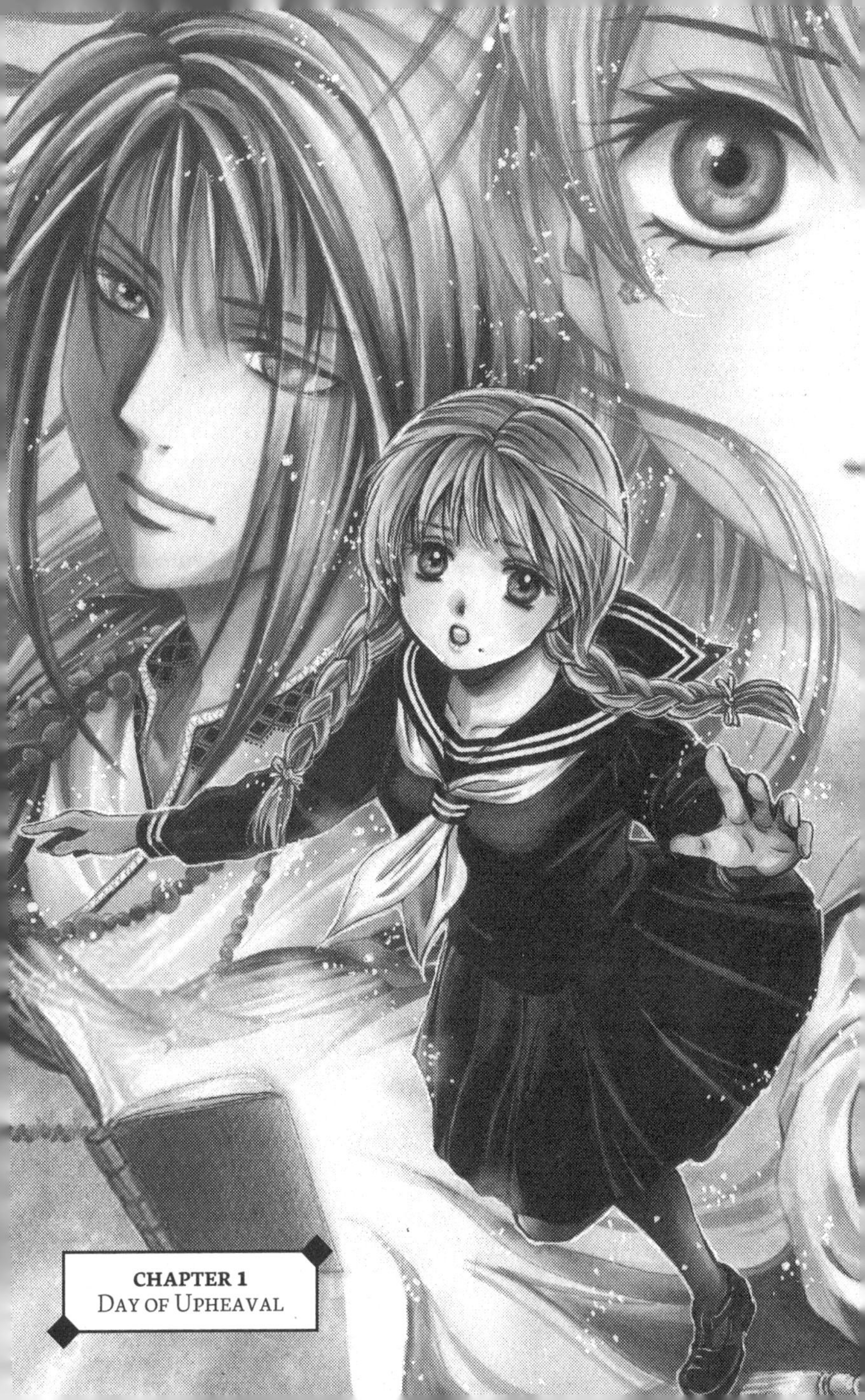

CHAPTER 1
Day of Upheaval

Fushigi Yûgi
BYAKKO SENKI

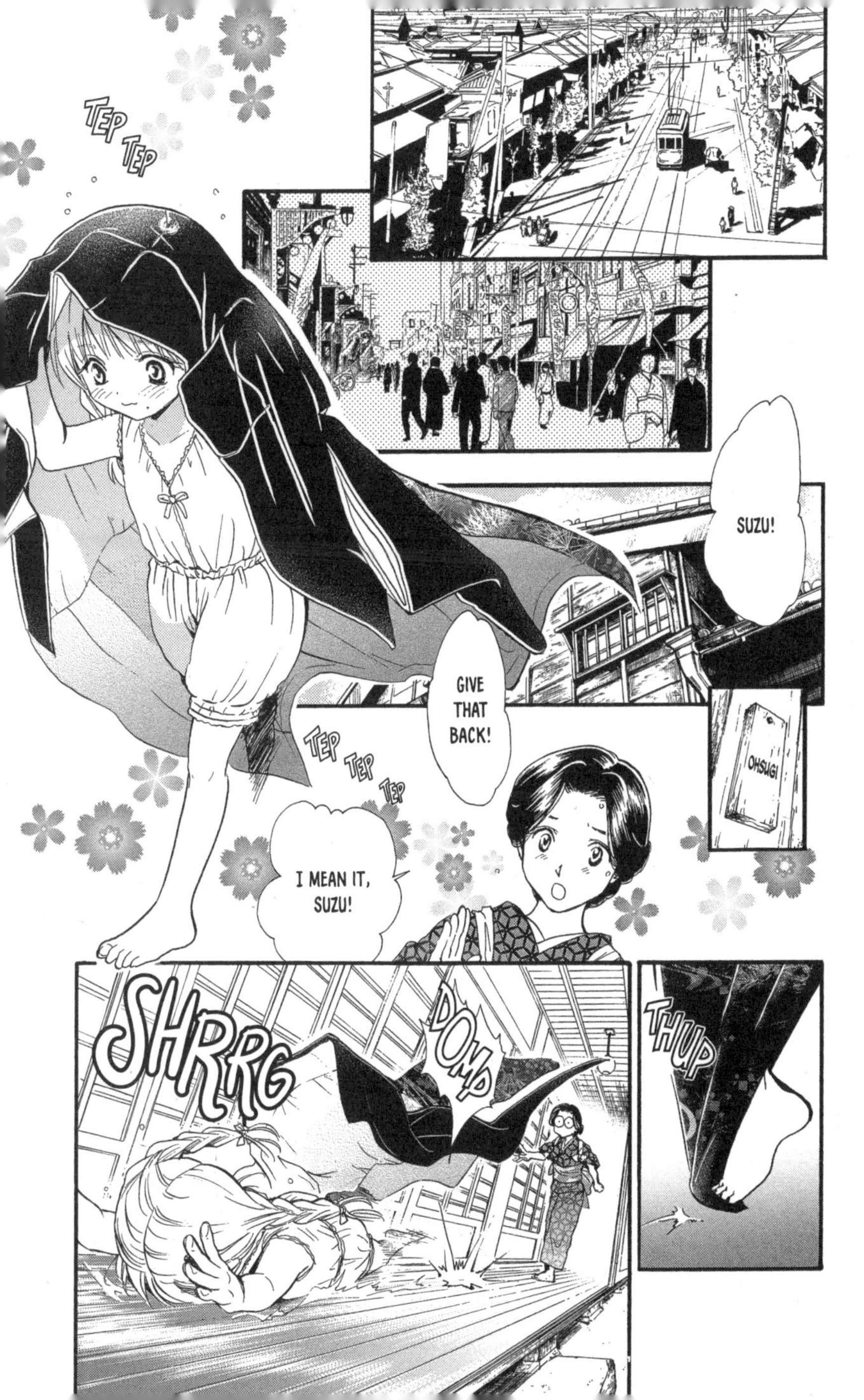
TEP TEP
SUZU!
OHSUGI
GIVE THAT BACK!
TEP TEP TEP
I MEAN IT, SUZU!
THUP
SHRRG
DOMP

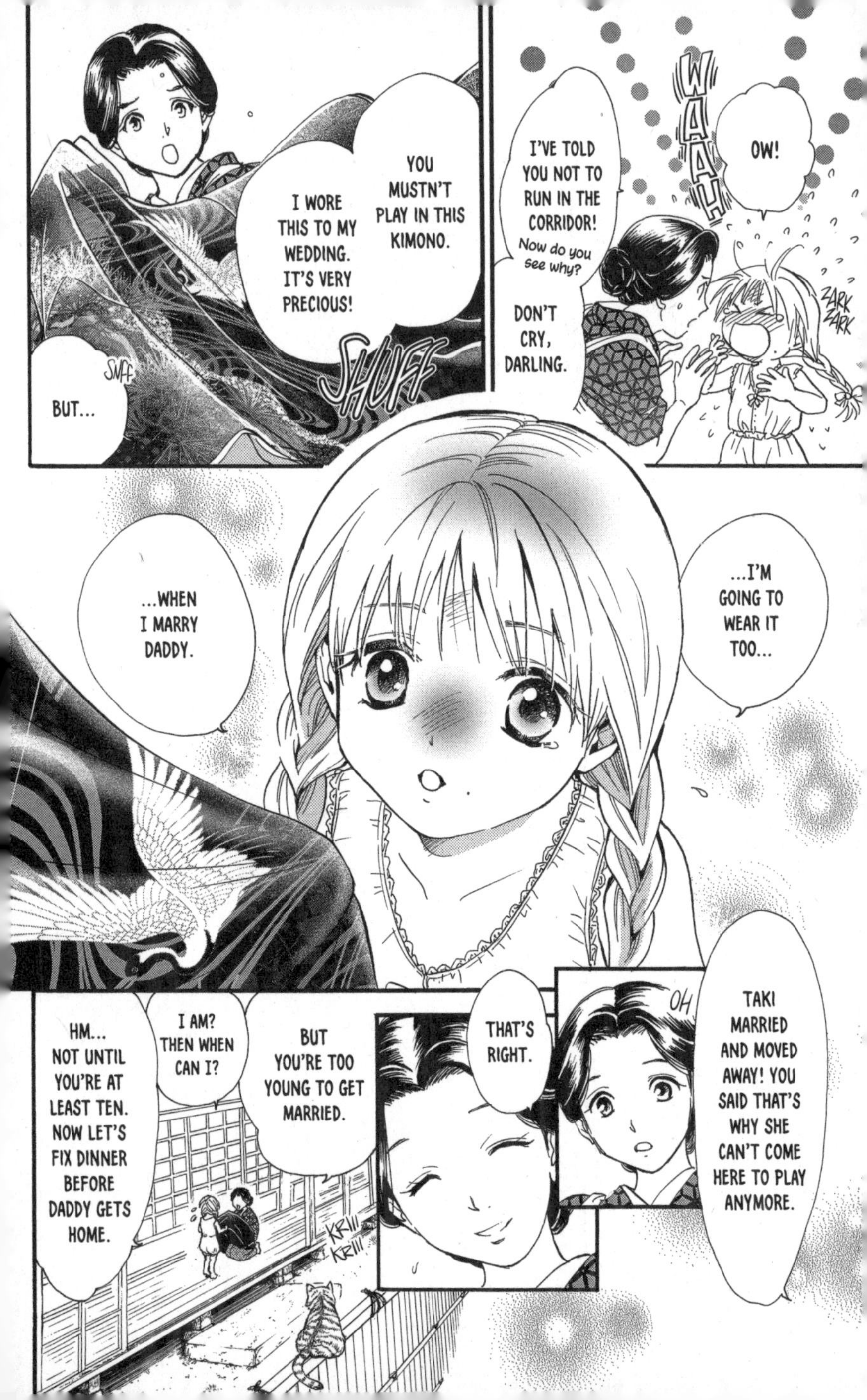
OW!
WAAAH
ZARK ZARK
I'VE TOLD YOU NOT TO RUN IN THE CORRIDOR! Now do you see why?
DON'T CRY, DARLING.
YOU MUSTN'T PLAY IN THIS KIMONO.
I WORE THIS TO MY WEDDING. IT'S VERY PRECIOUS!
SHUFF
SNFF
BUT...
...I'M GOING TO WEAR IT TOO...
...WHEN I MARRY DADDY.
OH
TAKI MARRIED AND MOVED AWAY! YOU SAID THAT'S WHY SHE CAN'T COME HERE TO PLAY ANYMORE.
THAT'S RIGHT.
BUT YOU'RE TOO YOUNG TO GET MARRIED.
I AM? THEN WHEN CAN I?
HM... NOT UNTIL YOU'RE AT LEAST TEN. NOW LET'S FIX DINNER BEFORE DADDY GETS HOME.
KRIII KRIII

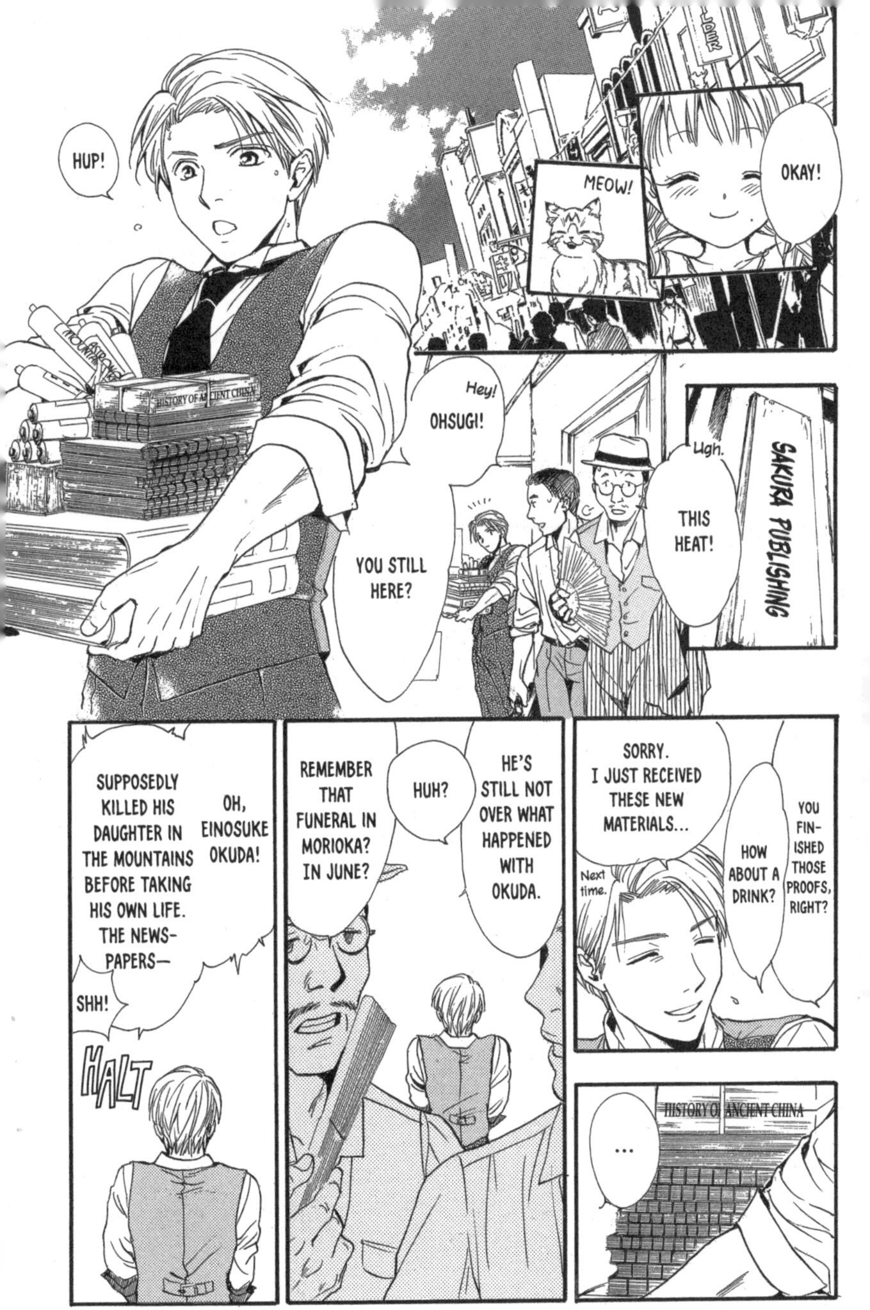
OKAY!
MEOW!
SAKURA PUBLISHING
Ugh.
THIS HEAT!
Hey!
OHSUGI!
YOU STILL HERE?
HUP!
HISTORY OF ANCIENT CHINA
YOU FINISHED THOSE PROOFS, RIGHT?
HOW ABOUT A DRINK?
SORRY. I JUST RECEIVED THESE NEW MATERIALS...
Next time.
HISTORY OF ANCIENT CHINA
...
HE'S STILL NOT OVER WHAT HAPPENED WITH OKUDA.
HUH?
REMEMBER THAT FUNERAL IN MORIOKA? IN JUNE?
OH, EINOSUKE OKUDA!
SUPPOSEDLY KILLED HIS DAUGHTER IN THE MOUNTAINS BEFORE TAKING HIS OWN LIFE. THE NEWSPAPERS—
SHH!
HALT

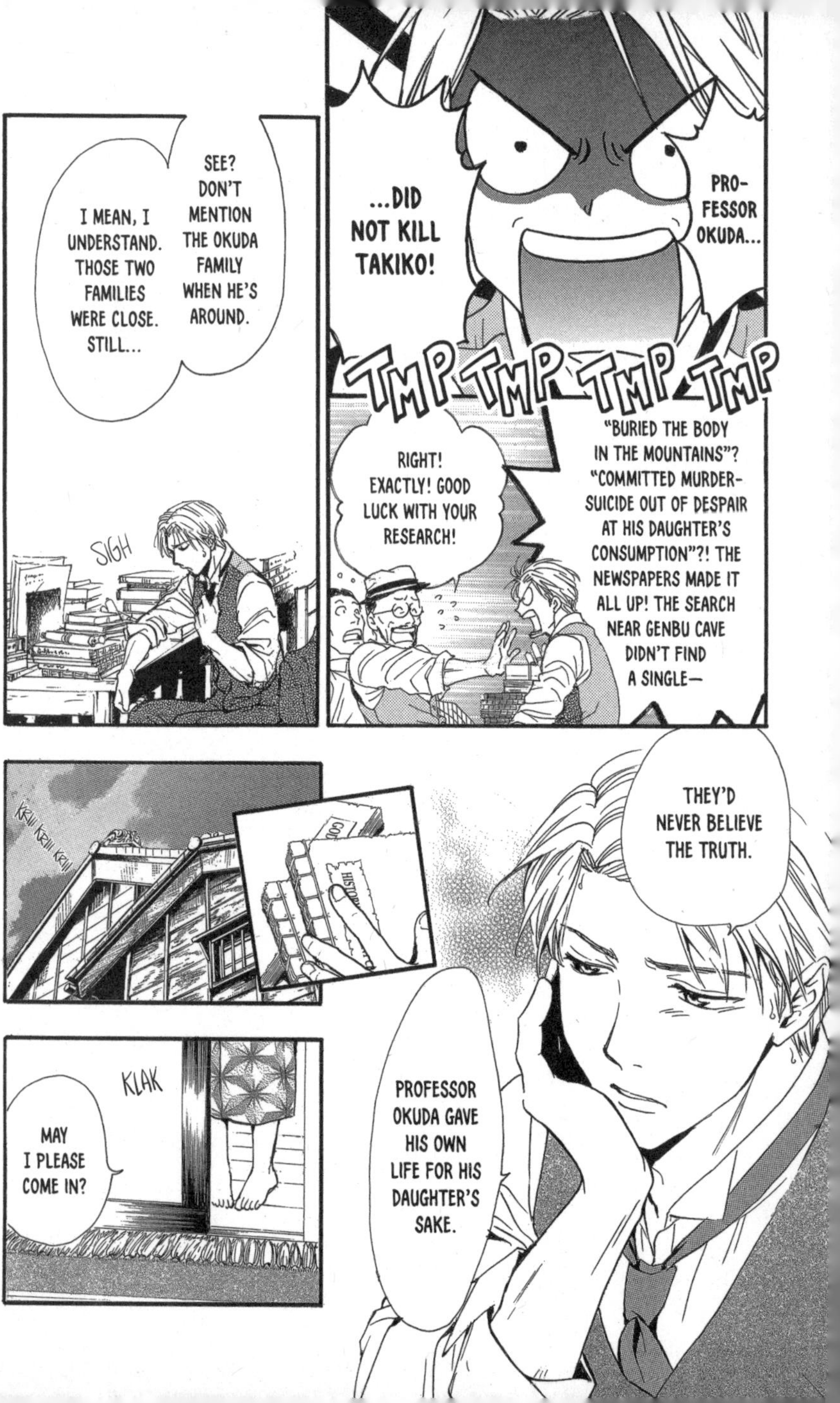
PRO-
FESSOR
OKUDA...
...DID NOT KILL TAKIKO!
TMP TMP TMP TMP
"BURIED THE BODY IN THE MOUNTAINS"? "COMMITTED MURDER-SUICIDE OUT OF DESPAIR AT HIS DAUGHTER'S CONSUMPTION"?! THE NEWSPAPERS MADE IT ALL UP! THE SEARCH NEAR GENBU CAVE DIDN'T FIND A SINGLE—
RIGHT! EXACTLY! GOOD LUCK WITH YOUR RESEARCH!
SEE? DON'T MENTION THE OKUDA FAMILY WHEN HE'S AROUND.
I MEAN, I UNDERSTAND. THOSE TWO FAMILIES WERE CLOSE. STILL...
SIGH
THEY'D NEVER BELIEVE THE TRUTH.
PROFESSOR OKUDA GAVE HIS OWN LIFE FOR HIS DAUGHTER'S SAKE.
KRIII KRIII KRIII
KLAK
MAY I PLEASE COME IN?

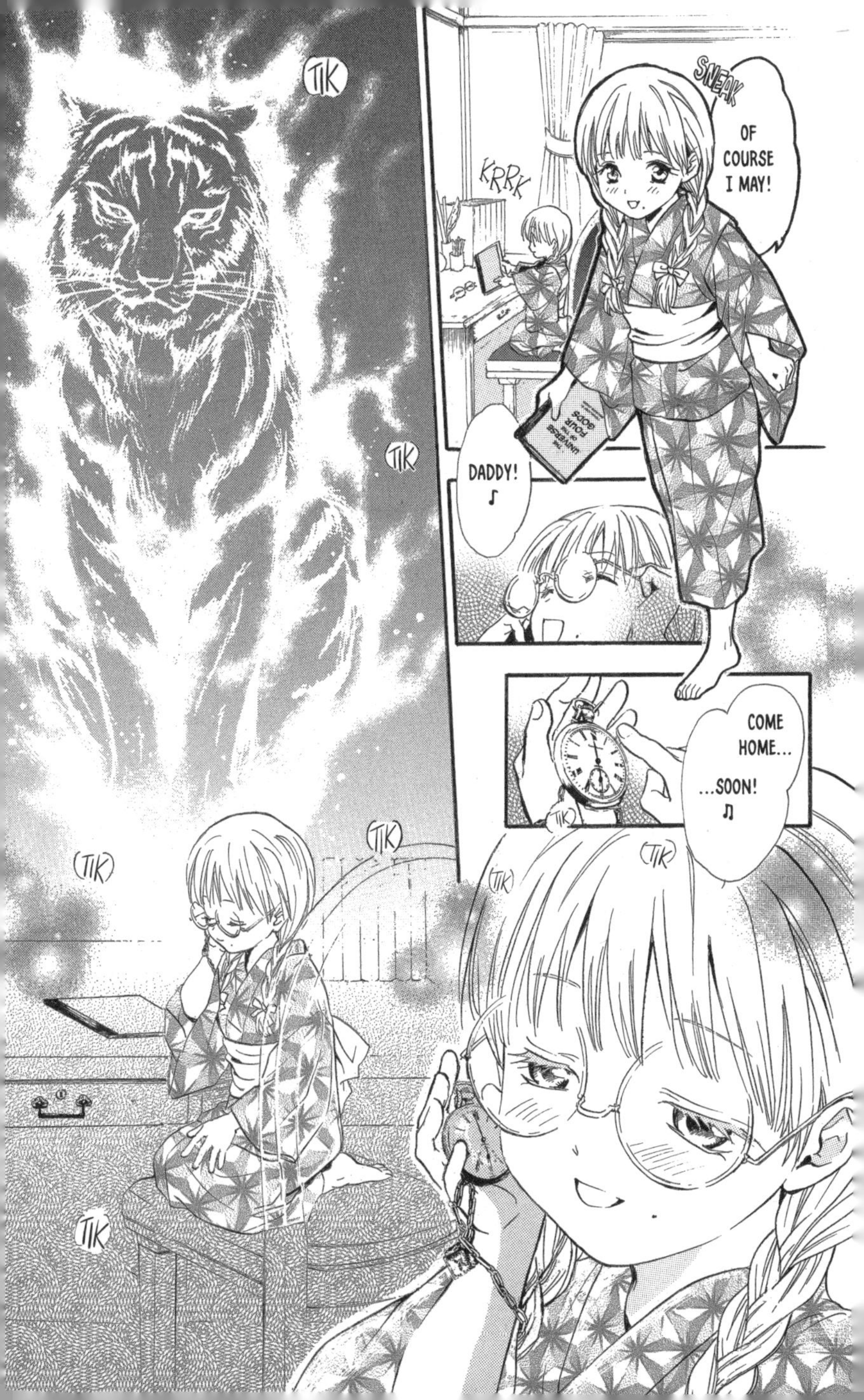

SNEAK
OF COURSE I MAY!
KRRK
DADDY! ♪
COME HOME...
...SOON! ♫
TIK
TIK
(TIK)
TIK
TIK
TIK
(TIK)
TIK

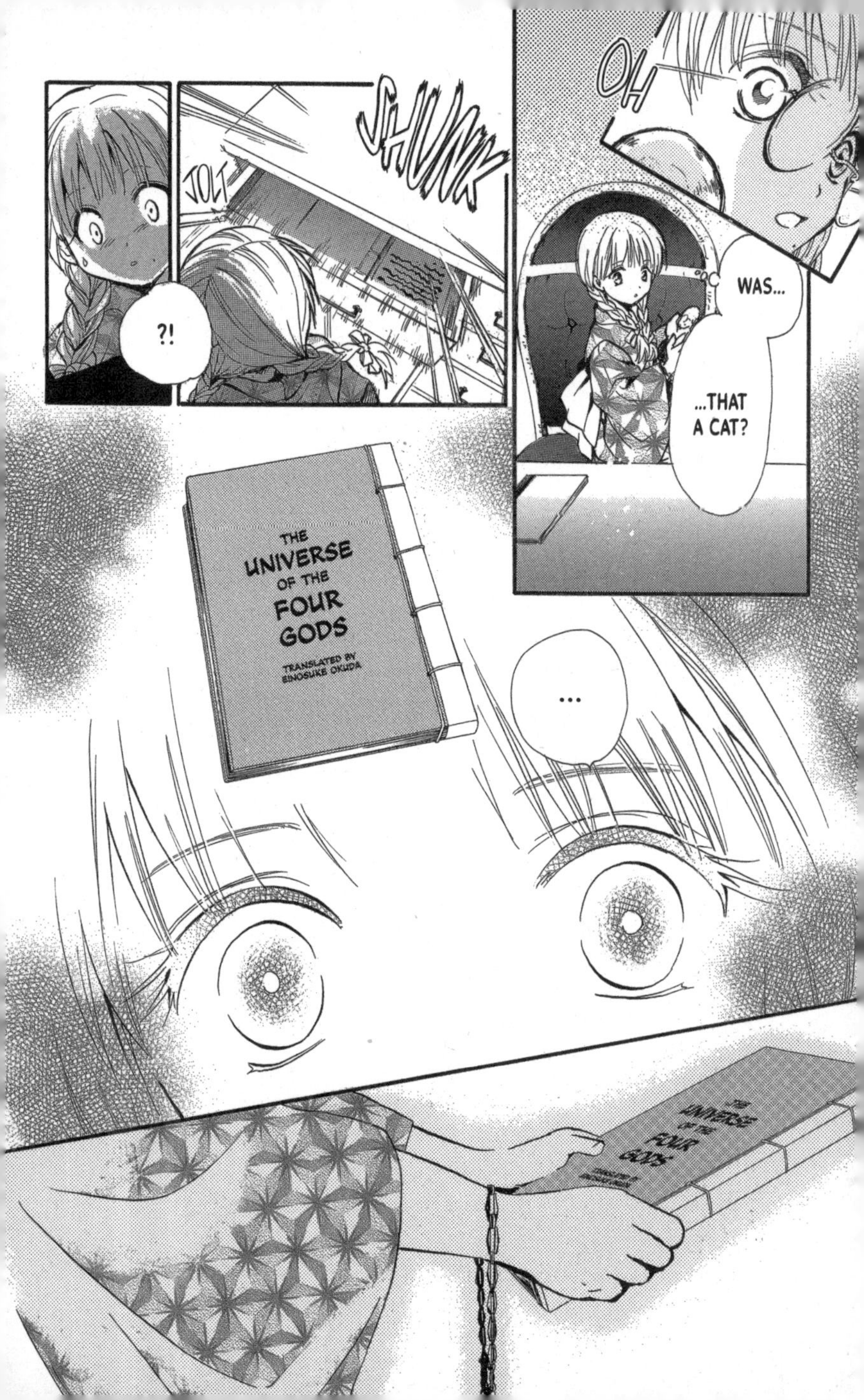
OH
WAS...
...THAT A CAT?
SHUNK
JOLT
?!
THE UNIVERSE OF THE FOUR GODS
TRANSLATED BY EINOSUKE OKUDA
...
THE UNIVERSE OF THE FOUR GODS

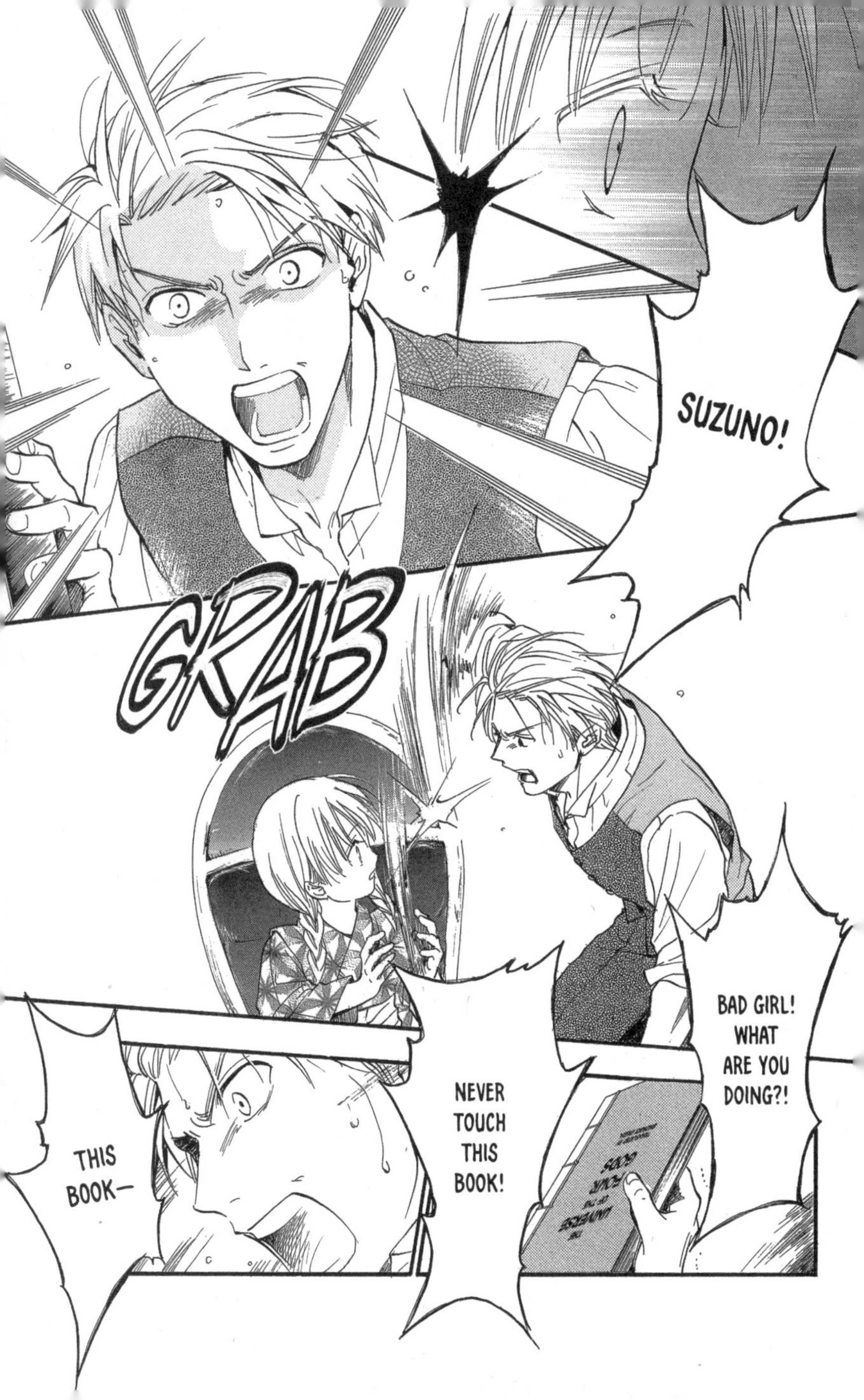
SUZUNO!
GRAB
BAD GIRL! WHAT ARE YOU DOING?!
NEVER TOUCH THIS BOOK!
THIS BOOK—

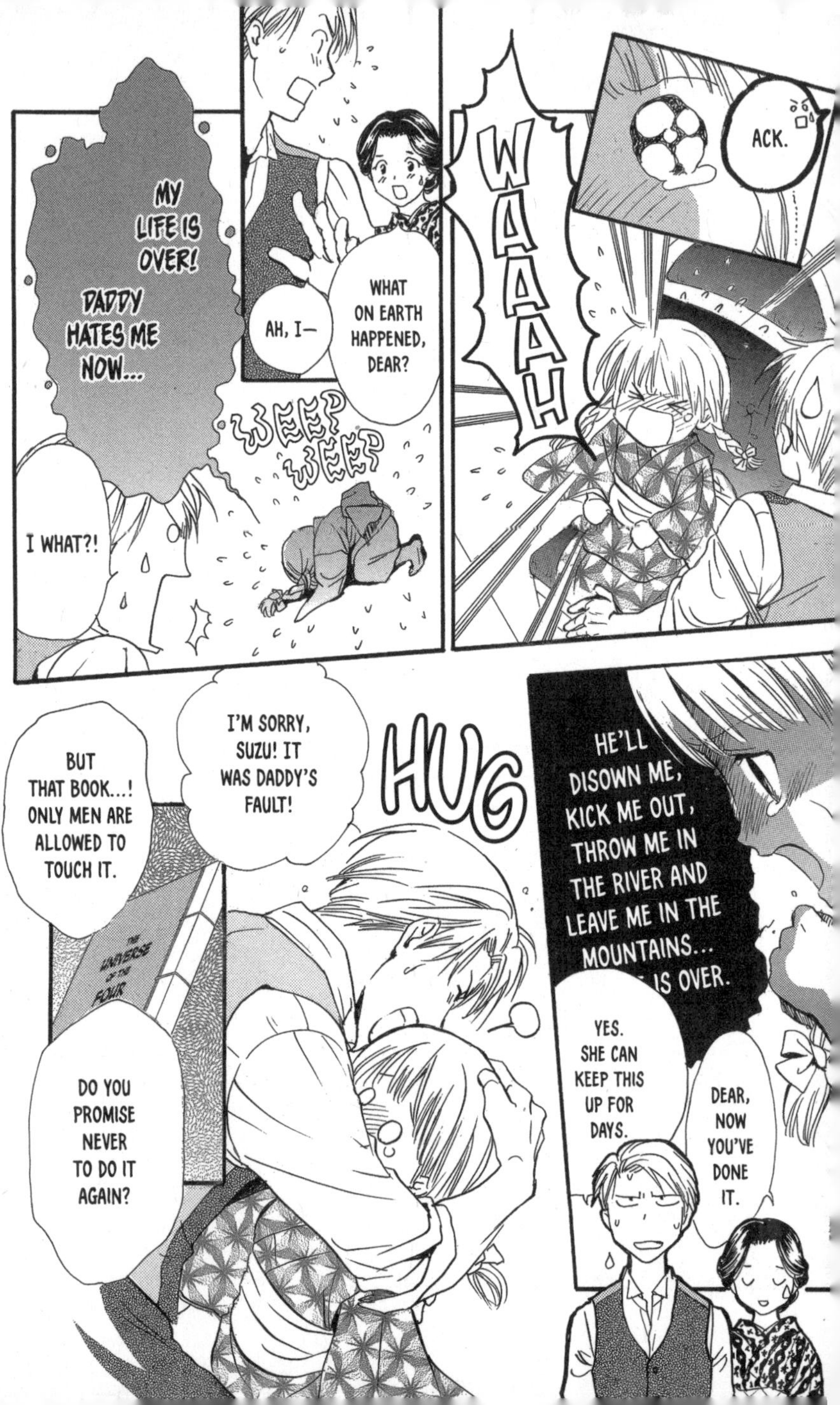
ACK.
WAAAAH
WHAT ON EARTH HAPPENED, DEAR?
AH, I—
WEEP WEEP
MY LIFE IS OVER!
DADDY HATES ME NOW...
I WHAT?!
HE'LL DISOWN ME, KICK ME OUT, THROW ME IN THE RIVER AND LEAVE ME IN THE MOUNTAINS... IS OVER.
DEAR, NOW YOU'VE DONE IT.
YES. SHE CAN KEEP THIS UP FOR DAYS.
HUG
I'M SORRY, SUZU! IT WAS DADDY'S FAULT!
BUT THAT BOOK...! ONLY MEN ARE ALLOWED TO TOUCH IT.
THE UNIVERSE OF THE FOUR
DO YOU PROMISE NEVER TO DO IT AGAIN?

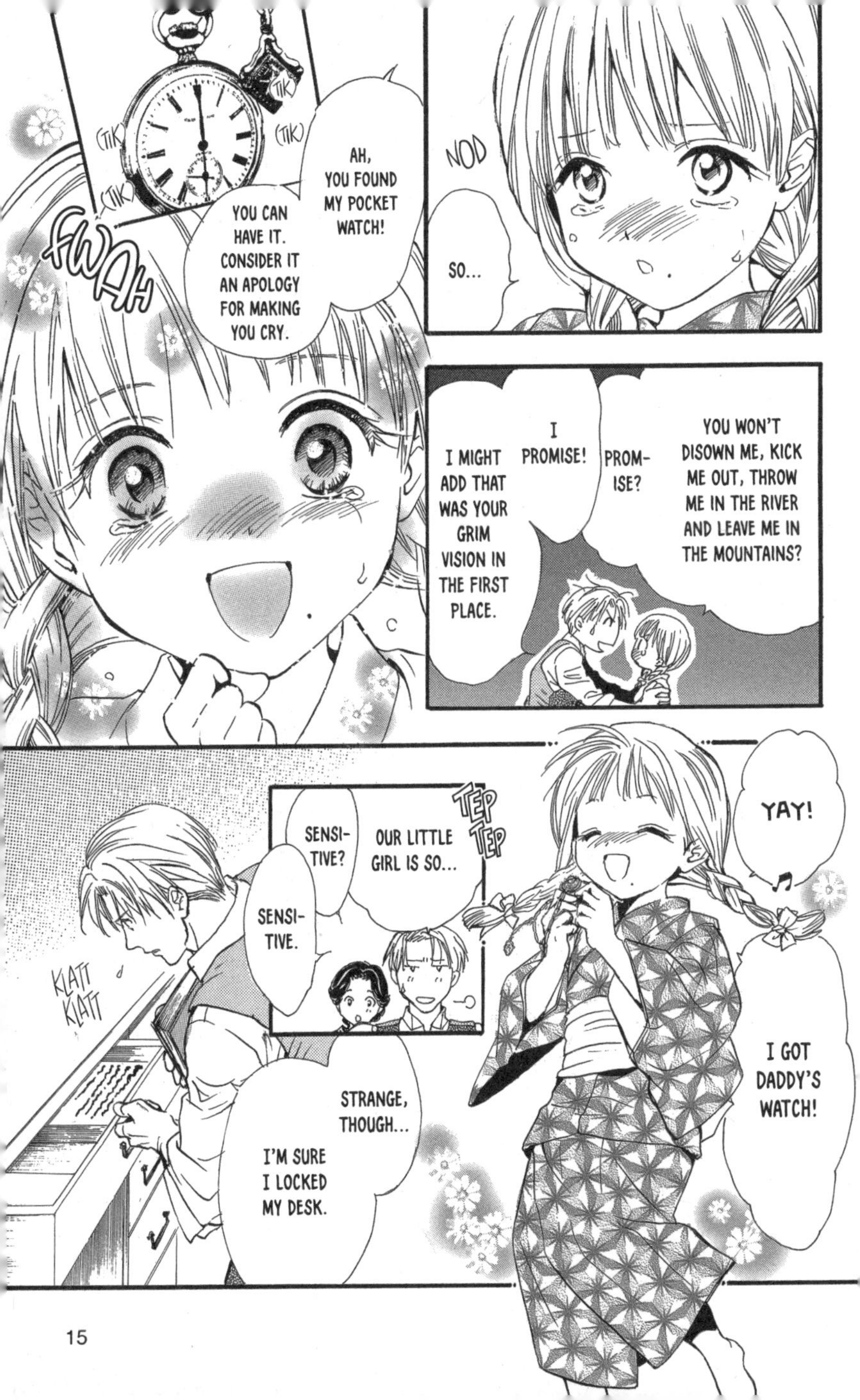
NOD
SO...
YOU WON'T DISOWN ME, KICK ME OUT, THROW ME IN THE RIVER AND LEAVE ME IN THE MOUNTAINS?
PROM-ISE?
I PROMISE!
I MIGHT ADD THAT WAS YOUR GRIM VISION IN THE FIRST PLACE.
(TIK)
(TIK)
(TIK)
(TIK)
AH, YOU FOUND MY POCKET WATCH!
YOU CAN HAVE IT. CONSIDER IT AN APOLOGY FOR MAKING YOU CRY.
FWAH
YAY!
I GOT DADDY'S WATCH!
TEP TEP
OUR LITTLE GIRL IS SO...
SENSI-TIVE?
SENSI-TIVE.
KLATT KLATT
STRANGE, THOUGH...
I'M SURE I LOCKED MY DESK.

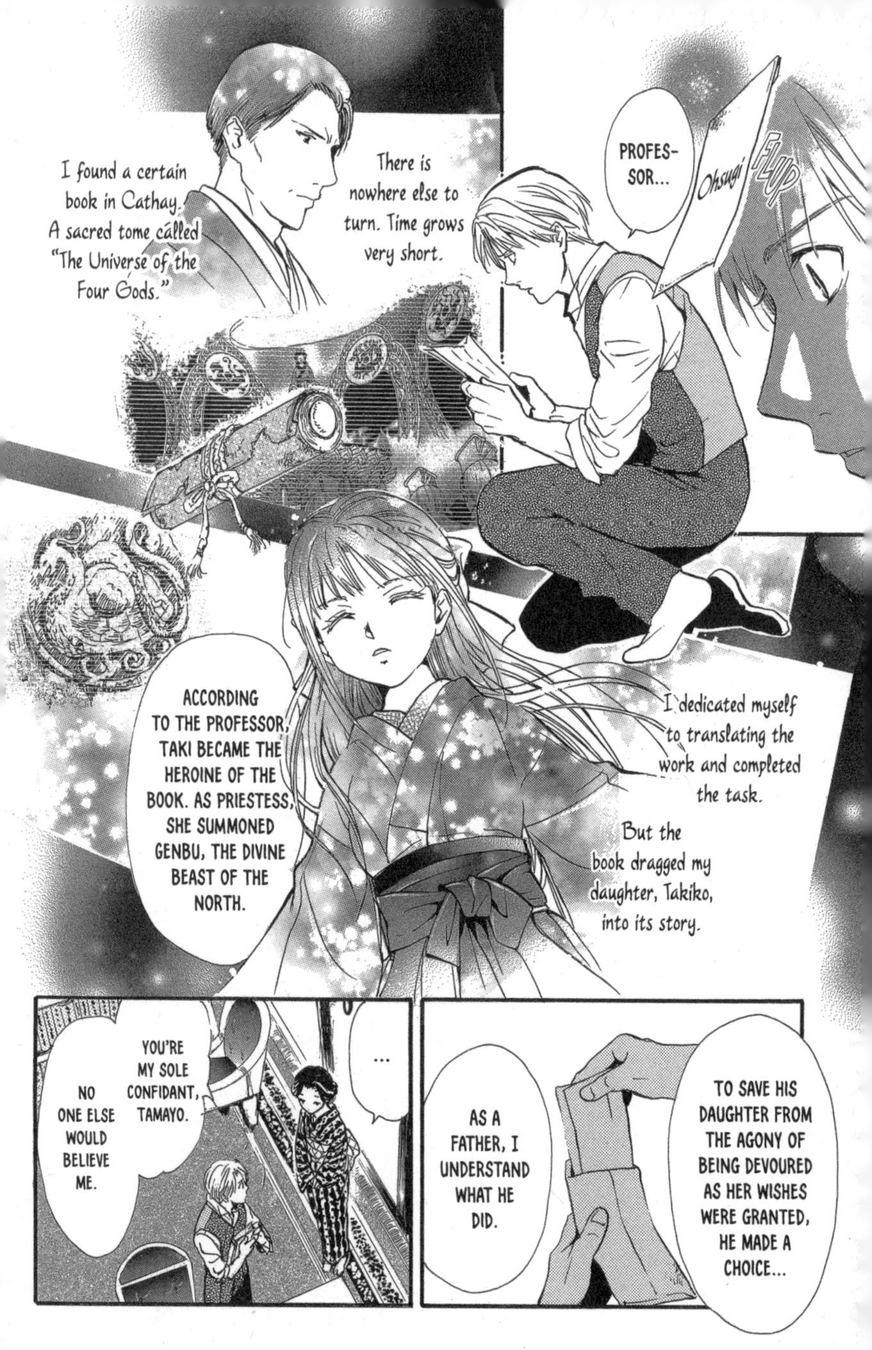
PROFES-SOR...
Ohsugi
FLIP
There is nowhere else to turn. Time grows very short.
I found a certain book in Cathay. A sacred tome called "The Universe of the Four Gods."
I dedicated myself to translating the work and completed the task.
But the book dragged my daughter, Takiko, into its story.
ACCORDING TO THE PROFESSOR, TAKI BECAME THE HEROINE OF THE BOOK. AS PRIESTESS, SHE SUMMONED GENBU, THE DIVINE BEAST OF THE NORTH.
TO SAVE HIS DAUGHTER FROM THE AGONY OF BEING DEVOURED AS HER WISHES WERE GRANTED, HE MADE A CHOICE...
AS A FATHER, I UNDERSTAND WHAT HE DID.
...
YOU'RE MY SOLE CONFIDANT, TAMAYO.
NO ONE ELSE WOULD BELIEVE ME.

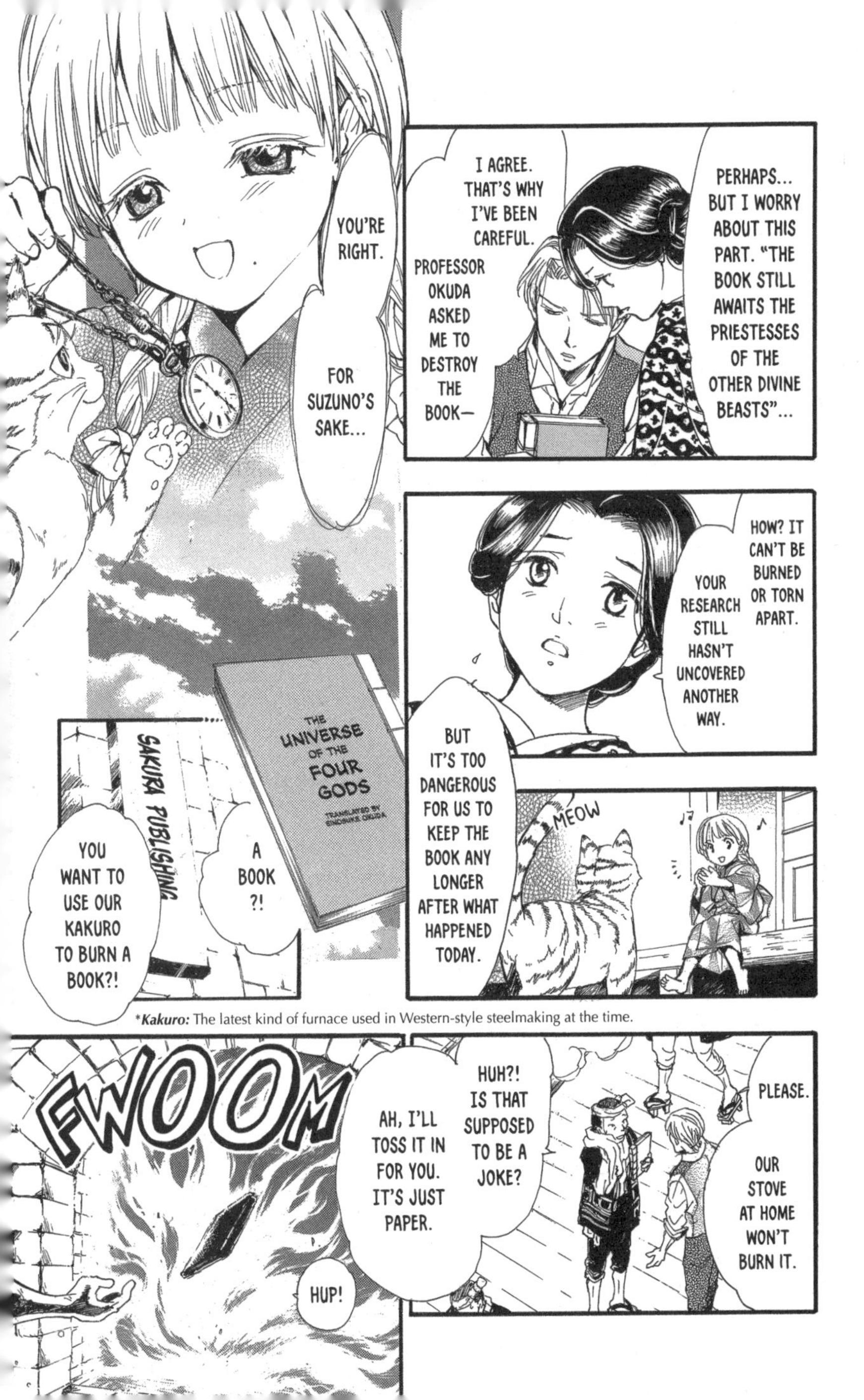
PERHAPS... BUT I WORRY ABOUT THIS PART. "THE BOOK STILL AWAITS THE PRIESTESSES OF THE OTHER DIVINE BEASTS"...
I AGREE. THAT'S WHY I'VE BEEN CAREFUL.
PROFESSOR OKUDA ASKED ME TO DESTROY THE BOOK—
HOW? IT CAN'T BE BURNED OR TORN APART.
YOUR RESEARCH STILL HASN'T UNCOVERED ANOTHER WAY.
BUT IT'S TOO DANGEROUS FOR US TO KEEP THE BOOK ANY LONGER AFTER WHAT HAPPENED TODAY.
MEOW
YOU'RE RIGHT.
FOR SUZUNO'S SAKE...
THE UNIVERSE OF THE FOUR GODS
SAKURA PUBLISHING
A BOOK ?!
YOU WANT TO USE OUR KAKURO TO BURN A BOOK?!
PLEASE.
OUR STOVE AT HOME WON'T BURN IT.
HUH?! IS THAT SUPPOSED TO BE A JOKE?
AH, I'LL TOSS IT IN FOR YOU. IT'S JUST PAPER.
HUP!
FWOOM

****Kakuro:*** The latest kind of furnace used in Western-style steelmaking at the time.

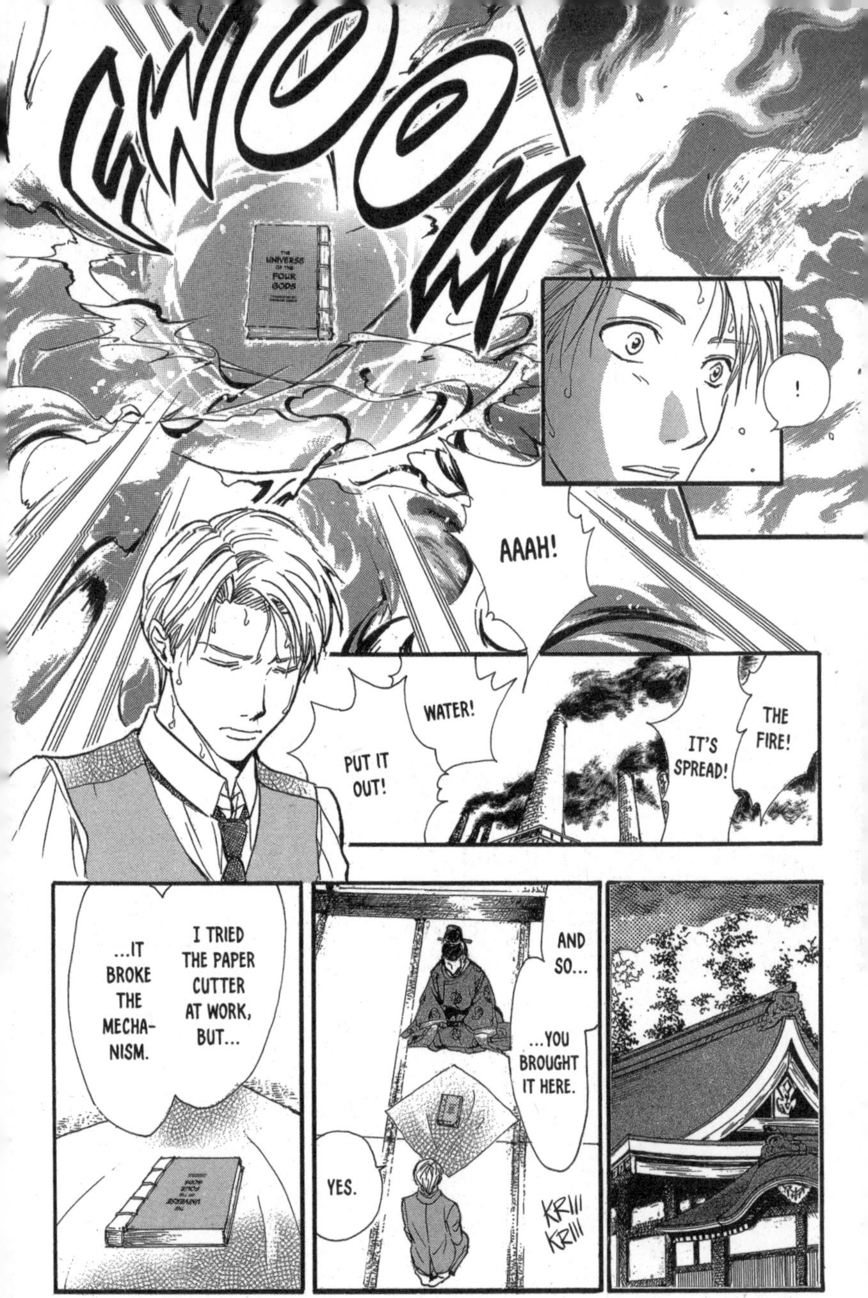
GWOOM
THE UNIVERSE OF THE FOUR GODS
!
AAAH!
THE FIRE!
IT'S SPREAD!
WATER!
PUT IT OUT!
AND SO...
...YOU BROUGHT IT HERE.
YES.
KRIII KRIII
I TRIED THE PAPER CUTTER AT WORK, BUT...
...IT BROKE THE MECHANISM.

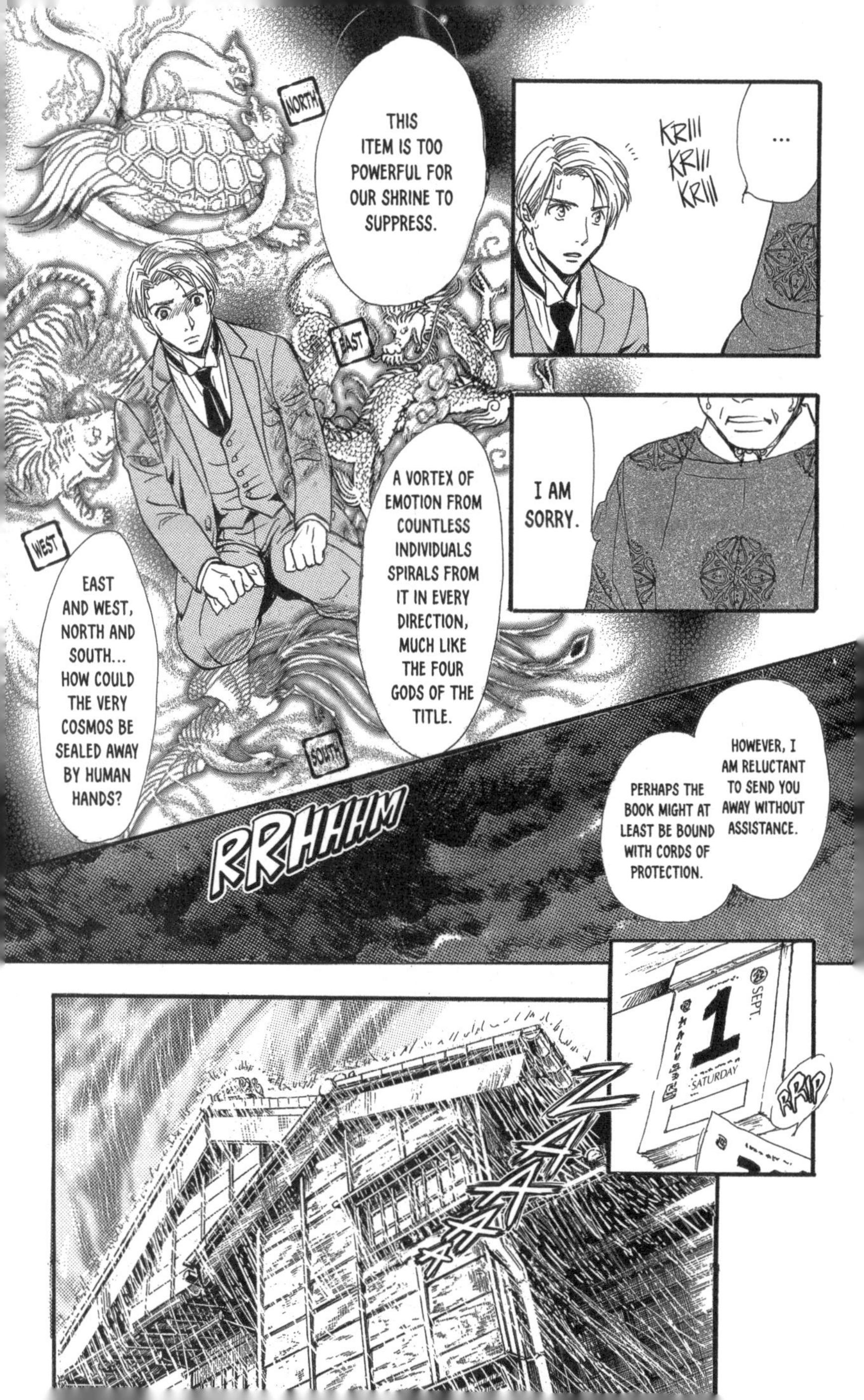
...
KRIII KRIII KRIII
I AM SORRY.
THIS ITEM IS TOO POWERFUL FOR OUR SHRINE TO SUPPRESS.
NORTH
EAST
WEST
SOUTH
A VORTEX OF EMOTION FROM COUNTLESS INDIVIDUALS SPIRALS FROM IT IN EVERY DIRECTION, MUCH LIKE THE FOUR GODS OF THE TITLE.
EAST AND WEST, NORTH AND SOUTH... HOW COULD THE VERY COSMOS BE SEALED AWAY BY HUMAN HANDS?
HOWEVER, I AM RELUCTANT TO SEND YOU AWAY WITHOUT ASSISTANCE.
PERHAPS THE BOOK MIGHT AT LEAST BE BOUND WITH CORDS OF PROTECTION.
RRHHHM
SEPT.
1
SATURDAY
RRIP
ZAAAA

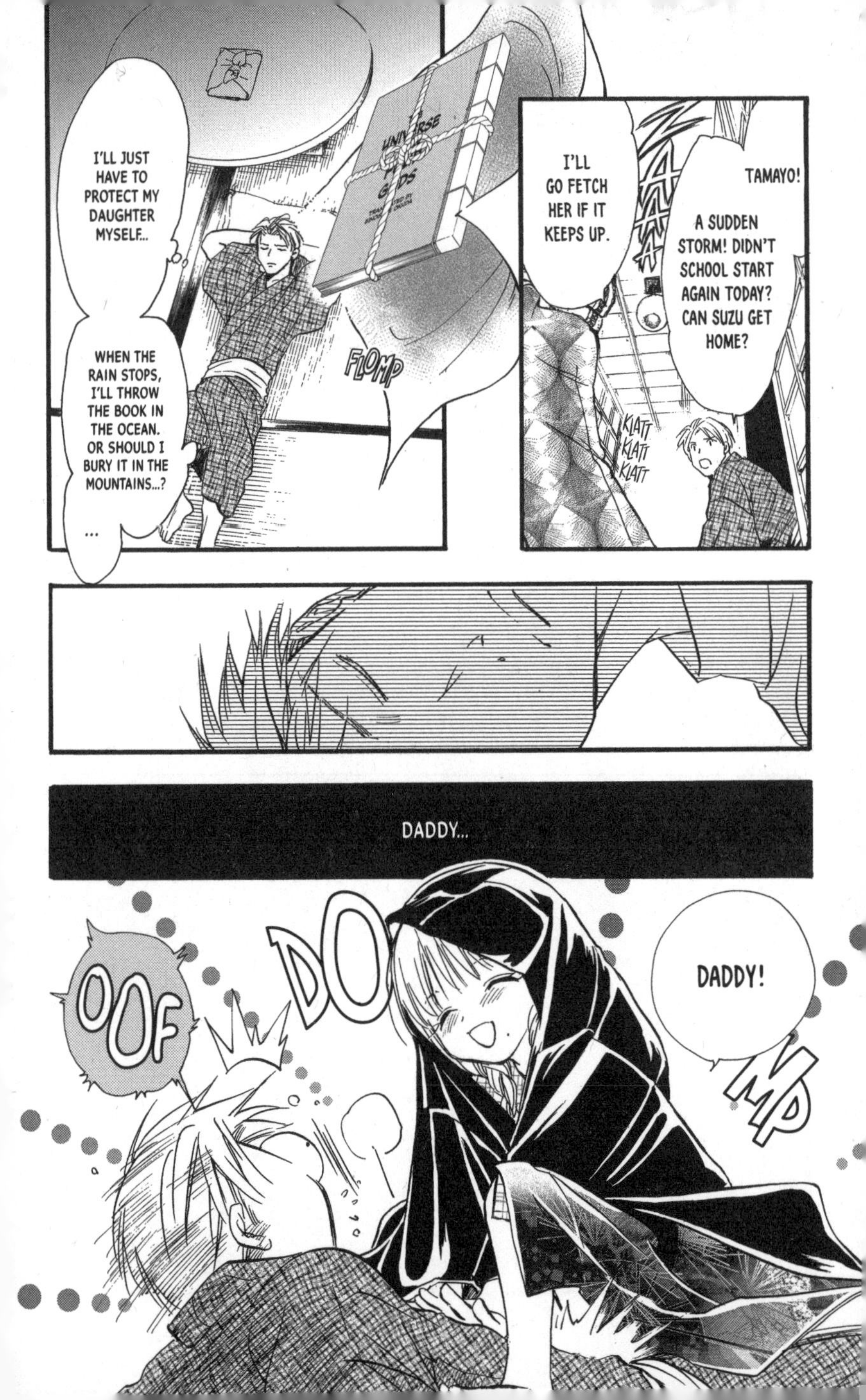
TAMAYO!
A SUDDEN STORM! DIDN'T SCHOOL START AGAIN TODAY? CAN SUZU GET HOME?
I'LL GO FETCH HER IF IT KEEPS UP.
KLATT KLATT KLATT
I'LL JUST HAVE TO PROTECT MY DAUGHTER MYSELF...
WHEN THE RAIN STOPS, I'LL THROW THE BOOK IN THE OCEAN. OR SHOULD I BURY IT IN THE MOUNTAINS...?
FLOMP
...
DADDY...
DADDY!
DO
MP
OOF

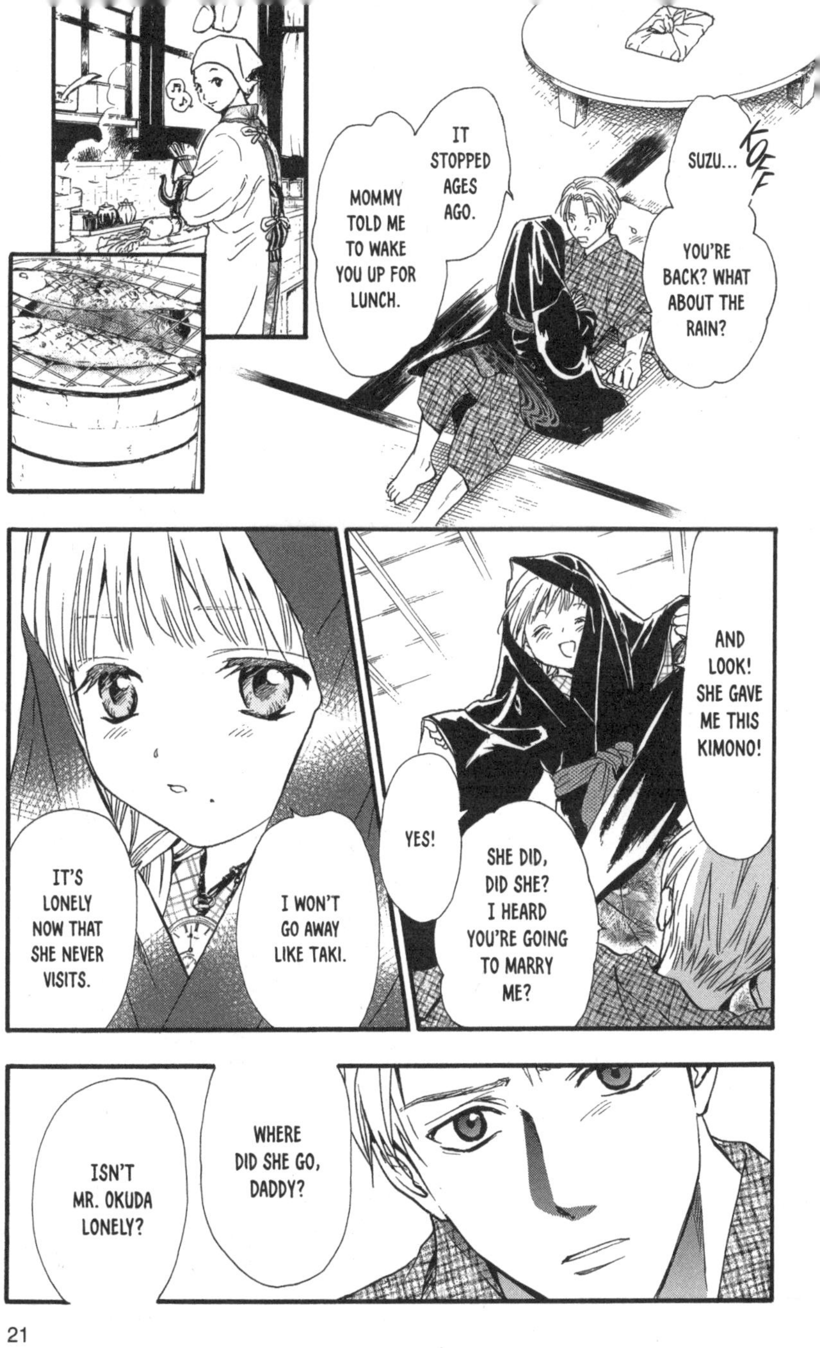
SUZU...
KOFF
YOU'RE BACK? WHAT ABOUT THE RAIN?
IT STOPPED AGES AGO.
MOMMY TOLD ME TO WAKE YOU UP FOR LUNCH.
AND LOOK! SHE GAVE ME THIS KIMONO!
SHE DID, DID SHE? I HEARD YOU'RE GOING TO MARRY ME?
YES!
I WON'T GO AWAY LIKE TAKI.
IT'S LONELY NOW THAT SHE NEVER VISITS.
WHERE DID SHE GO, DADDY?
ISN'T MR. OKUDA LONELY?

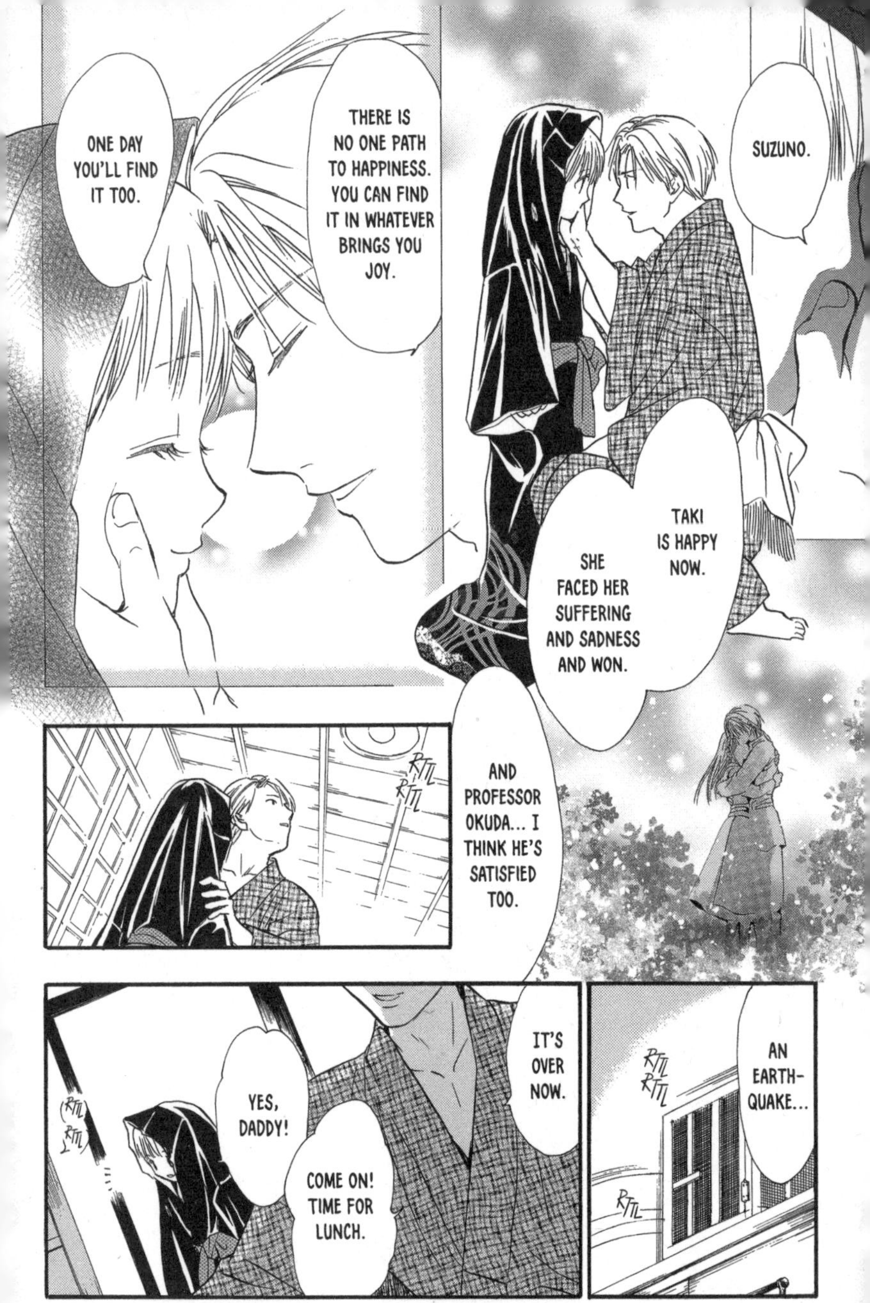
SUZUNO.
TAKI IS HAPPY NOW.
SHE FACED HER SUFFERING AND SADNESS AND WON.
AND PROFESSOR OKUDA... I THINK HE'S SATISFIED TOO.
THERE IS NO ONE PATH TO HAPPINESS. YOU CAN FIND IT IN WHATEVER BRINGS YOU JOY.
ONE DAY YOU'LL FIND IT TOO.
RTTL RTTL
AN EARTH-QUAKE...
RTTL RTTL
RTTL
IT'S OVER NOW.
COME ON! TIME FOR LUNCH.
YES, DADDY!
(RTTL RTTL)
...

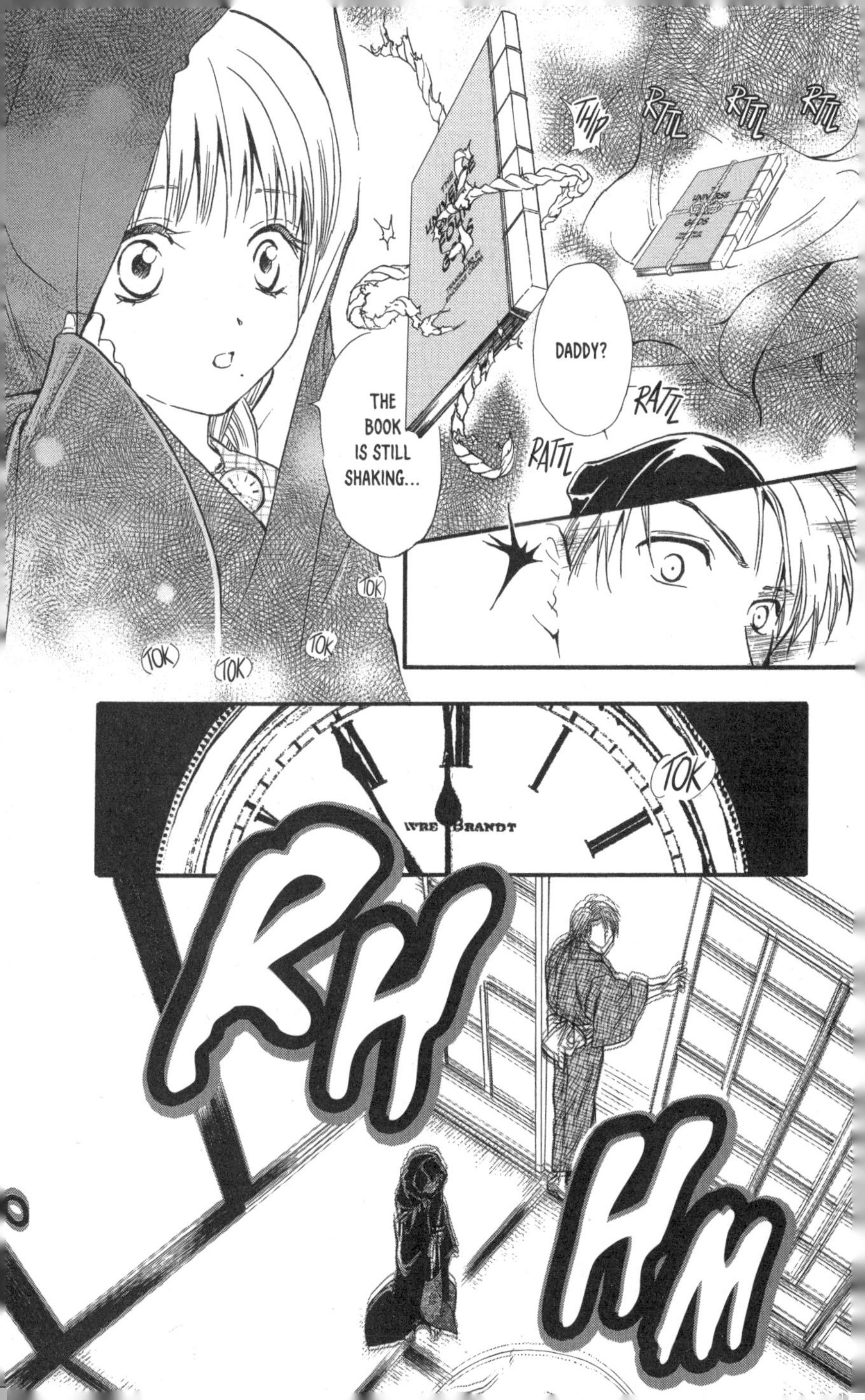

RTTL
RTTL
RTTL
THP
DADDY?
RATTL
RATTL
THE BOOK IS STILL SHAKING...
TOK
TOK
TOK
TOK
TOK
WRE BRANDT

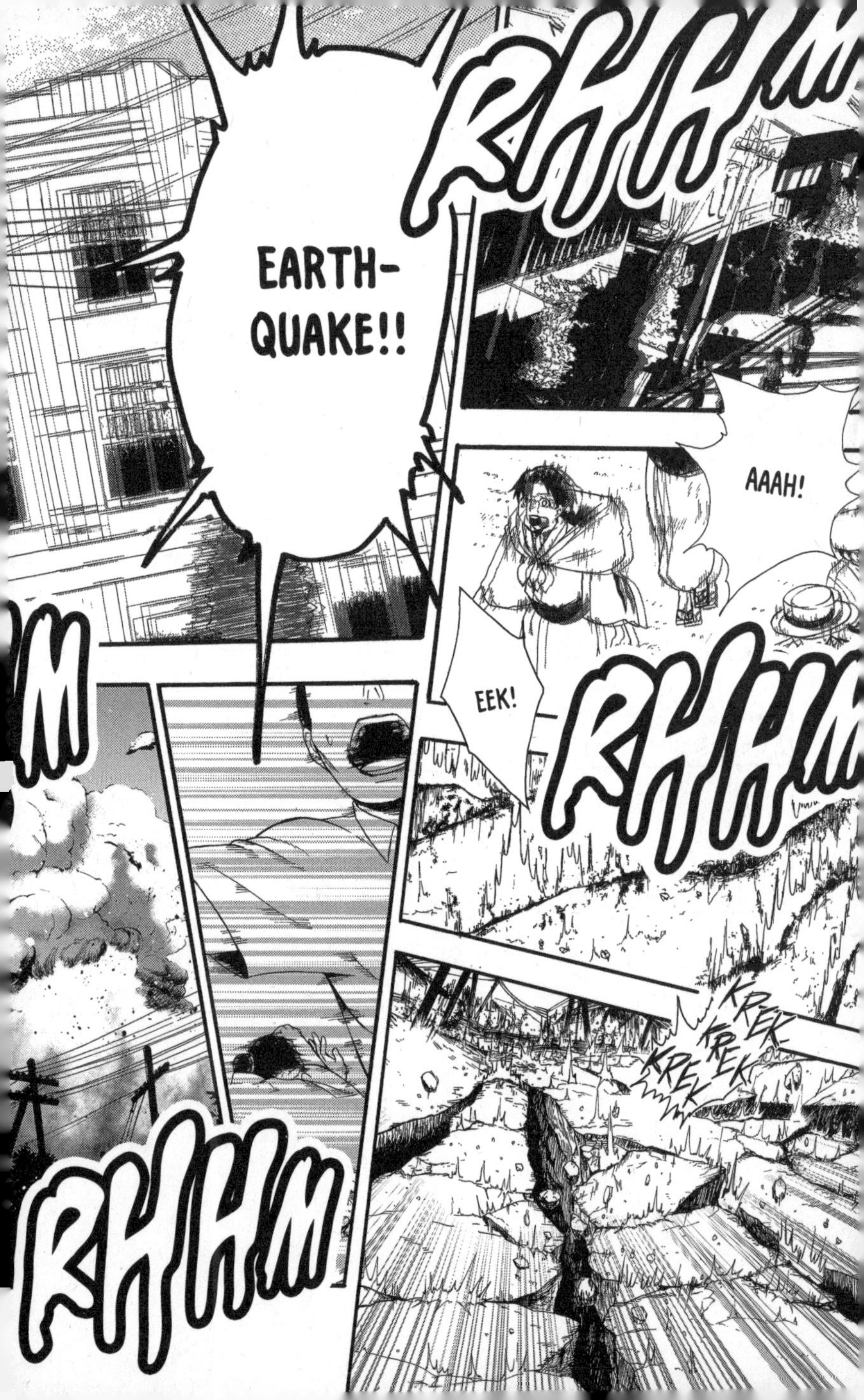
RHH
EARTH-QUAKE!!
AAAH!
EEK!
RHH
KREK KREK KREK
RHHM

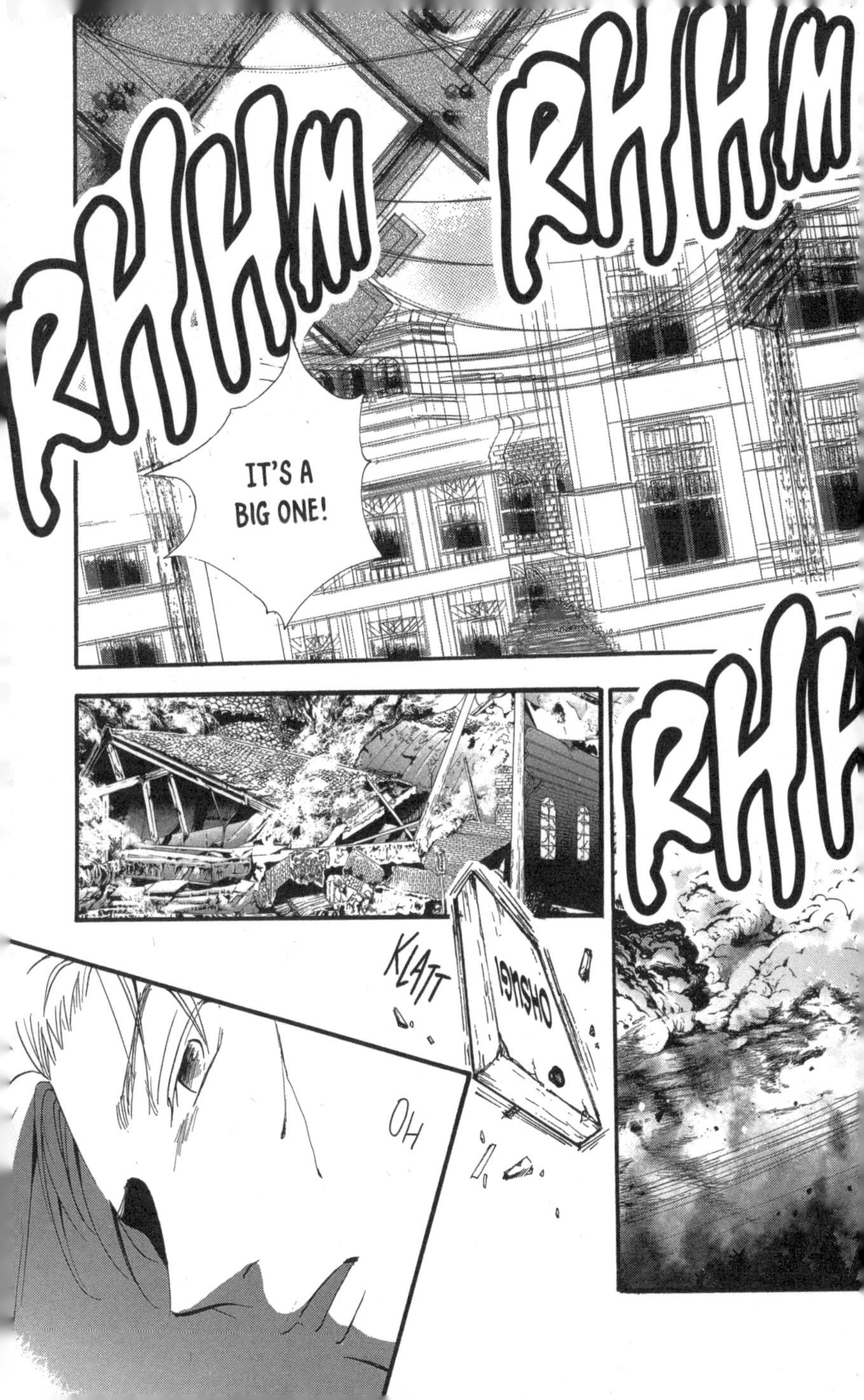
RHHM
RHHM
IT'S A BIG ONE!
KLATT
OH

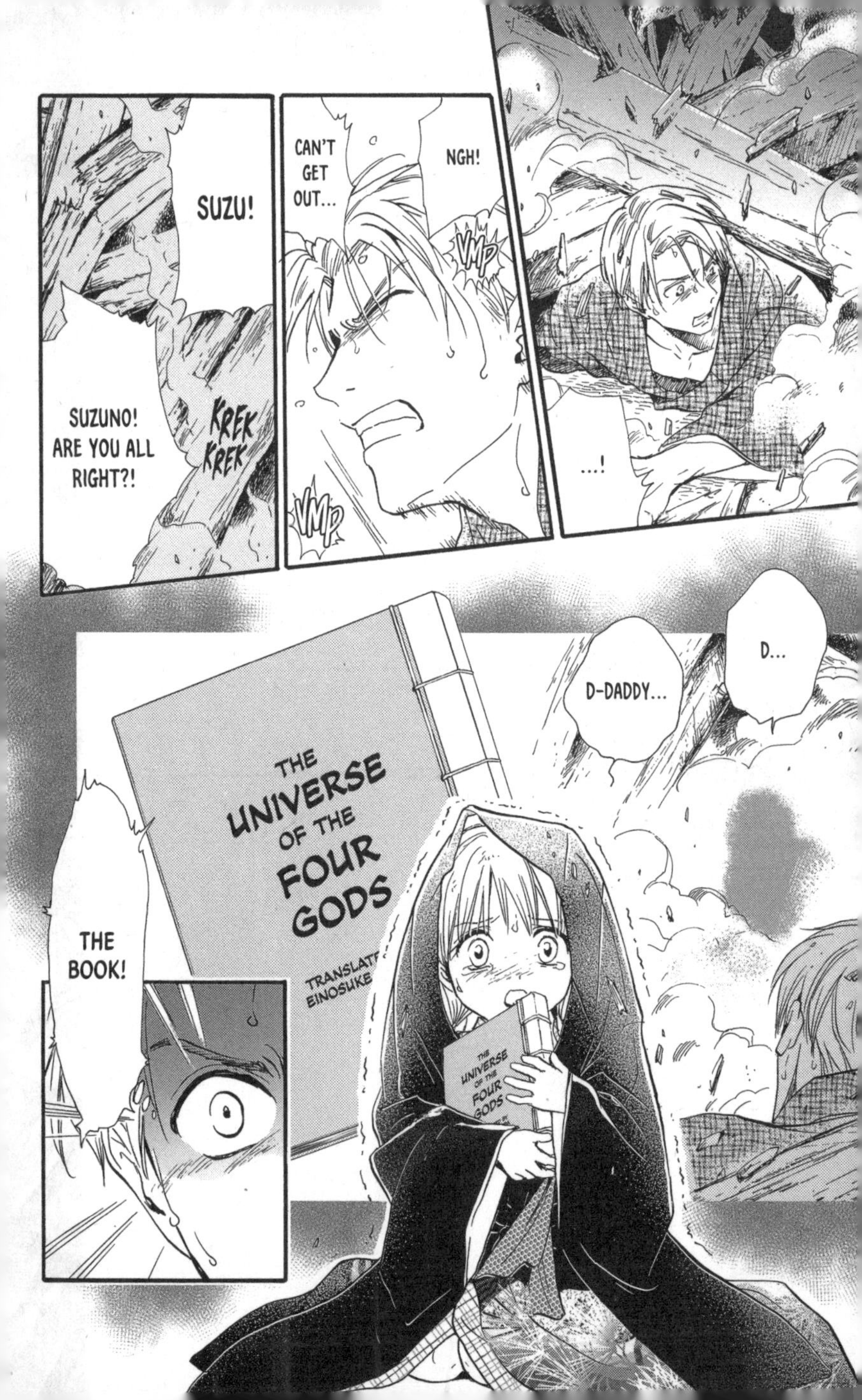
...!
NGH!
VMP
CAN'T GET OUT...
VMP
SUZU!
SUZUNO! ARE YOU ALL RIGHT?!
KREK KREK
D...
D-DADDY...
THE UNIVERSE OF THE FOUR GODS
THE UNIVERSE OF THE FOUR GODS
THE BOOK!

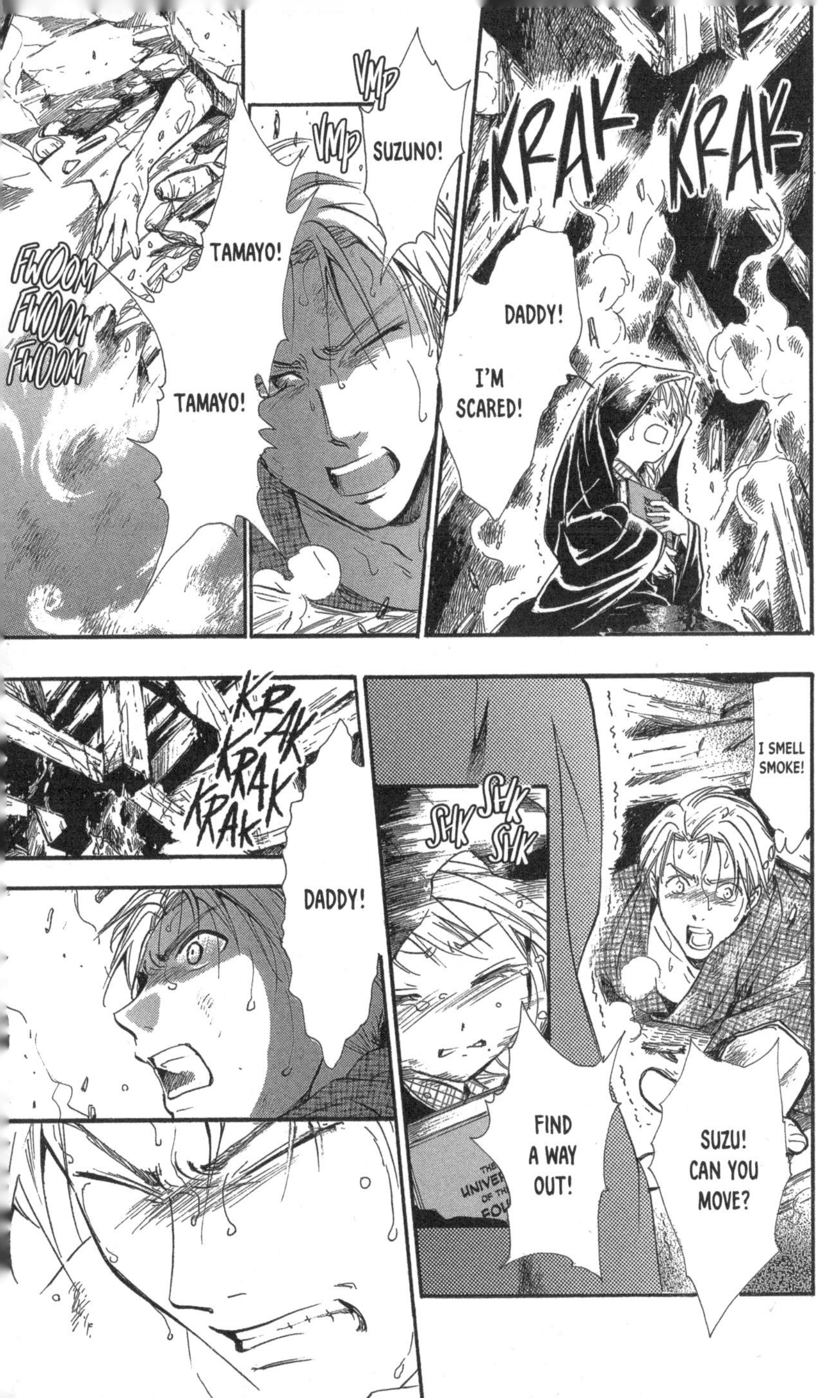
KRAK KRAK
DADDY!
I'M SCARED!
VMP
VMP
SUZUNO!
FWOOM FWOOM FWOOM
TAMAYO!
TAMAYO!
I SMELL SMOKE!
SHK SHK SHK SHK
SUZU! CAN YOU MOVE?
FIND A WAY OUT!
KRAK KRAK KRAK KRAK
DADDY!

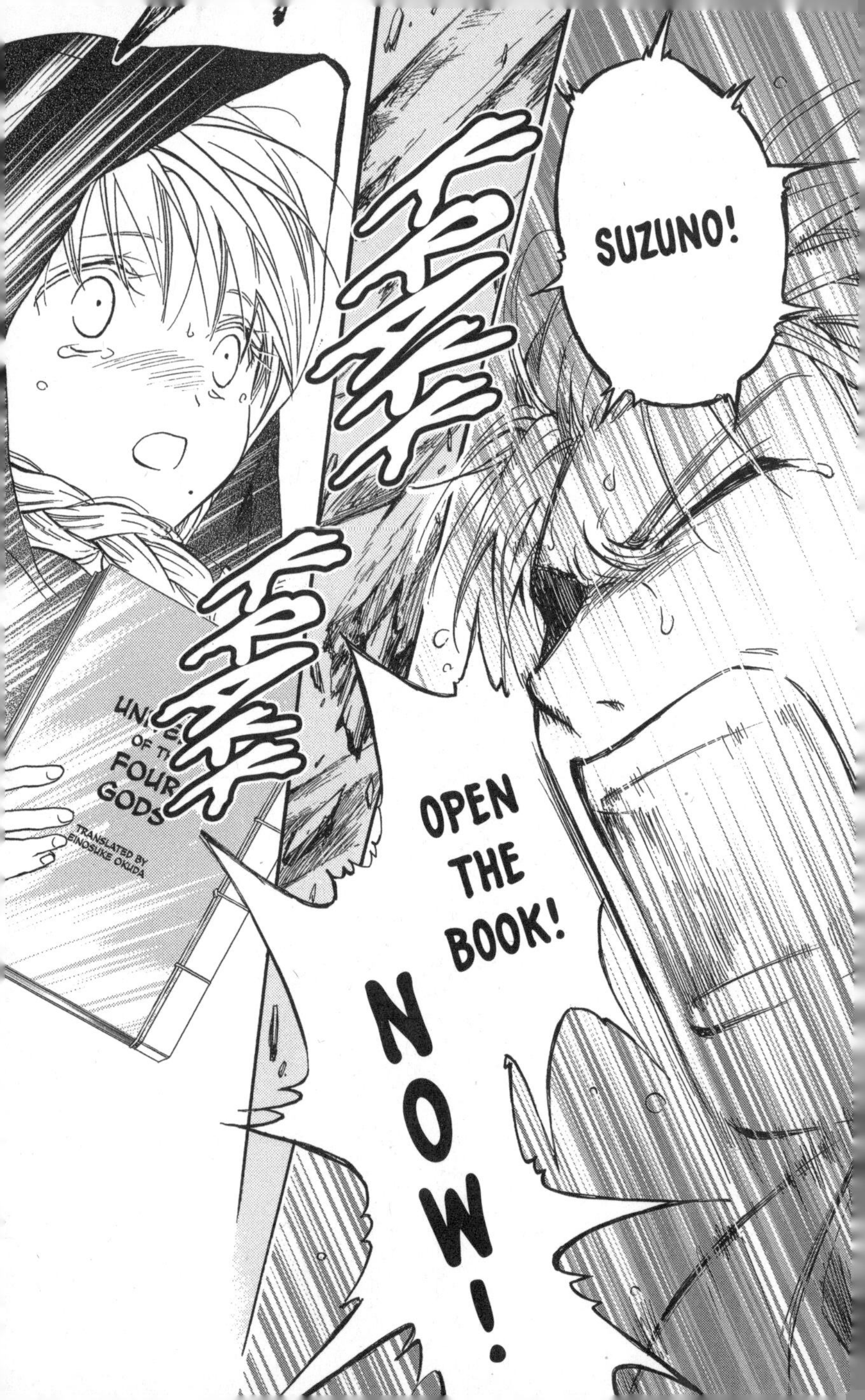
SUZUNO!
OPEN THE BOOK!
NOW!!
FOUR GODS
TRANSLATED BY EINOSUKE OKUDA

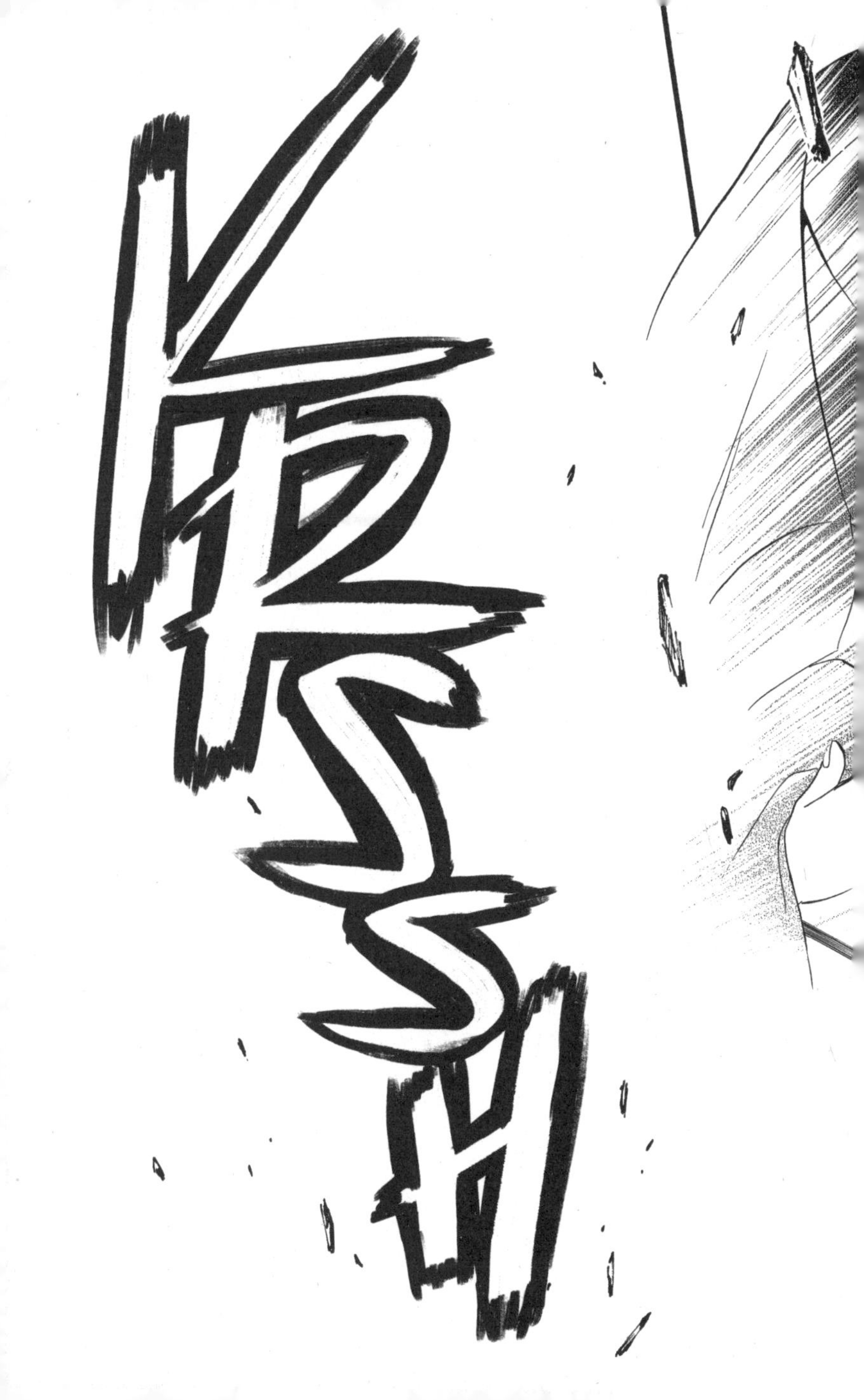
KRSSH

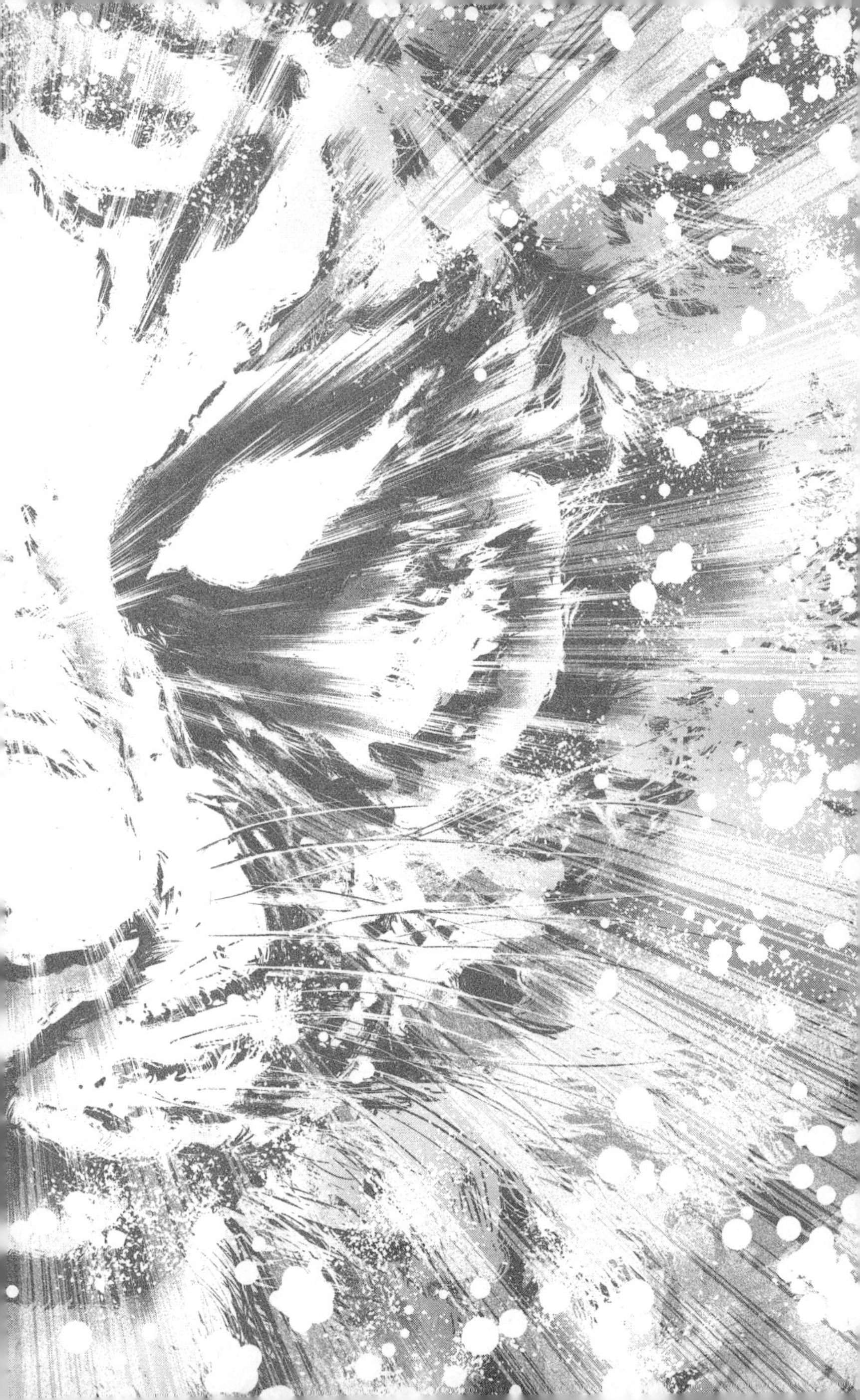

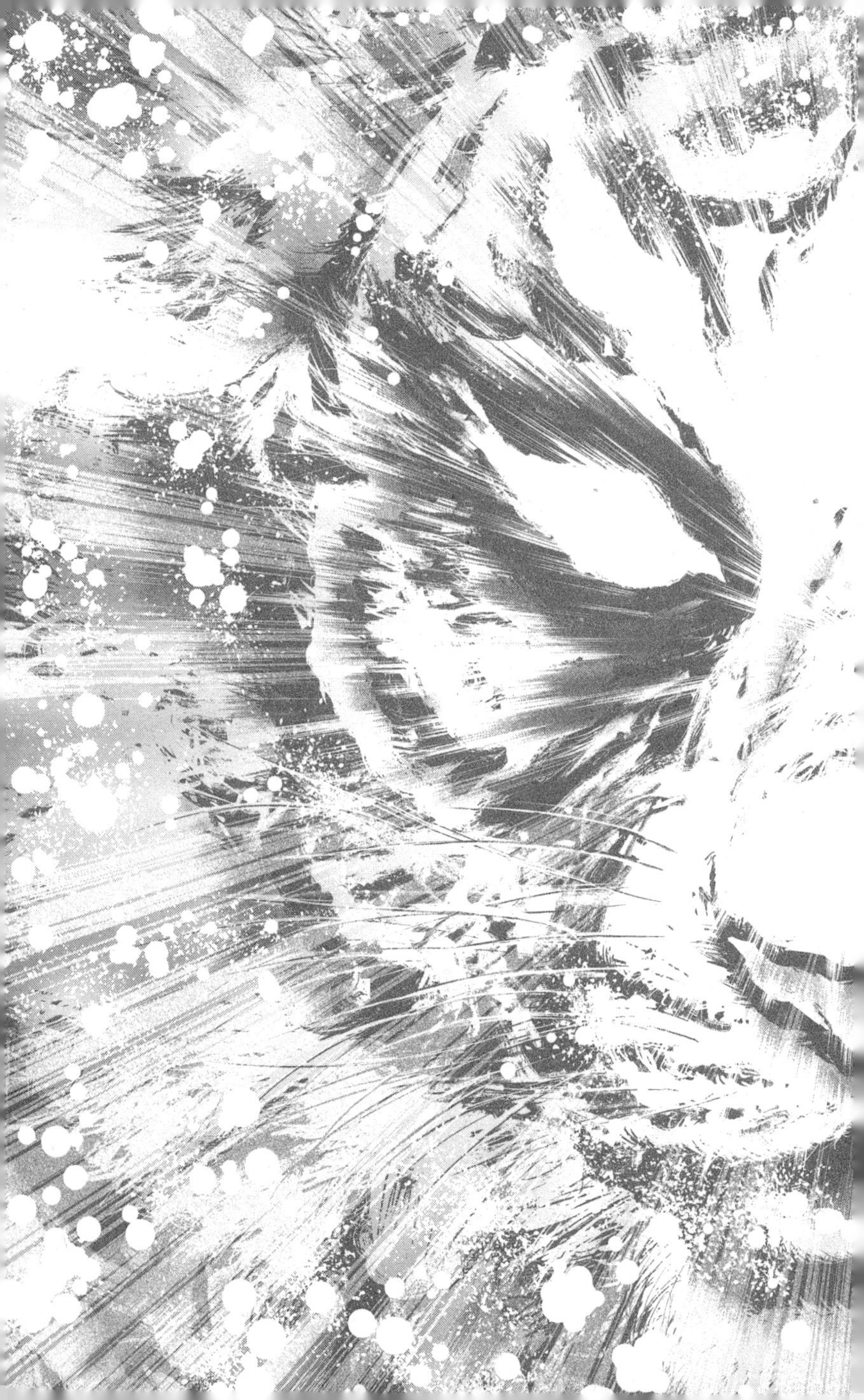

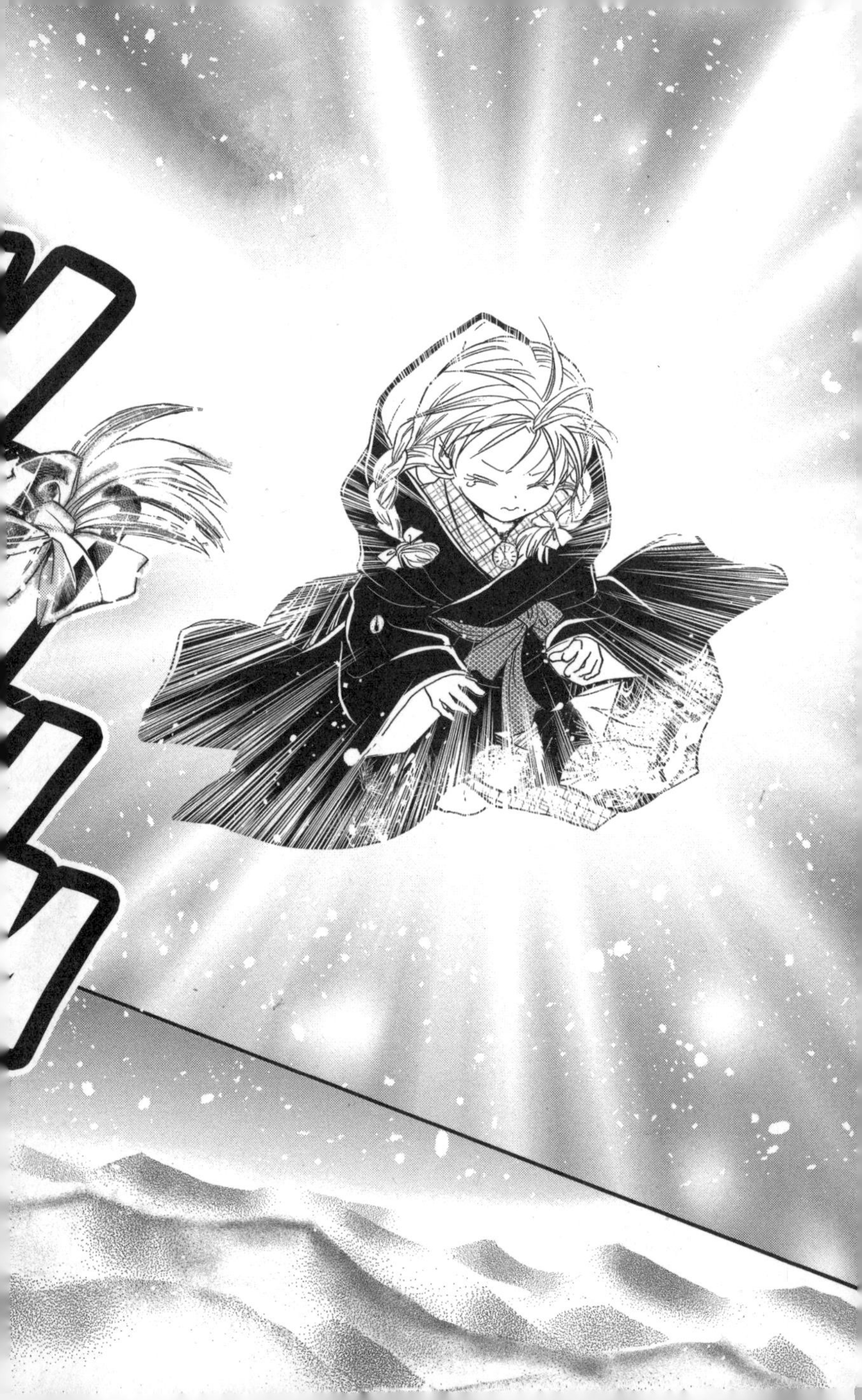

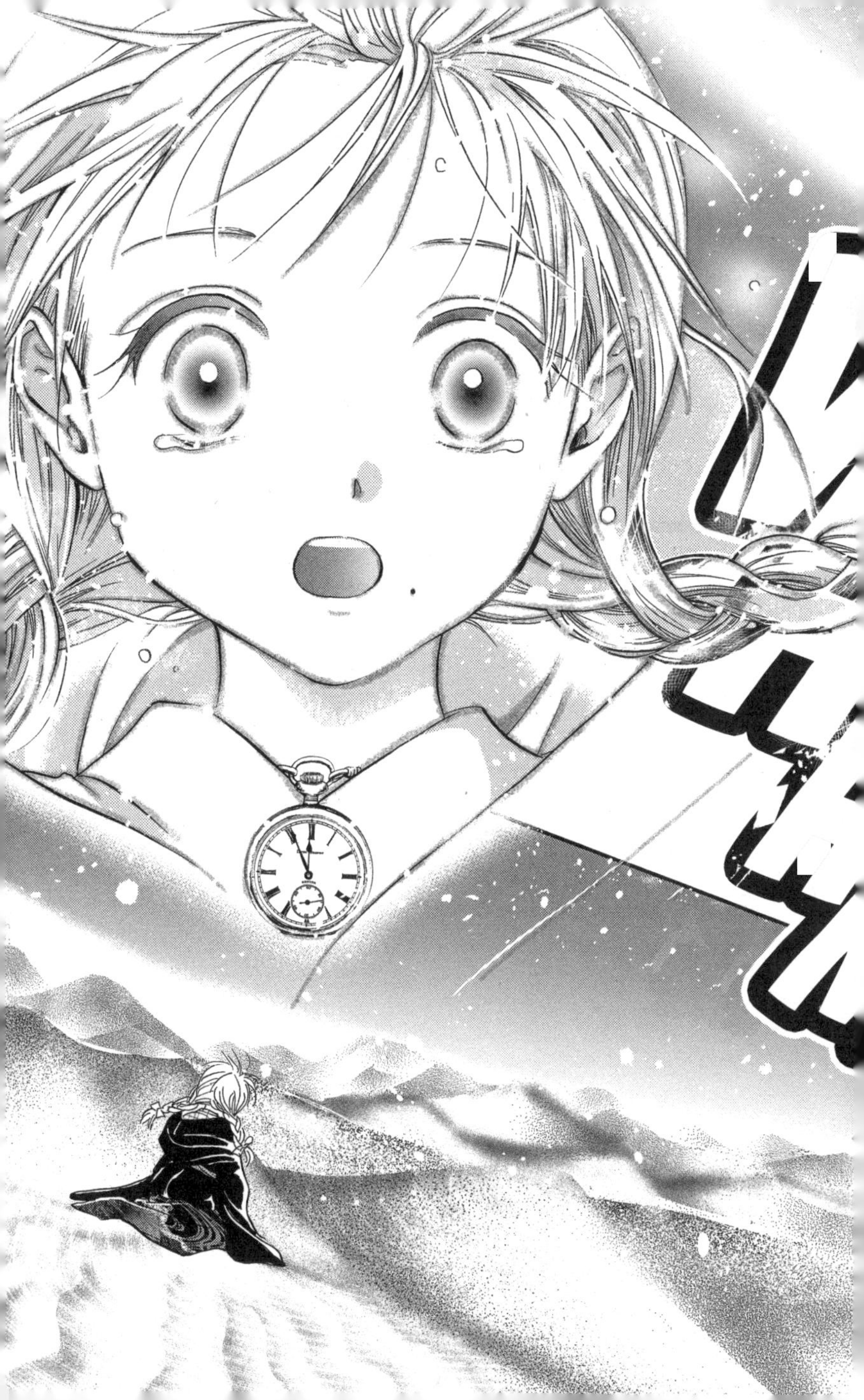

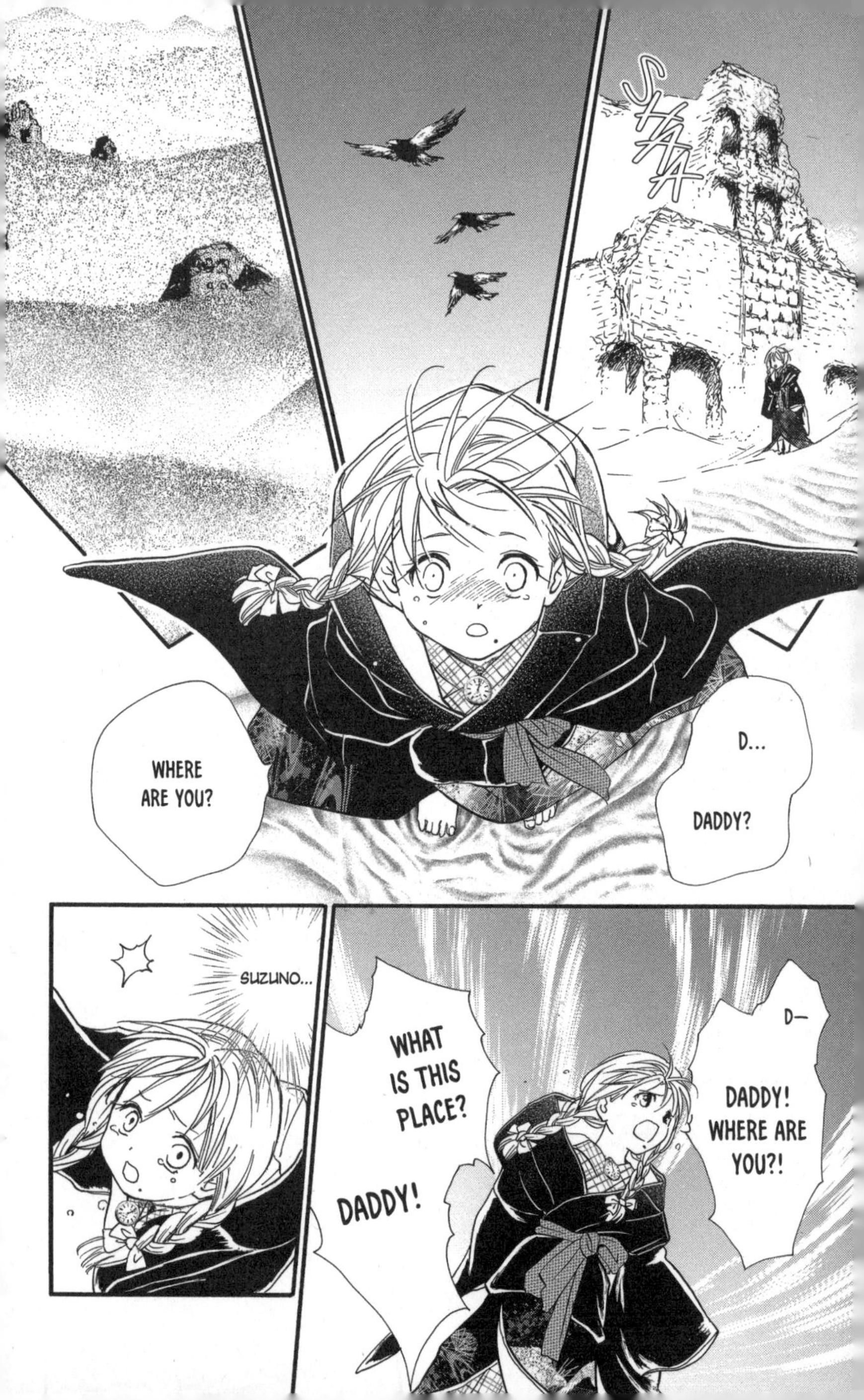
SHAAA
D...
DADDY?
WHERE ARE YOU?
D—
DADDY! WHERE ARE YOU?!
WHAT IS THIS PLACE?
DADDY!
SUZUNO...

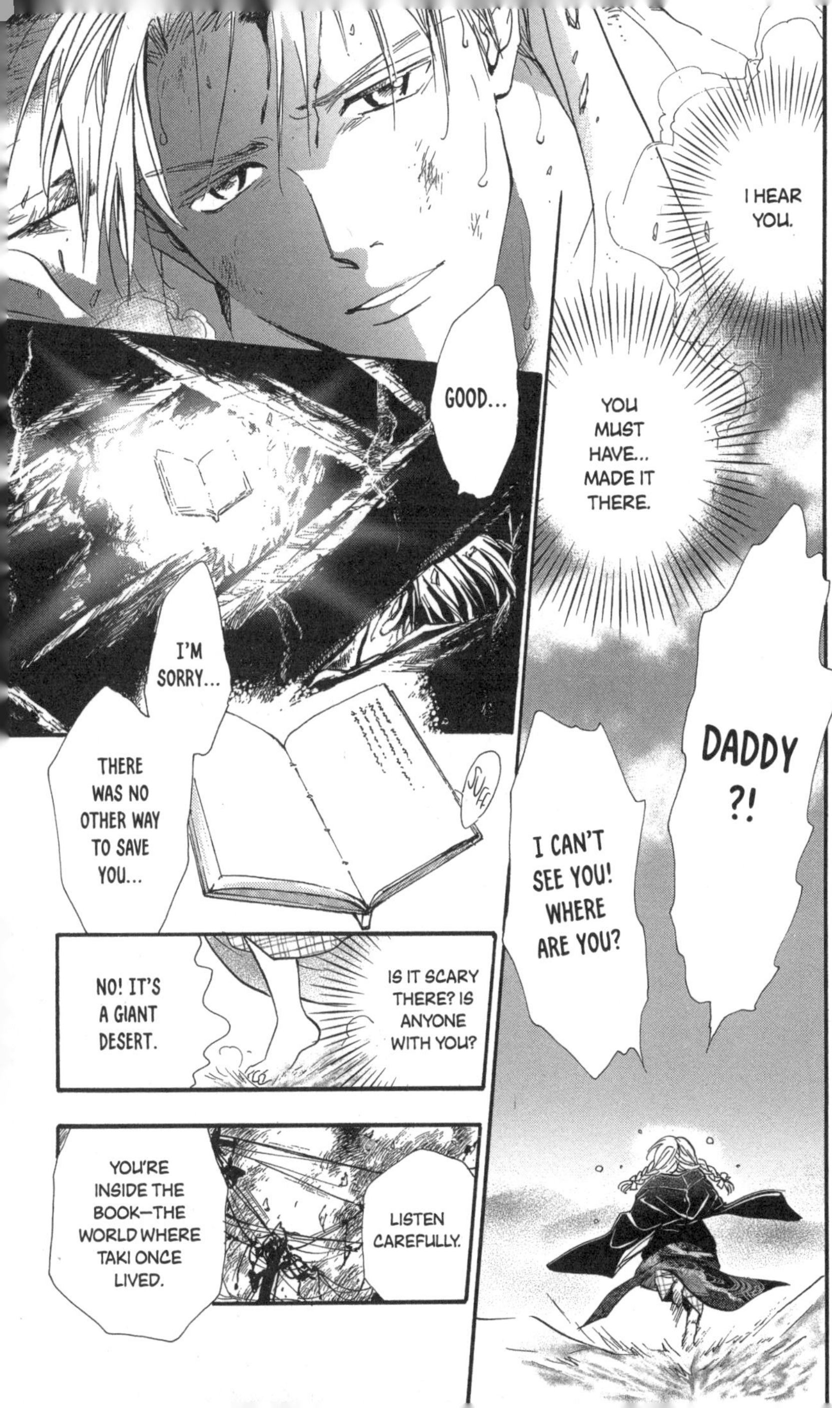
I HEAR YOU.
YOU MUST HAVE... MADE IT THERE.
DADDY?!
I CAN'T SEE YOU! WHERE ARE YOU?
GOOD...
I'M SORRY...
THERE WAS NO OTHER WAY TO SAVE YOU...
SUFF
IS IT SCARY THERE? IS ANYONE WITH YOU?
NO! IT'S A GIANT DESERT.
LISTEN CAREFULLY.
YOU'RE INSIDE THE BOOK—THE WORLD WHERE TAKI ONCE LIVED.

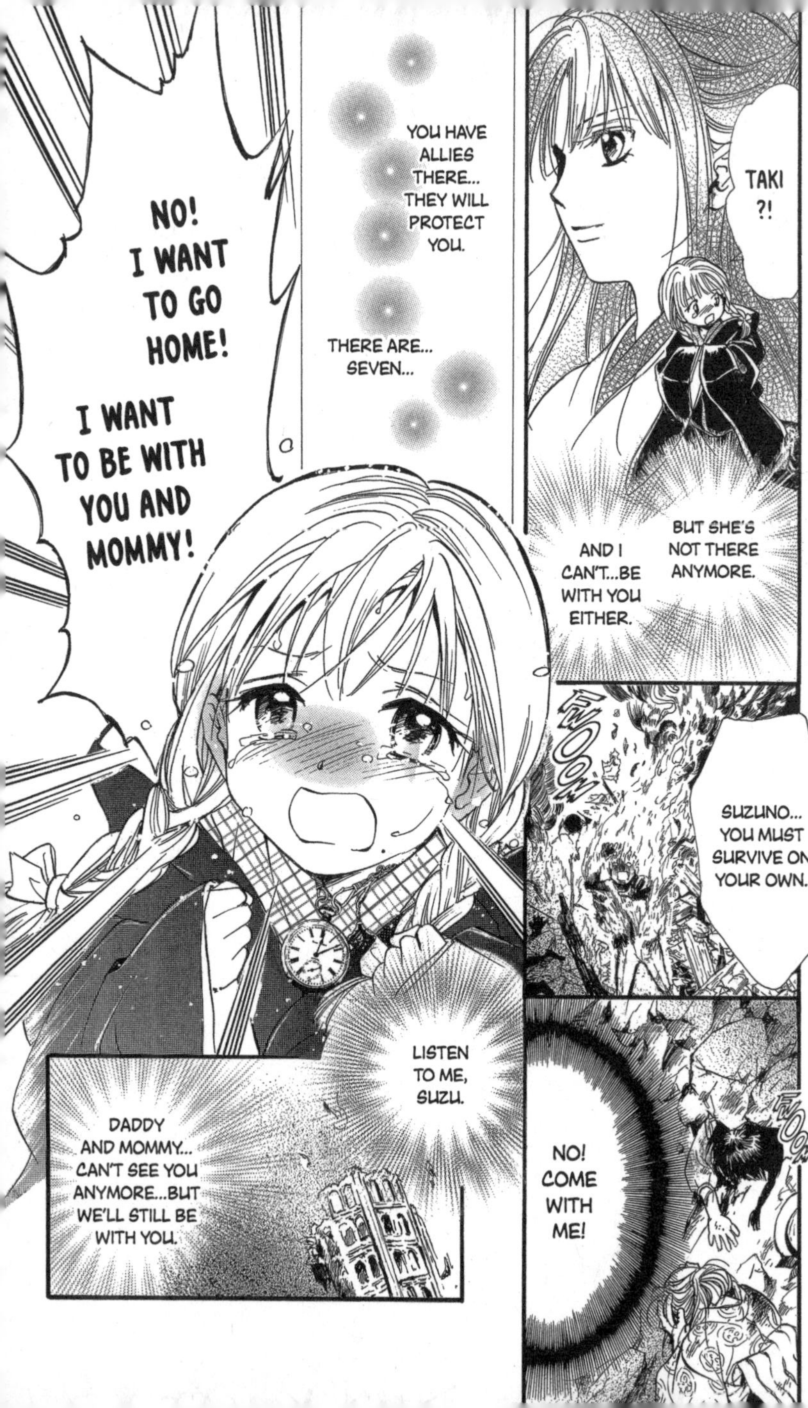
TAKI ?!
BUT SHE'S NOT THERE ANYMORE.
AND I CAN'T...BE WITH YOU EITHER.
YOU HAVE ALLIES THERE... THEY WILL PROTECT YOU.
THERE ARE... SEVEN...
NO! I WANT TO GO HOME!
I WANT TO BE WITH YOU AND MOMMY!
FWOOOM
SUZUNO... YOU MUST SURVIVE ON YOUR OWN.
FWOOOM
NO! COME WITH ME!
LISTEN TO ME, SUZU.
DADDY AND MOMMY... CAN'T SEE YOU ANYMORE...BUT WE'LL STILL BE WITH YOU.

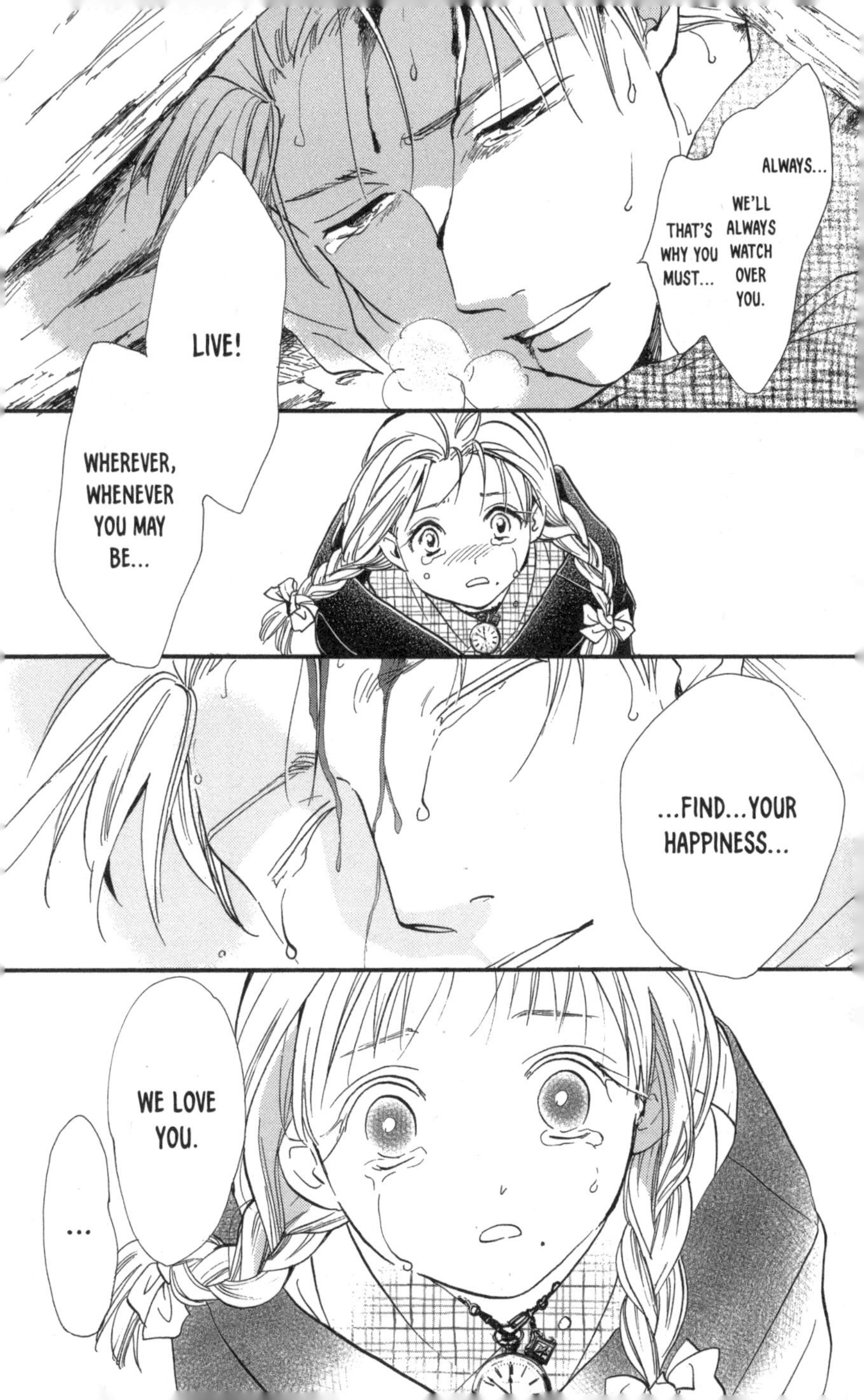
ALWAYS...
WE'LL ALWAYS WATCH OVER YOU.
THAT'S WHY YOU MUST...
LIVE!
WHEREVER, WHENEVER YOU MAY BE...
...FIND...YOUR HAPPINESS...
WE LOVE YOU.
...

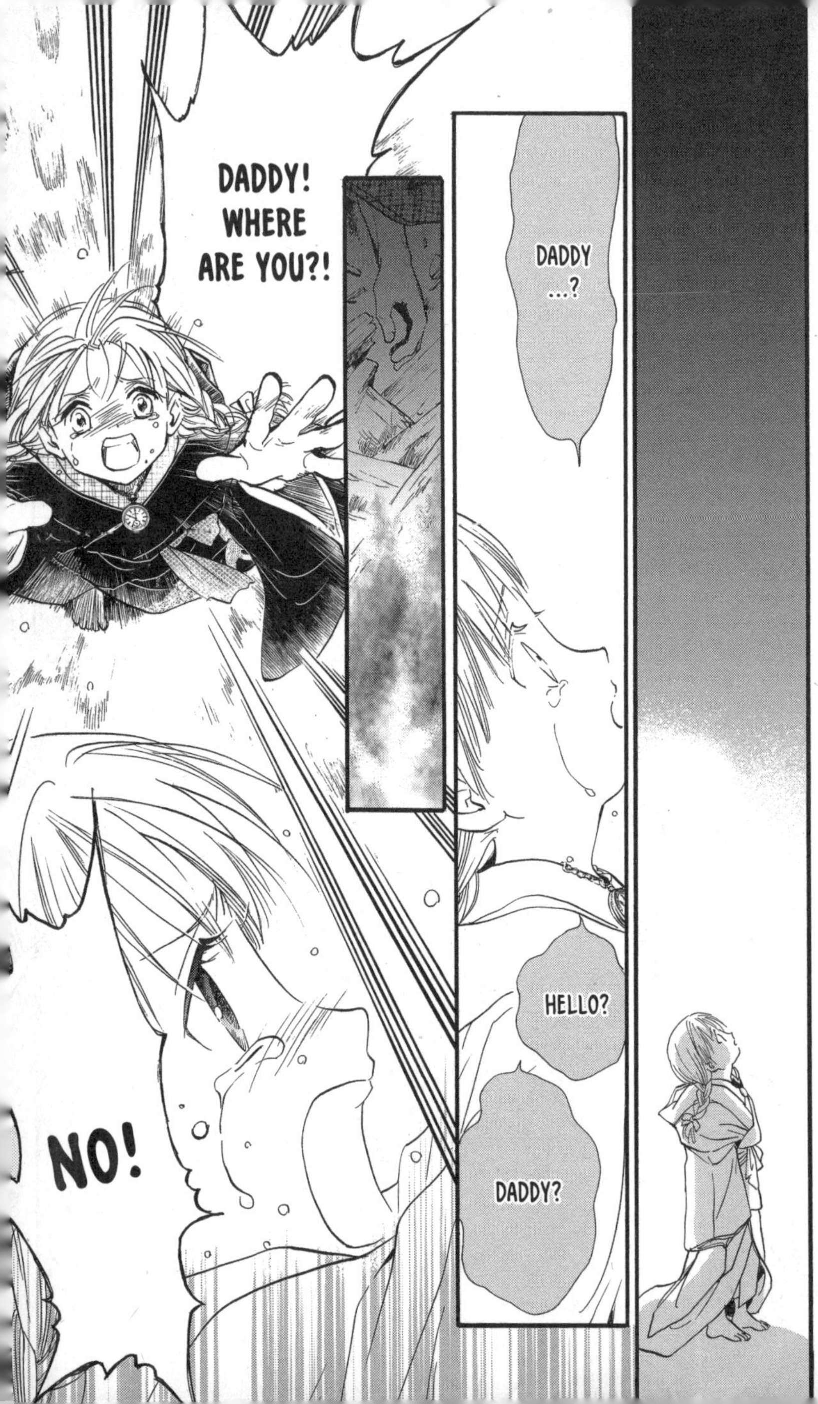
DADDY ...?
HELLO?
DADDY?
DADDY! WHERE ARE YOU?!
NO!

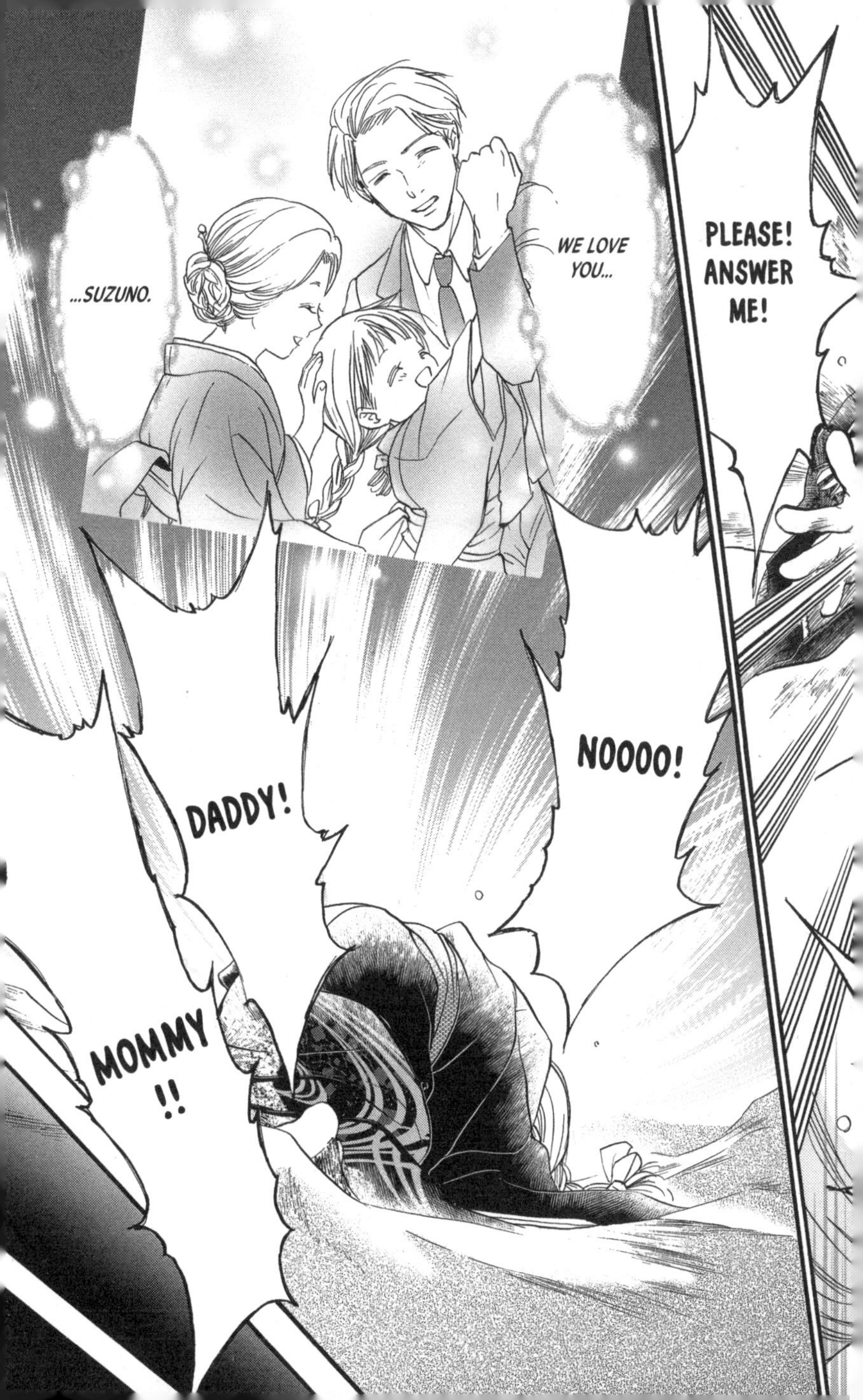
PLEASE! ANSWER ME!
WE LOVE YOU...
...SUZUNO.
NOOOO!
DADDY!
MOMMY!!

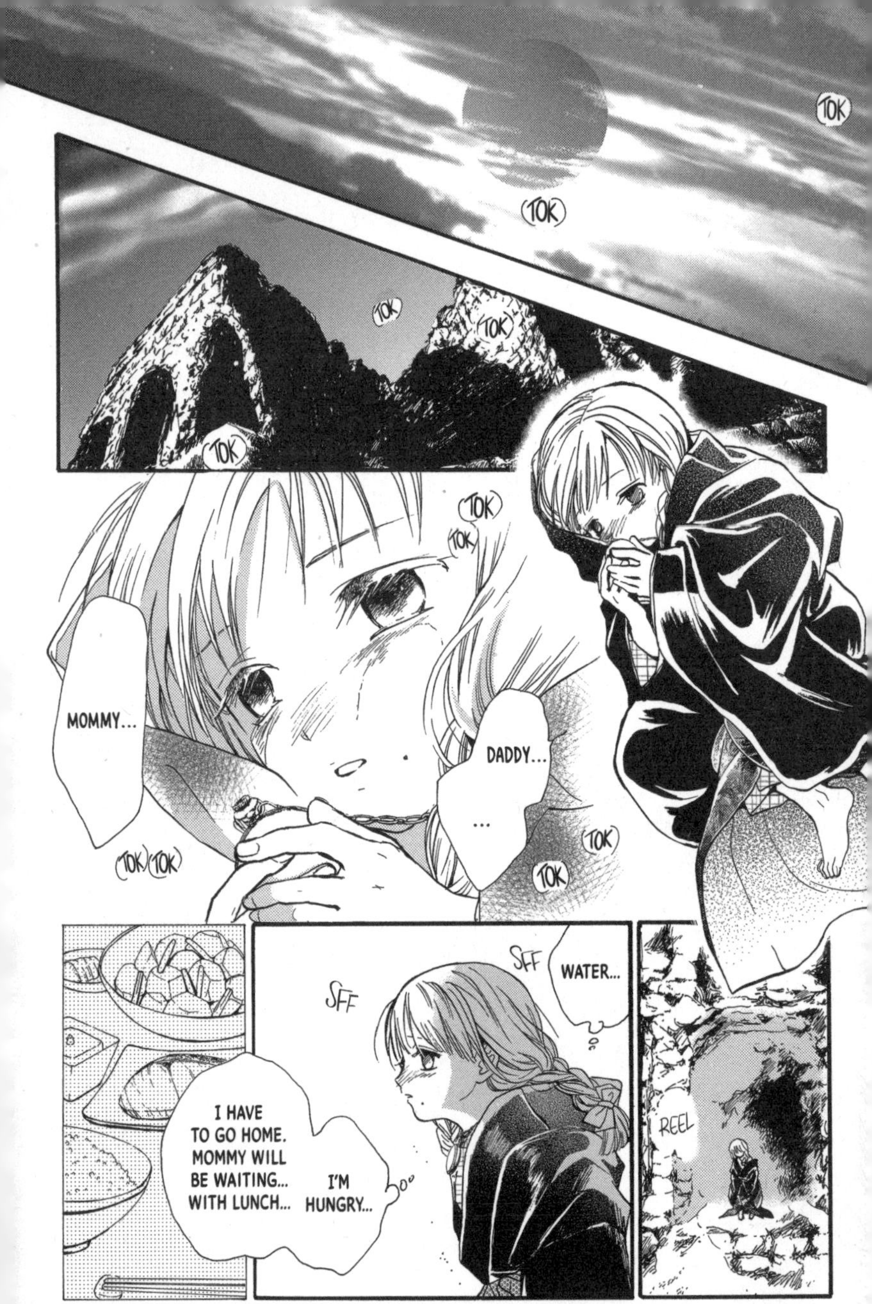
TOK
TOK
TOK
TOK
TOK
TOK
TOK
DADDY...
MOMMY...
...
TOK
TOK
TOK
TOK
REEL
SFF
WATER...
SFF
I'M HUNGRY...
I HAVE TO GO HOME. MOMMY WILL BE WAITING... WITH LUNCH...

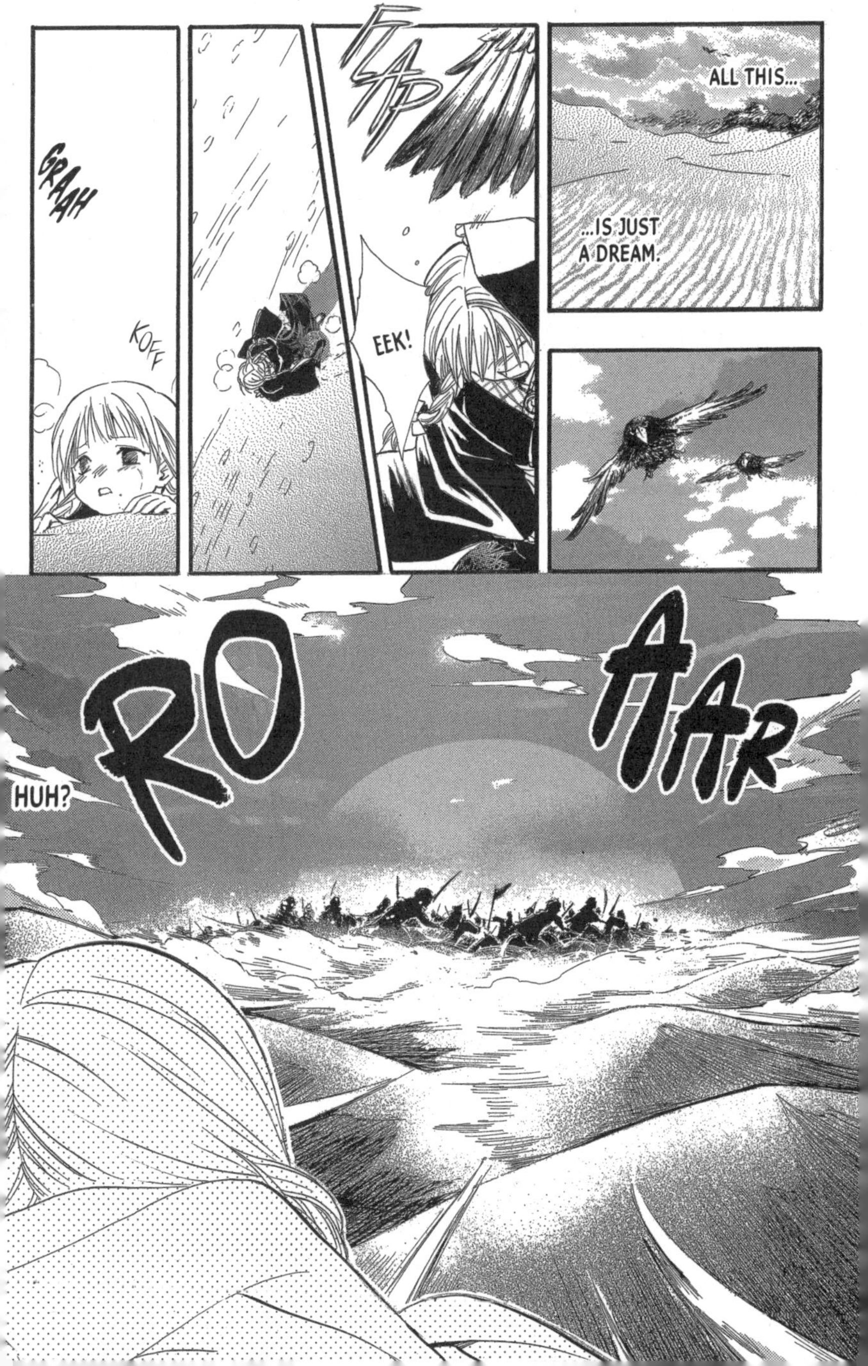
ALL THIS...
...IS JUST A DREAM.
FLAP
EEK!
GRAAH
KOFF
RO AAR
HUH?

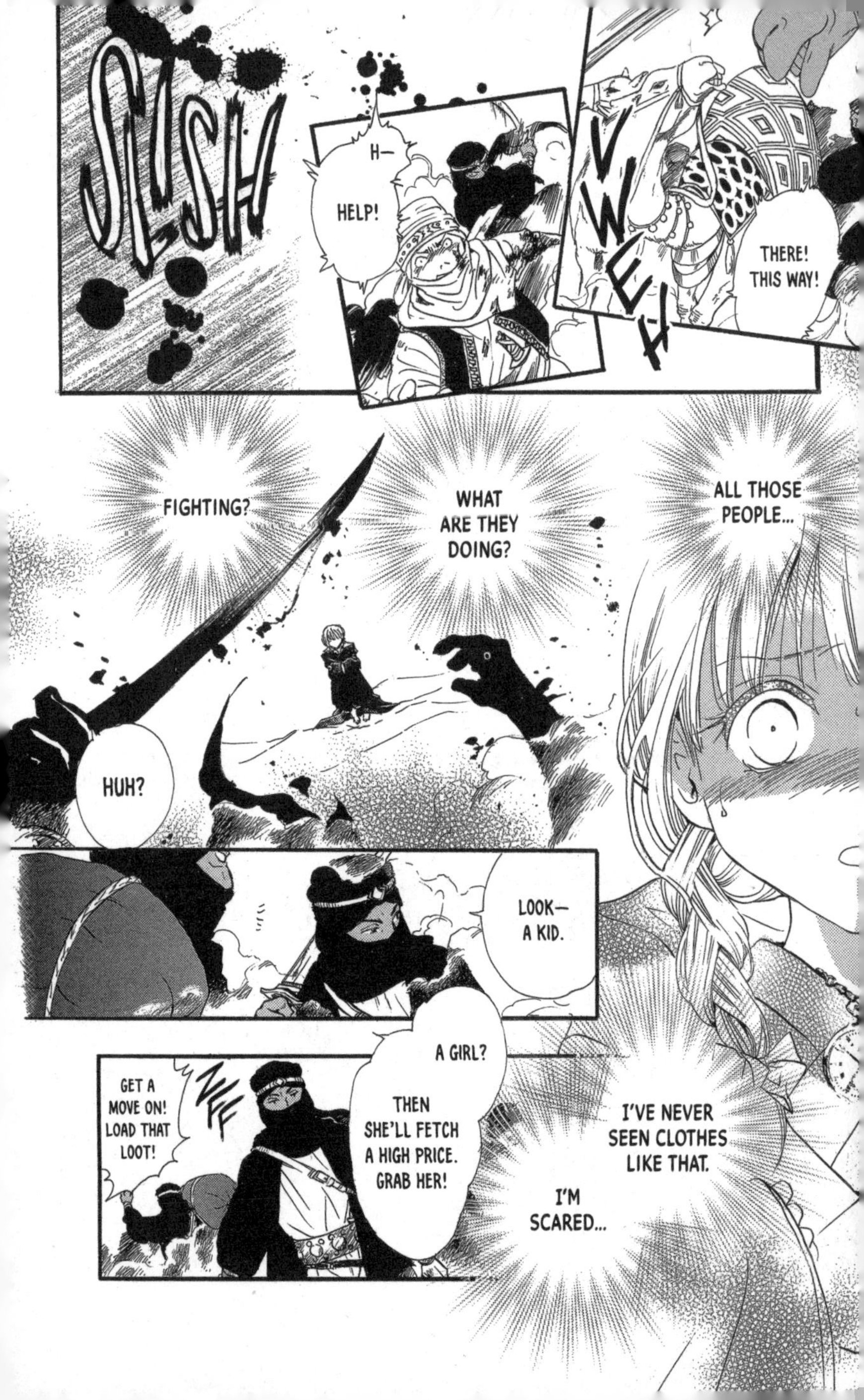
VWEH
THERE! THIS WAY!
H—
HELP!
SLASH
ALL THOSE PEOPLE...
I'VE NEVER SEEN CLOTHES LIKE THAT.
I'M SCARED...
WHAT ARE THEY DOING?
FIGHTING?
HUH?
LOOK— A KID.
A GIRL?
THEN SHE'LL FETCH A HIGH PRICE. GRAB HER!
GET A MOVE ON! LOAD THAT LOOT!

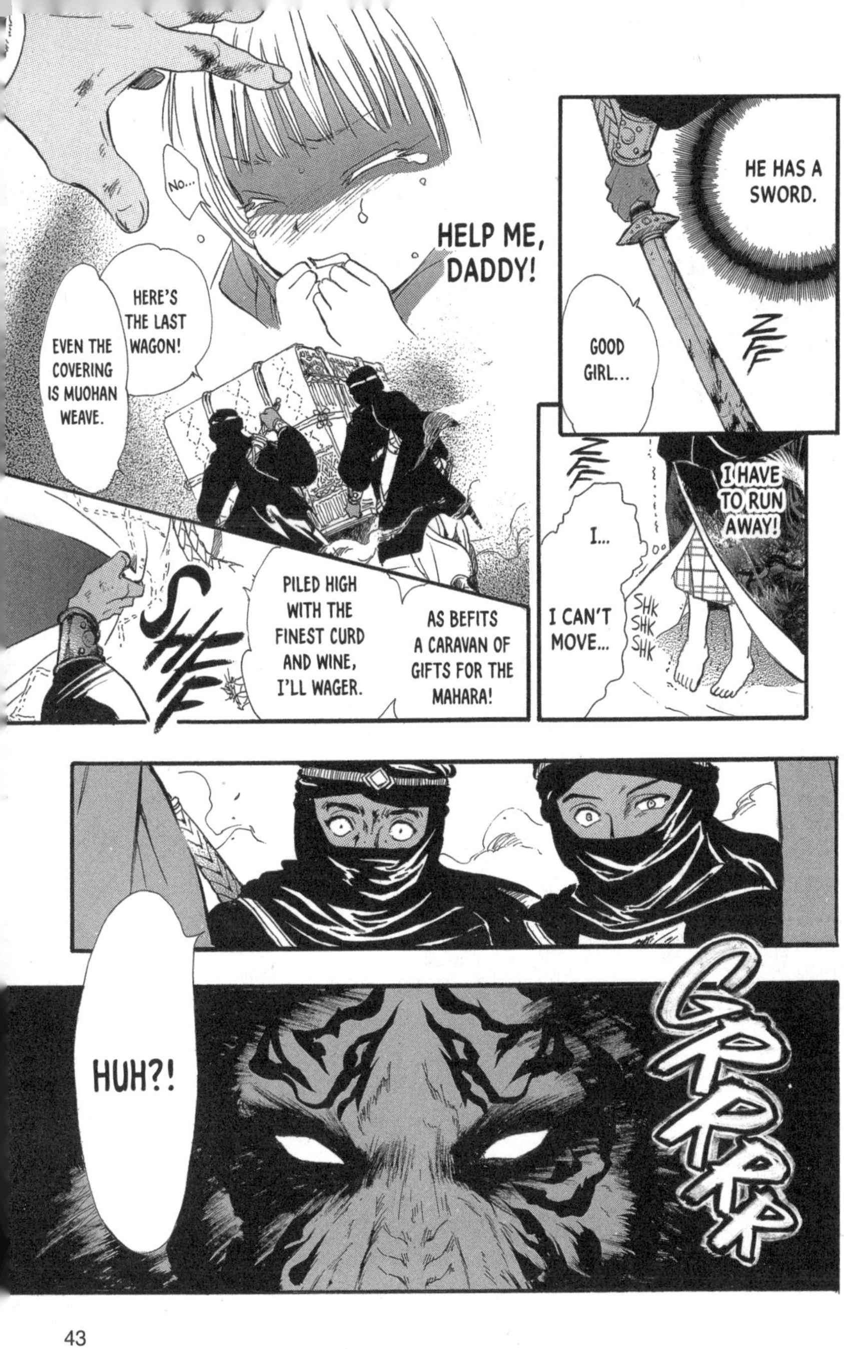
HE HAS A SWORD.
ZFF
GOOD GIRL...
I HAVE TO RUN AWAY!
ZFF
I...
I CAN'T MOVE...
SHK SHK SHK
NO...
HELP ME, DADDY!
HERE'S THE LAST WAGON!
EVEN THE COVERING IS MUOHAN WEAVE.
AS BEFITS A CARAVAN OF GIFTS FOR THE MAHARA!
PILED HIGH WITH THE FINEST CURD AND WINE, I'LL WAGER.
SHFF
HUH?!
GRRRR

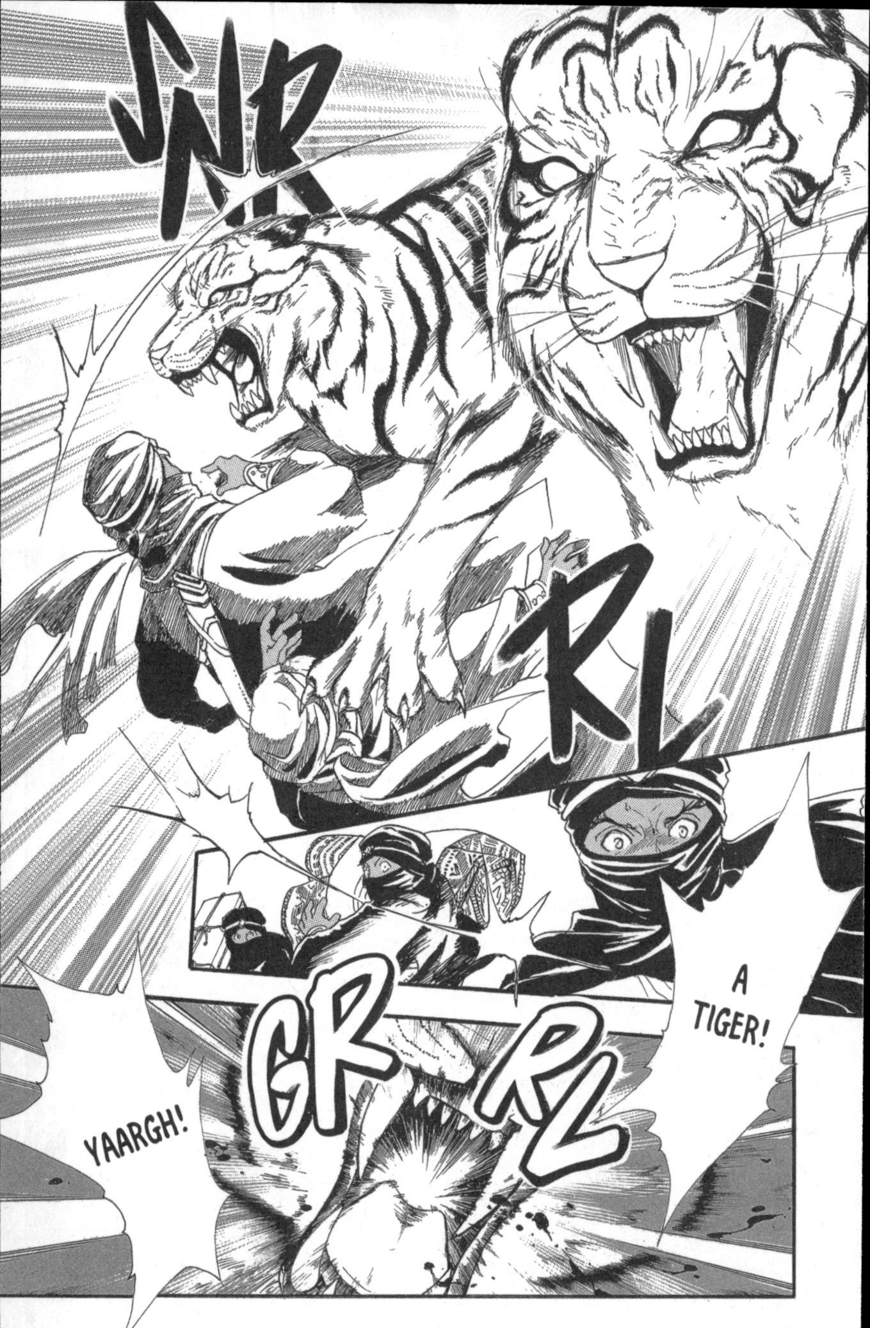
SNR
RL
A TIGER!
GRRL
YAARGH!

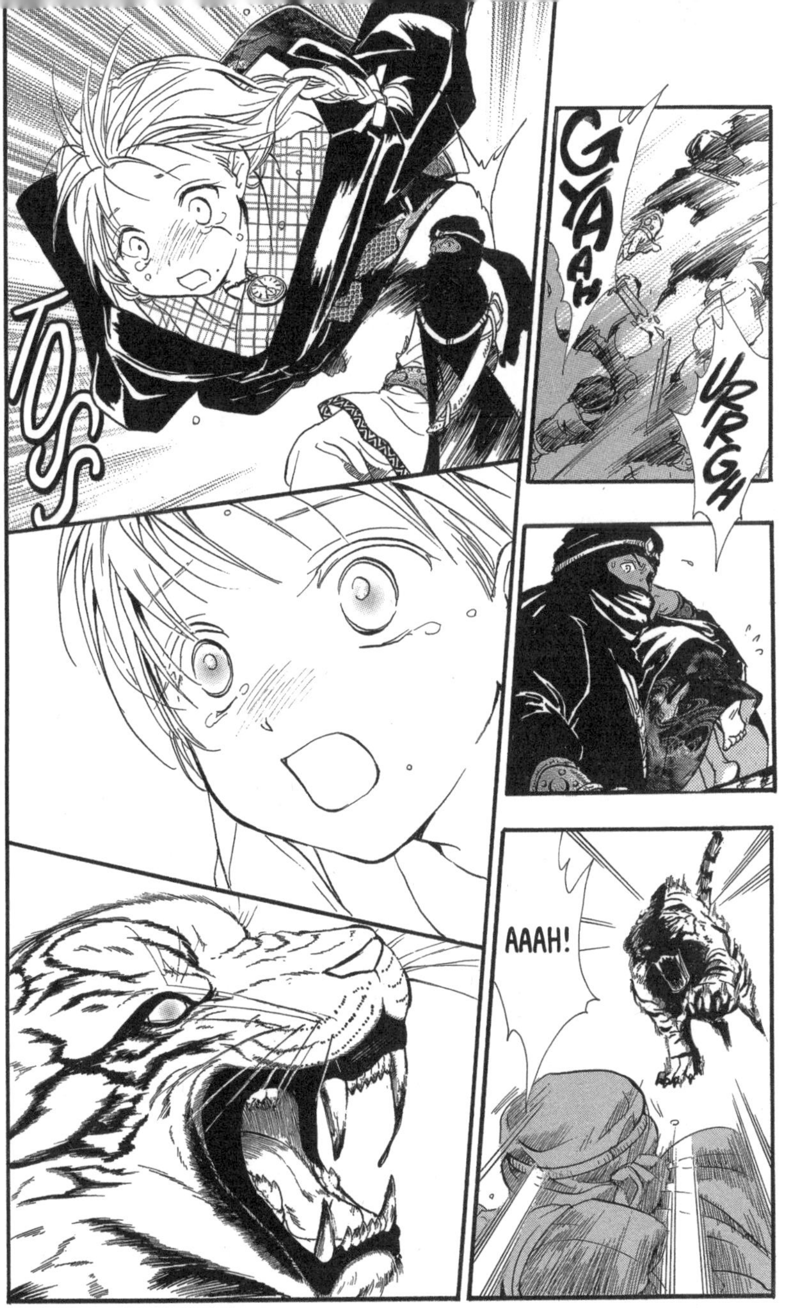
GYAAH
URRGH
AAAH!
TOSS

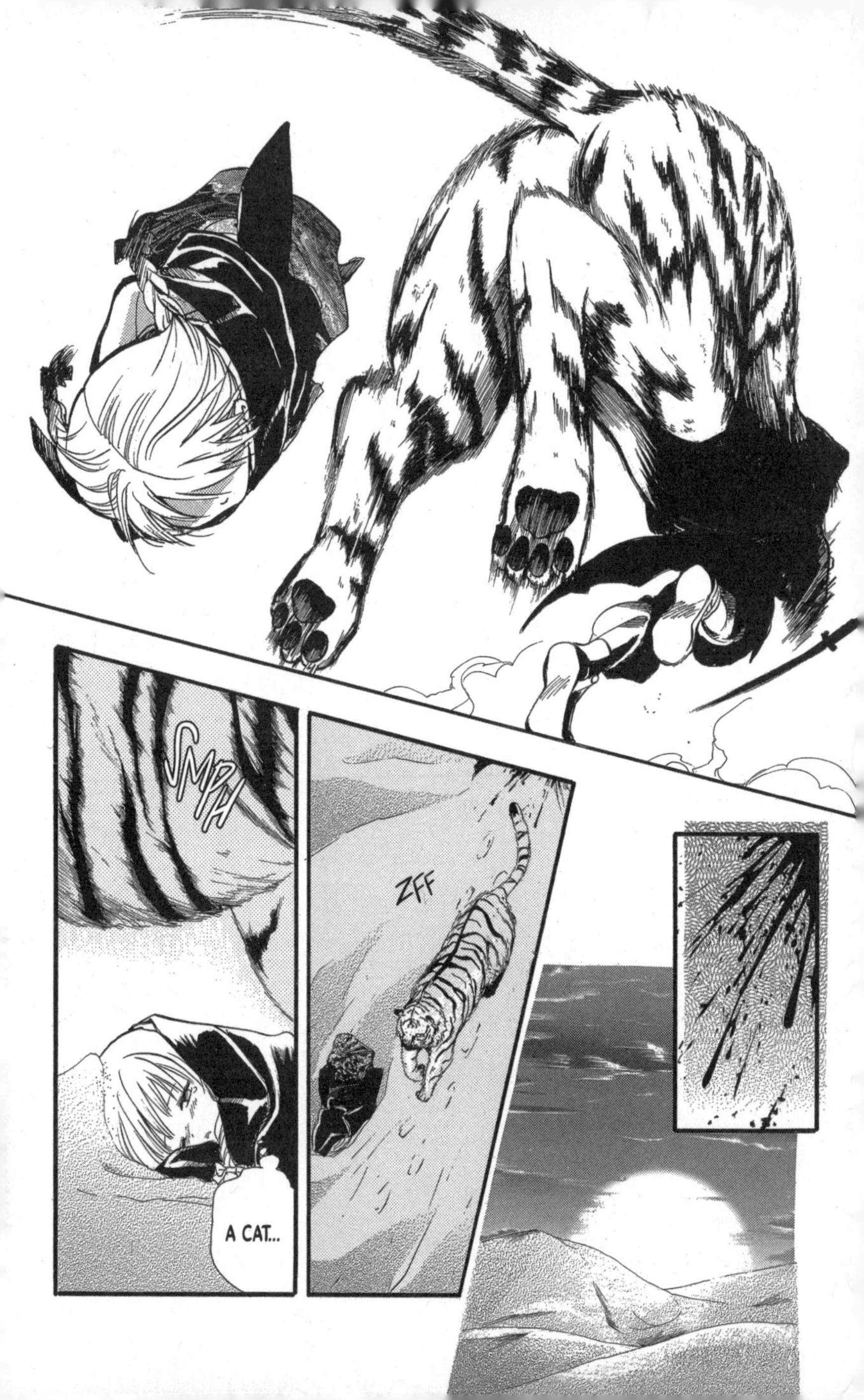
ZFF
SMPH
A CAT...

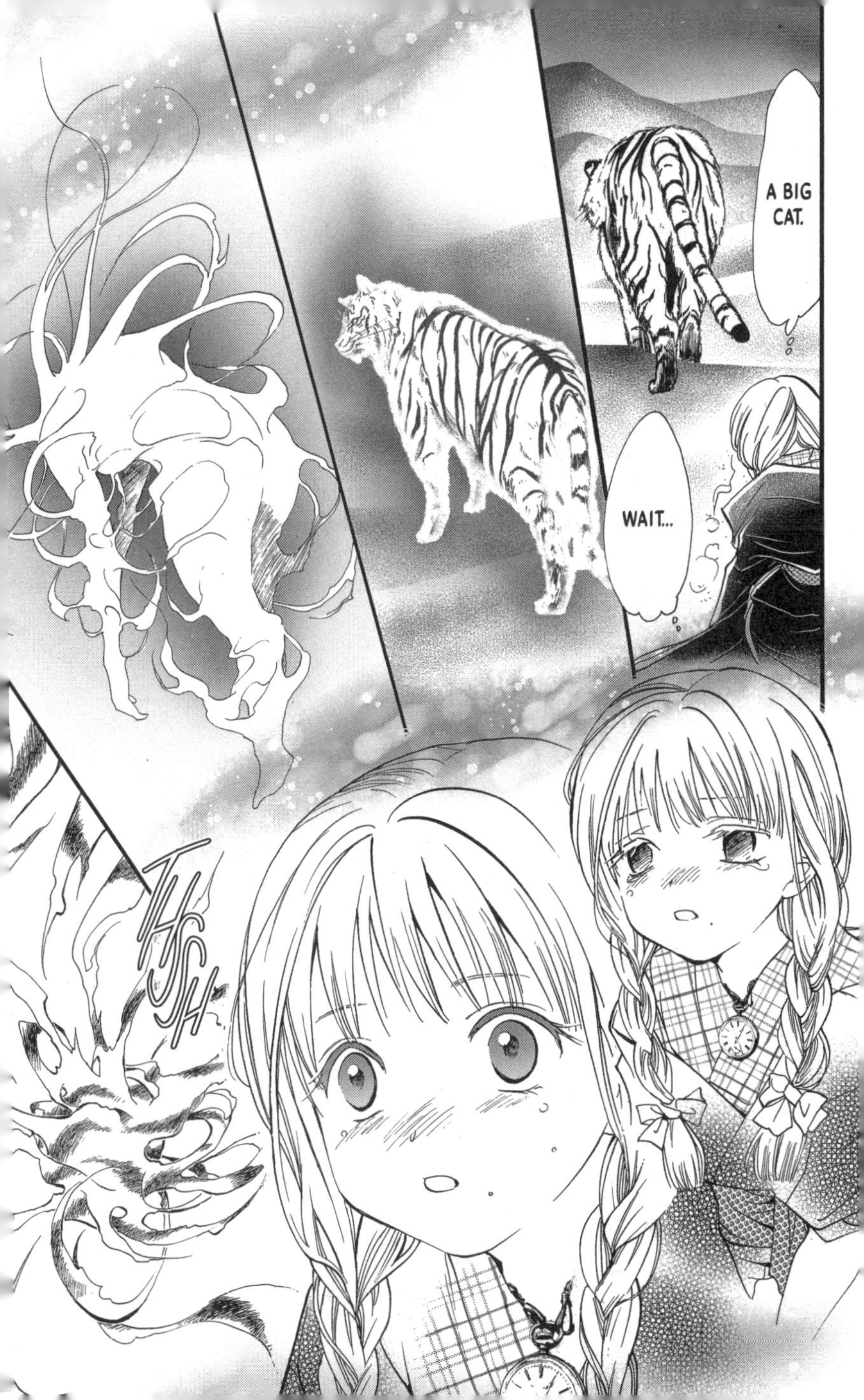
A BIG CAT.
WAIT...
THSSH

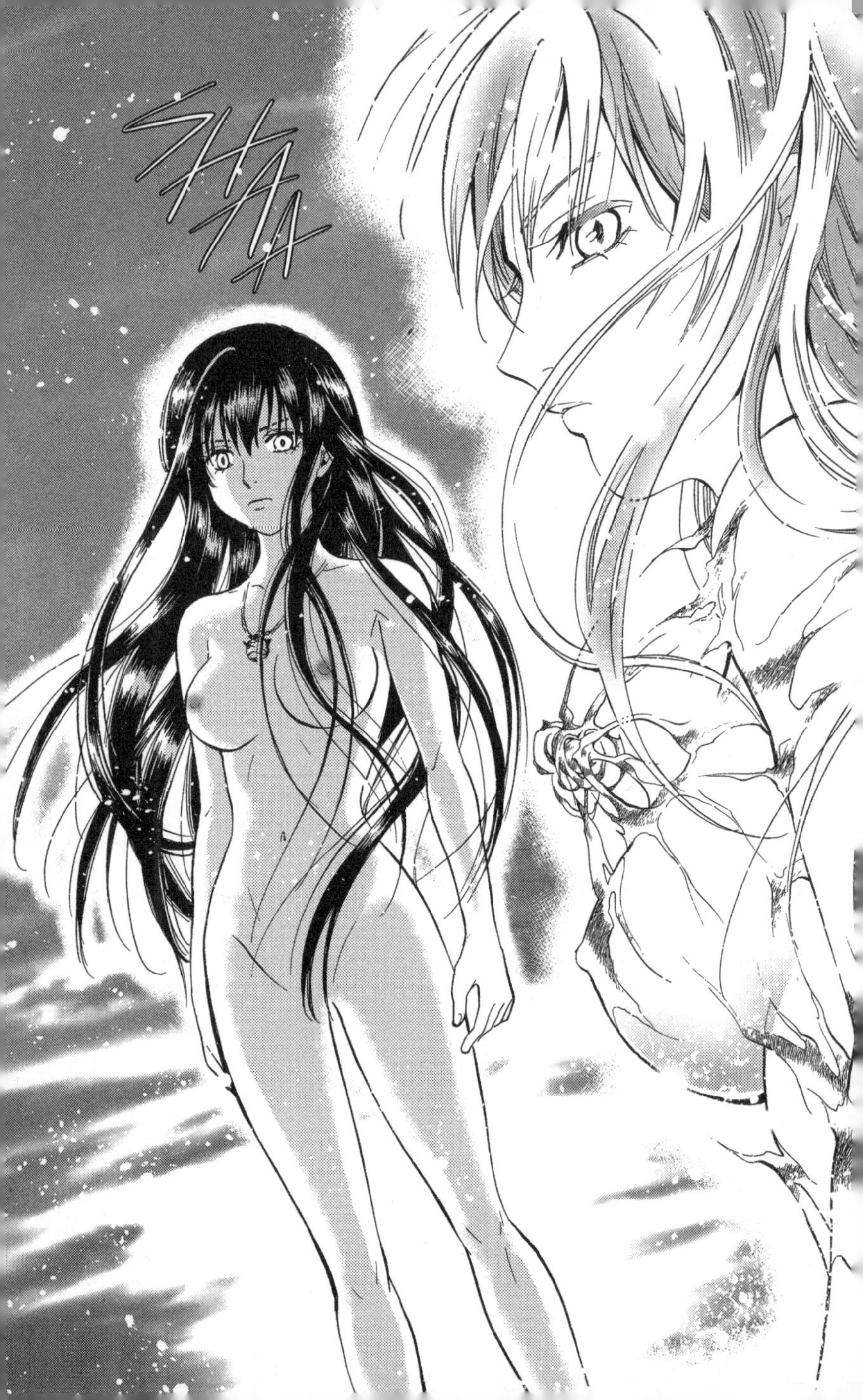
SHAA

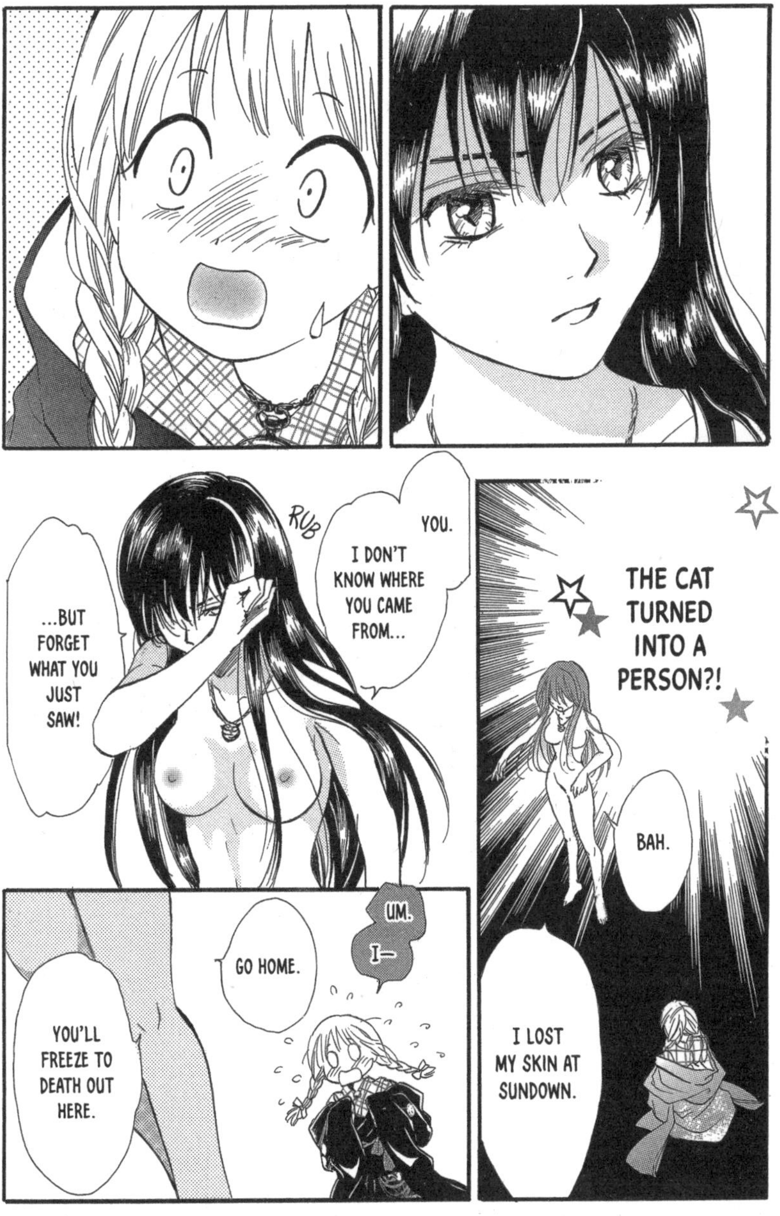
THE CAT TURNED INTO A PERSON?!
BAH.
I LOST MY SKIN AT SUNDOWN.
RUB
YOU.
I DON'T KNOW WHERE YOU CAME FROM...
...BUT FORGET WHAT YOU JUST SAW!
UM.
I—
GO HOME.
YOU'LL FREEZE TO DEATH OUT HERE.

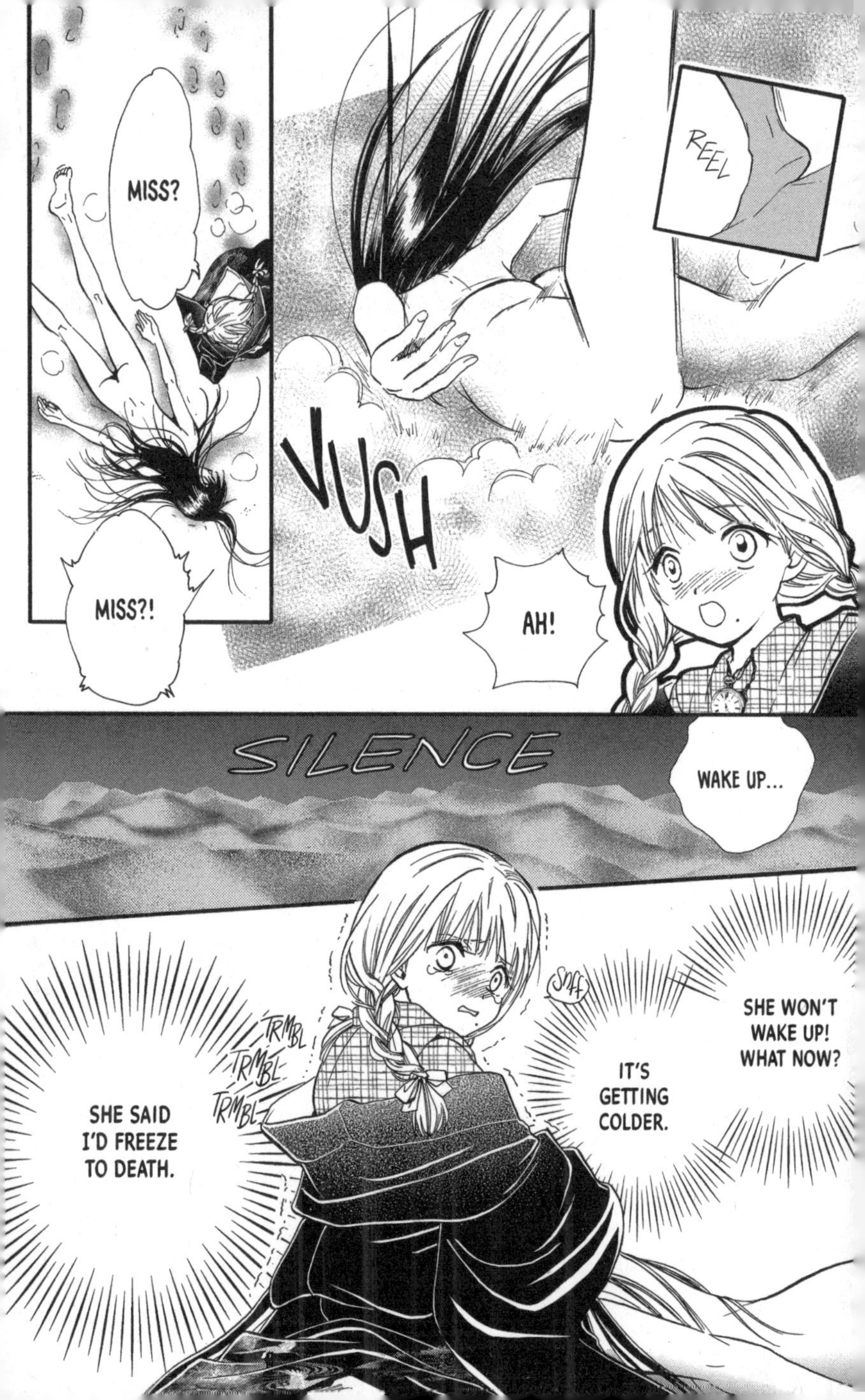
REEL
VUSH
AH!
MISS?
MISS?!
SILENCE
WAKE UP...
SHE WON'T WAKE UP! WHAT NOW?
SNFF
IT'S GETTING COLDER.
TRMBL TRMBL TRMBL
SHE SAID I'D FREEZE TO DEATH.

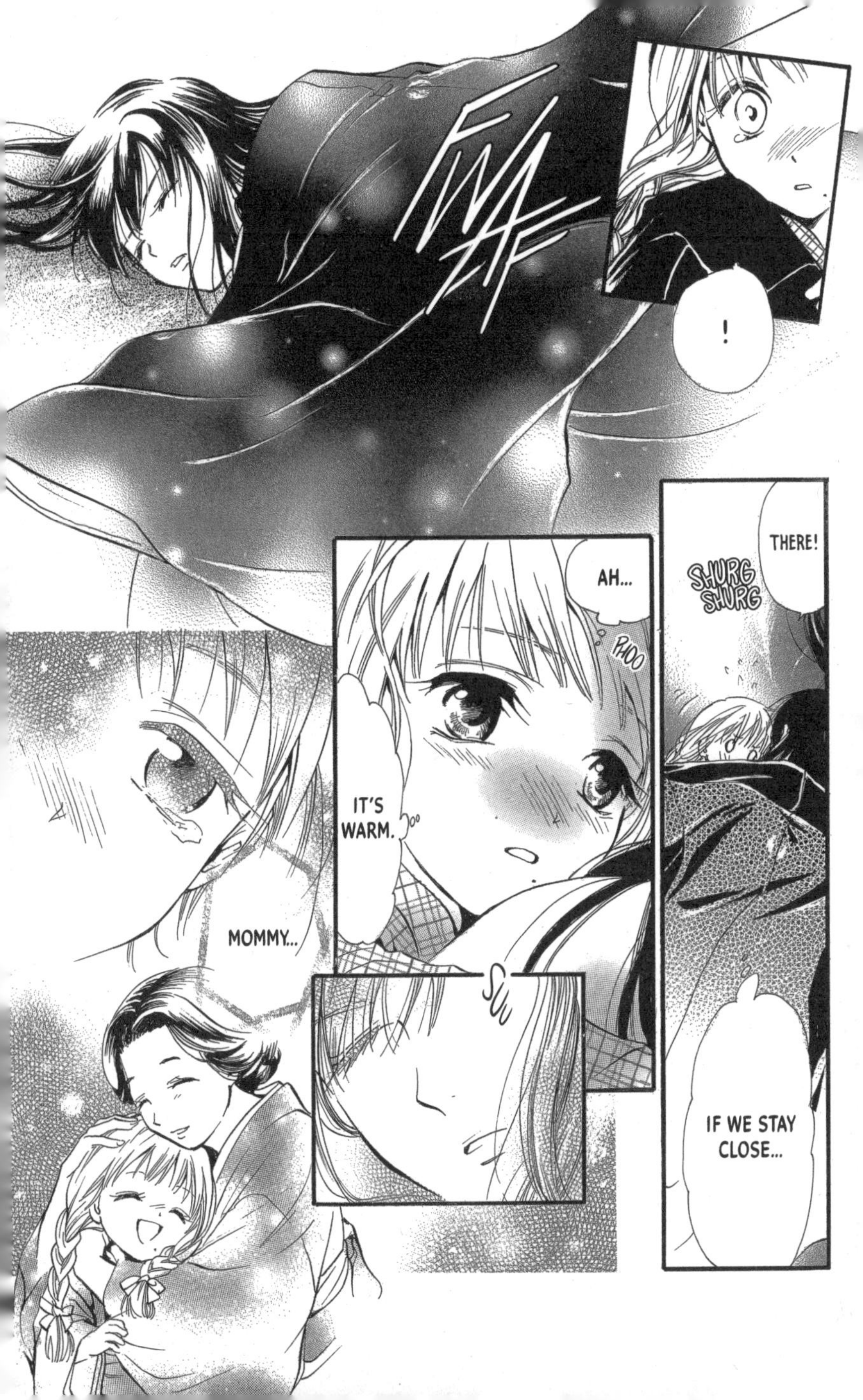
!
FWAFF
THERE!
SHURG SHURG
IF WE STAY CLOSE...
AH...
PHOO
IT'S WARM.
SUU
MOMMY...

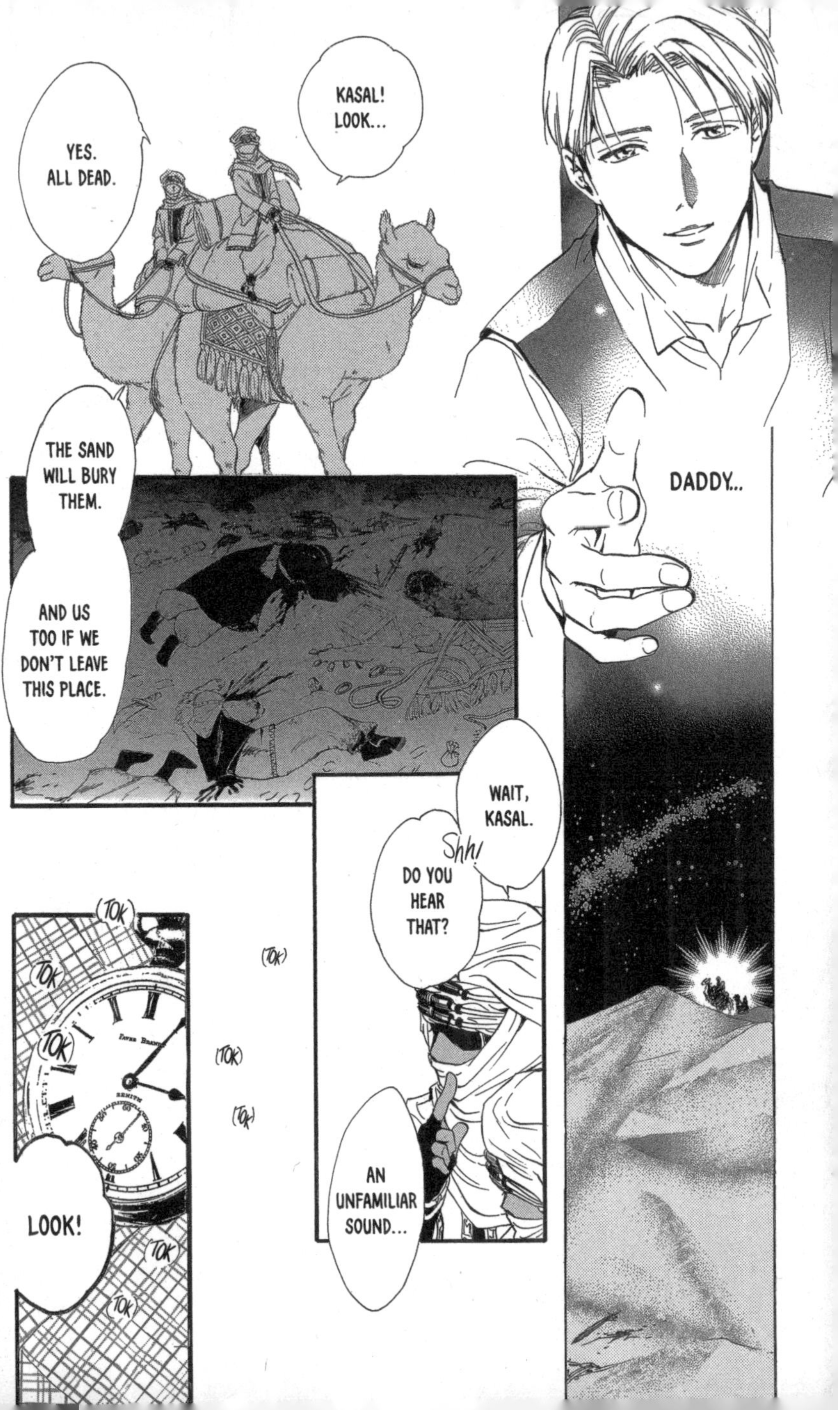
DADDY...
KASAL! LOOK...
YES. ALL DEAD.
THE SAND WILL BURY THEM.
AND US TOO IF WE DON'T LEAVE THIS PLACE.
WAIT, KASAL.
Shh!
DO YOU HEAR THAT?
AN UNFAMILIAR SOUND...
(TOK)
(TOK)
(TOK)
(TOK)
(TOK)
(TOK)
(TOK)
(TOK)
LOOK!

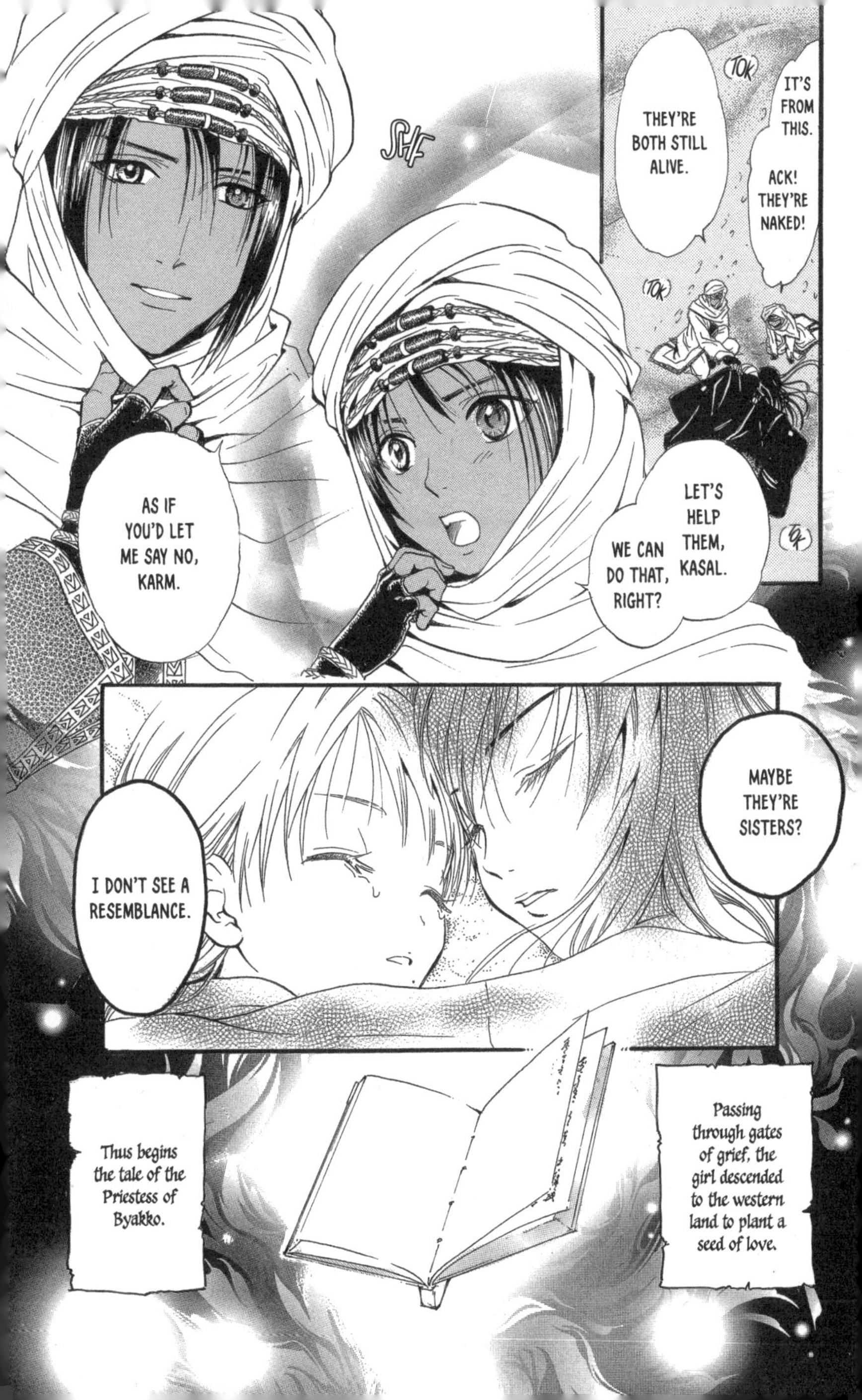
TOK
IT'S FROM THIS.
ACK! THEY'RE NAKED!
THEY'RE BOTH STILL ALIVE.
TOK
TOK
SHF
LET'S HELP THEM, KASAL.
WE CAN DO THAT, RIGHT?
AS IF YOU'D LET ME SAY NO, KARM.
MAYBE THEY'RE SISTERS?
I DON'T SEE A RESEMBLANCE.
Passing through gates of grief, the girl descended to the western land to plant a seed of love.
Thus begins the tale of the Priestess of Byakko.

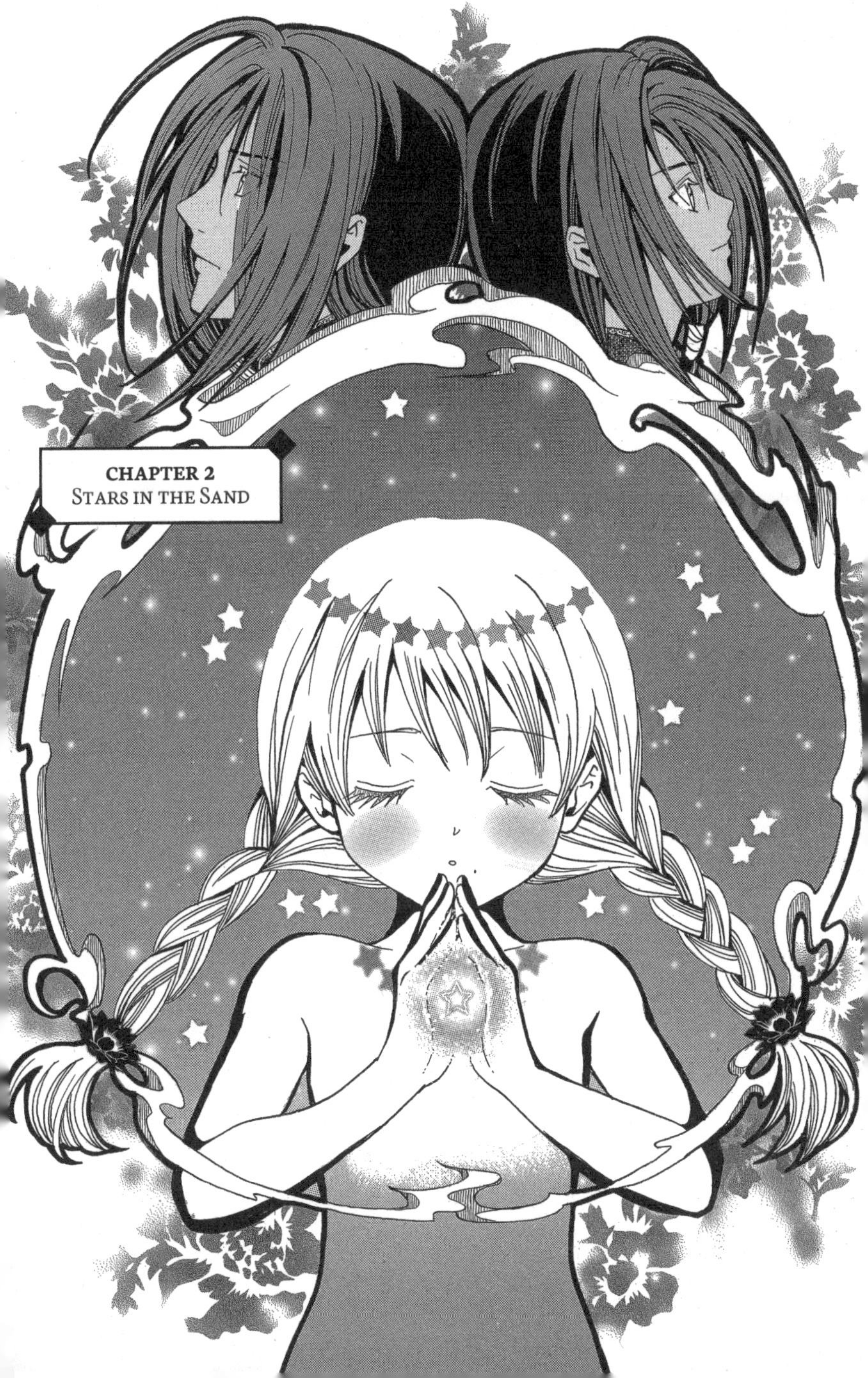
CHAPTER 2
Stars in the Sand

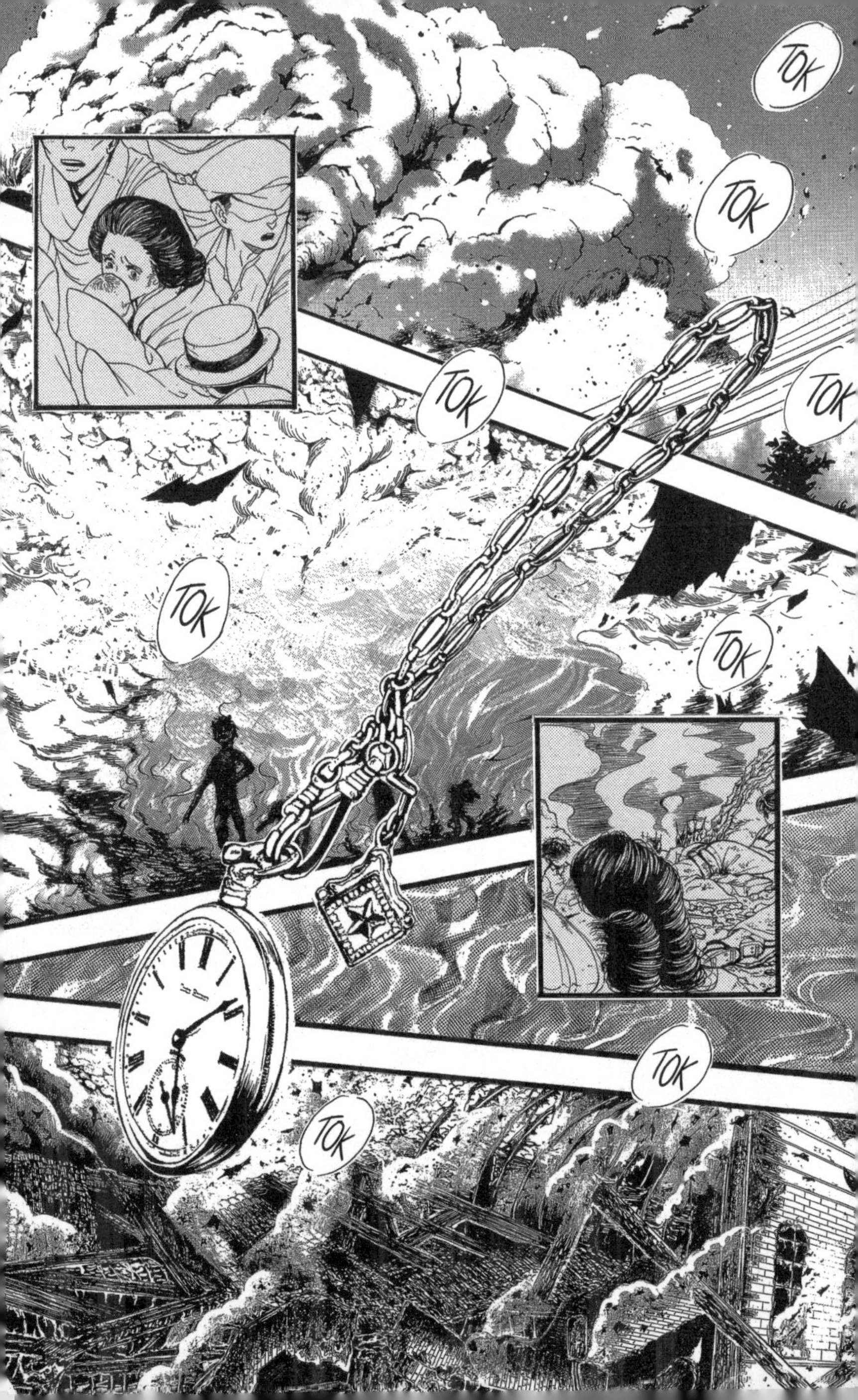
TOK
TOK
TOK
TOK
TOK
TOK
TOK
TOK
TOK

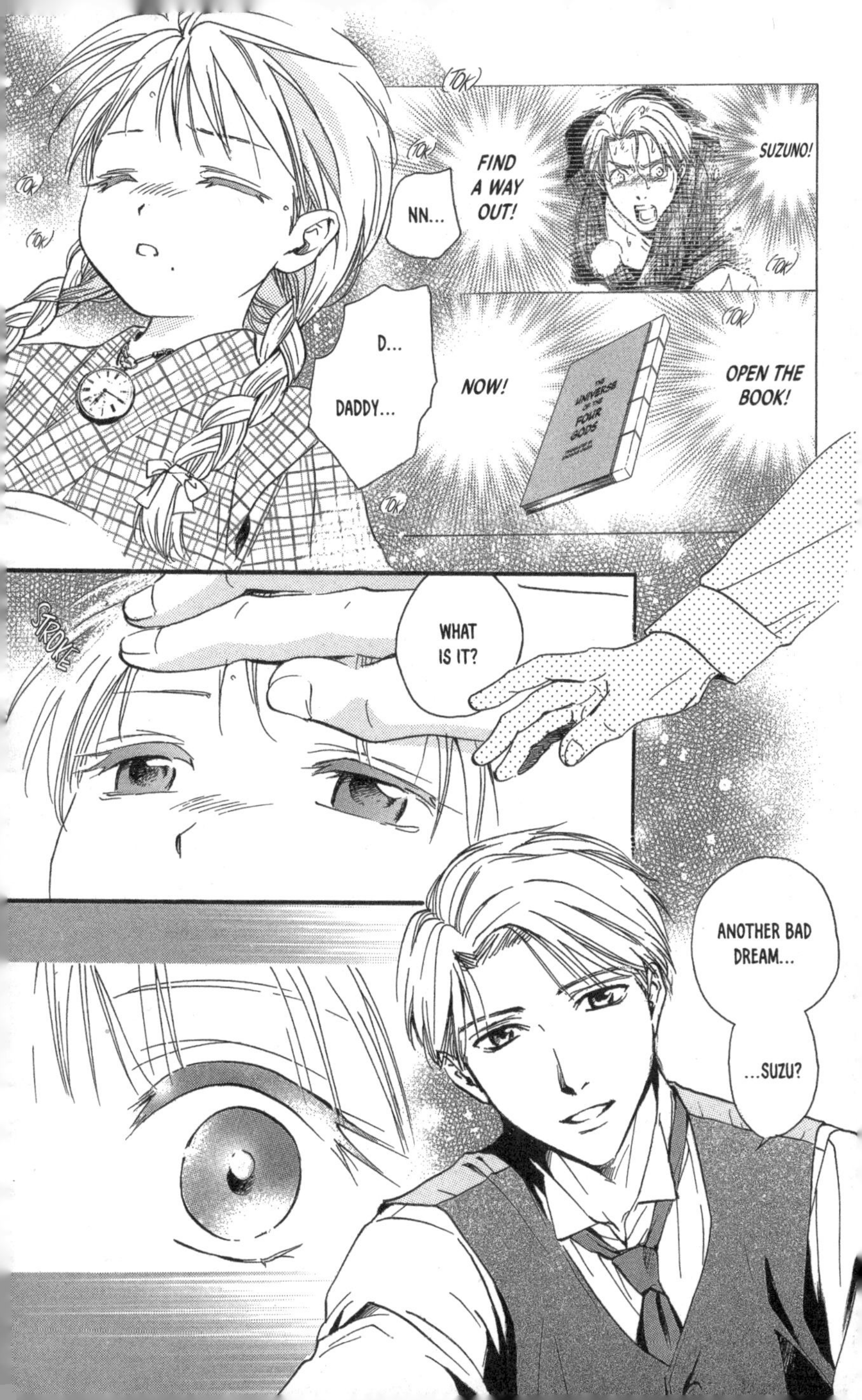
(TOK)
SUZUNO!
FIND A WAY OUT!
(TOK)
(TOK)
OPEN THE BOOK!
NOW!
THE UNIVERSE OF THE FOUR GODS
(TOK)
(TOK)
NN...
(TOK)
(TOK)
D...
DADDY...
WHAT IS IT?
STROKE
ANOTHER BAD DREAM...
...SUZU?

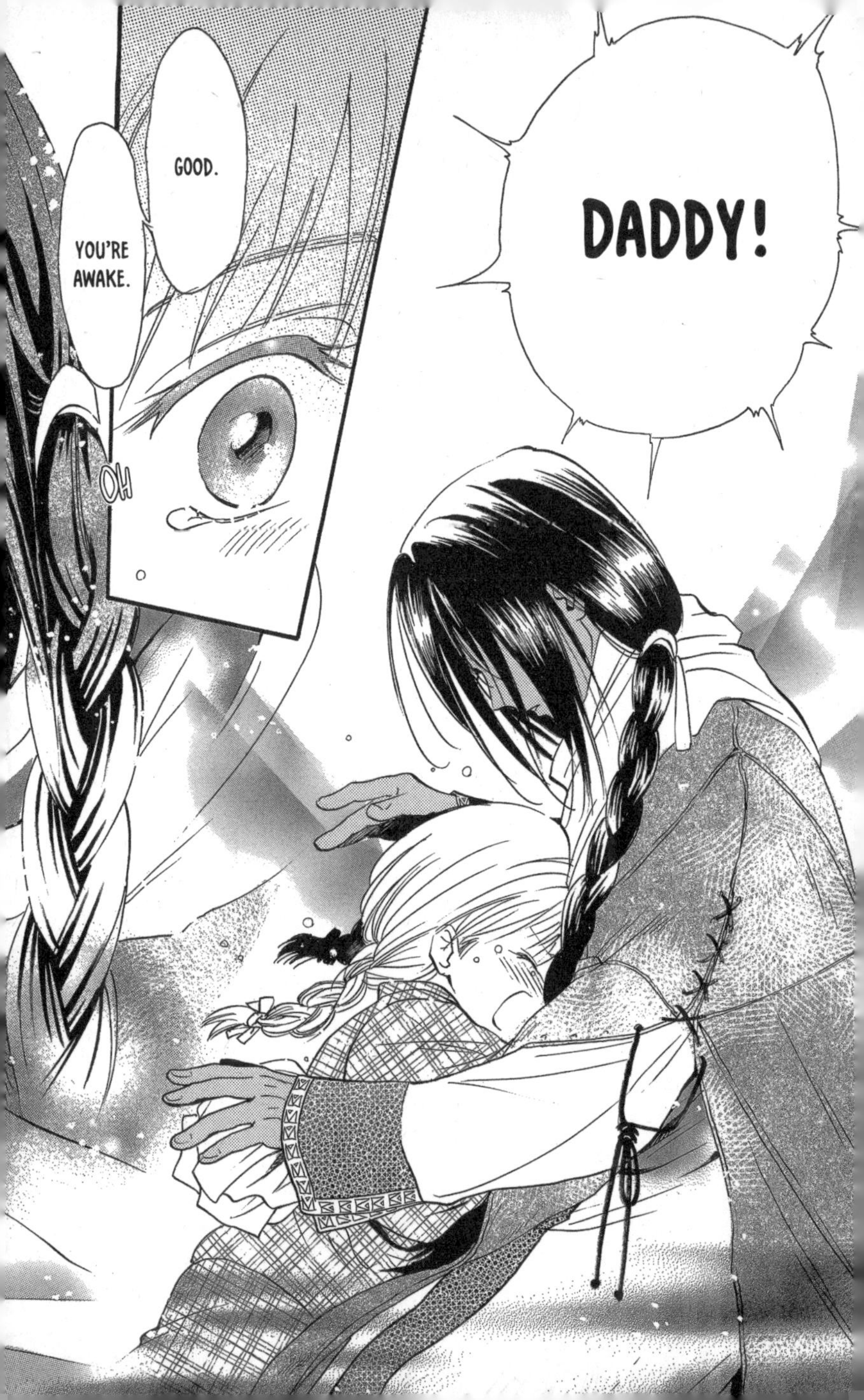
DADDY!
GOOD.
YOU'RE AWAKE.
OH

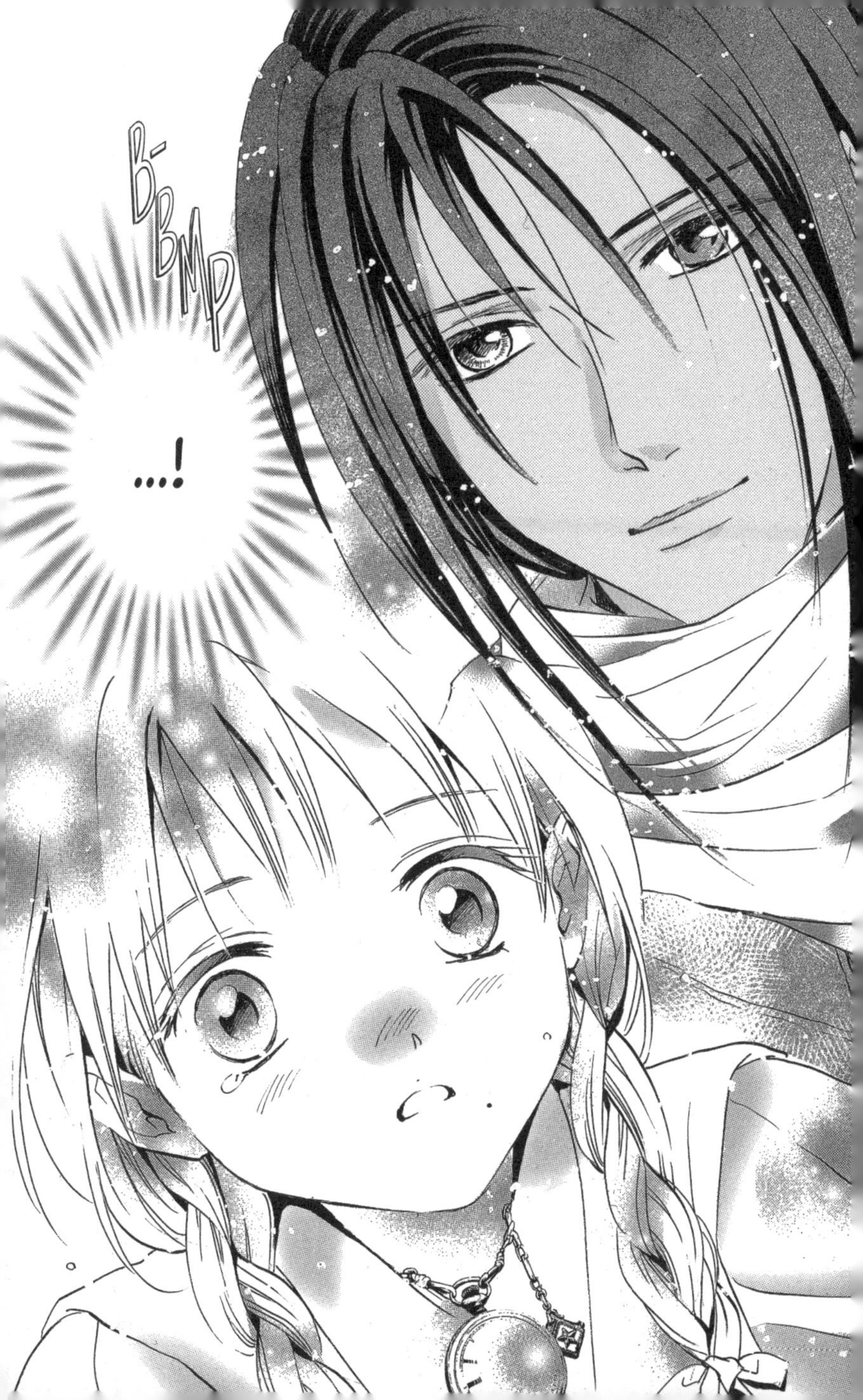
B-BMP
...!

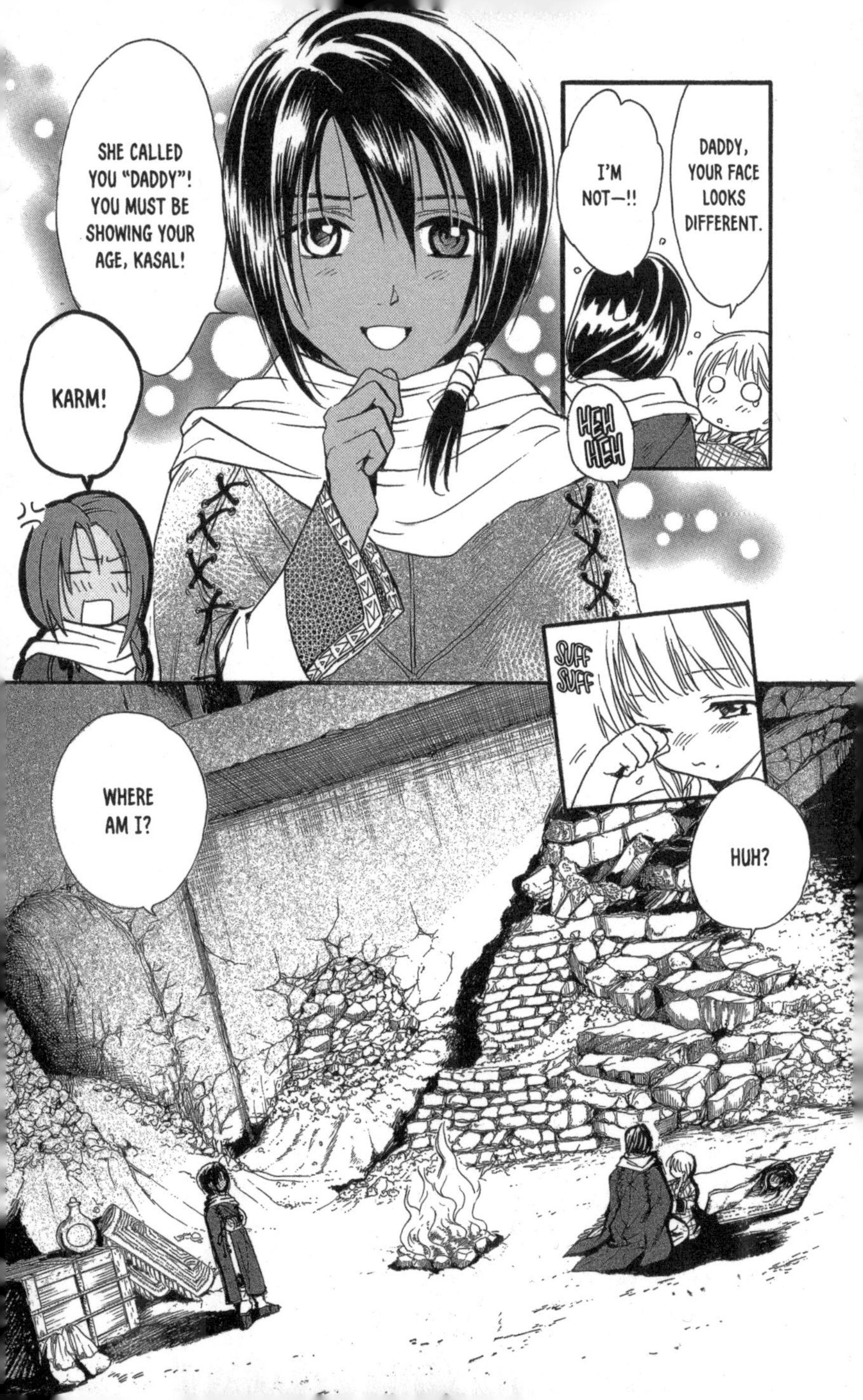
DADDY, YOUR FACE LOOKS DIFFERENT.
I'M NOT—!!
HEH HEH
SHE CALLED YOU "DADDY"! YOU MUST BE SHOWING YOUR AGE, KASAL!
KARM!
SUFF SUFF
HUH?
WHERE AM I?

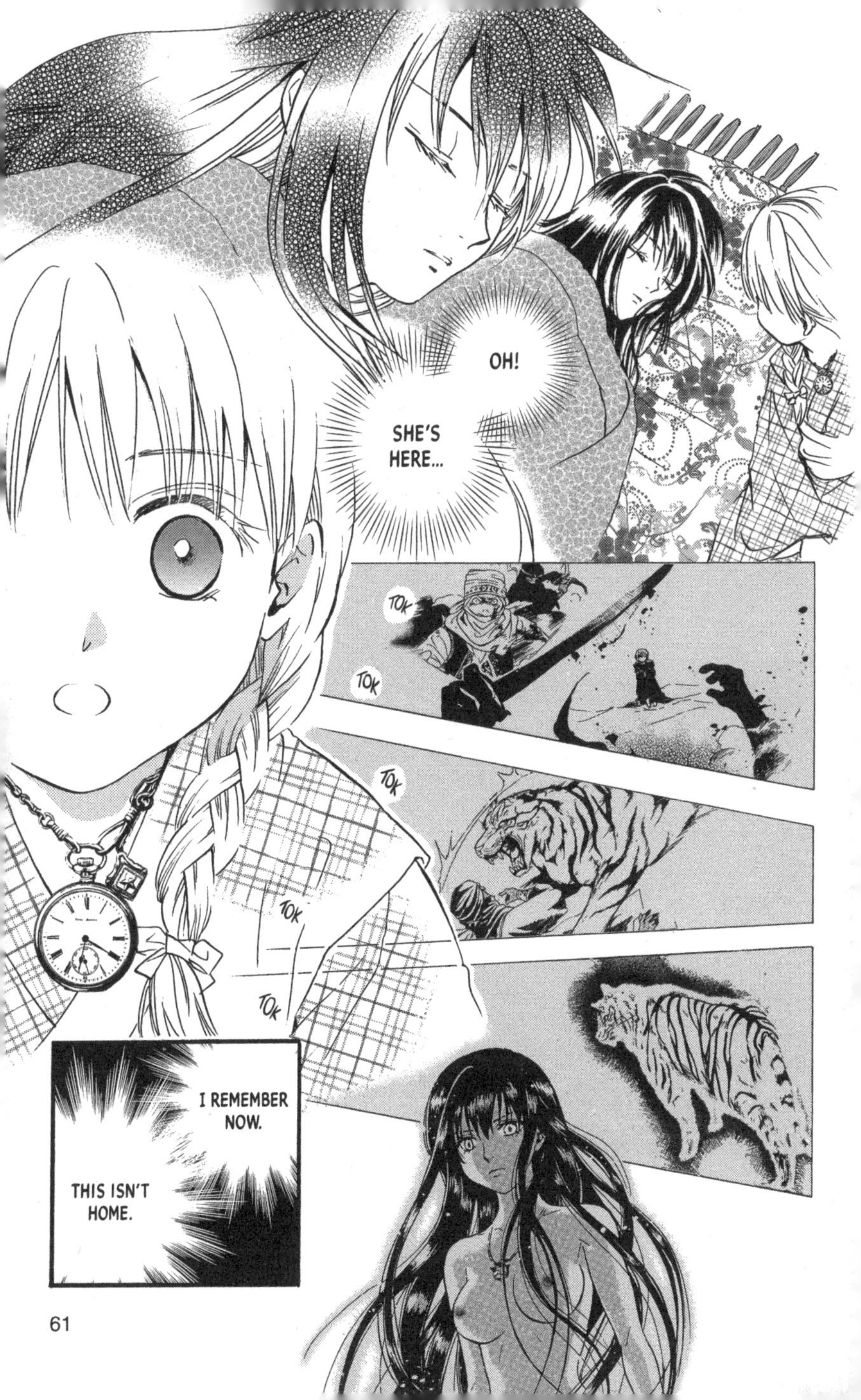
OH!
SHE'S HERE...
TOK
TOK
TOK
TOK
TOK
I REMEMBER NOW.
THIS ISN'T HOME.

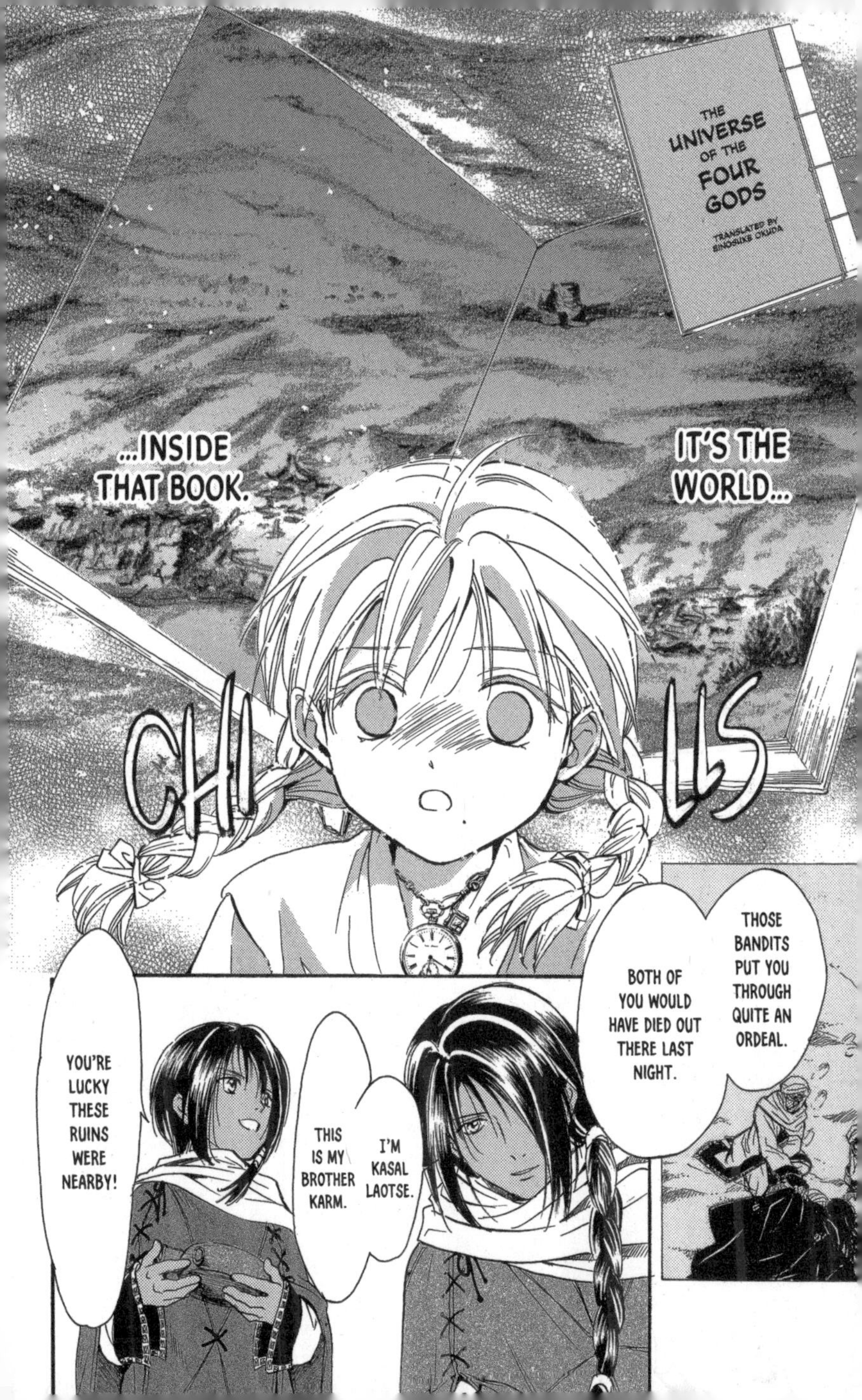
THE UNIVERSE OF THE FOUR GODS
TRANSLATED BY EINOSUKE OKUDA
IT'S THE WORLD...
...INSIDE THAT BOOK.
CHI LLS
THOSE BANDITS PUT YOU THROUGH QUITE AN ORDEAL.
BOTH OF YOU WOULD HAVE DIED OUT THERE LAST NIGHT.
I'M KASAL LAOTSE.
THIS IS MY BROTHER KARM.
YOU'RE LUCKY THESE RUINS WERE NEARBY!

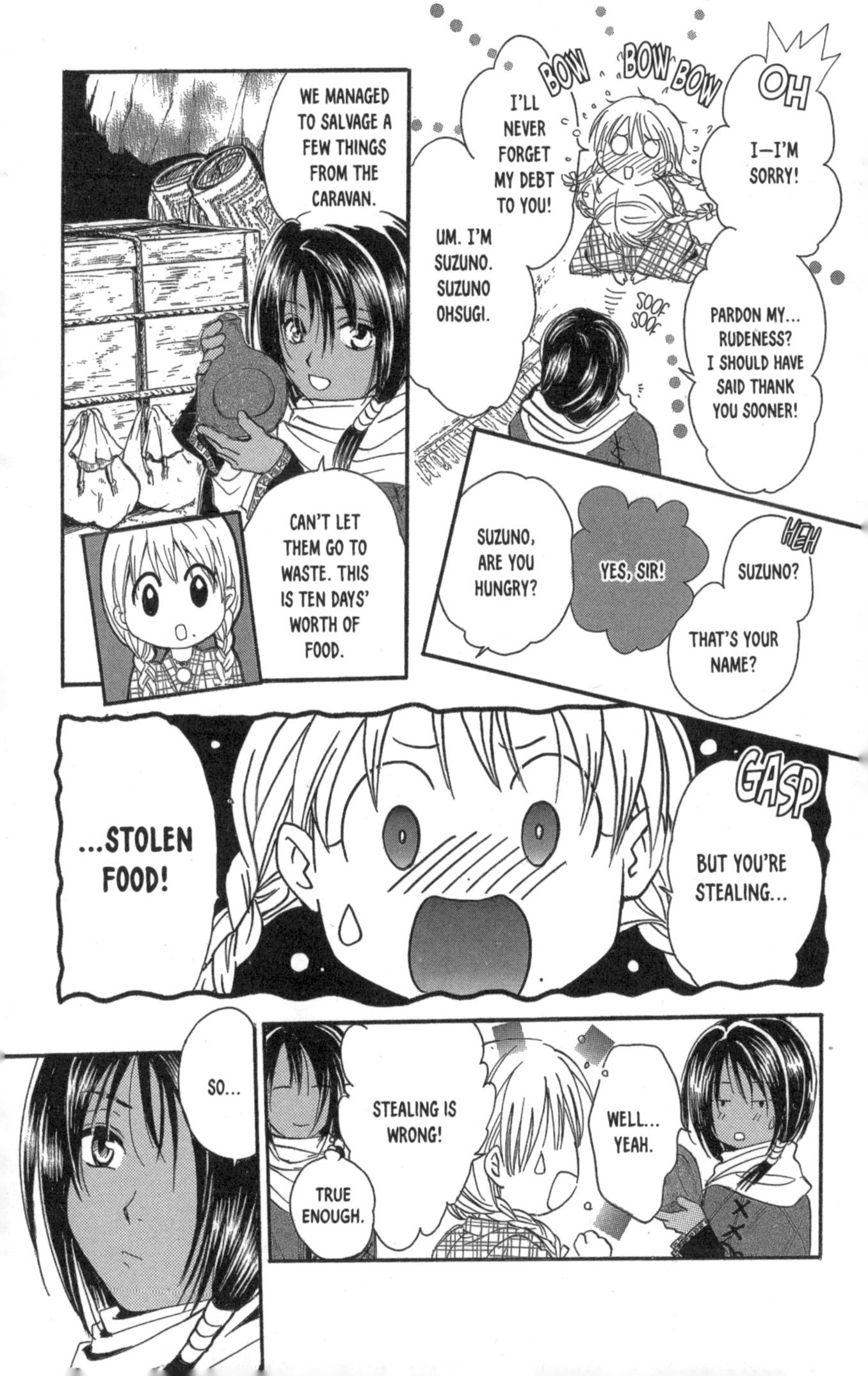
OH
I—I'M SORRY!
BOW BOW BOW
I'LL NEVER FORGET MY DEBT TO YOU!
PARDON MY... RUDENESS? I SHOULD HAVE SAID THANK YOU SOONER!
UM. I'M SUZUNO. SUZUNO OHSUGI.
SOOF SOOF
HEH
SUZUNO?
THAT'S YOUR NAME?
YES, SIR!
SUZUNO, ARE YOU HUNGRY?
WE MANAGED TO SALVAGE A FEW THINGS FROM THE CARAVAN.
CAN'T LET THEM GO TO WASTE. THIS IS TEN DAYS' WORTH OF FOOD.
GASP
BUT YOU'RE STEALING...
...STOLEN FOOD!
WELL... YEAH.
STEALING IS WRONG!
TRUE ENOUGH.
SO...

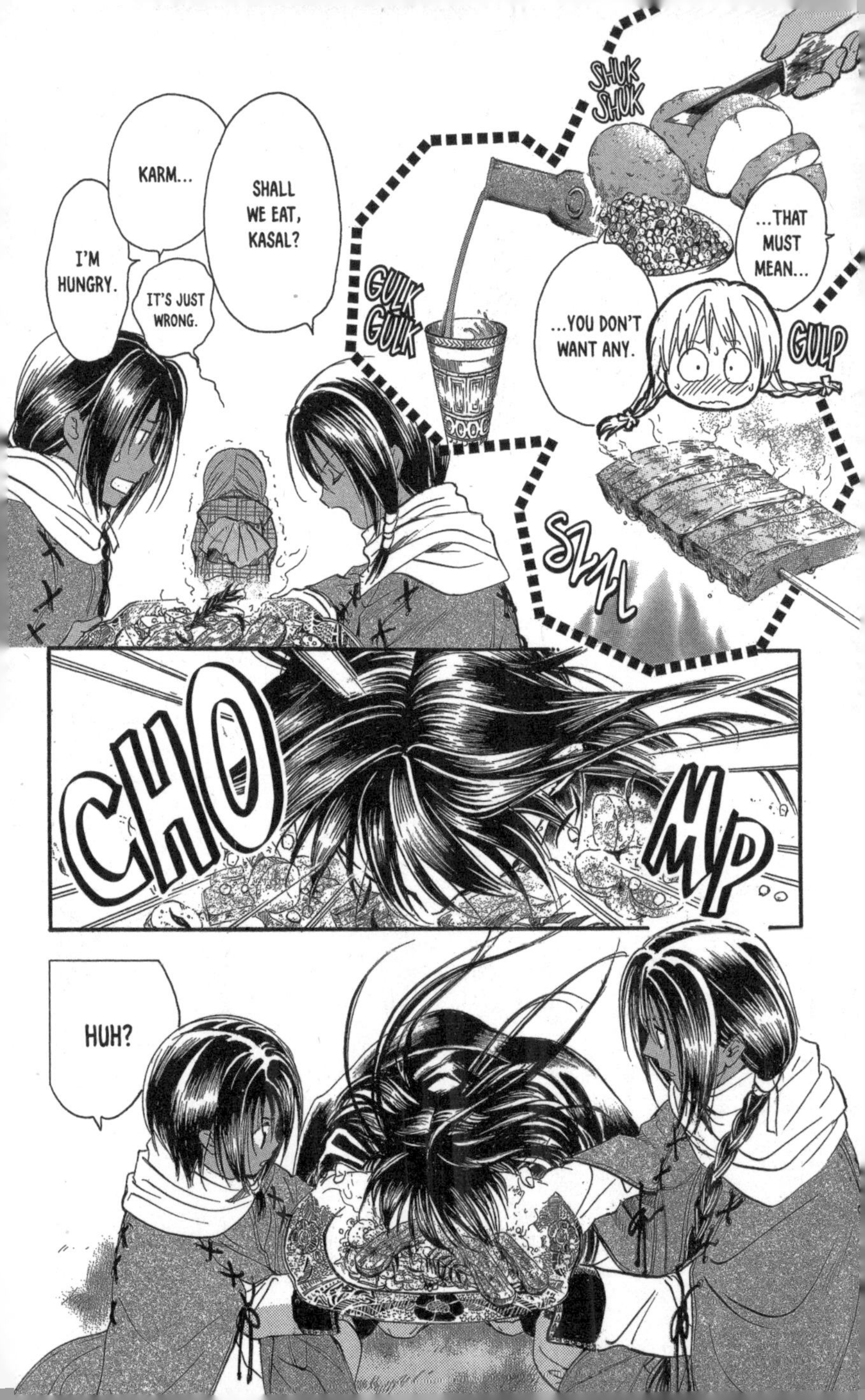
SHUK SHUK
...THAT MUST MEAN...
GULP
...YOU DON'T WANT ANY.
GULK GULK
SHALL WE EAT, KASAL?
KARM...
IT'S JUST WRONG.
I'M HUNGRY.
CHOMP
HUH?

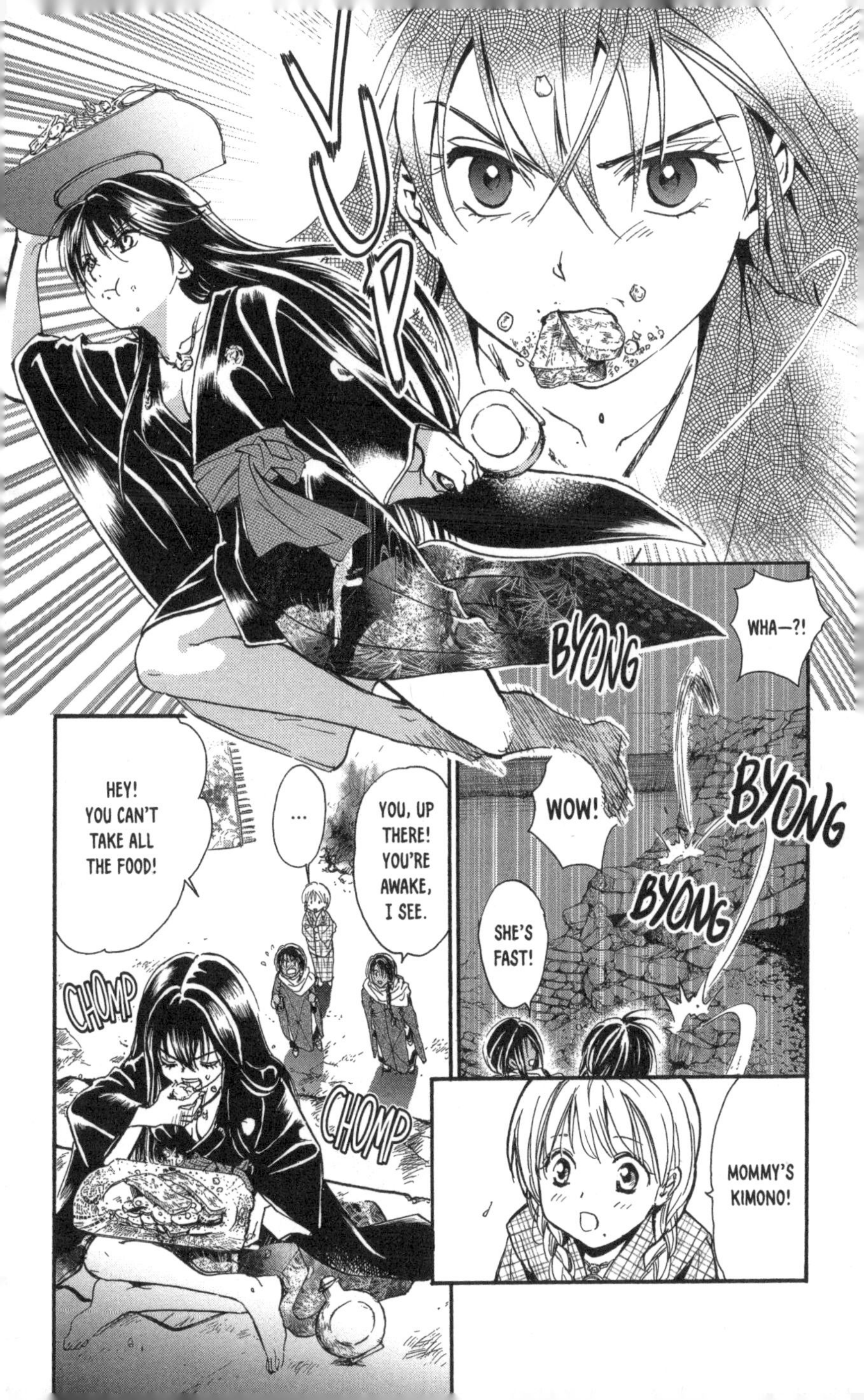
VUP
WHA—?!
BYONG
BYONG
WOW!
BYONG
SHE'S FAST!
MOMMY'S KIMONO!
YOU, UP THERE! YOU'RE AWAKE, I SEE.
...
HEY! YOU CAN'T TAKE ALL THE FOOD!
CHOMP
CHOMP

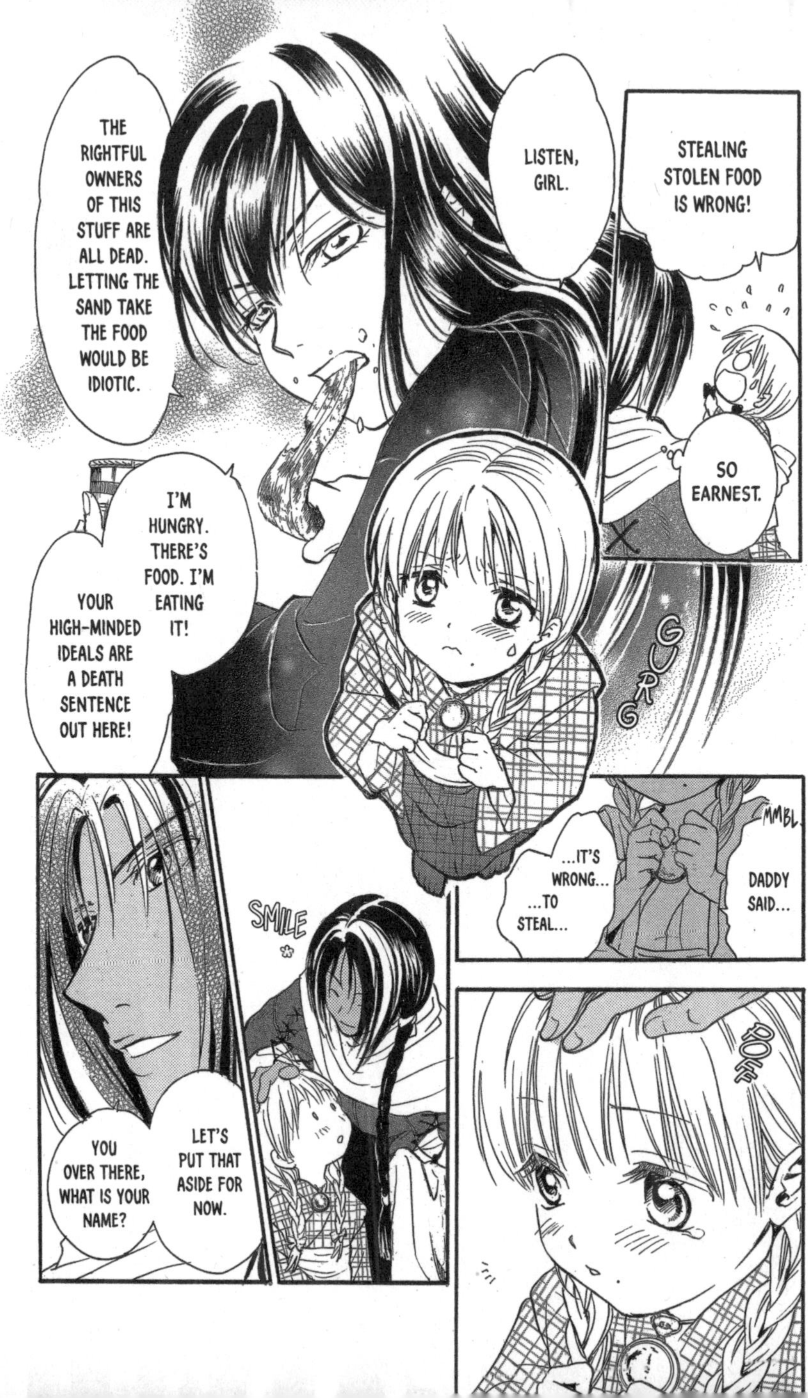
STEALING STOLEN FOOD IS WRONG!
SO EARNEST.
LISTEN, GIRL.
THE RIGHTFUL OWNERS OF THIS STUFF ARE ALL DEAD. LETTING THE SAND TAKE THE FOOD WOULD BE IDIOTIC.
I'M HUNGRY. THERE'S FOOD. I'M EATING IT!
YOUR HIGH-MINDED IDEALS ARE A DEATH SENTENCE OUT HERE!
GURG
GURG
DADDY SAID...
MMBL
...IT'S WRONG...
...TO STEAL...
POFF
SMILE
LET'S PUT THAT ASIDE FOR NOW.
YOU OVER THERE, WHAT IS YOUR NAME?

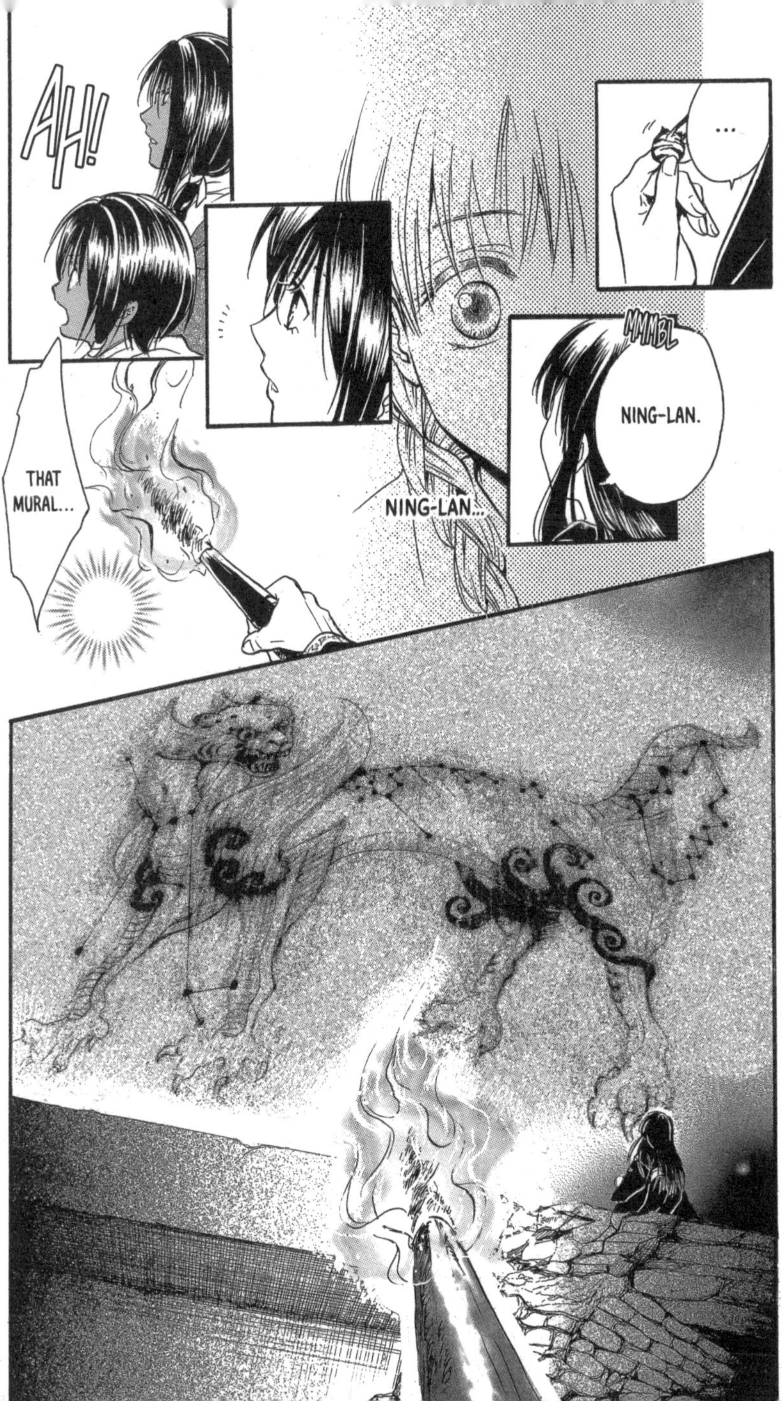
...
MMMBL
NING-LAN.
NING-LAN...
AH!
THAT MURAL...

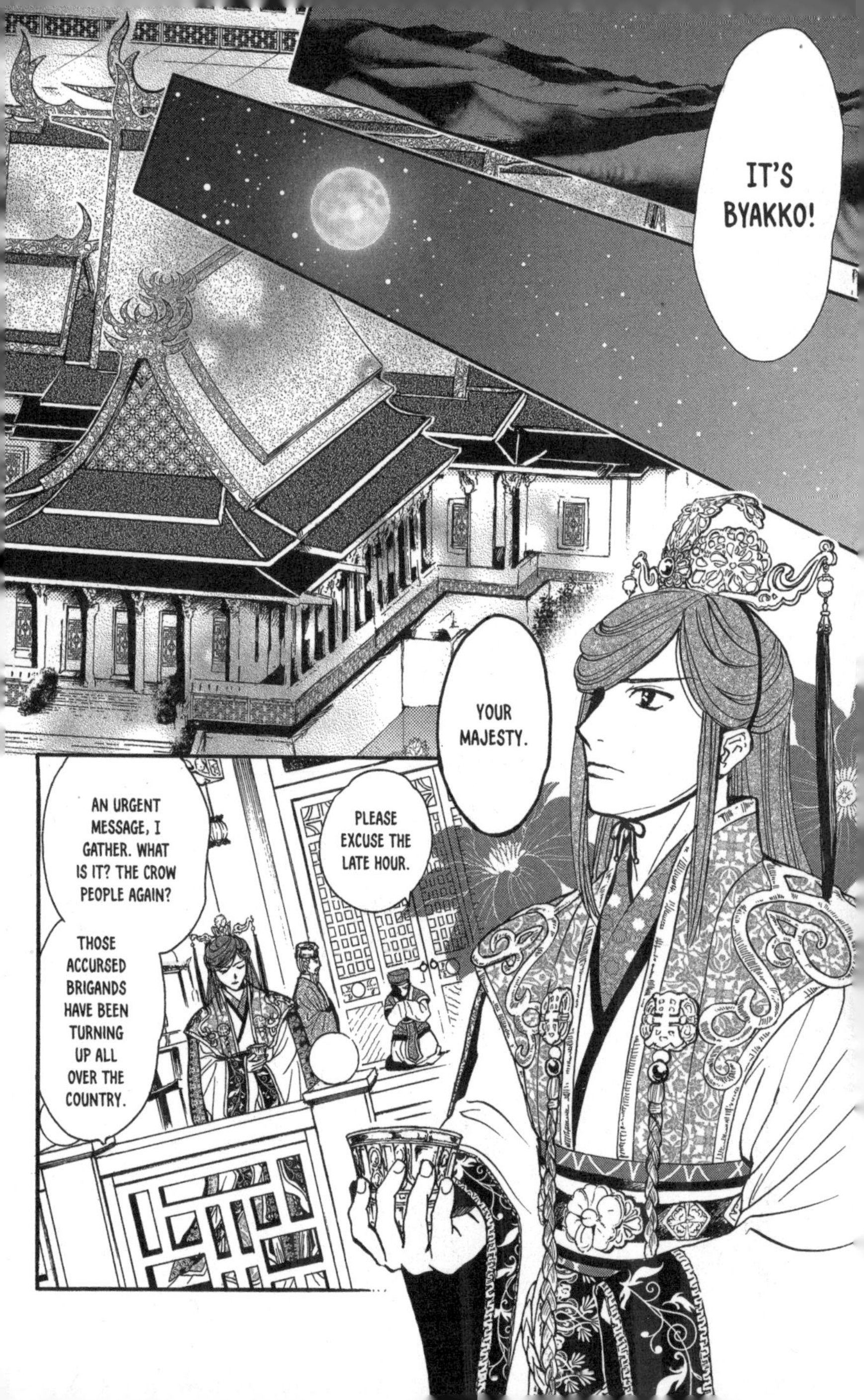
IT'S BYAKKO!
YOUR MAJESTY.
PLEASE EXCUSE THE LATE HOUR.
AN URGENT MESSAGE, I GATHER. WHAT IS IT? THE CROW PEOPLE AGAIN?
THOSE ACCURSED BRIGANDS HAVE BEEN TURNING UP ALL OVER THE COUNTRY.

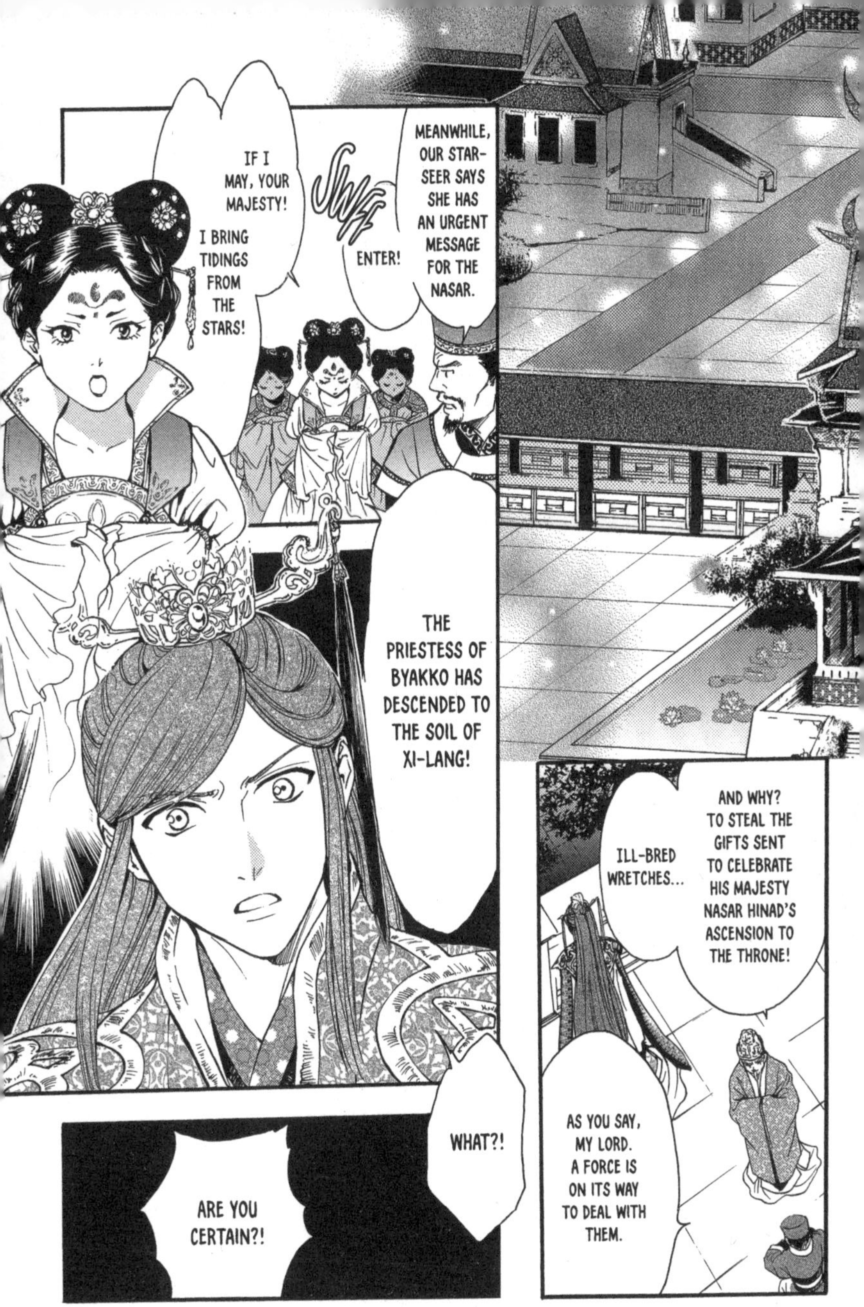

AND WHY? TO STEAL THE GIFTS SENT TO CELEBRATE HIS MAJESTY NASAR HINAD'S ASCENSION TO THE THRONE!
ILL-BRED WRETCHES...
AS YOU SAY, MY LORD. A FORCE IS ON ITS WAY TO DEAL WITH THEM.
MEANWHILE, OUR STAR-SEER SAYS SHE HAS AN URGENT MESSAGE FOR THE NASAR.
ENTER!
SWFF
IF I MAY, YOUR MAJESTY!
I BRING TIDINGS FROM THE STARS!
THE PRIESTESS OF BYAKKO HAS DESCENDED TO THE SOIL OF XI-LANG!
WHAT?!
ARE YOU CERTAIN?!

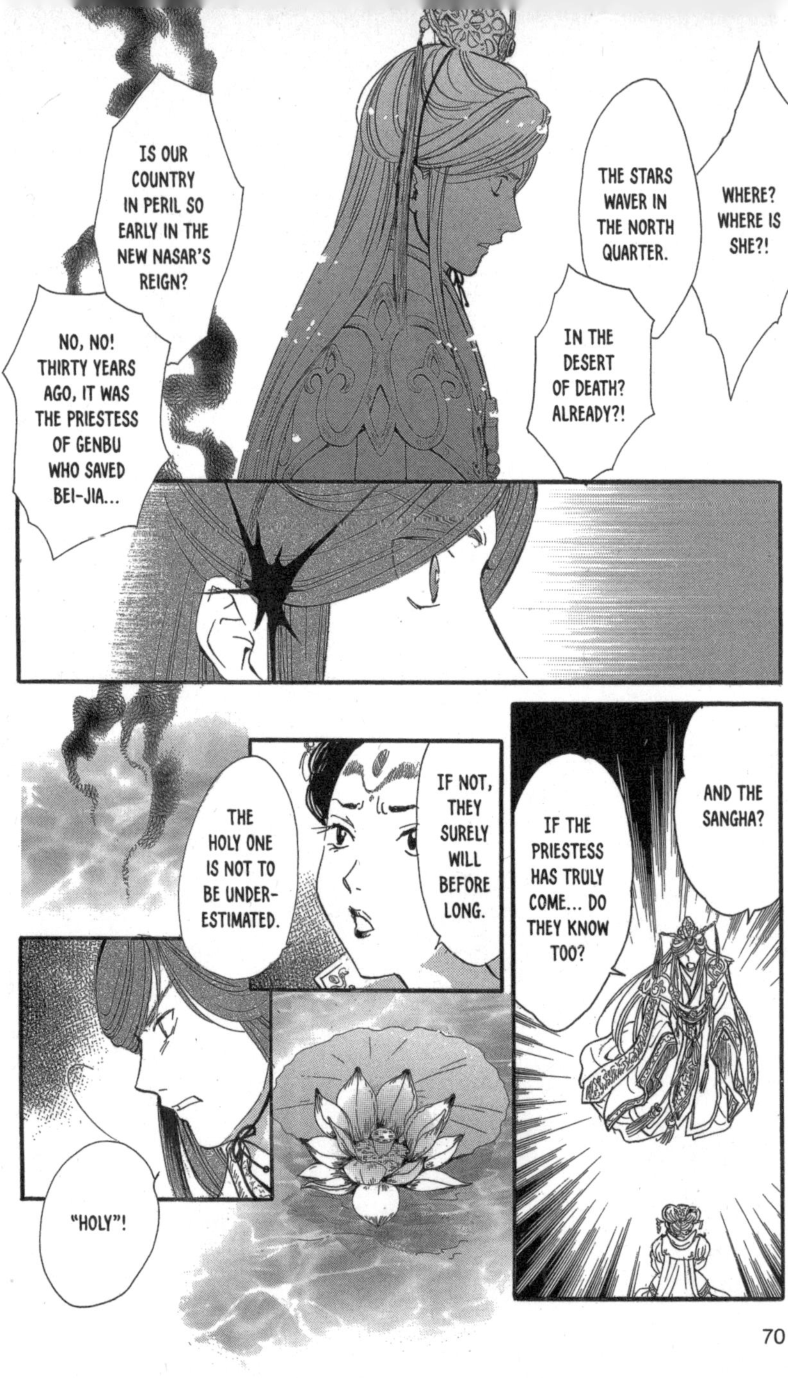
WHERE? WHERE IS SHE?!
THE STARS WAVER IN THE NORTH QUARTER.
IN THE DESERT OF DEATH? ALREADY?!
IS OUR COUNTRY IN PERIL SO EARLY IN THE NEW NASAR'S REIGN?
NO, NO! THIRTY YEARS AGO, IT WAS THE PRIESTESS OF GENBU WHO SAVED BEI-JIA...
AND THE SANGHA?
IF THE PRIESTESS HAS TRULY COME... DO THEY KNOW TOO?
IF NOT, THEY SURELY WILL BEFORE LONG.
THE HOLY ONE IS NOT TO BE UNDER-ESTIMATED.
"HOLY"!

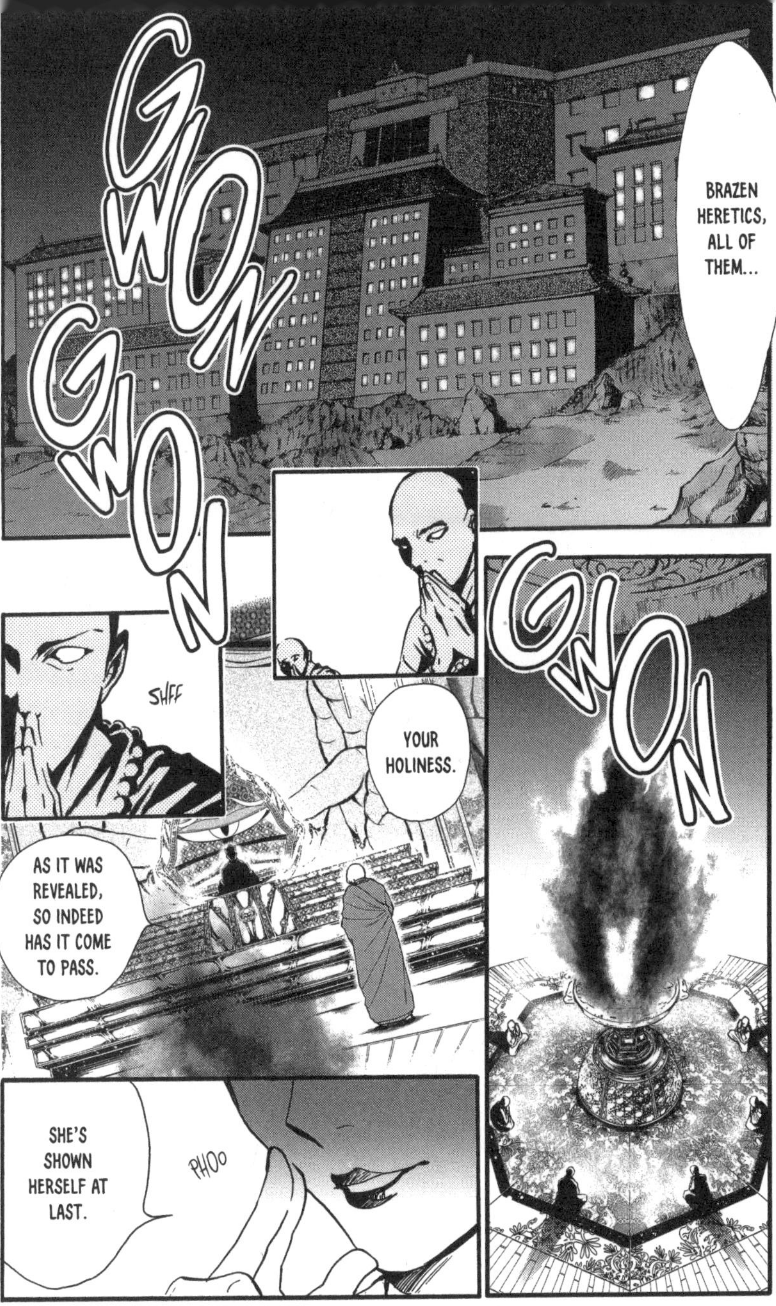
BRAZEN HERETICS, ALL OF THEM...
GWON
GWON
GWON
YOUR HOLINESS.
SHFF
AS IT WAS REVEALED, SO INDEED HAS IT COME TO PASS.
SHE'S SHOWN HERSELF AT LAST.
PHOO

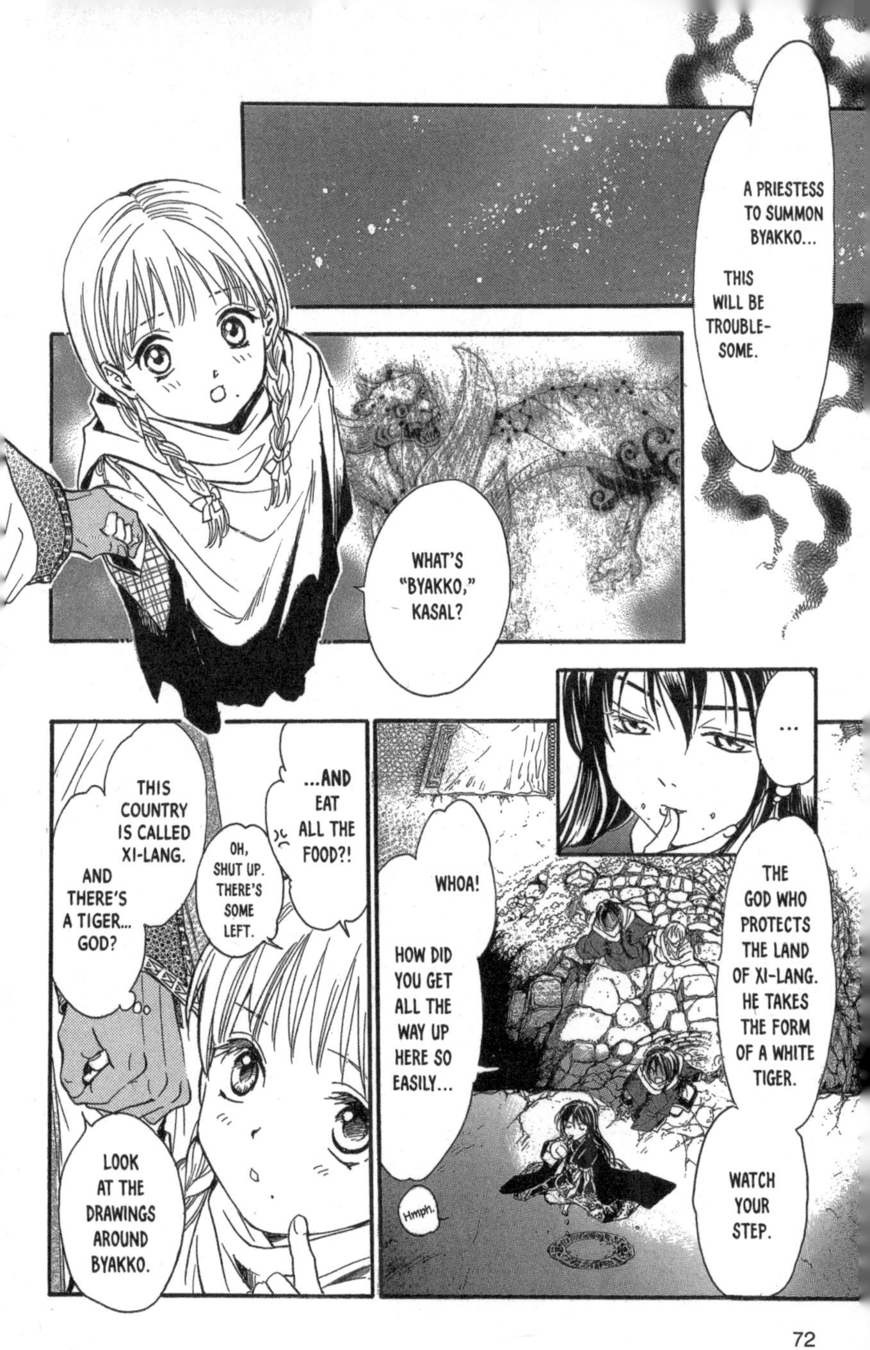

A PRIESTESS TO SUMMON BYAKKO...
THIS WILL BE TROUBLE-SOME.
WHAT'S "BYAKKO," KASAL?
...
THE GOD WHO PROTECTS THE LAND OF XI-LANG. HE TAKES THE FORM OF A WHITE TIGER.
WATCH YOUR STEP.
WHOA!
HOW DID YOU GET ALL THE WAY UP HERE SO EASILY...
Hmph.
...AND EAT ALL THE FOOD?!
OH, SHUT UP. THERE'S SOME LEFT.
THIS COUNTRY IS CALLED XI-LANG.
AND THERE'S A TIGER... GOD?
LOOK AT THE DRAWINGS AROUND BYAKKO.

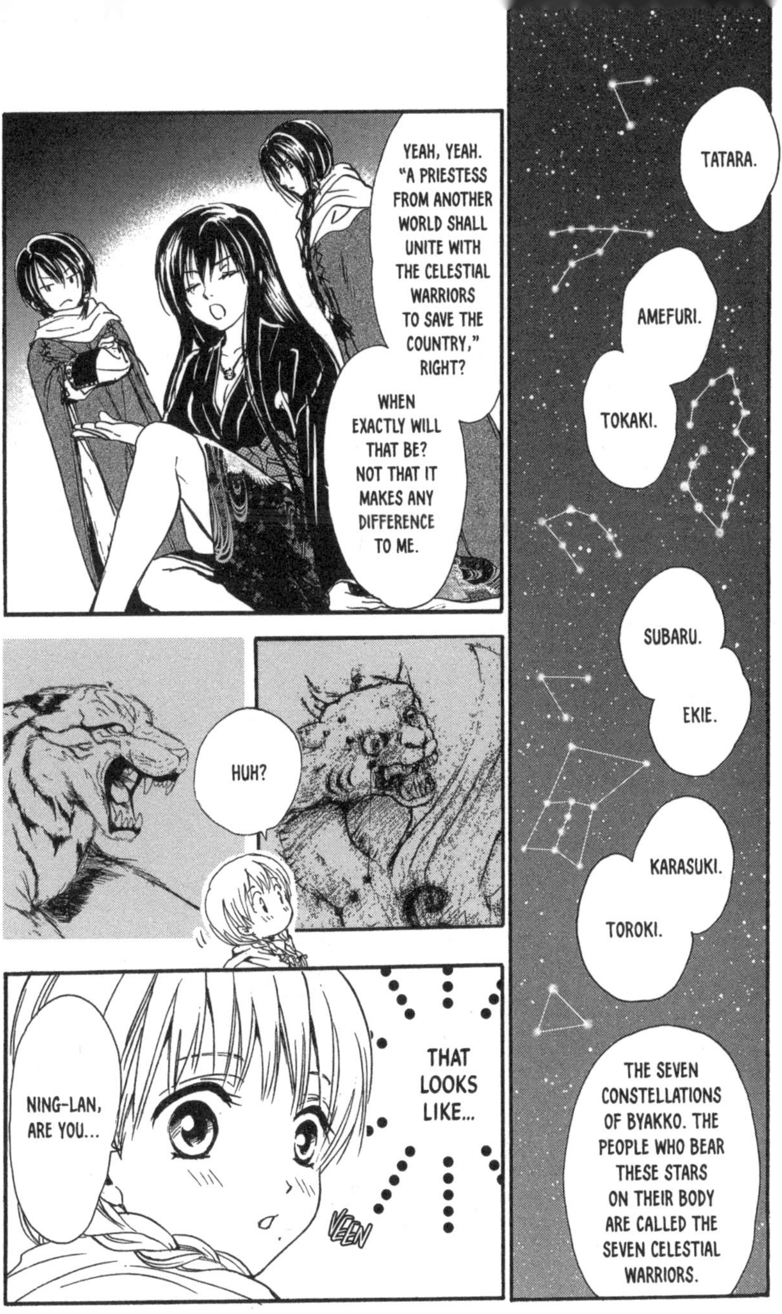
TATARA.
AMEFURI.
TOKAKI.
SUBARU.
EKIE.
KARASUKI.
TOROKI.
THE SEVEN CONSTELLATIONS OF BYAKKO. THE PEOPLE WHO BEAR THESE STARS ON THEIR BODY ARE CALLED THE SEVEN CELESTIAL WARRIORS.
YEAH, YEAH. "A PRIESTESS FROM ANOTHER WORLD SHALL UNITE WITH THE CELESTIAL WARRIORS TO SAVE THE COUNTRY," RIGHT?
WHEN EXACTLY WILL THAT BE? NOT THAT IT MAKES ANY DIFFERENCE TO ME.
HUH?
THAT LOOKS LIKE...
VEEN
NING-LAN, ARE YOU...

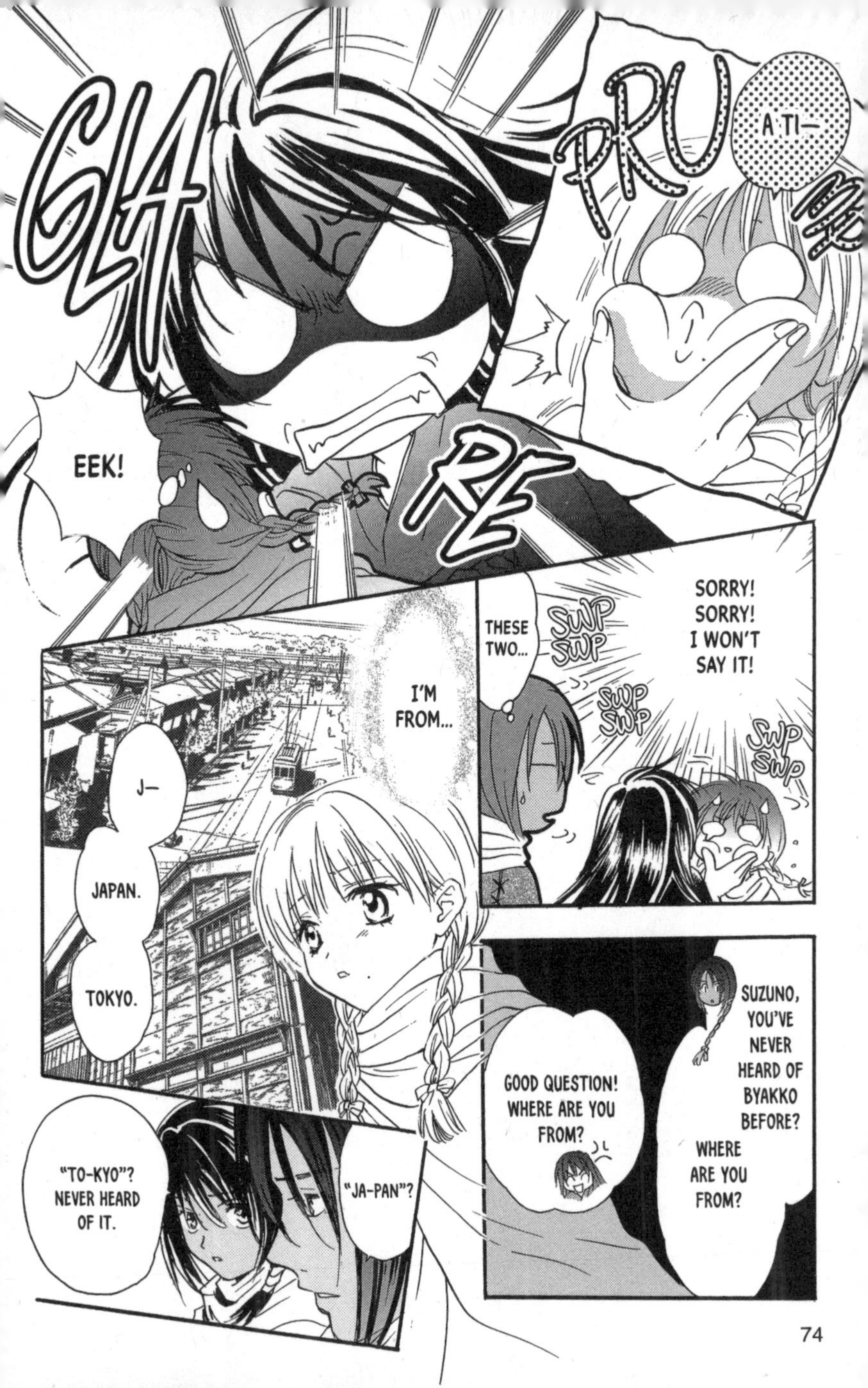
PRU
A TI—
MP
GLA
RE
EEK!
SORRY! SORRY! I WON'T SAY IT!
SWP SWP
SWP SWP
SWP SWP
THESE TWO...
I'M FROM...
J—
JAPAN.
TOKYO.
SUZUNO, YOU'VE NEVER HEARD OF BYAKKO BEFORE?
WHERE ARE YOU FROM?
GOOD QUESTION! WHERE ARE YOU FROM?
"JA-PAN"?
"TO-KYO"? NEVER HEARD OF IT.

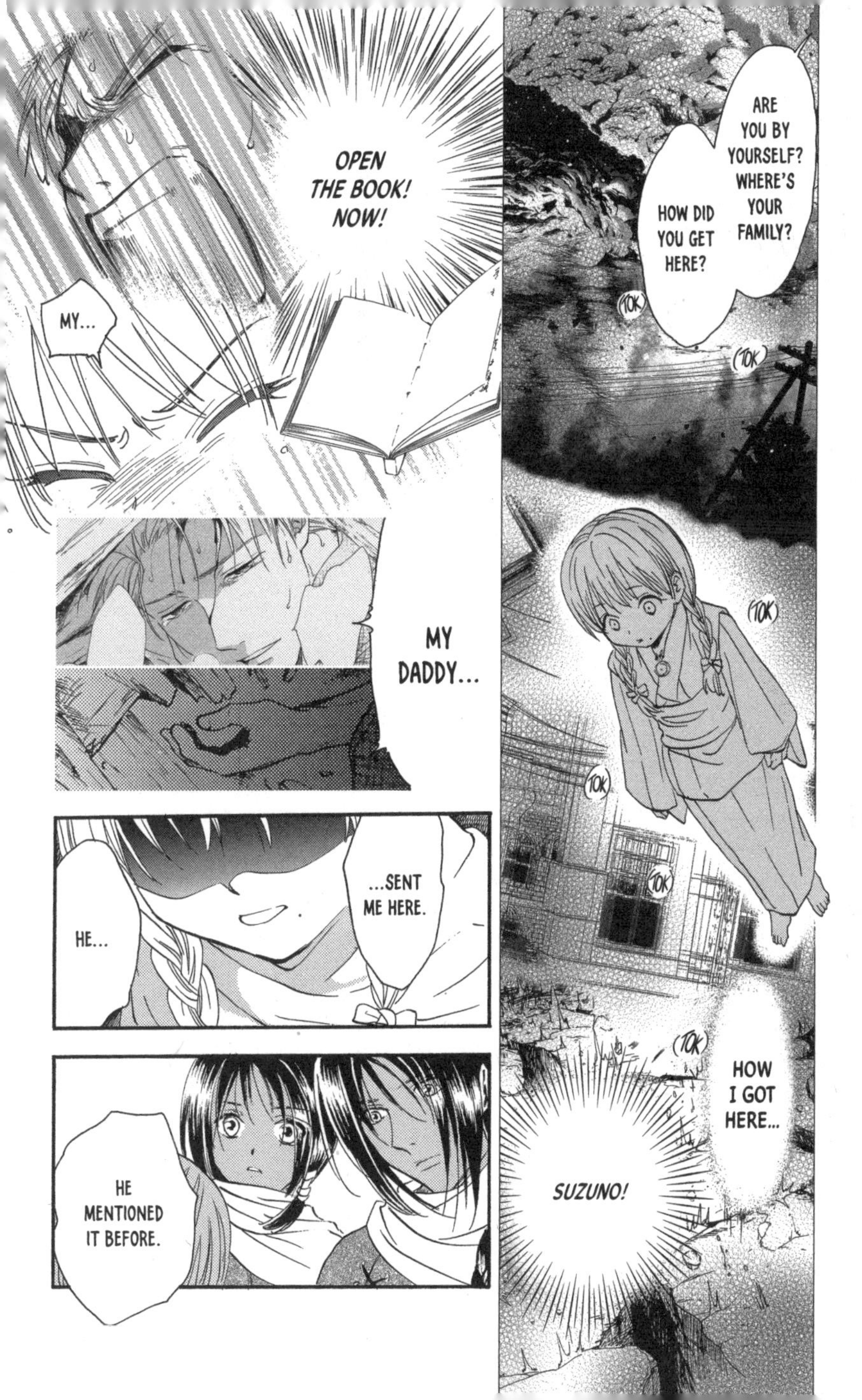
ARE YOU BY YOURSELF? WHERE'S YOUR FAMILY?
HOW DID YOU GET HERE?
TOK
TOK
TOK
TOK
TOK
TOK
HOW I GOT HERE...
SUZUNO!
OPEN THE BOOK! NOW!
MY...
MY DADDY...
...SENT ME HERE.
HE...
HE MENTIONED IT BEFORE.

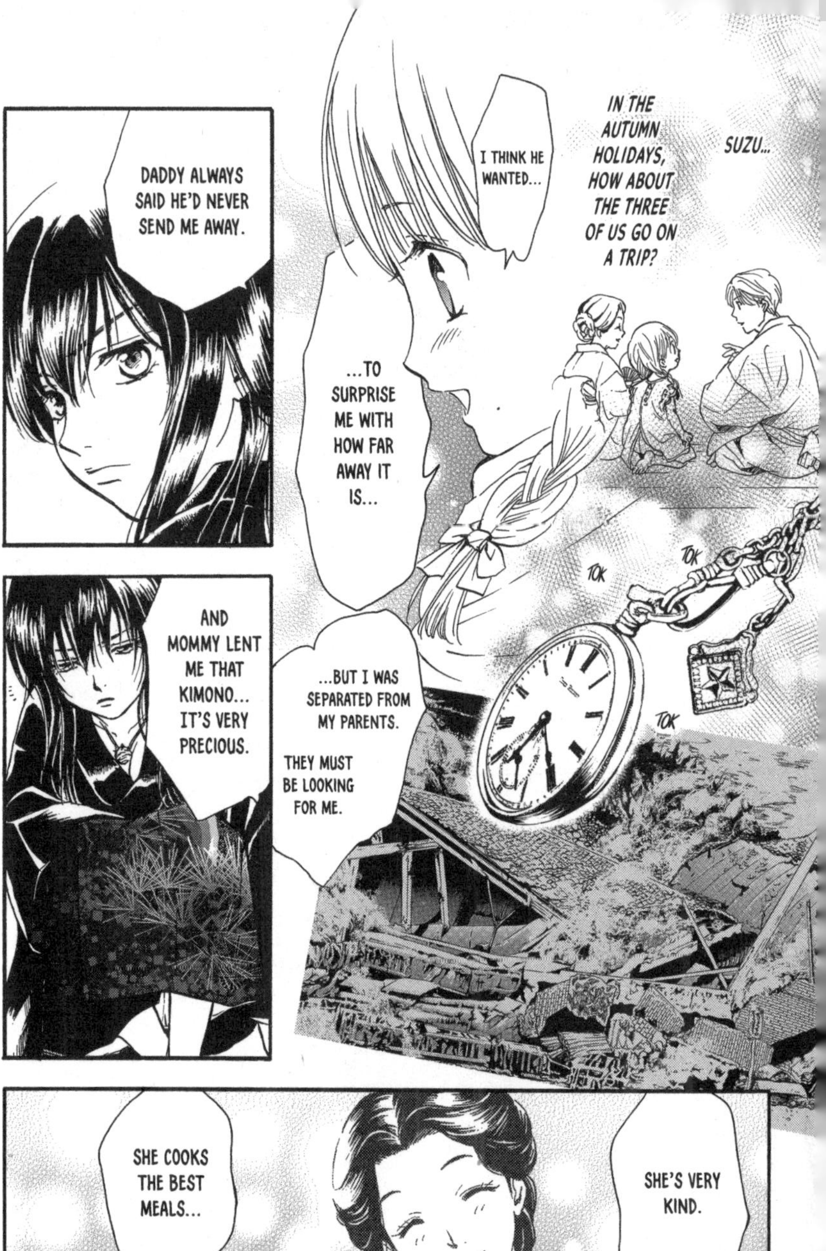
SUZU...
IN THE AUTUMN HOLIDAYS, HOW ABOUT THE THREE OF US GO ON A TRIP?
I THINK HE WANTED...
...TO SURPRISE ME WITH HOW FAR AWAY IT IS...
TOK
TOK
TOK
...BUT I WAS SEPARATED FROM MY PARENTS.
THEY MUST BE LOOKING FOR ME.
DADDY ALWAYS SAID HE'D NEVER SEND ME AWAY.
AND MOMMY LENT ME THAT KIMONO... IT'S VERY PRECIOUS.
SHE'S VERY KIND.
SHE COOKS THE BEST MEALS...

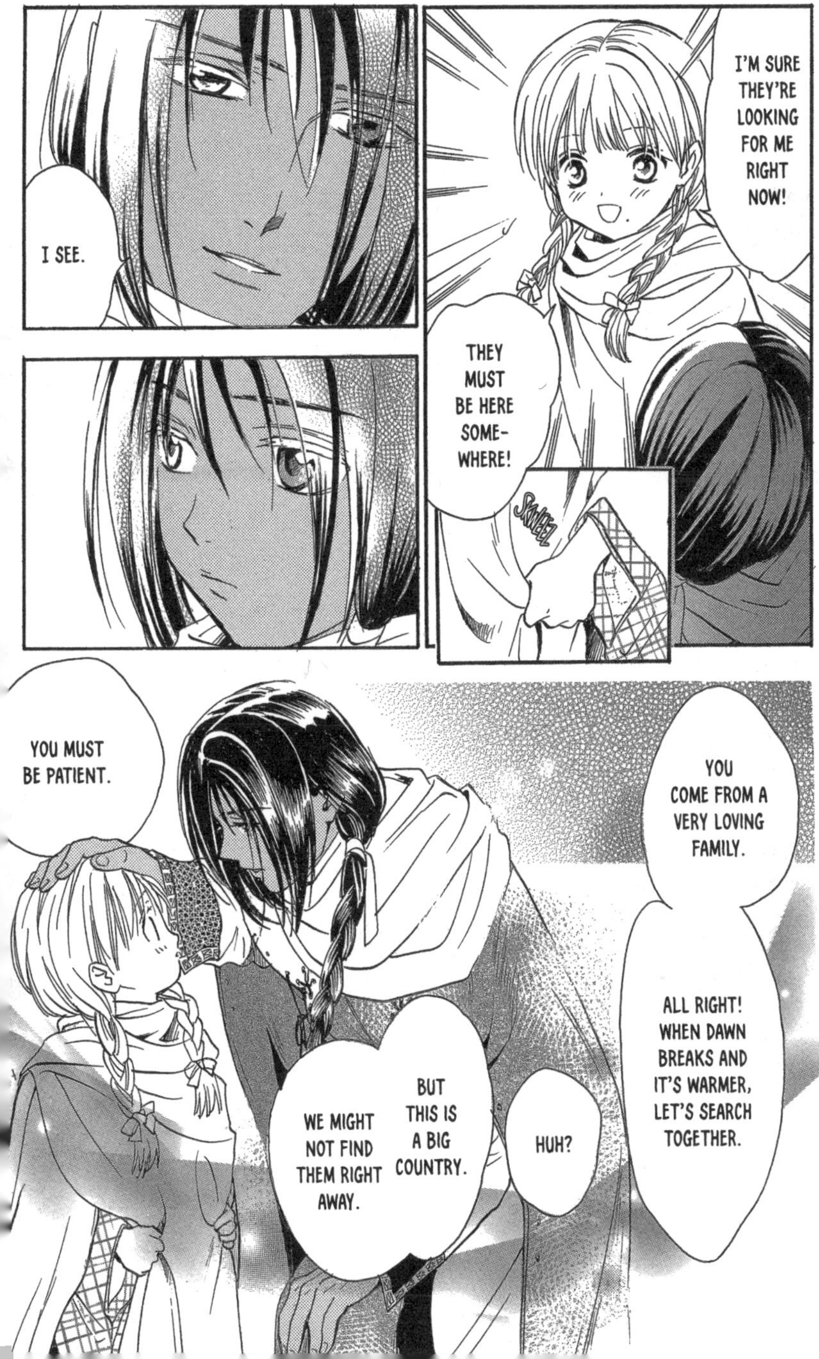
I'M SURE THEY'RE LOOKING FOR ME RIGHT NOW!
THEY MUST BE HERE SOME-WHERE!
SKWEEZ
I SEE.
YOU COME FROM A VERY LOVING FAMILY.
ALL RIGHT! WHEN DAWN BREAKS AND IT'S WARMER, LET'S SEARCH TOGETHER.
HUH?
BUT THIS IS A BIG COUNTRY.
WE MIGHT NOT FIND THEM RIGHT AWAY.
YOU MUST BE PATIENT.

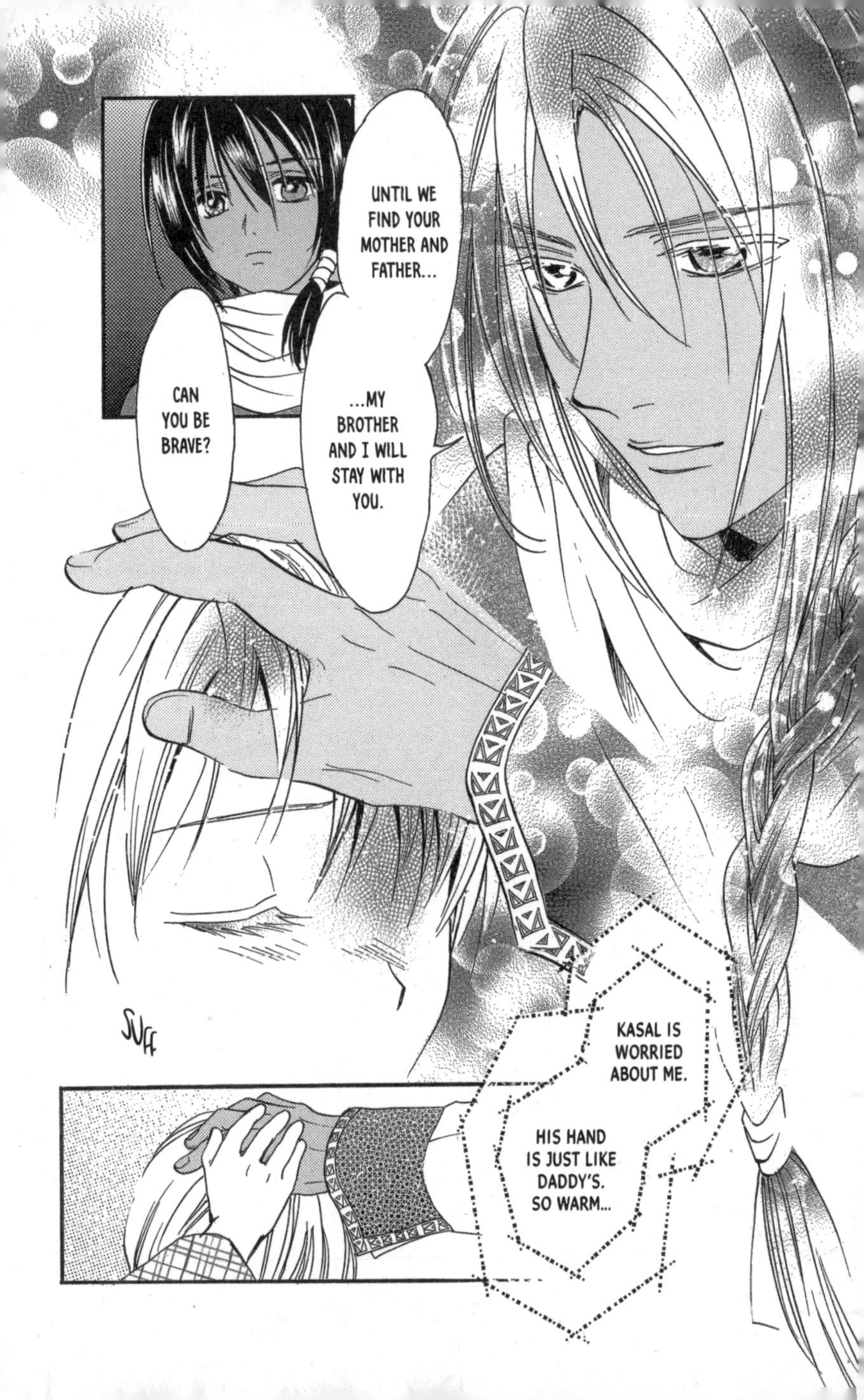
UNTIL WE FIND YOUR MOTHER AND FATHER...
...MY BROTHER AND I WILL STAY WITH YOU.
CAN YOU BE BRAVE?
SUFF
KASAL IS WORRIED ABOUT ME.
HIS HAND IS JUST LIKE DADDY'S. SO WARM...

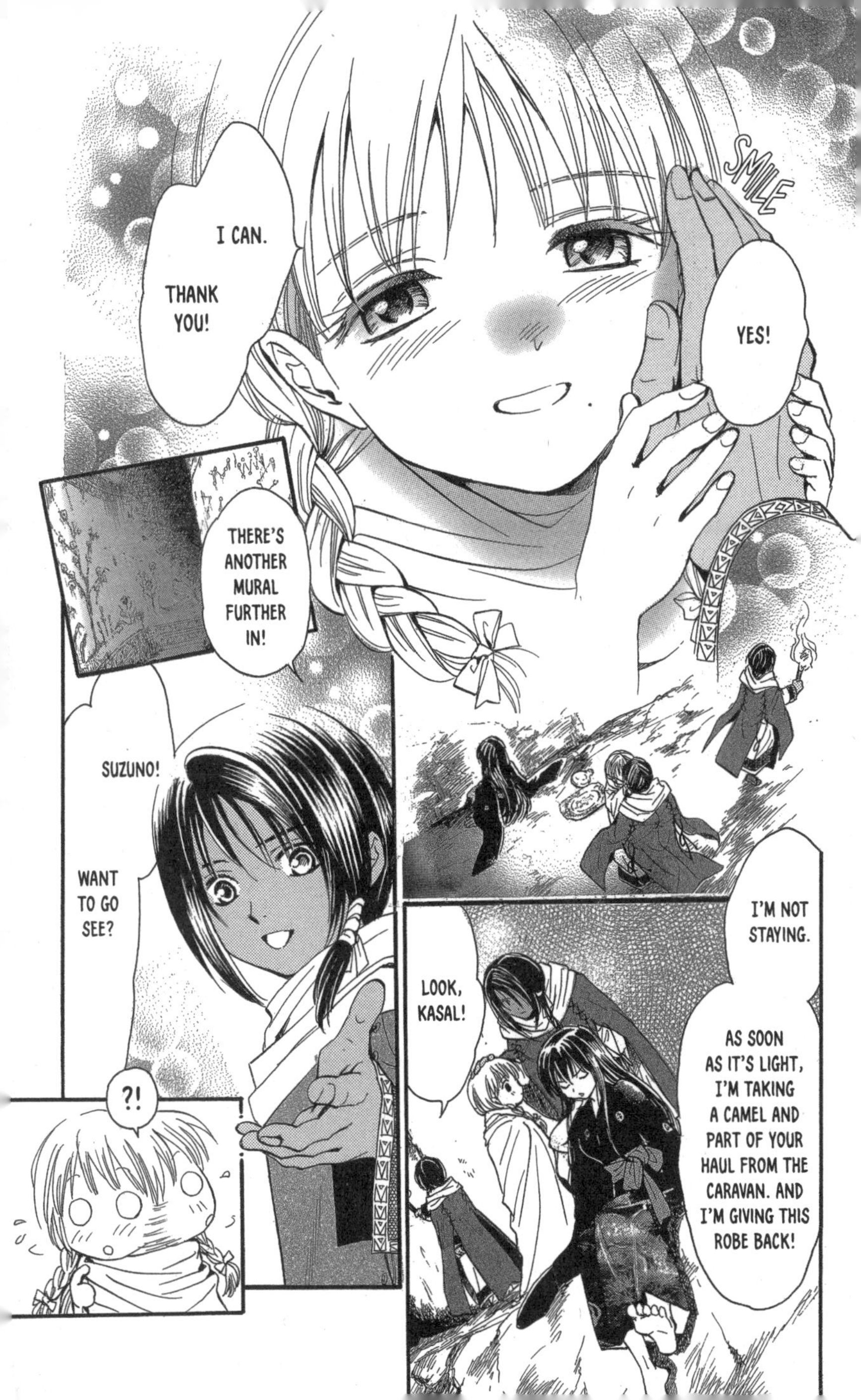
SMILE
YES!
I CAN.
THANK YOU!
THERE'S ANOTHER MURAL FURTHER IN!
SUZUNO!
WANT TO GO SEE?
I'M NOT STAYING.
AS SOON AS IT'S LIGHT, I'M TAKING A CAMEL AND PART OF YOUR HAUL FROM THE CARAVAN. AND I'M GIVING THIS ROBE BACK!
LOOK, KASAL!
?!

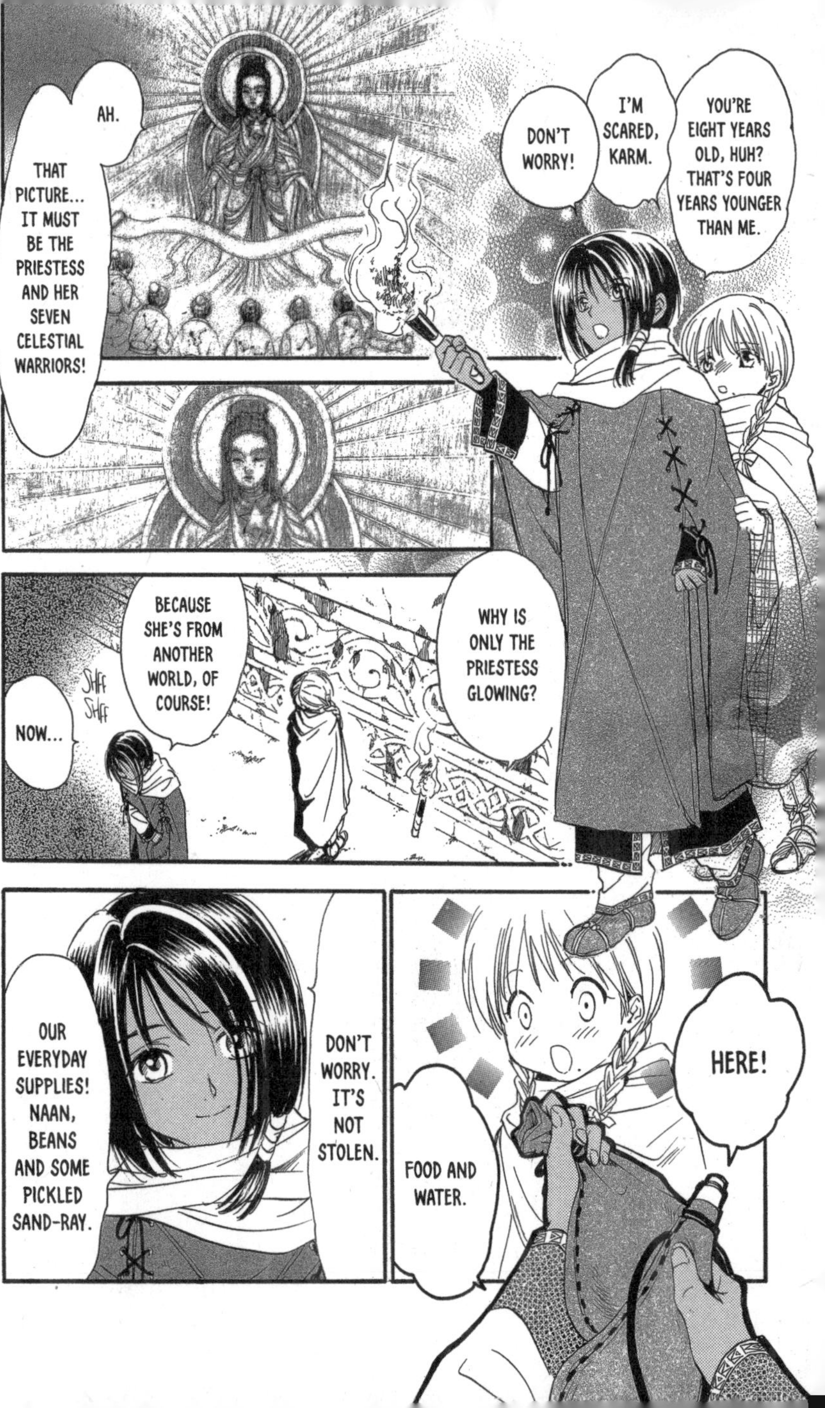
YOU'RE EIGHT YEARS OLD, HUH? THAT'S FOUR YEARS YOUNGER THAN ME.
I'M SCARED, KARM.
DON'T WORRY!
AH.
THAT PICTURE... IT MUST BE THE PRIESTESS AND HER SEVEN CELESTIAL WARRIORS!
WHY IS ONLY THE PRIESTESS GLOWING?
BECAUSE SHE'S FROM ANOTHER WORLD, OF COURSE!
SHFF SHFF
NOW...
HERE!
FOOD AND WATER.
DON'T WORRY. IT'S NOT STOLEN.
OUR EVERYDAY SUPPLIES! NAAN, BEANS AND SOME PICKLED SAND-RAY.

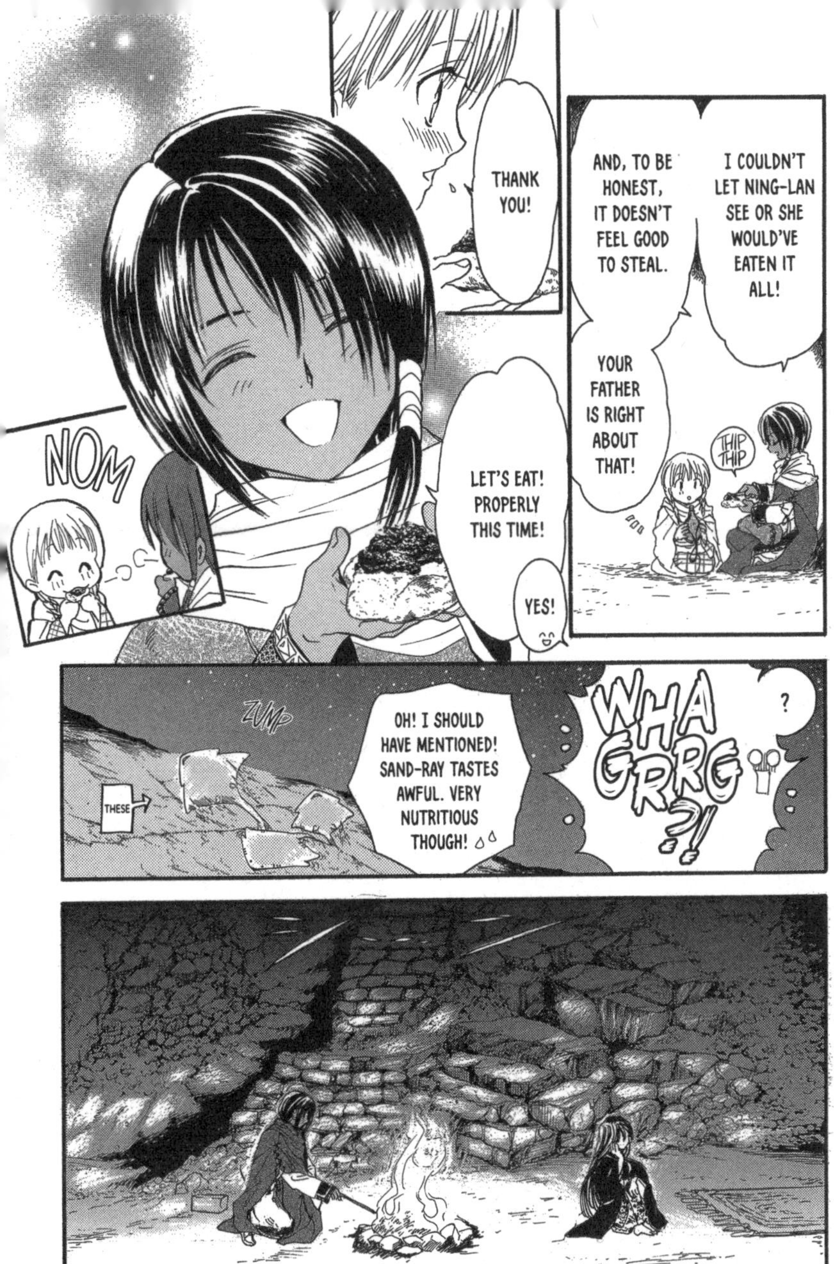
I COULDN'T LET NING-LAN SEE OR SHE WOULD'VE EATEN IT ALL!
AND, TO BE HONEST, IT DOESN'T FEEL GOOD TO STEAL.
YOUR FATHER IS RIGHT ABOUT THAT!
THIP THIP
THANK YOU!
LET'S EAT! PROPERLY THIS TIME!
YES!
NOM
?
WHA GRRG?!
OH! I SHOULD HAVE MENTIONED! SAND-RAY TASTES AWFUL. VERY NUTRITIOUS THOUGH!
ZUMP
THESE

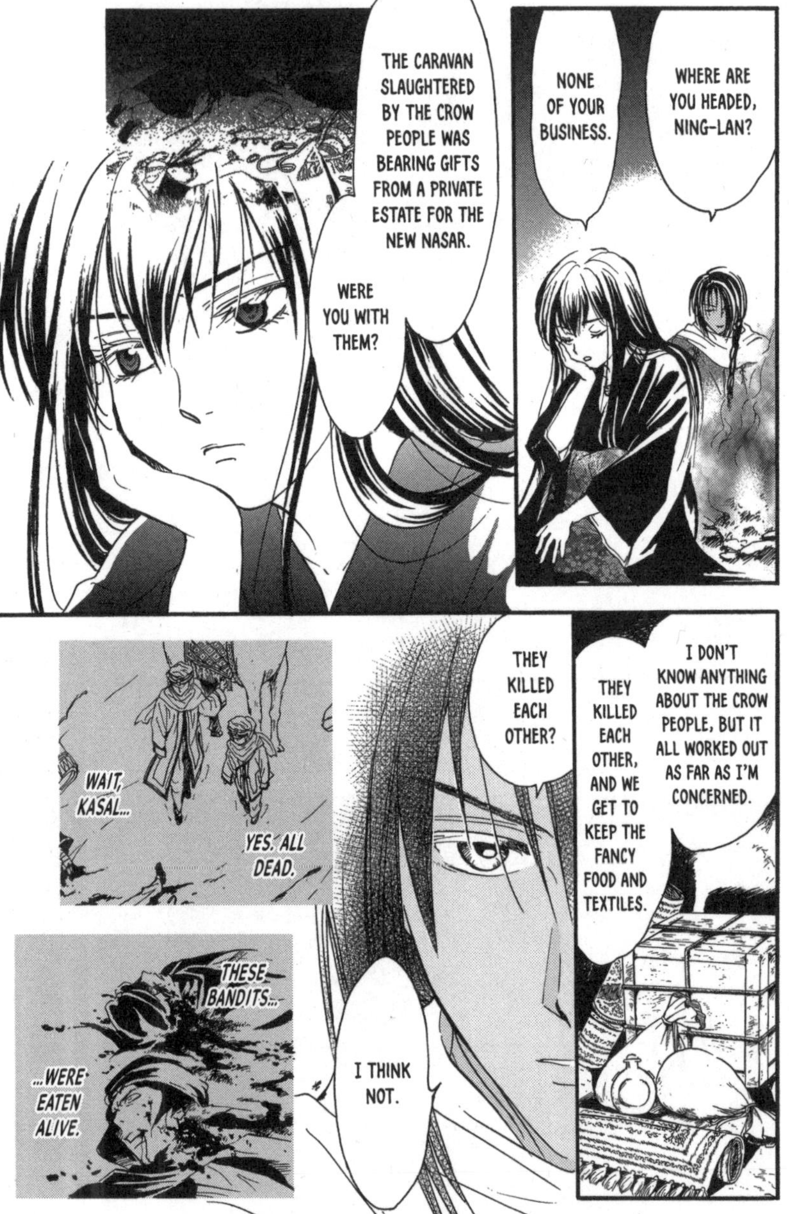
WHERE ARE YOU HEADED, NING-LAN?
NONE OF YOUR BUSINESS.
THE CARAVAN SLAUGHTERED BY THE CROW PEOPLE WAS BEARING GIFTS FROM A PRIVATE ESTATE FOR THE NEW NASAR.
WERE YOU WITH THEM?
I DON'T KNOW ANYTHING ABOUT THE CROW PEOPLE, BUT IT ALL WORKED OUT AS FAR AS I'M CONCERNED.
THEY KILLED EACH OTHER, AND WE GET TO KEEP THE FANCY FOOD AND TEXTILES.
THEY KILLED EACH OTHER?
I THINK NOT.
WAIT, KASAL...
YES. ALL DEAD.
THESE BANDITS...
...WERE EATEN ALIVE.

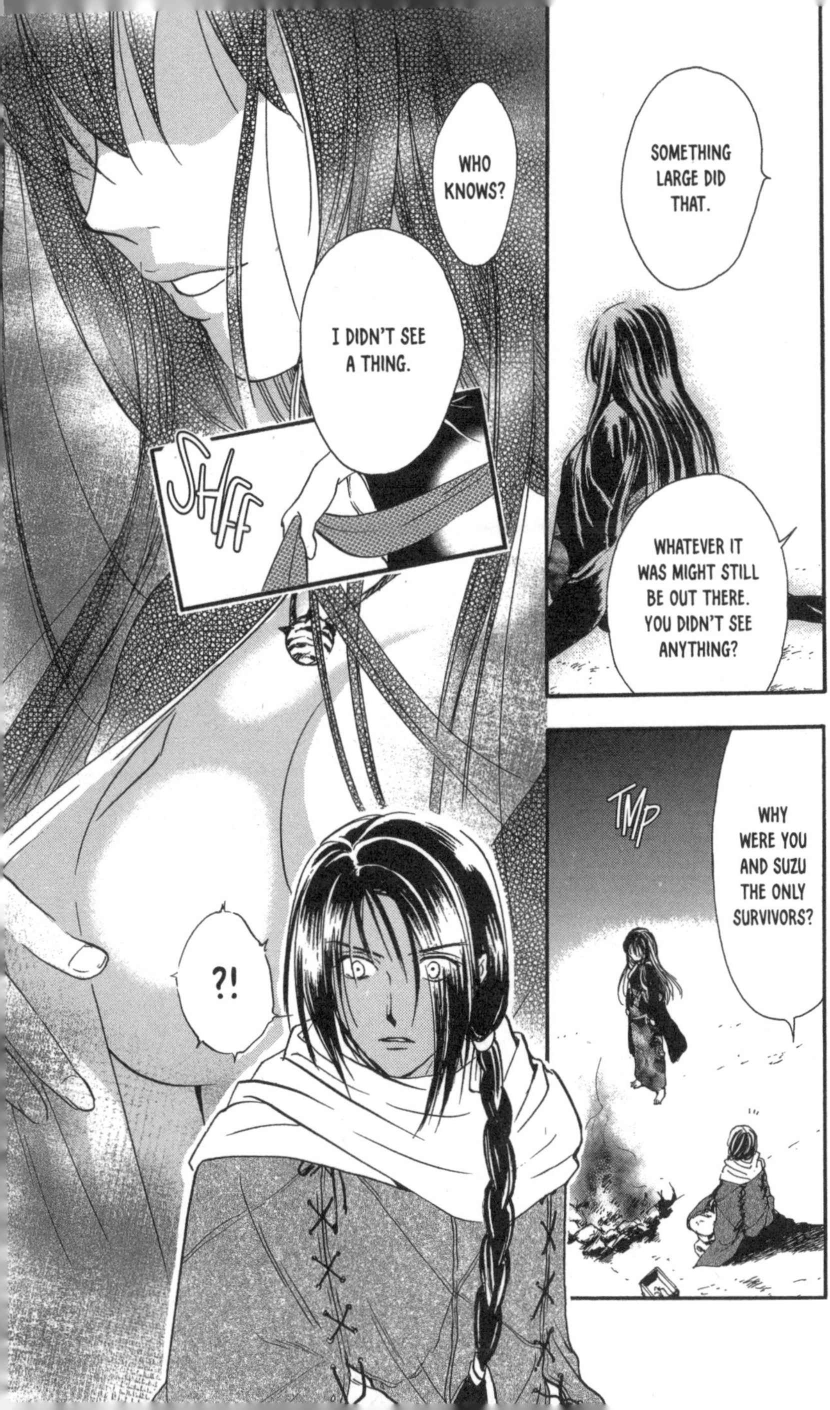
SOMETHING LARGE DID THAT.
WHATEVER IT WAS MIGHT STILL BE OUT THERE. YOU DIDN'T SEE ANYTHING?
TMP
WHY WERE YOU AND SUZU THE ONLY SURVIVORS?
WHO KNOWS?
I DIDN'T SEE A THING.
SHFF
?!

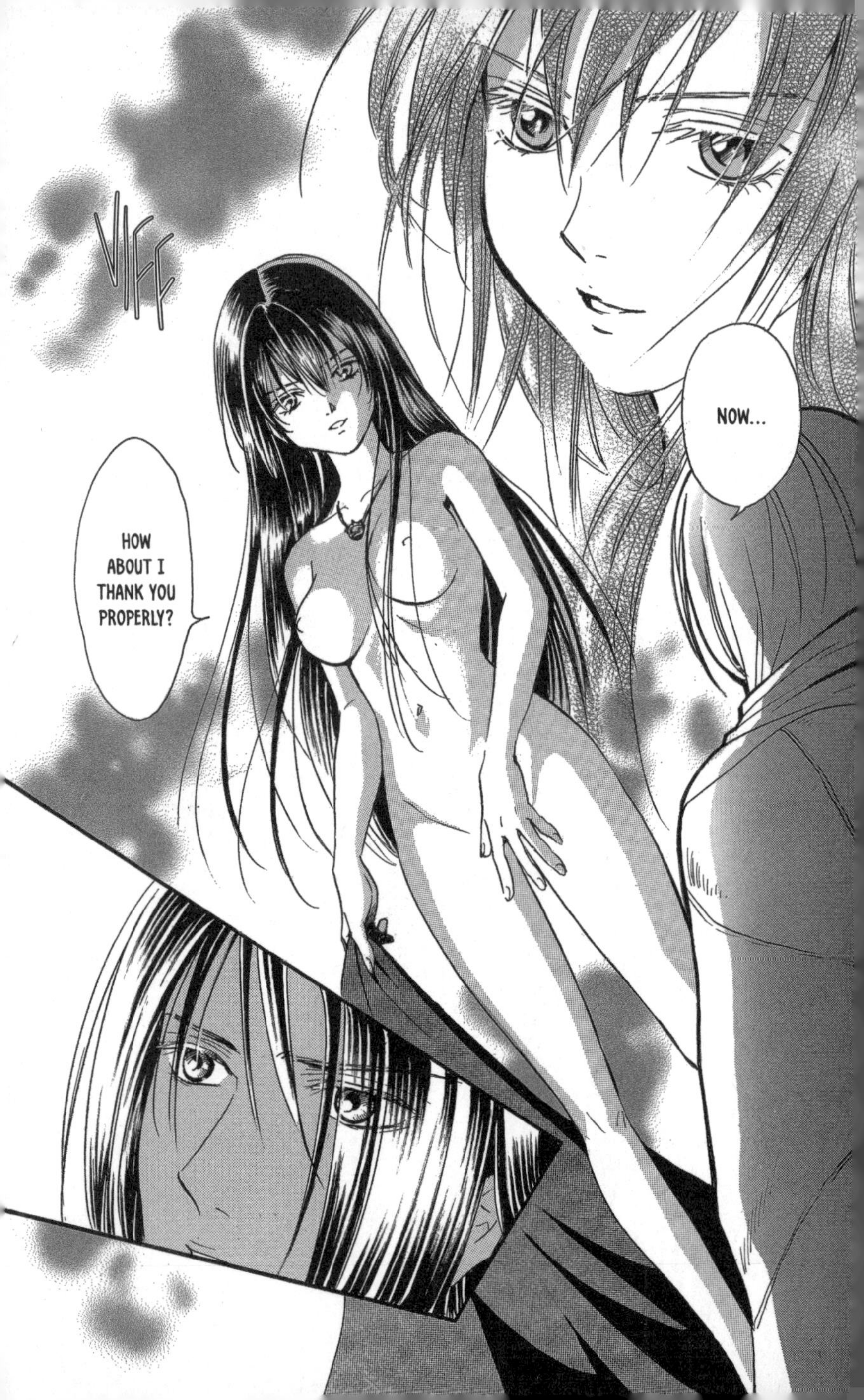
NOW...
VIFF
HOW ABOUT I THANK YOU PROPERLY?

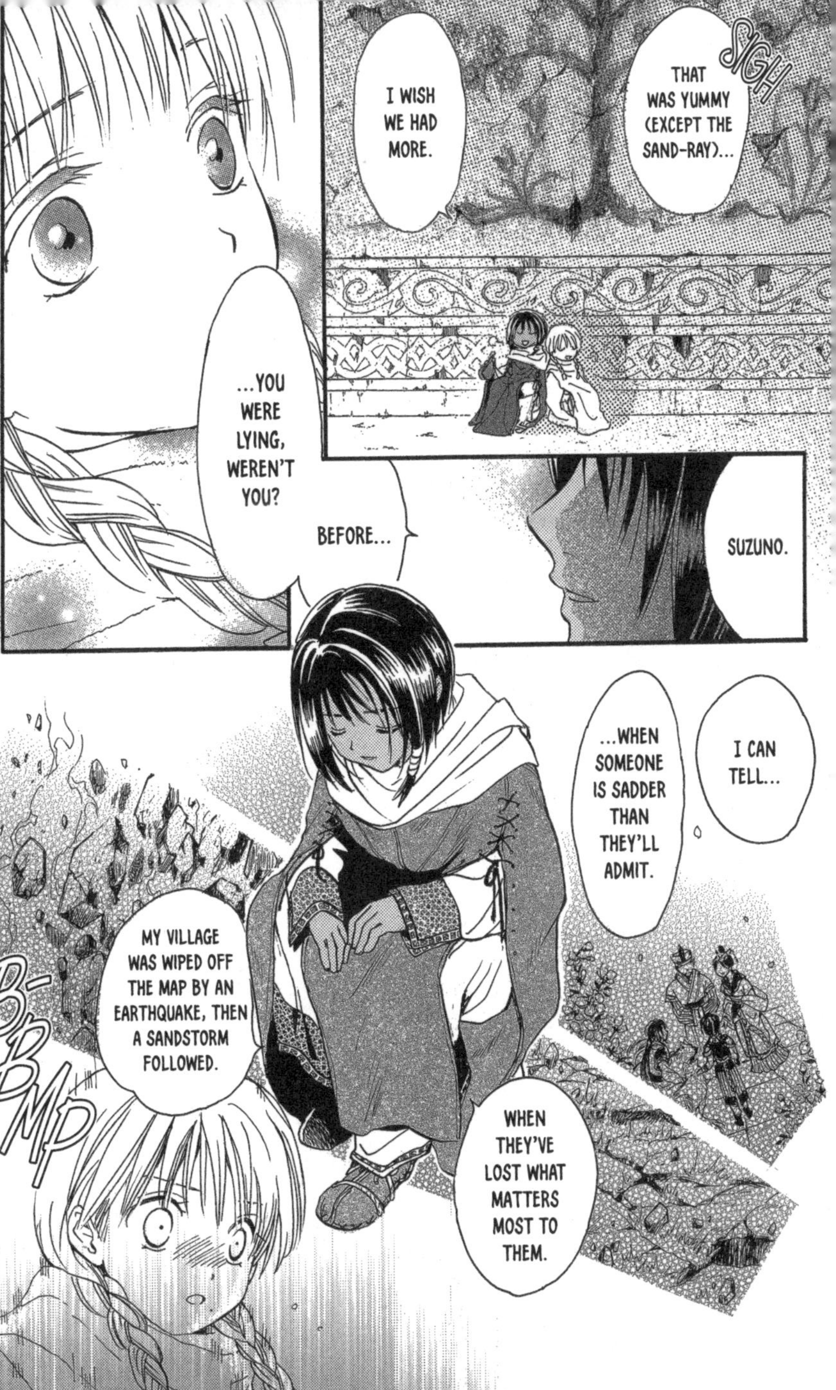
SIGH
THAT WAS YUMMY (EXCEPT THE SAND-RAY)...
I WISH WE HAD MORE.
SUZUNO.
BEFORE...
...YOU WERE LYING, WEREN'T YOU?
I CAN TELL...
...WHEN SOMEONE IS SADDER THAN THEY'LL ADMIT.
WHEN THEY'VE LOST WHAT MATTERS MOST TO THEM.
MY VILLAGE WAS WIPED OFF THE MAP BY AN EARTHQUAKE, THEN A SANDSTORM FOLLOWED.
B-BMP

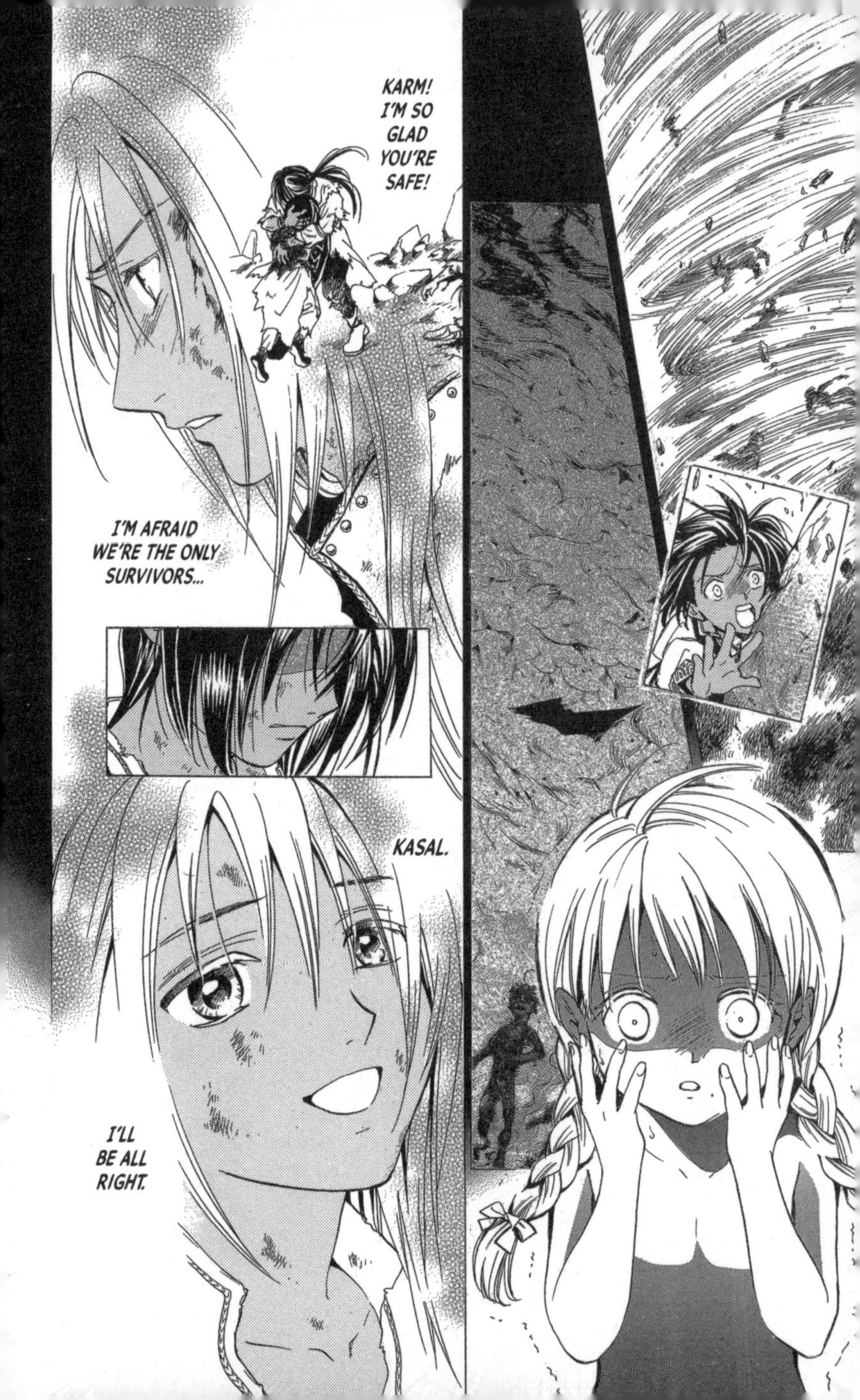
KARM! I'M SO GLAD YOU'RE SAFE!
I'M AFRAID WE'RE THE ONLY SURVIVORS...
KASAL.
I'LL BE ALL RIGHT.

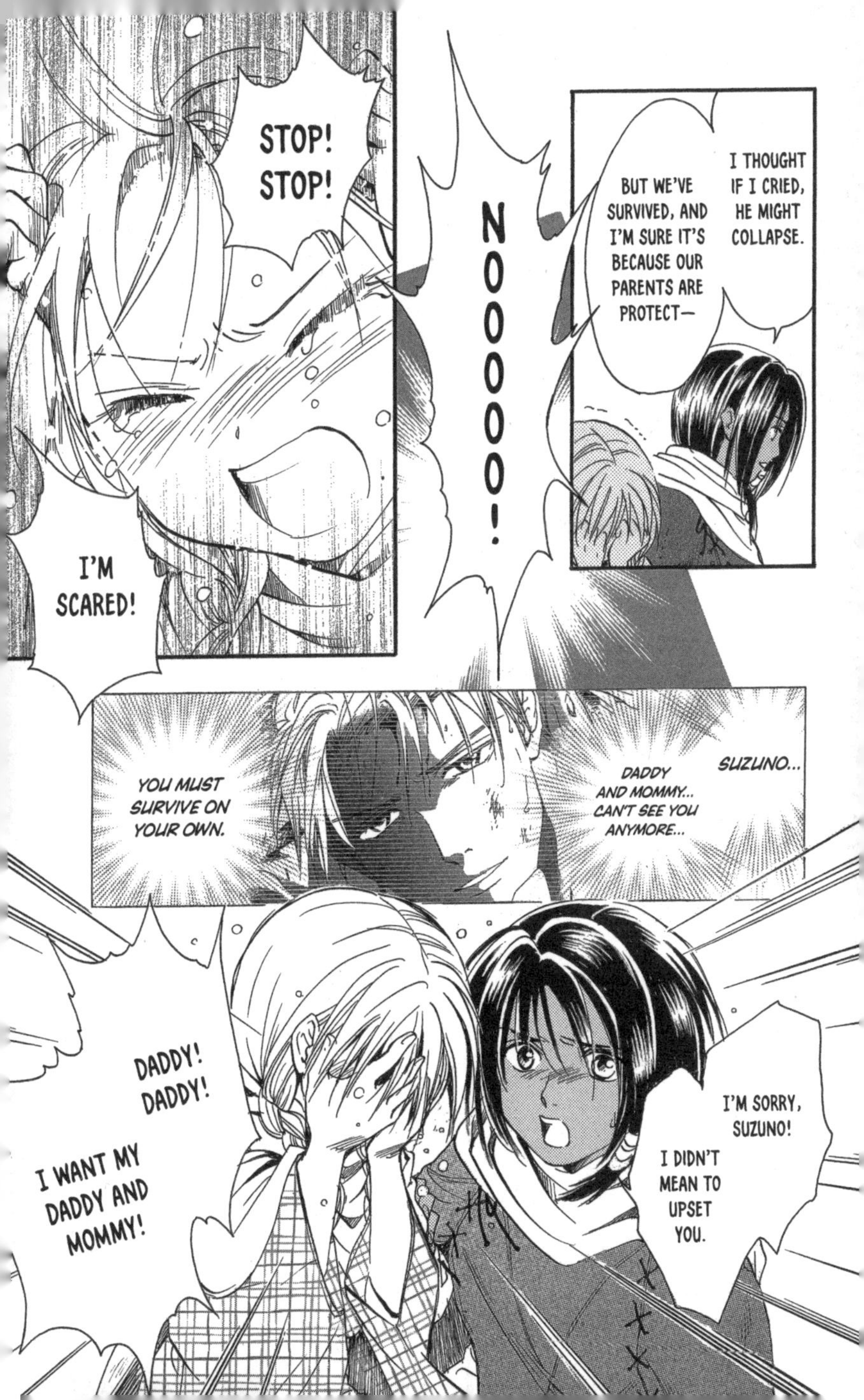
I THOUGHT IF I CRIED, HE MIGHT COLLAPSE.
BUT WE'VE SURVIVED, AND I'M SURE IT'S BECAUSE OUR PARENTS ARE PROTECT—
NOOOOOO!
STOP! STOP!
I'M SCARED!
SUZUNO...
DADDY AND MOMMY... CAN'T SEE YOU ANYMORE...
YOU MUST SURVIVE ON YOUR OWN.
I'M SORRY, SUZUNO!
I DIDN'T MEAN TO UPSET YOU.
DADDY! DADDY!
I WANT MY DADDY AND MOMMY!

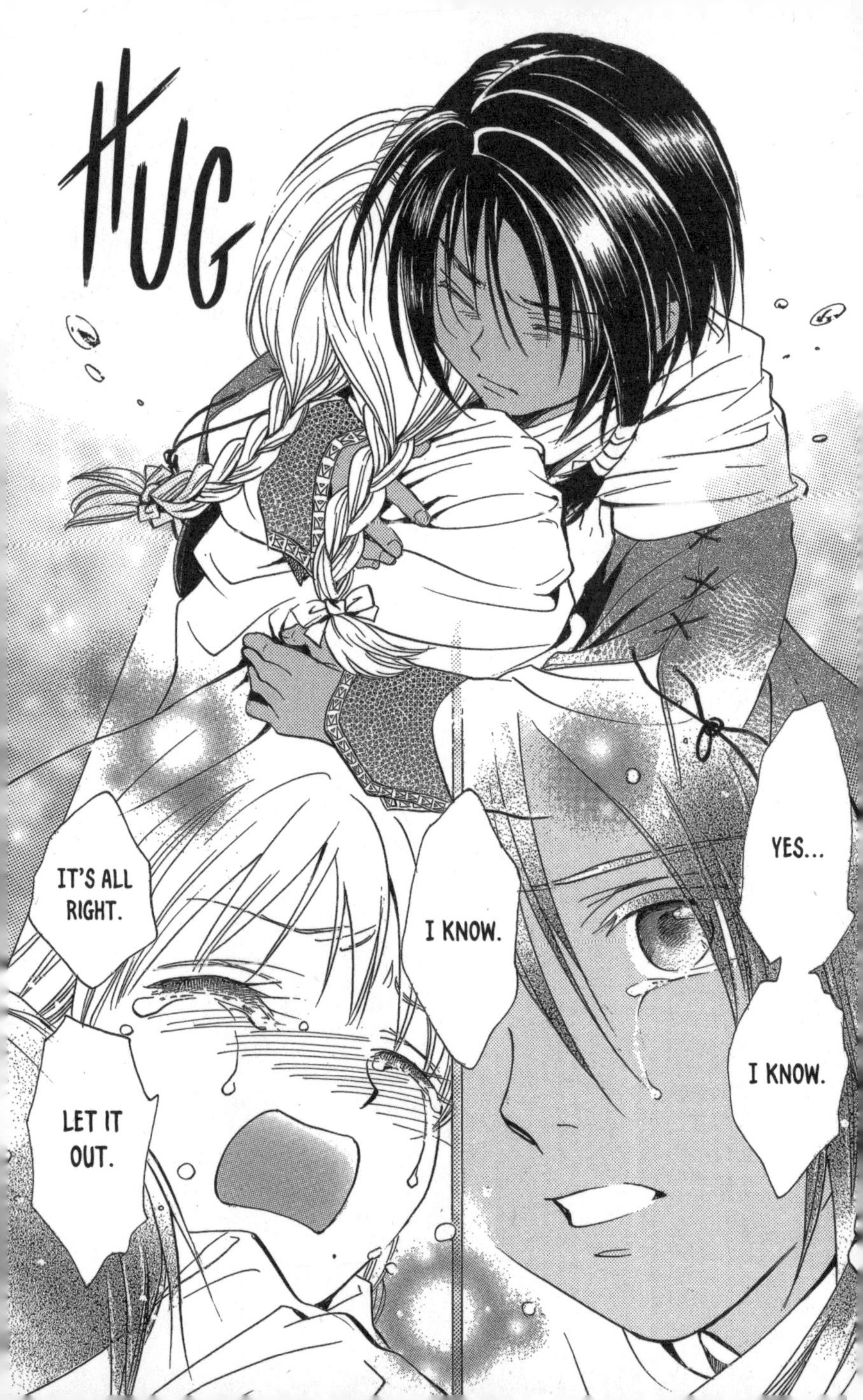
HUG
YES...
I KNOW.
I KNOW.
IT'S ALL RIGHT.
LET IT OUT.

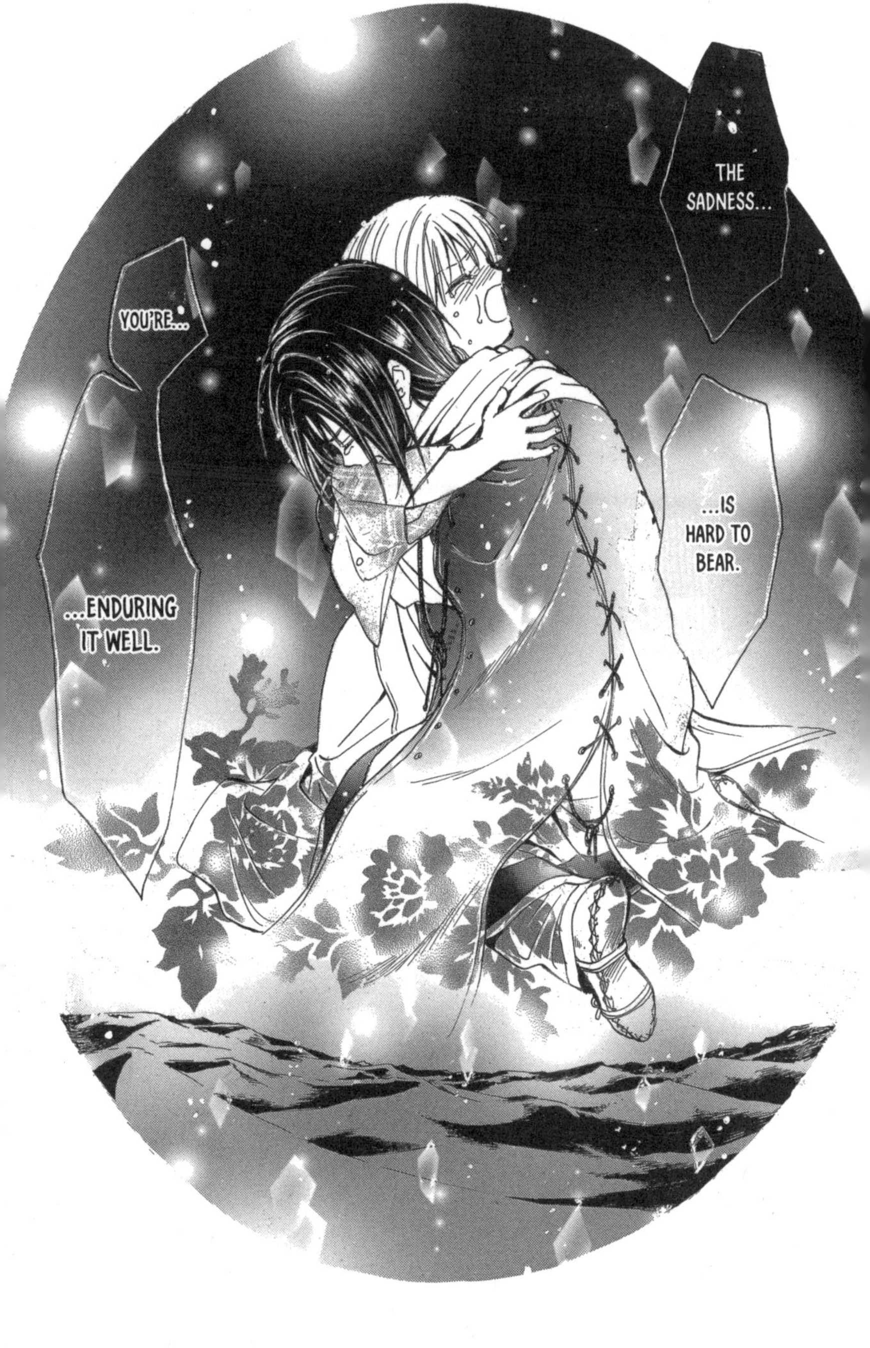
THE SADNESS...
...IS HARD TO BEAR.
YOU'RE...
...ENDURING IT WELL.

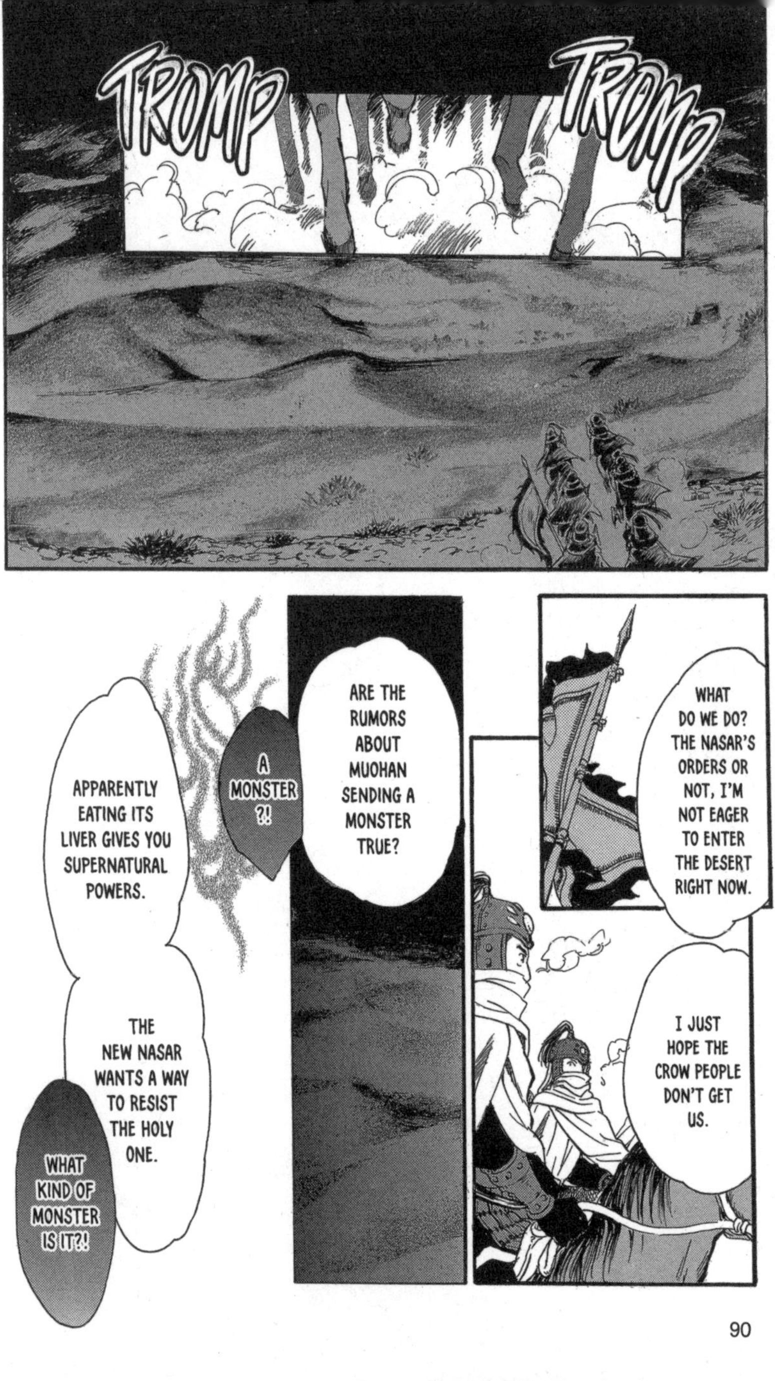
TROMP
TROMP
WHAT DO WE DO? THE NASAR'S ORDERS OR NOT, I'M NOT EAGER TO ENTER THE DESERT RIGHT NOW.
I JUST HOPE THE CROW PEOPLE DON'T GET US.
ARE THE RUMORS ABOUT MUOHAN SENDING A MONSTER TRUE?
A MONSTER?!
APPARENTLY EATING ITS LIVER GIVES YOU SUPERNATURAL POWERS.
THE NEW NASAR WANTS A WAY TO RESIST THE HOLY ONE.
WHAT KIND OF MONSTER IS IT?!

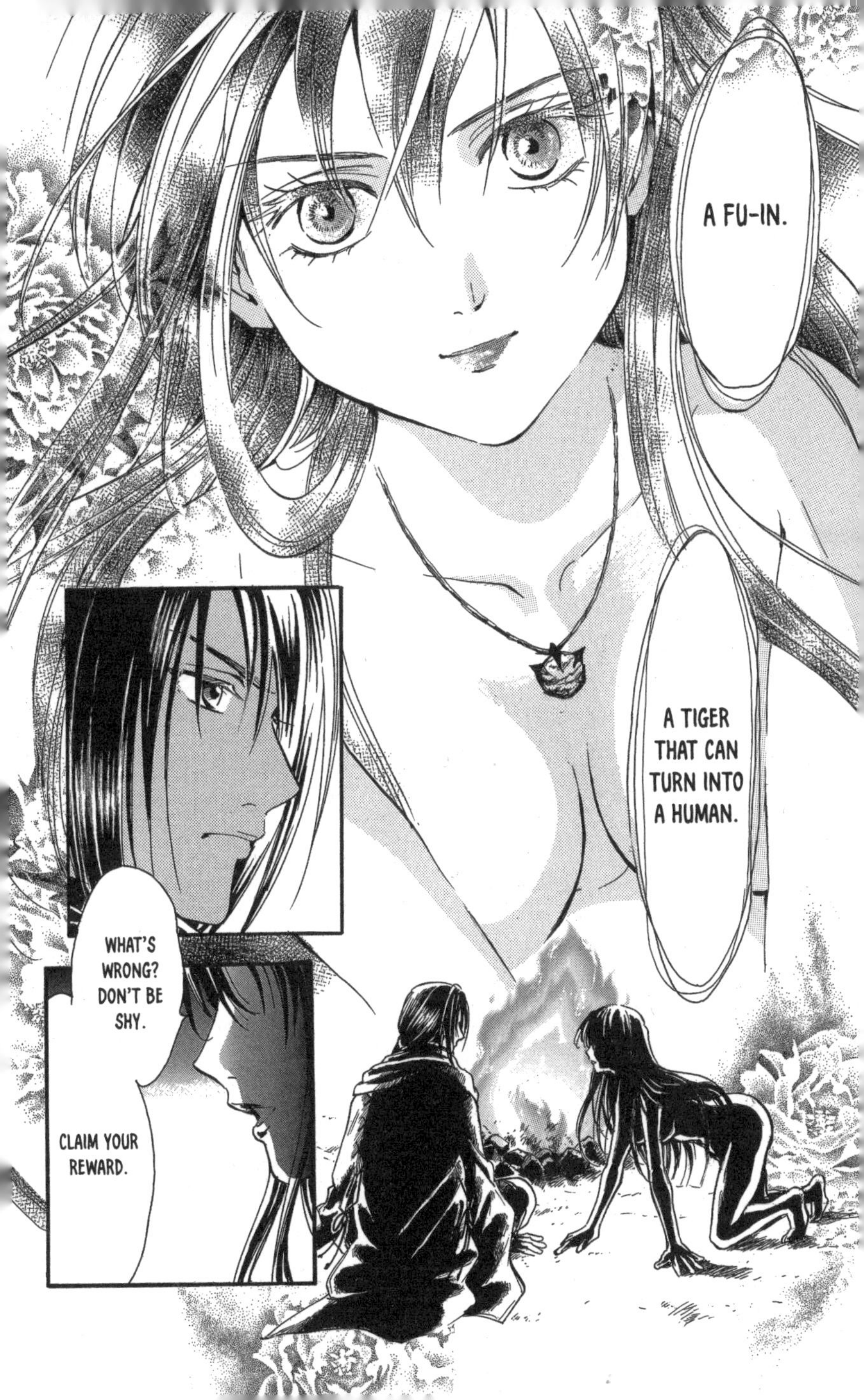
A FU-IN.
A TIGER THAT CAN TURN INTO A HUMAN.
WHAT'S WRONG? DON'T BE SHY.
CLAIM YOUR REWARD.

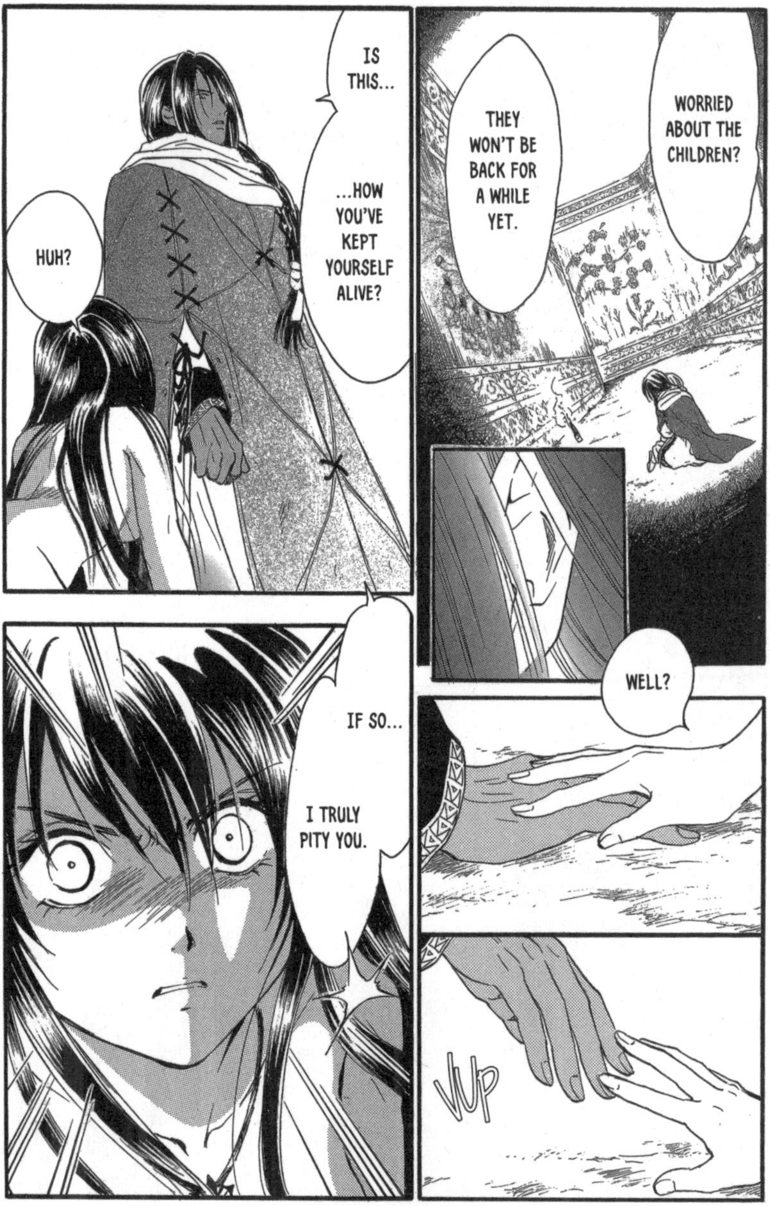
WORRIED ABOUT THE CHILDREN?
THEY WON'T BE BACK FOR A WHILE YET.
IS THIS...
...HOW YOU'VE KEPT YOURSELF ALIVE?
HUH?
WELL?
VUP
IF SO...
I TRULY PITY YOU.

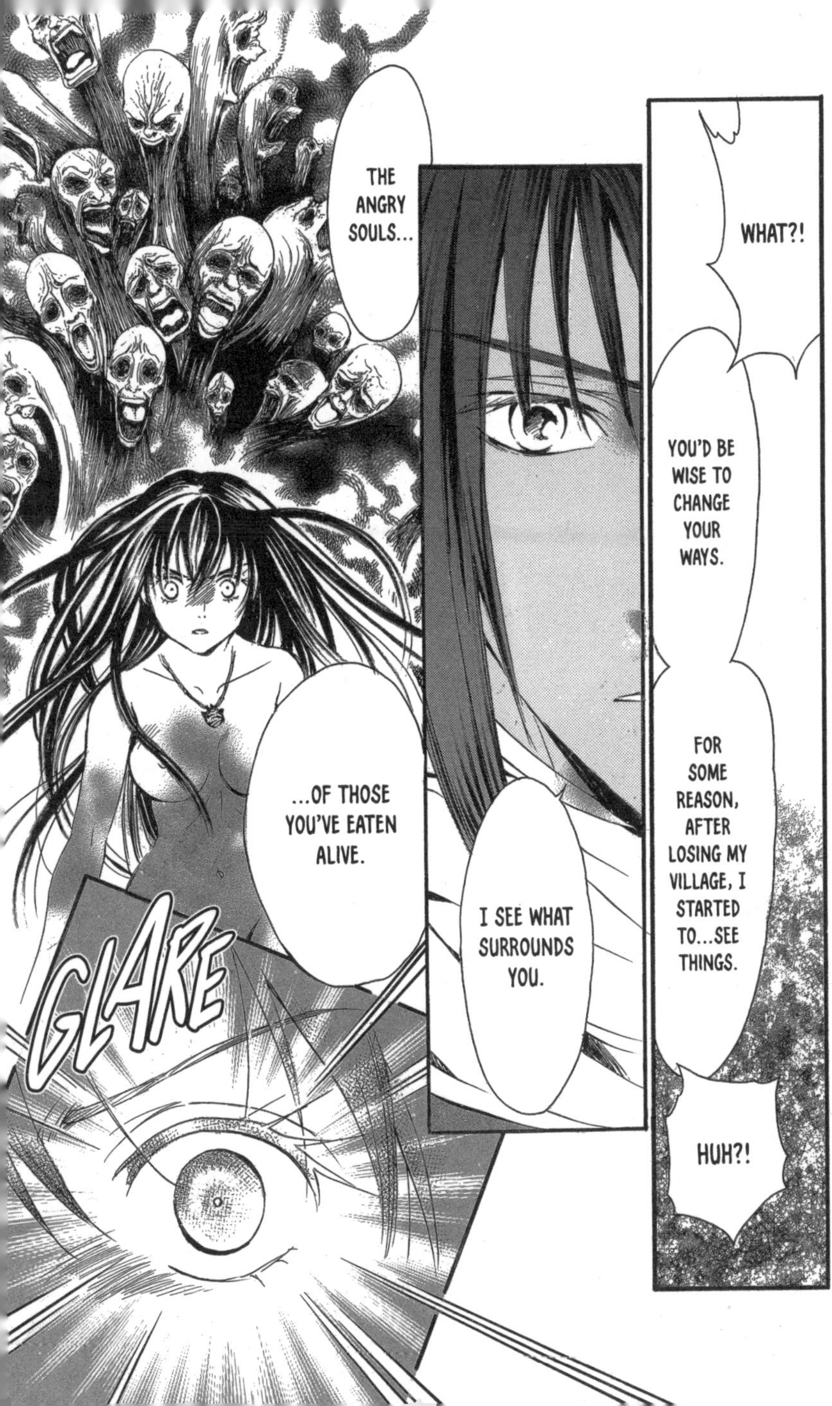
WHAT?!
YOU'D BE WISE TO CHANGE YOUR WAYS.
FOR SOME REASON, AFTER LOSING MY VILLAGE, I STARTED TO...SEE THINGS.
HUH?!
I SEE WHAT SURROUNDS YOU.
THE ANGRY SOULS...
...OF THOSE YOU'VE EATEN ALIVE.
GLARE

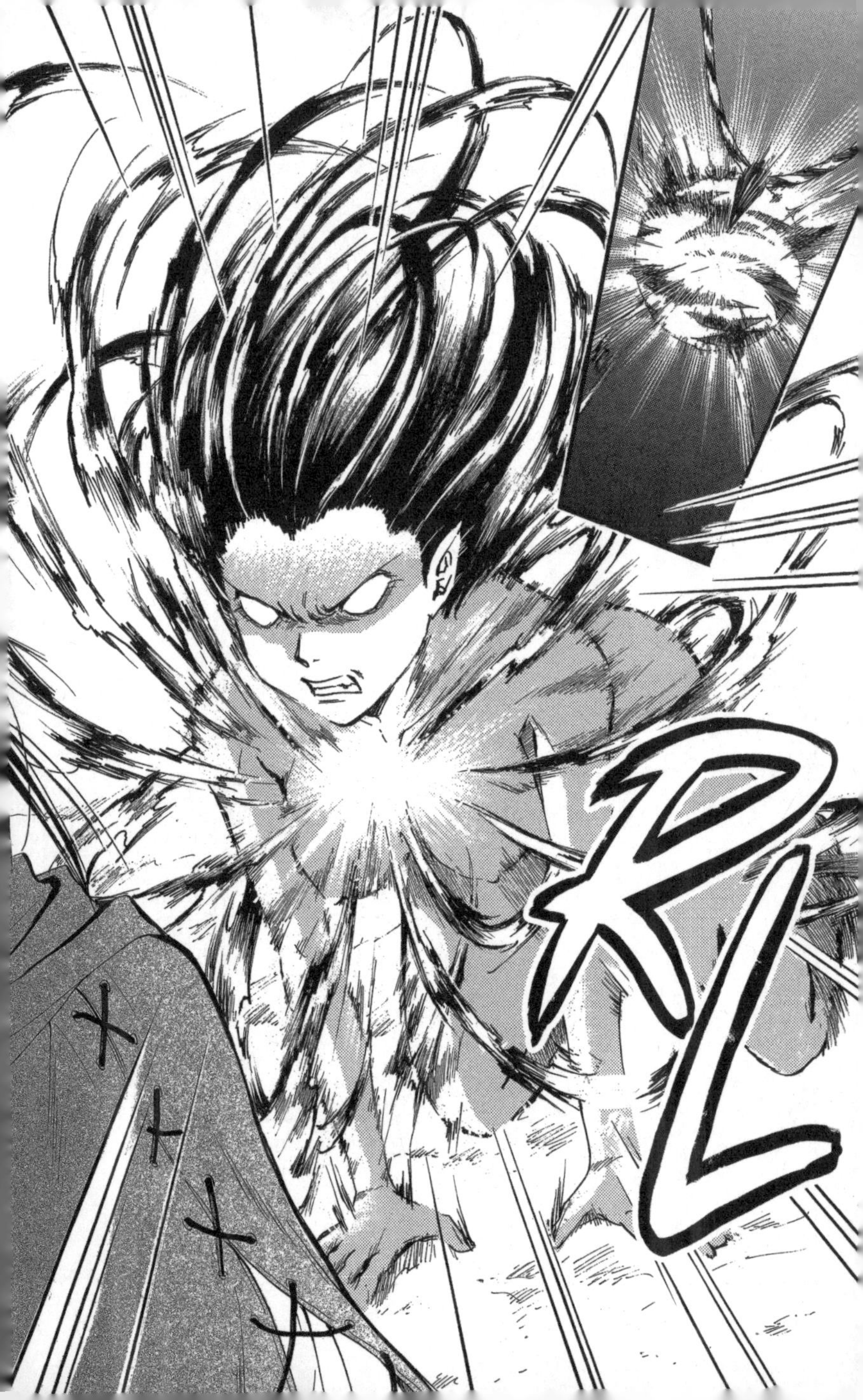

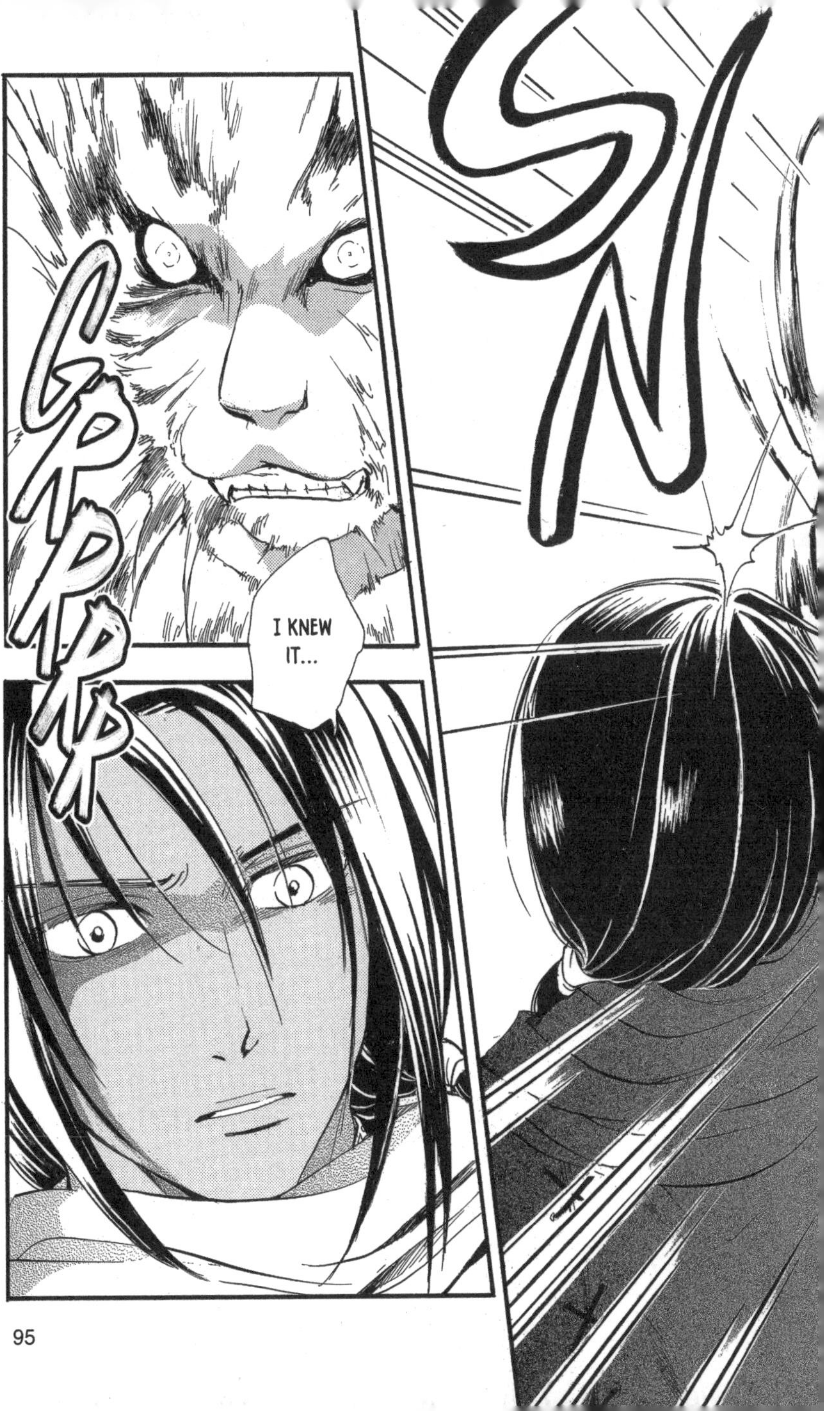
SN
GRRRR
I KNEW IT...

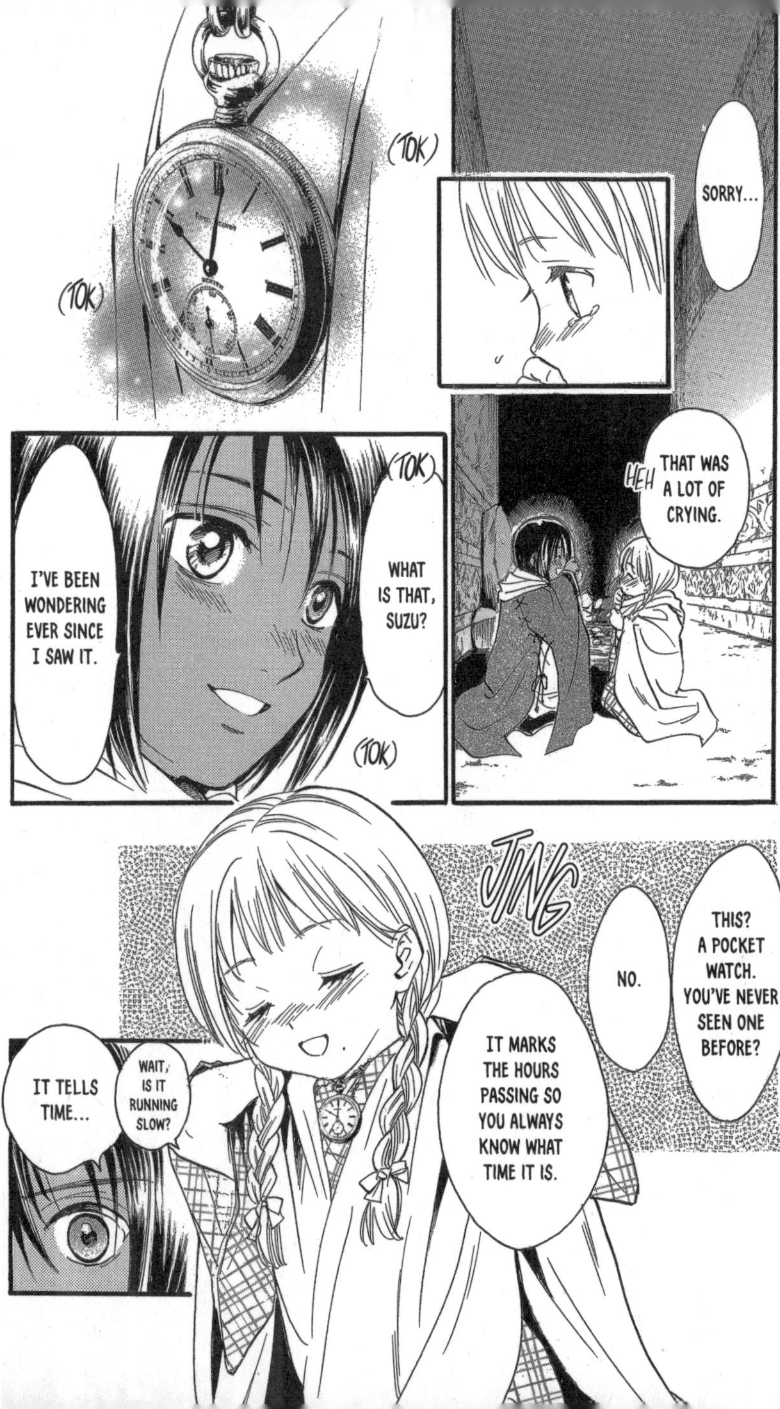
SORRY...
(TOK)
(TOK)
HEH
THAT WAS A LOT OF CRYING.
(TOK)
WHAT IS THAT, SUZU?
I'VE BEEN WONDERING EVER SINCE I SAW IT.
(TOK)
JING
THIS? A POCKET WATCH. YOU'VE NEVER SEEN ONE BEFORE?
NO.
IT MARKS THE HOURS PASSING SO YOU ALWAYS KNOW WHAT TIME IT IS.
WAIT, IS IT RUNNING SLOW?
IT TELLS TIME...

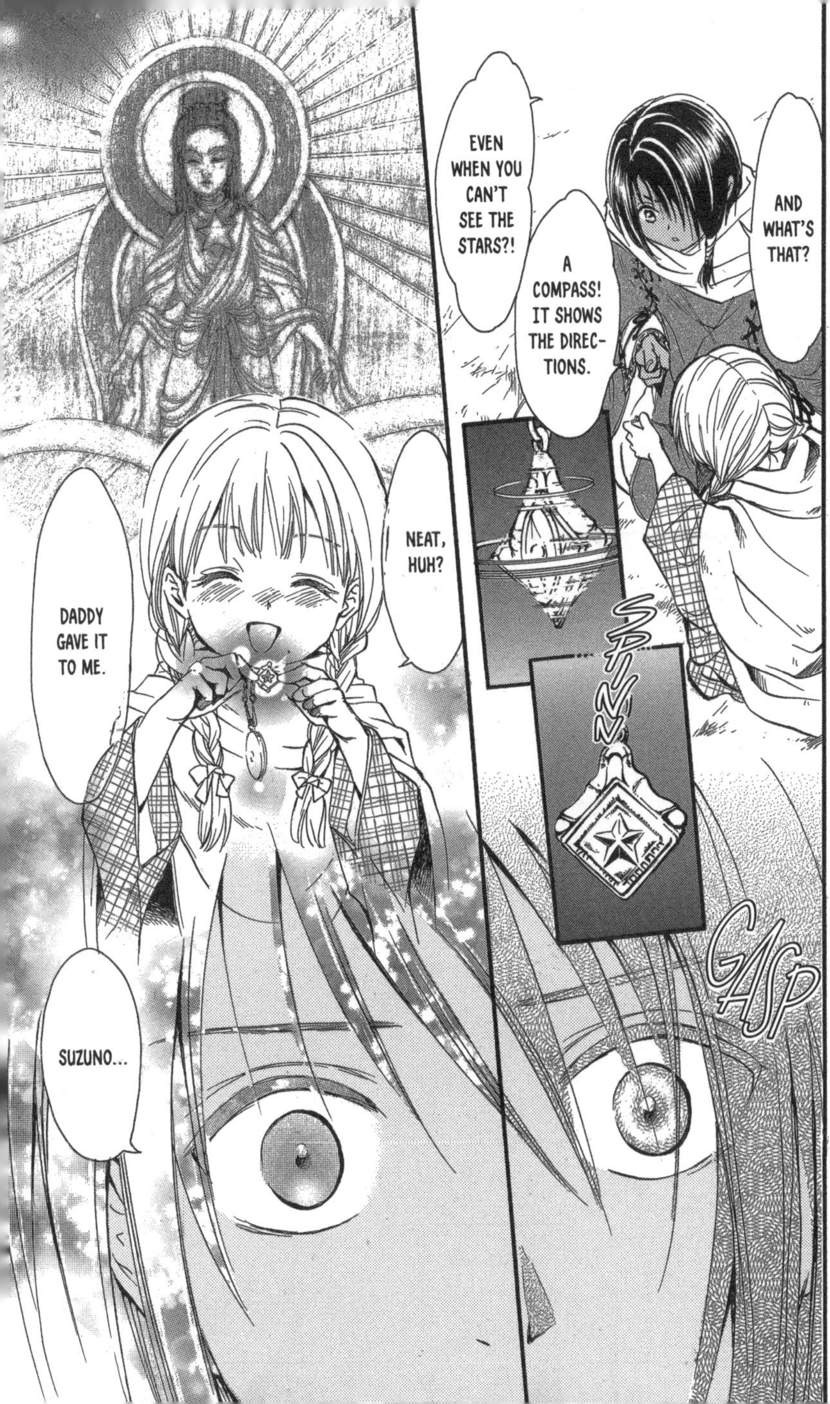
AND WHAT'S THAT?
A COMPASS! IT SHOWS THE DIREC-TIONS.
EVEN WHEN YOU CAN'T SEE THE STARS?!
SPINNN
GASP
NEAT, HUH?
DADDY GAVE IT TO ME.
SUZUNO...

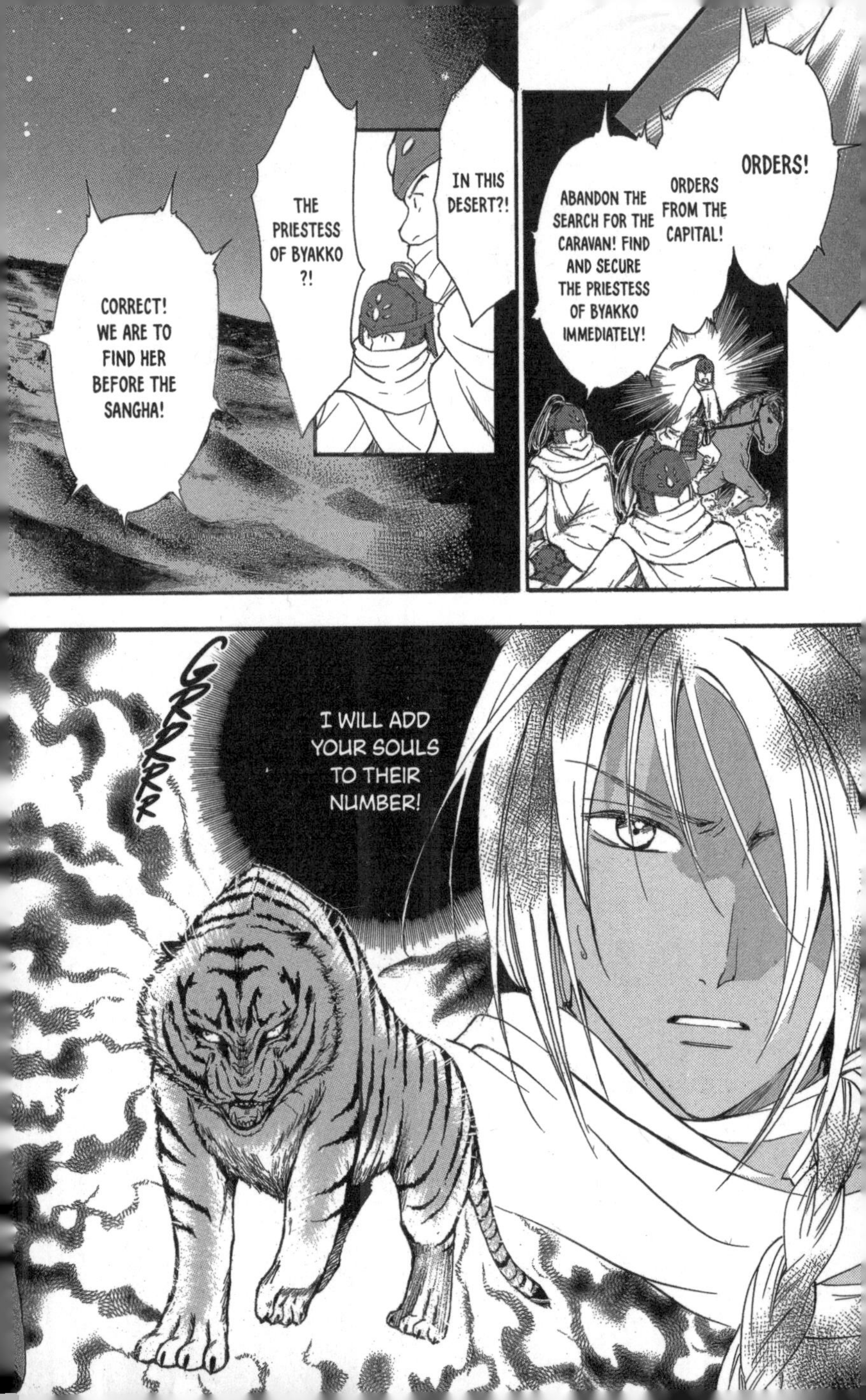
ORDERS!
ORDERS FROM THE CAPITAL!
ABANDON THE SEARCH FOR THE CARAVAN! FIND AND SECURE THE PRIESTESS OF BYAKKO IMMEDIATELY!
IN THIS DESERT?!
THE PRIESTESS OF BYAKKO ?!
CORRECT! WE ARE TO FIND HER BEFORE THE SANGHA!
I WILL ADD YOUR SOULS TO THEIR NUMBER!
GRRRRR

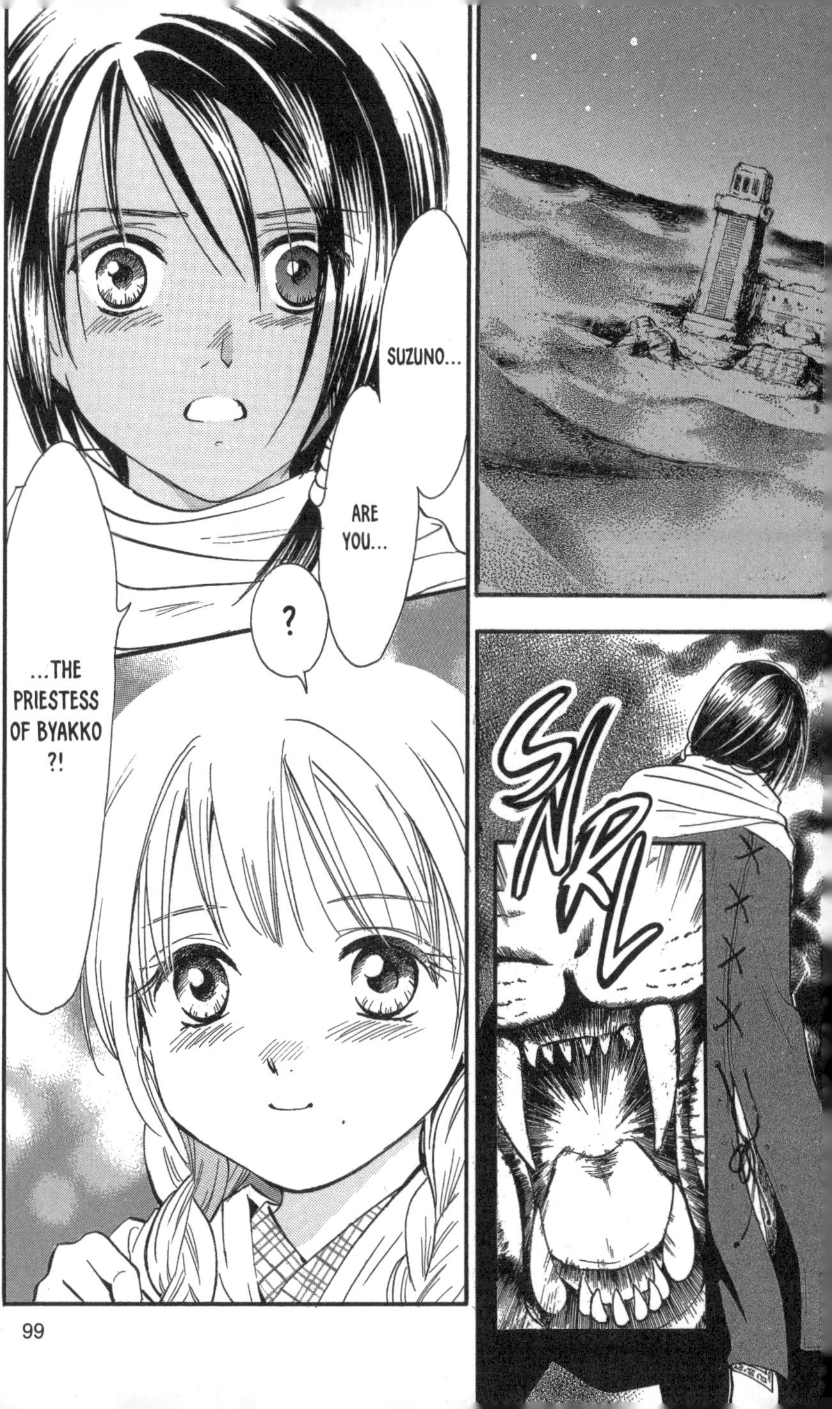
SNRL
SUZUNO...
ARE YOU...
?
...THE PRIESTESS OF BYAKKO ?!

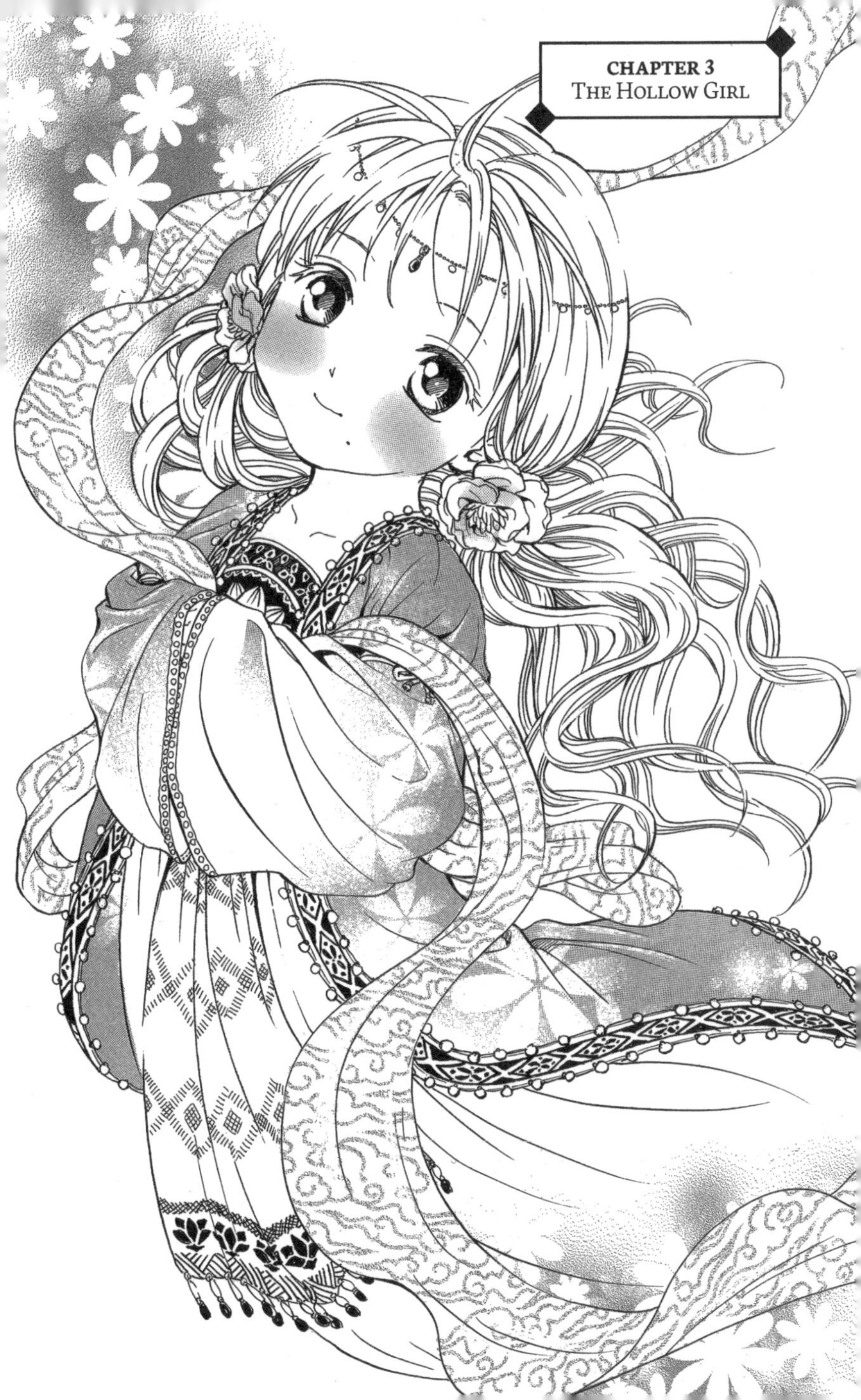
CHAPTER 3
THE HOLLOW GIRL

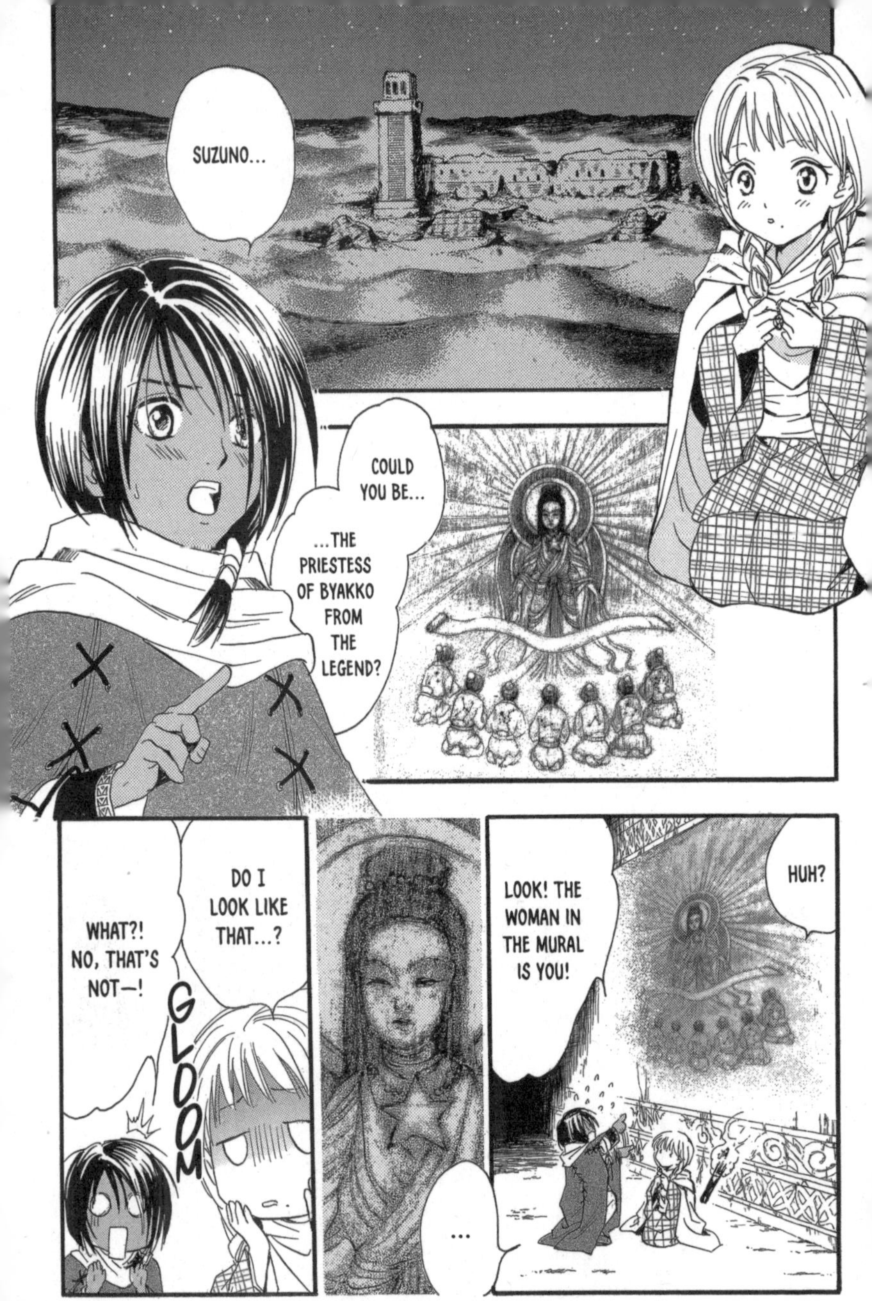
SUZUNO...
COULD YOU BE...
...THE PRIESTESS OF BYAKKO FROM THE LEGEND?
HUH?
LOOK! THE WOMAN IN THE MURAL IS YOU!
...
DO I LOOK LIKE THAT...?
WHAT?! NO, THAT'S NOT—!
GLOOM

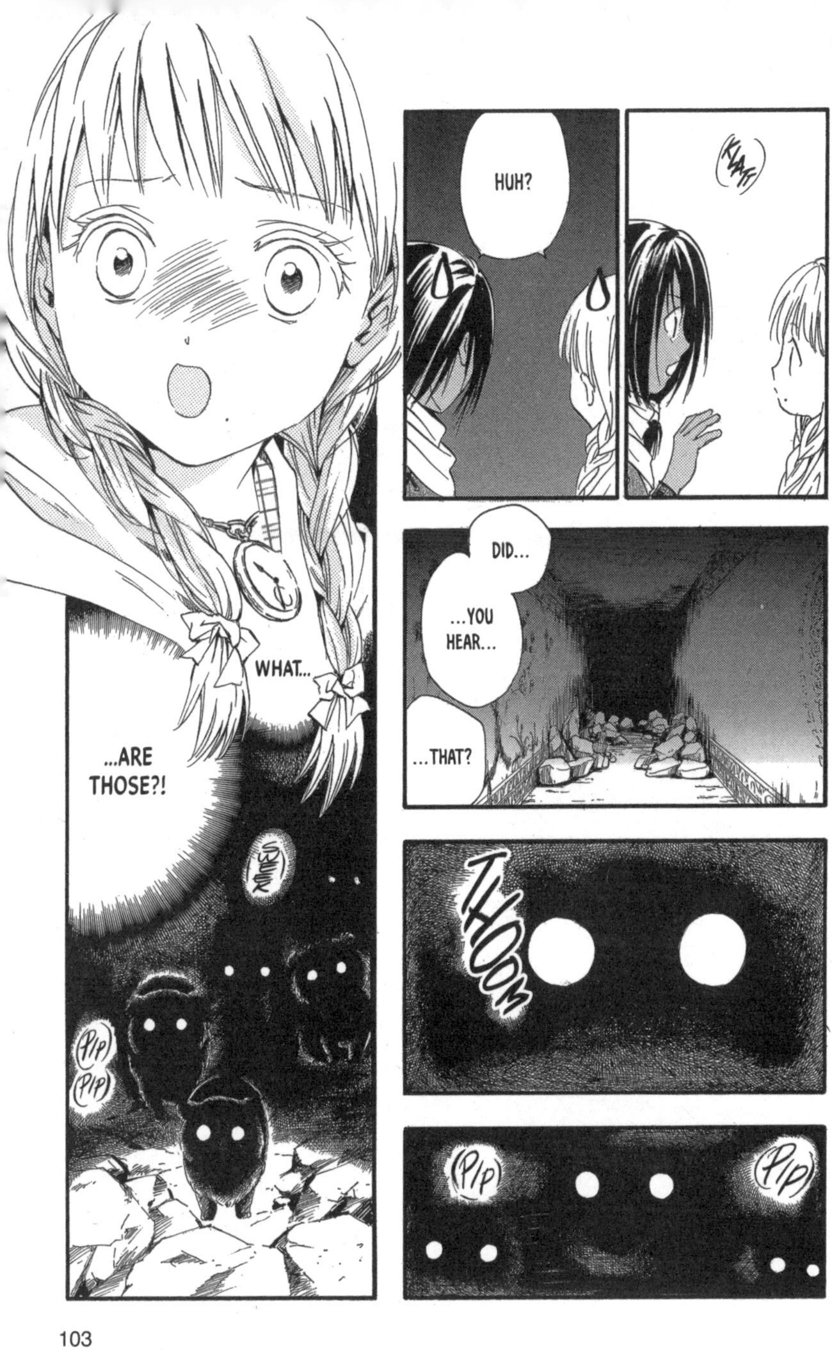
KLAFF
HUH?
DID...
...YOU HEAR...
...THAT?
THOOM
PIP
PIP
WHAT...
...ARE THOSE?!
SWEEK
PIP
PIP

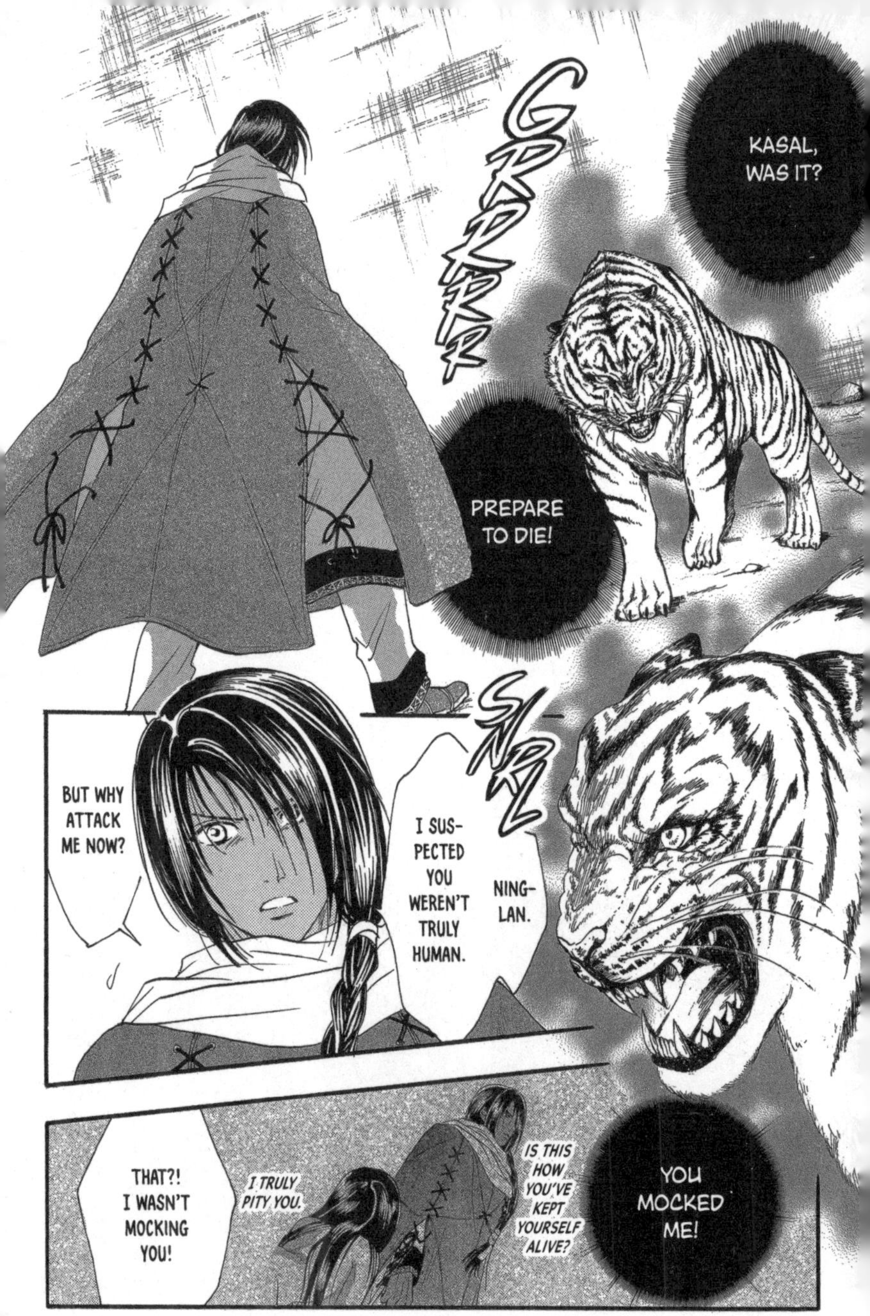
KASAL, WAS IT?
GRRRRR
PREPARE TO DIE!
SNRL
NING-LAN.
I SUSPECTED YOU WEREN'T TRULY HUMAN.
BUT WHY ATTACK ME NOW?
YOU MOCKED ME!
IS THIS HOW YOU'VE KEPT YOURSELF ALIVE?
I TRULY PITY YOU.
THAT?! I WASN'T MOCKING YOU!

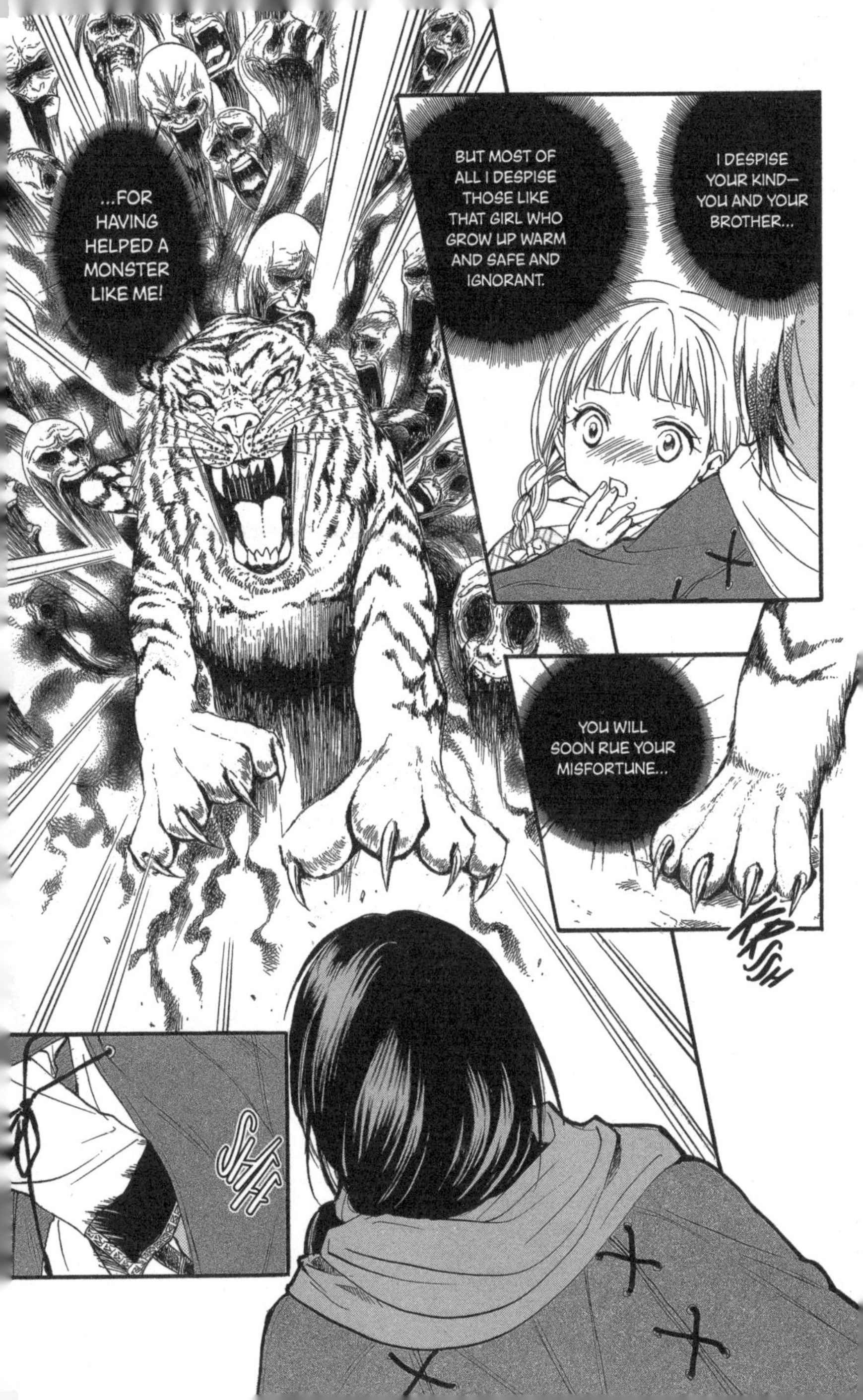
I DESPISE YOUR KIND—YOU AND YOUR BROTHER...
BUT MOST OF ALL I DESPISE THOSE LIKE THAT GIRL WHO GROW UP WARM AND SAFE AND IGNORANT.
YOU WILL SOON RUE YOUR MISFORTUNE...
KRSSH
...FOR HAVING HELPED A MONSTER LIKE ME!
SHFF

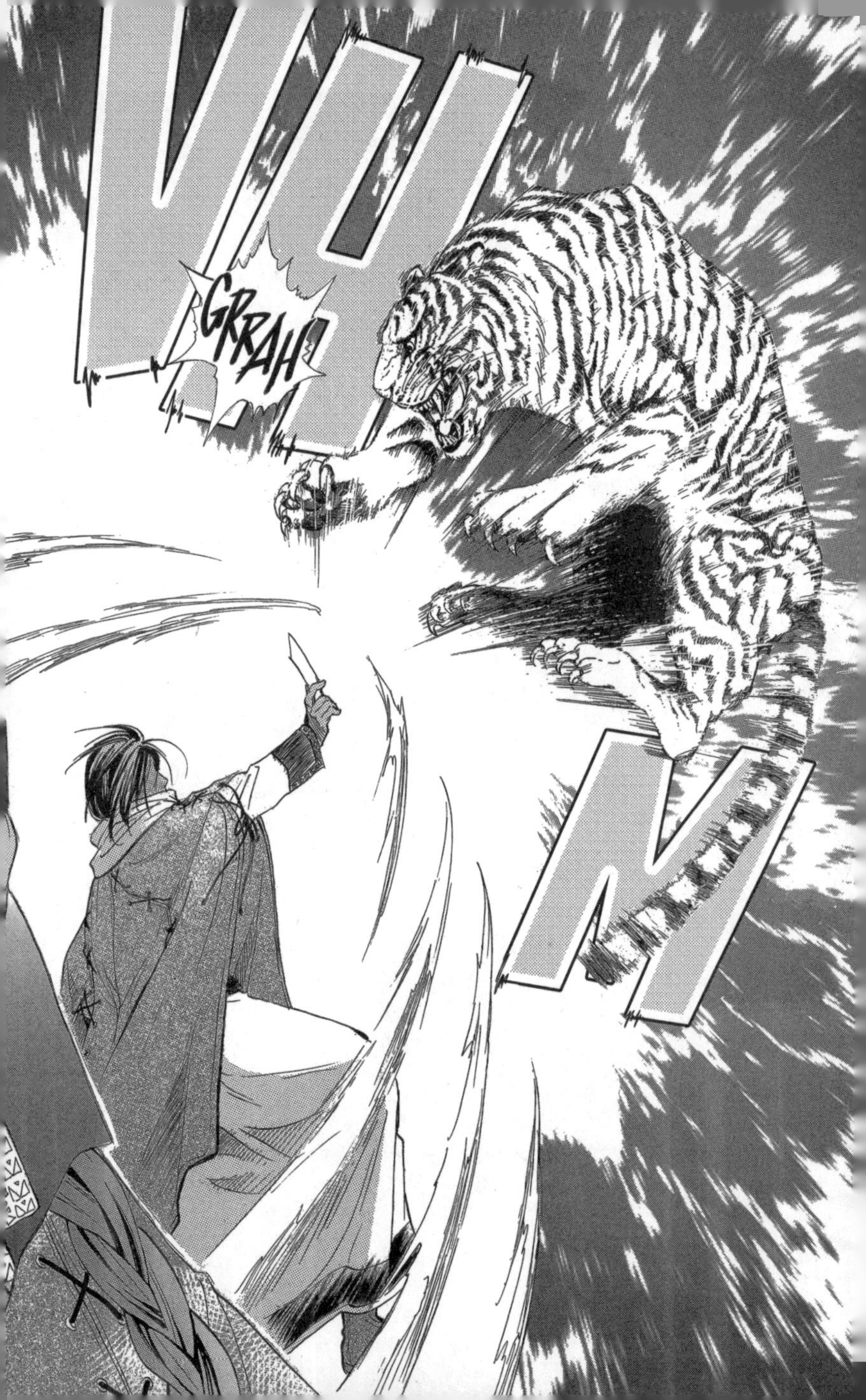
GRRAH
N

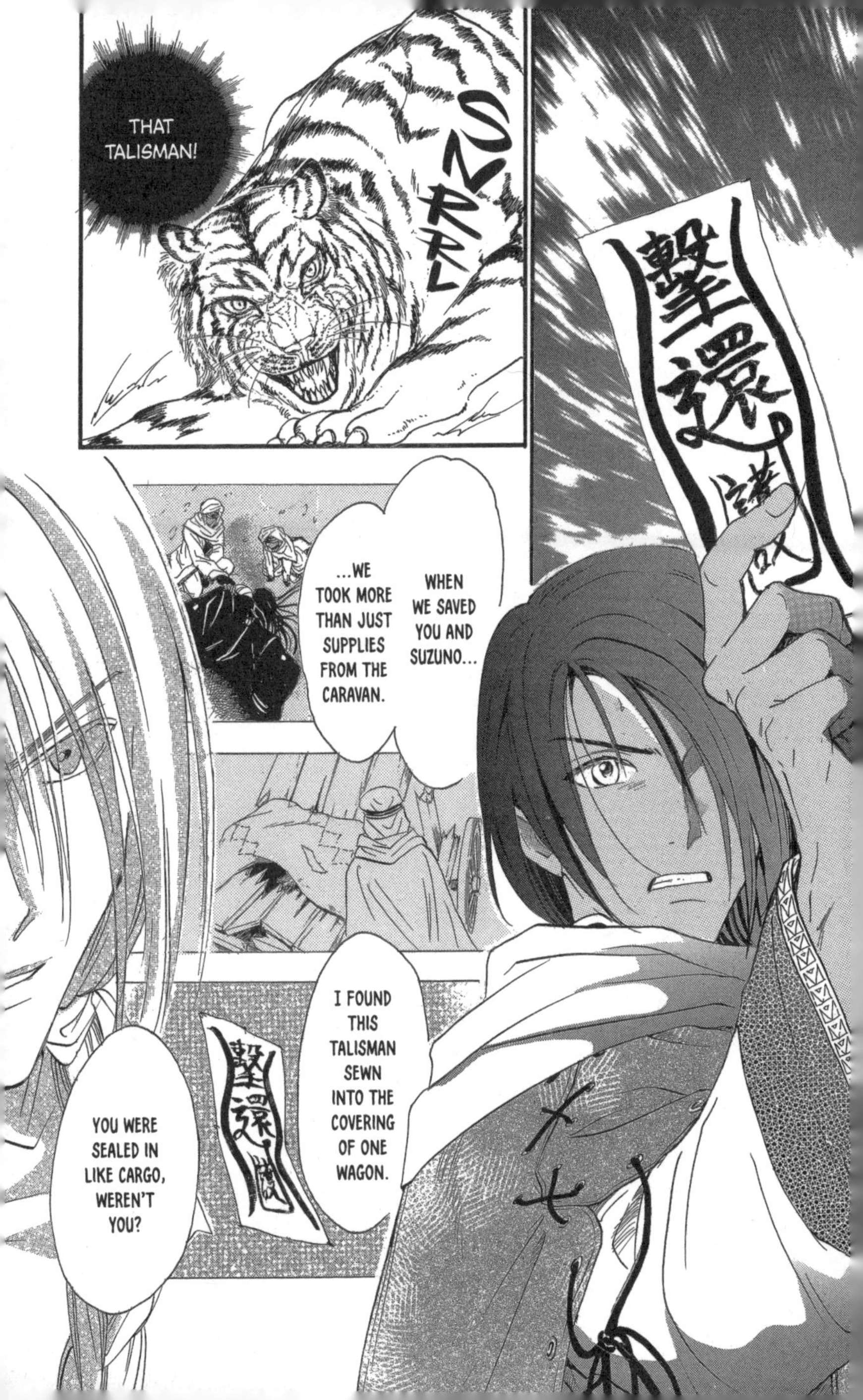
撃還
SNRRL
THAT TALISMAN!
WHEN WE SAVED YOU AND SUZUNO...
...WE TOOK MORE THAN JUST SUPPLIES FROM THE CARAVAN.
I FOUND THIS TALISMAN SEWN INTO THE COVERING OF ONE WAGON.
YOU WERE SEALED IN LIKE CARGO, WEREN'T YOU?

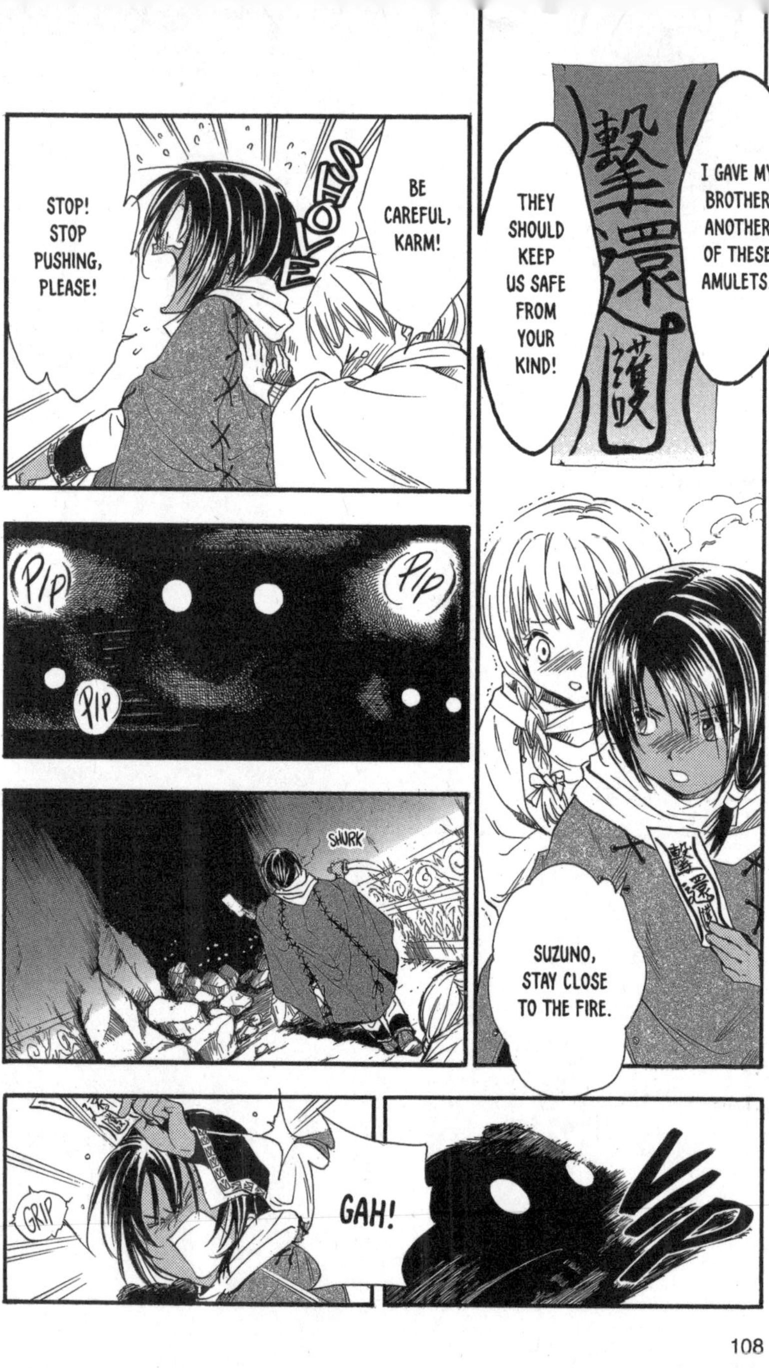
I GAVE MY BROTHER ANOTHER OF THESE AMULETS.
THEY SHOULD KEEP US SAFE FROM YOUR KIND!
SUZUNO, STAY CLOSE TO THE FIRE.
BE CAREFUL, KARM!
SHOVE
STOP! STOP PUSHING, PLEASE!
PIP
PIP
PIP
SHURK
GAH!
GRIP

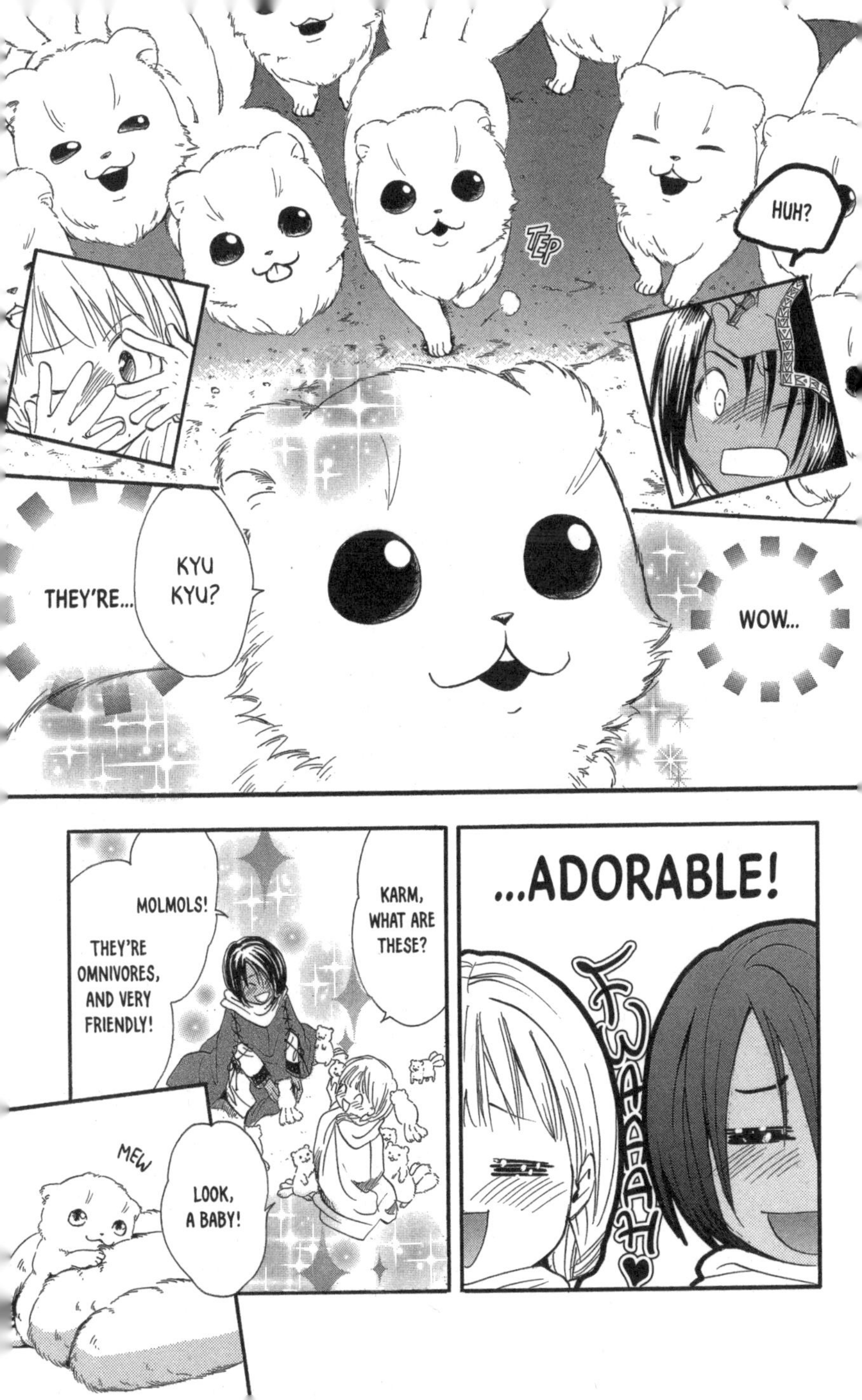
HUH?
TEP
WOW...
KYU KYU?
THEY'RE...
...ADORABLE!
KARM, WHAT ARE THESE?
MOLMOLS!
THEY'RE OMNIVORES, AND VERY FRIENDLY!
LOOK, A BABY!
MEW

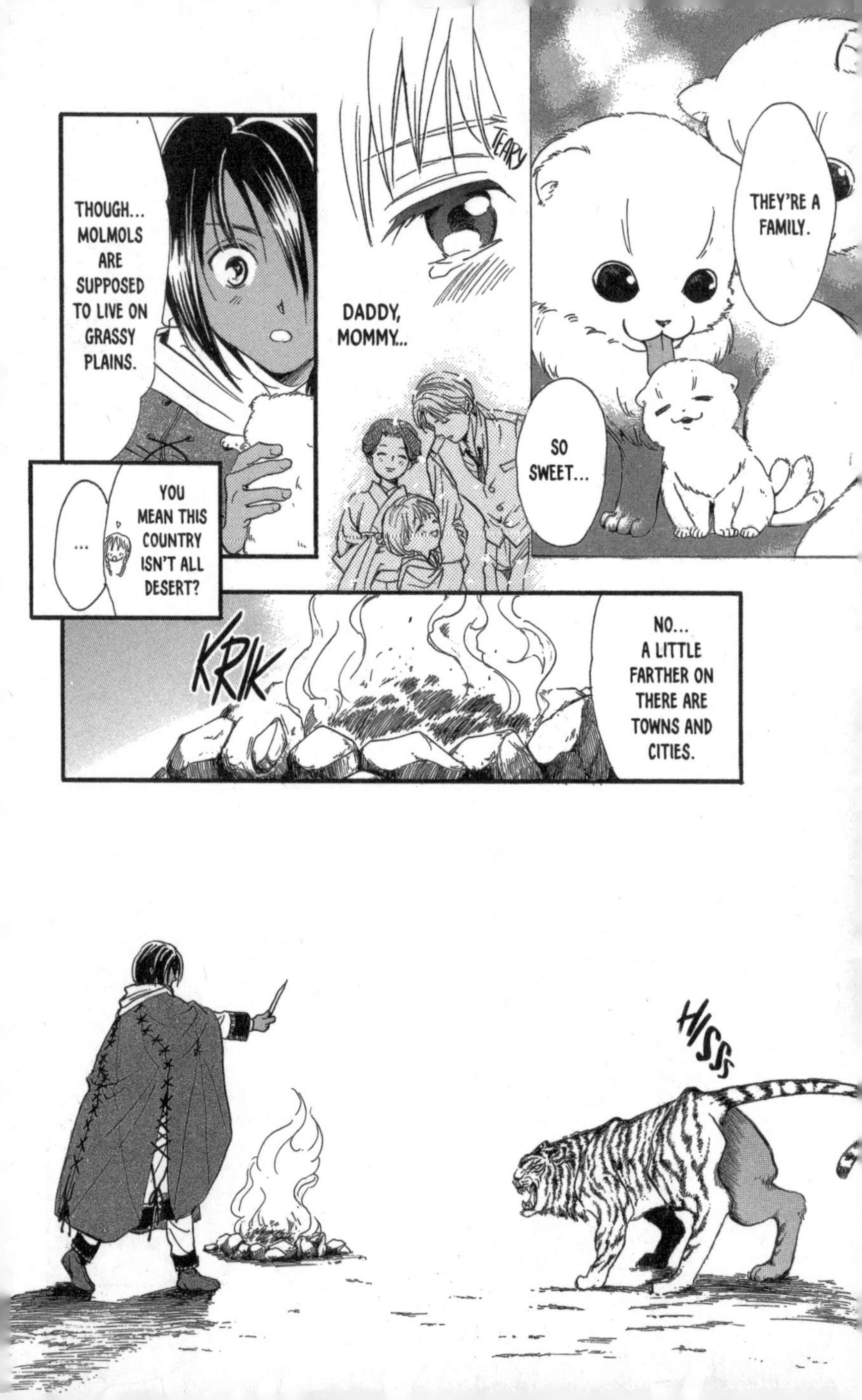
THEY'RE A FAMILY.
SO SWEET...
TEARY
DADDY, MOMMY...
THOUGH... MOLMOLS ARE SUPPOSED TO LIVE ON GRASSY PLAINS.
YOU MEAN THIS COUNTRY ISN'T ALL DESERT?
...
NO... A LITTLE FARTHER ON THERE ARE TOWNS AND CITIES.
KRIK
HISSS

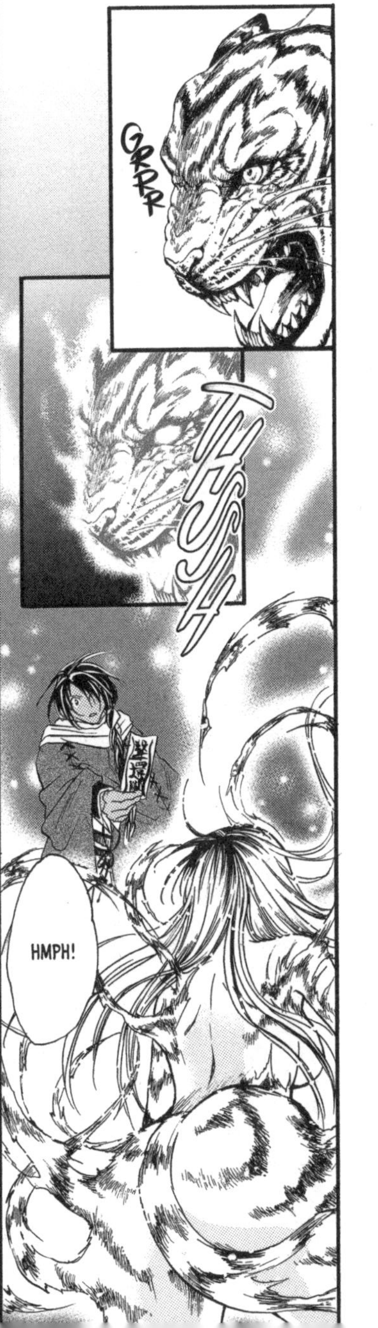
GRRR
THSSH
HMPH!
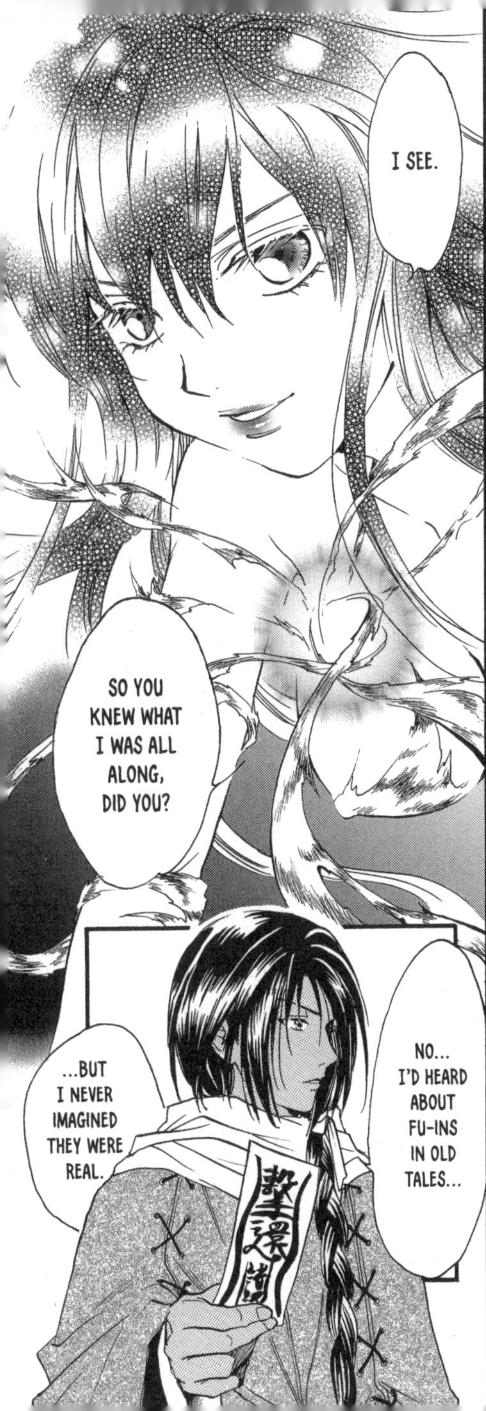
I SEE.
SO YOU KNEW WHAT I WAS ALL ALONG, DID YOU?
NO... I'D HEARD ABOUT FU-INS IN OLD TALES...
...BUT I NEVER IMAGINED THEY WERE REAL.

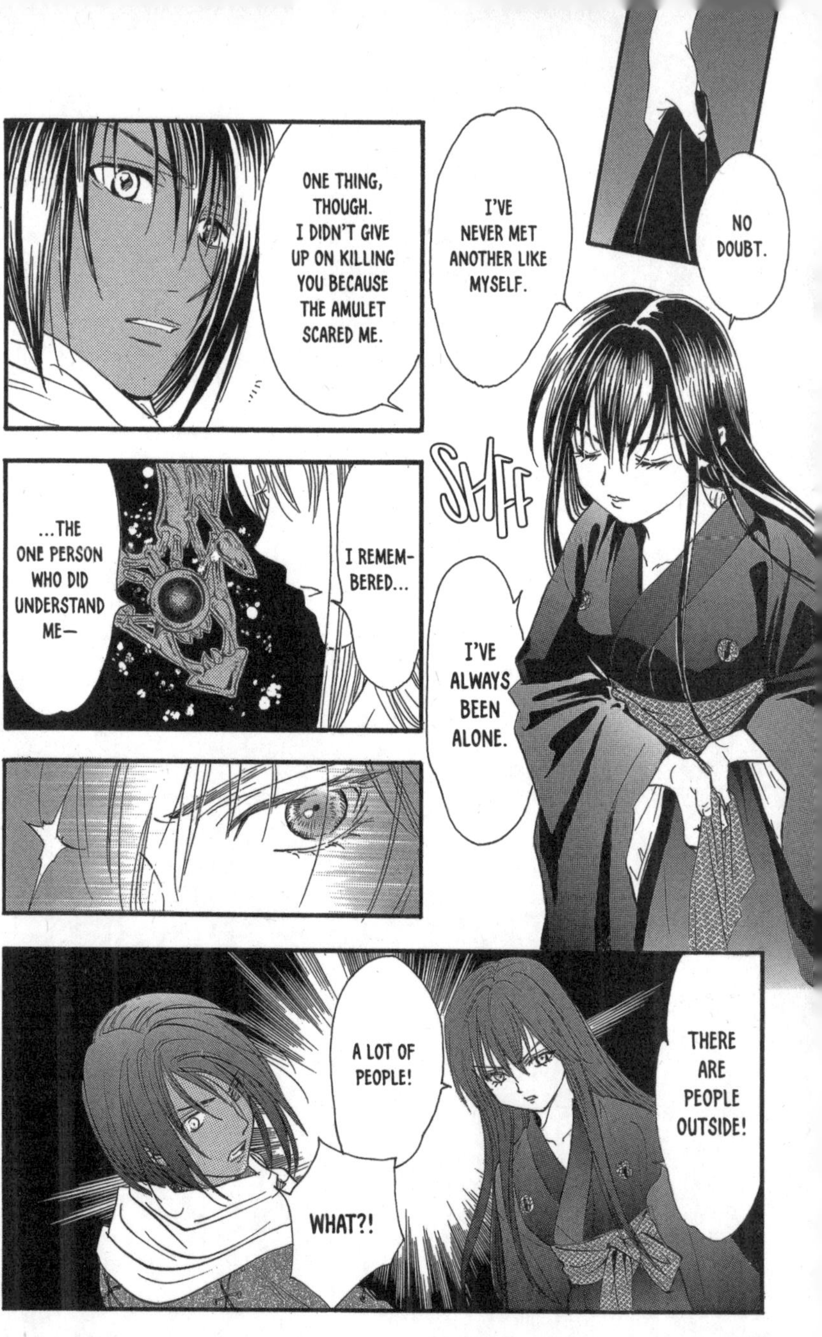
NO DOUBT.
I'VE NEVER MET ANOTHER LIKE MYSELF.
SHFF
I'VE ALWAYS BEEN ALONE.
ONE THING, THOUGH. I DIDN'T GIVE UP ON KILLING YOU BECAUSE THE AMULET SCARED ME.
I REMEMBERED...
...THE ONE PERSON WHO DID UNDERSTAND ME—
THERE ARE PEOPLE OUTSIDE!
A LOT OF PEOPLE!
WHAT?!

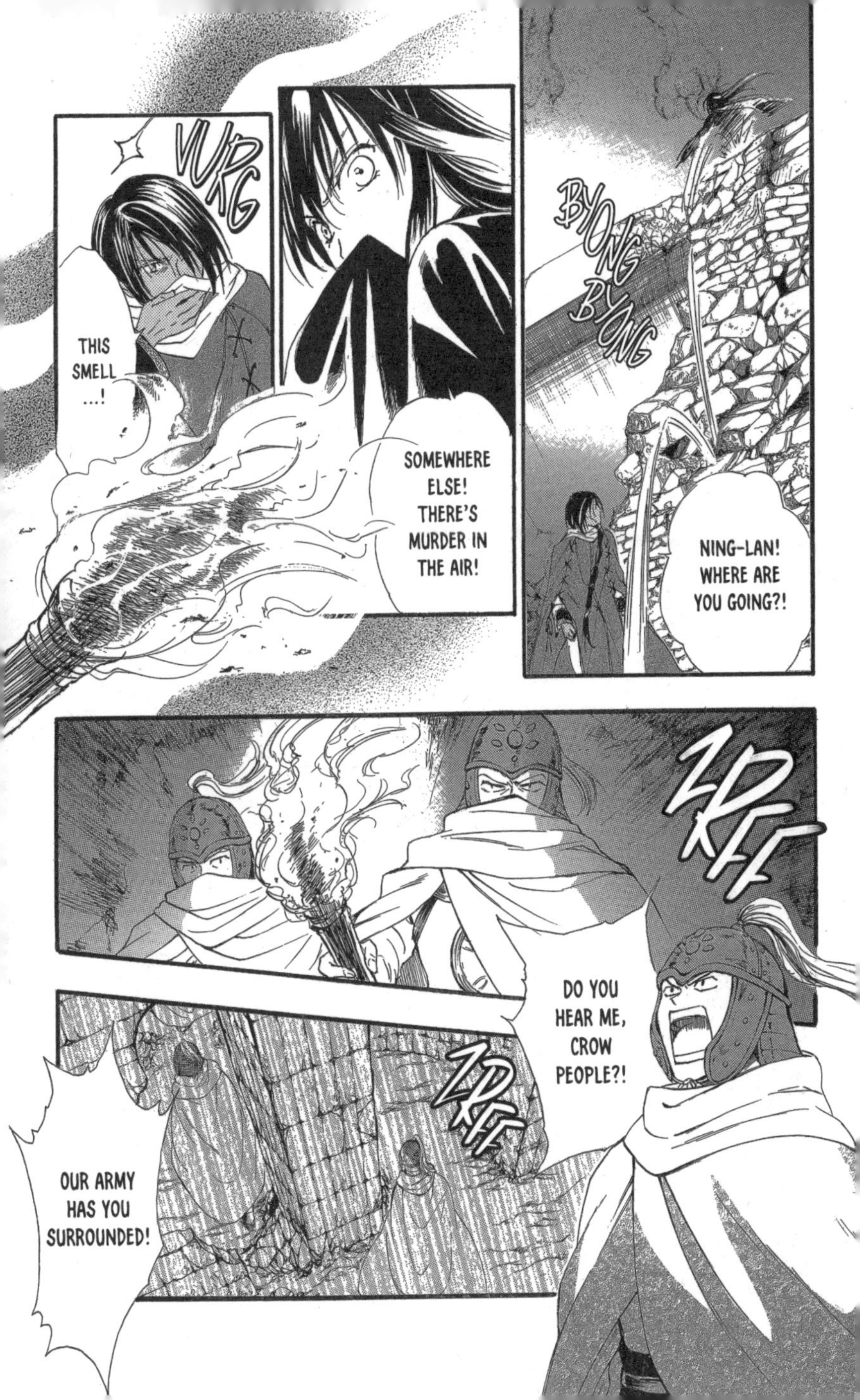
BYONG BYONG
NING-LAN! WHERE ARE YOU GOING?!
SOMEWHERE ELSE! THERE'S MURDER IN THE AIR!
VURG
THIS SMELL ...!
ZRFF
DO YOU HEAR ME, CROW PEOPLE?!
ZRFF
OUR ARMY HAS YOU SURROUNDED!

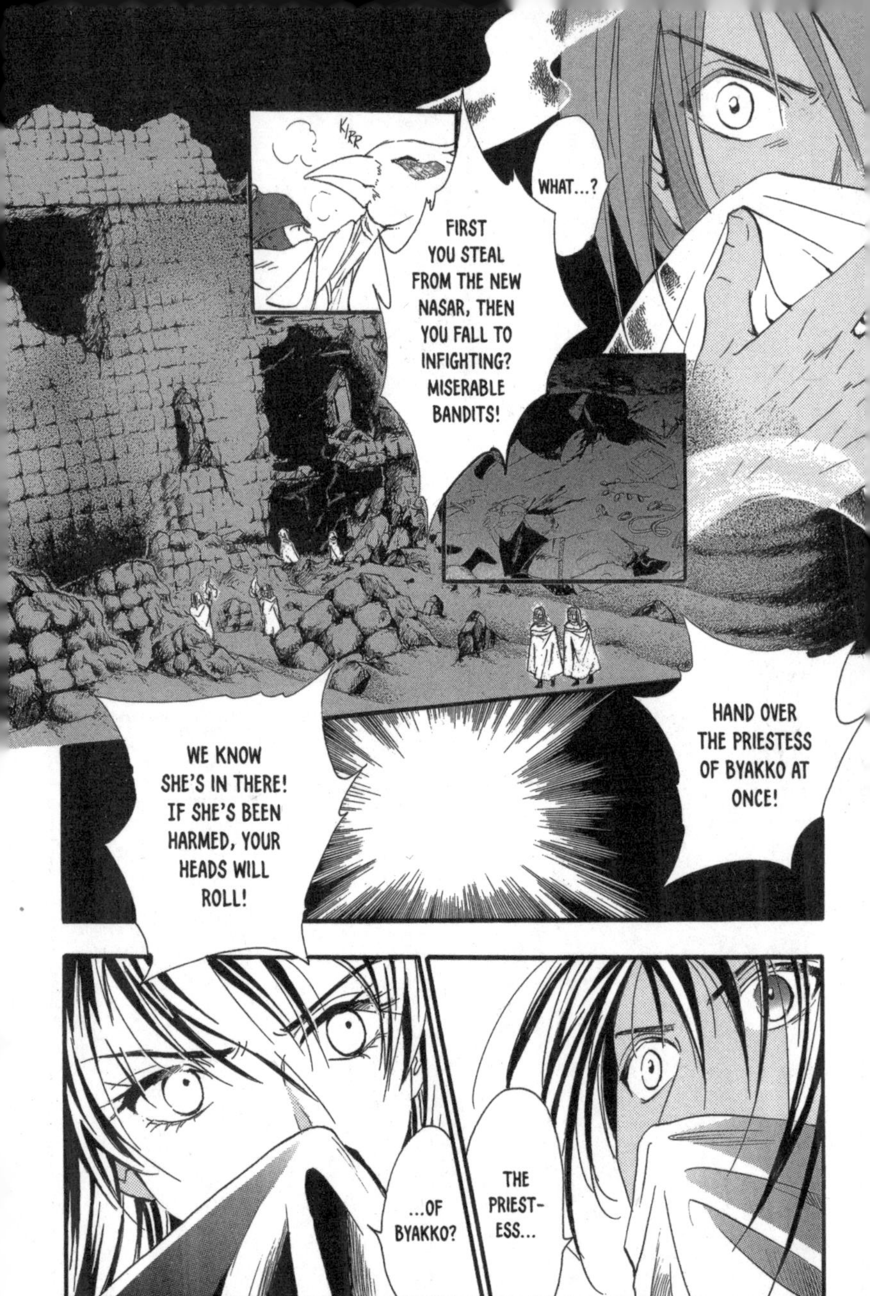
WHAT...?
KIRR
FIRST YOU STEAL FROM THE NEW NASAR, THEN YOU FALL TO INFIGHTING? MISERABLE BANDITS!
HAND OVER THE PRIESTESS OF BYAKKO AT ONCE!
WE KNOW SHE'S IN THERE! IF SHE'S BEEN HARMED, YOUR HEADS WILL ROLL!
THE PRIEST-ESS...
...OF BYAKKO?

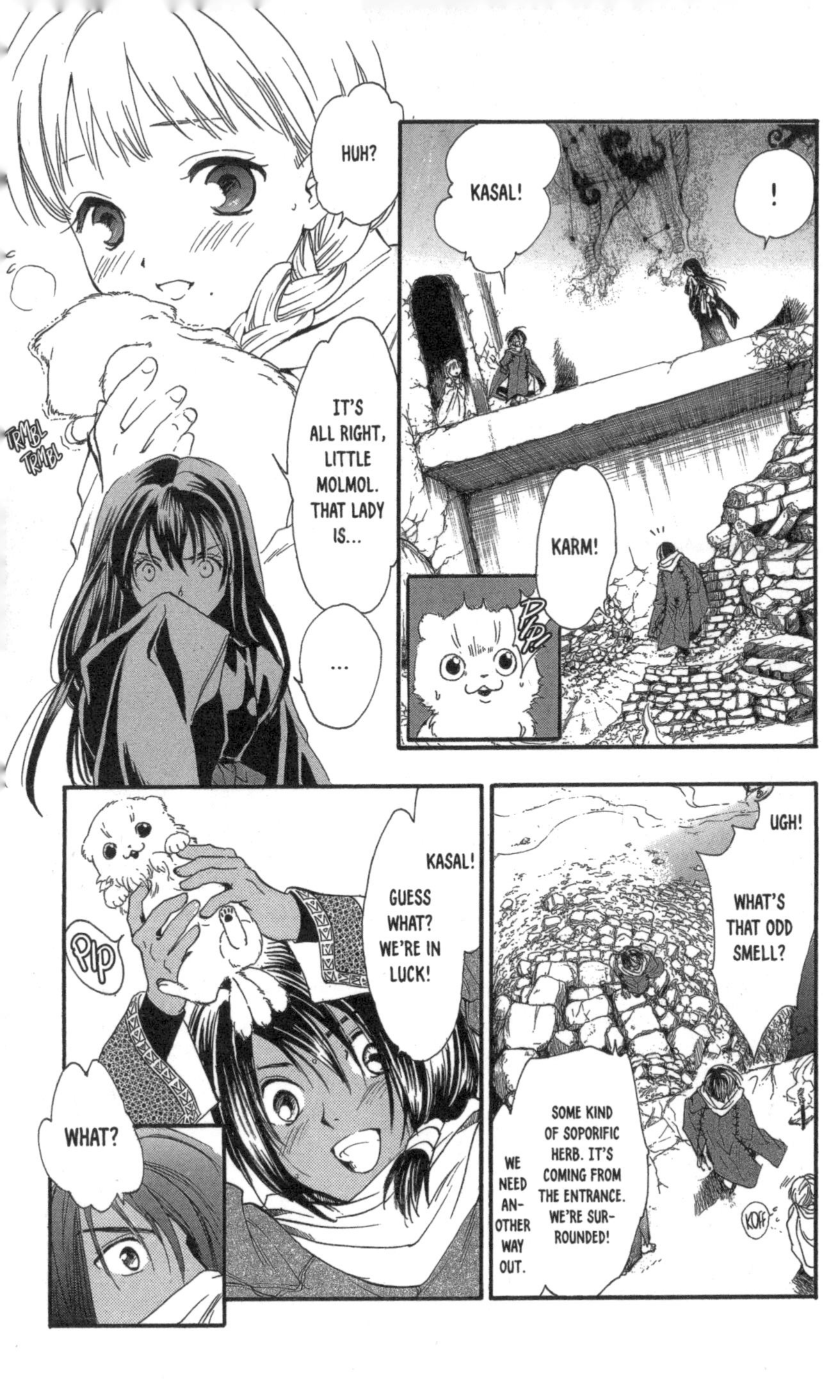
!
KASAL!
KARM!
PIP!
HUH?
TRMBL TRMBL
IT'S ALL RIGHT, LITTLE MOLMOL. THAT LADY IS...
...
UGH!
WHAT'S THAT ODD SMELL?
SOME KIND OF SOPORIFIC HERB. IT'S COMING FROM THE ENTRANCE. WE'RE SUR-ROUNDED!
WE NEED AN-OTHER WAY OUT.
KOFF
KASAL!
GUESS WHAT? WE'RE IN LUCK!
PIP
WHAT?

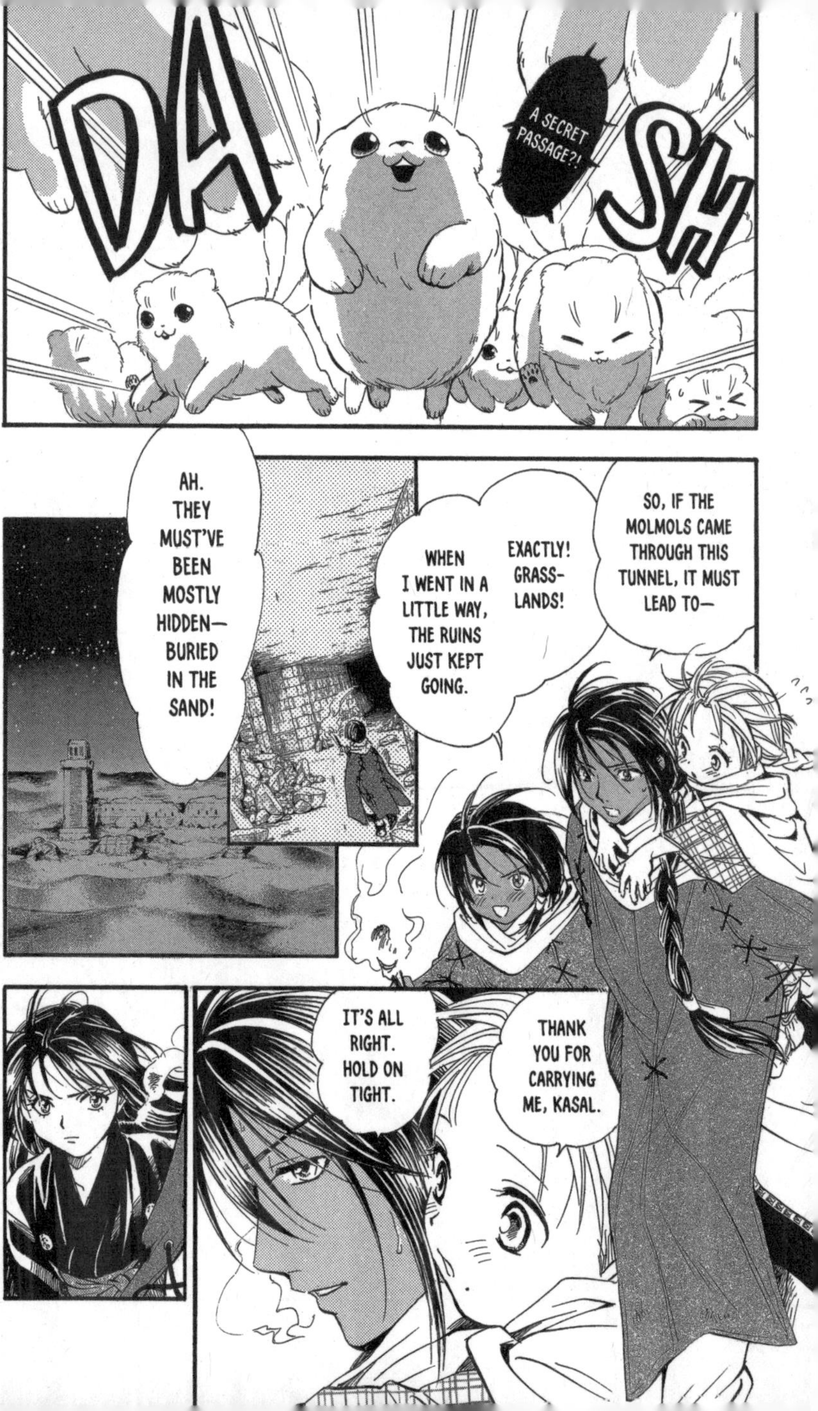
A SECRET PASSAGE?!
DASH
SO, IF THE MOLMOLS CAME THROUGH THIS TUNNEL, IT MUST LEAD TO—
EXACTLY! GRASS-LANDS!
WHEN I WENT IN A LITTLE WAY, THE RUINS JUST KEPT GOING.
AH. THEY MUST'VE BEEN MOSTLY HIDDEN—BURIED IN THE SAND!
THANK YOU FOR CARRYING ME, KASAL.
IT'S ALL RIGHT. HOLD ON TIGHT.

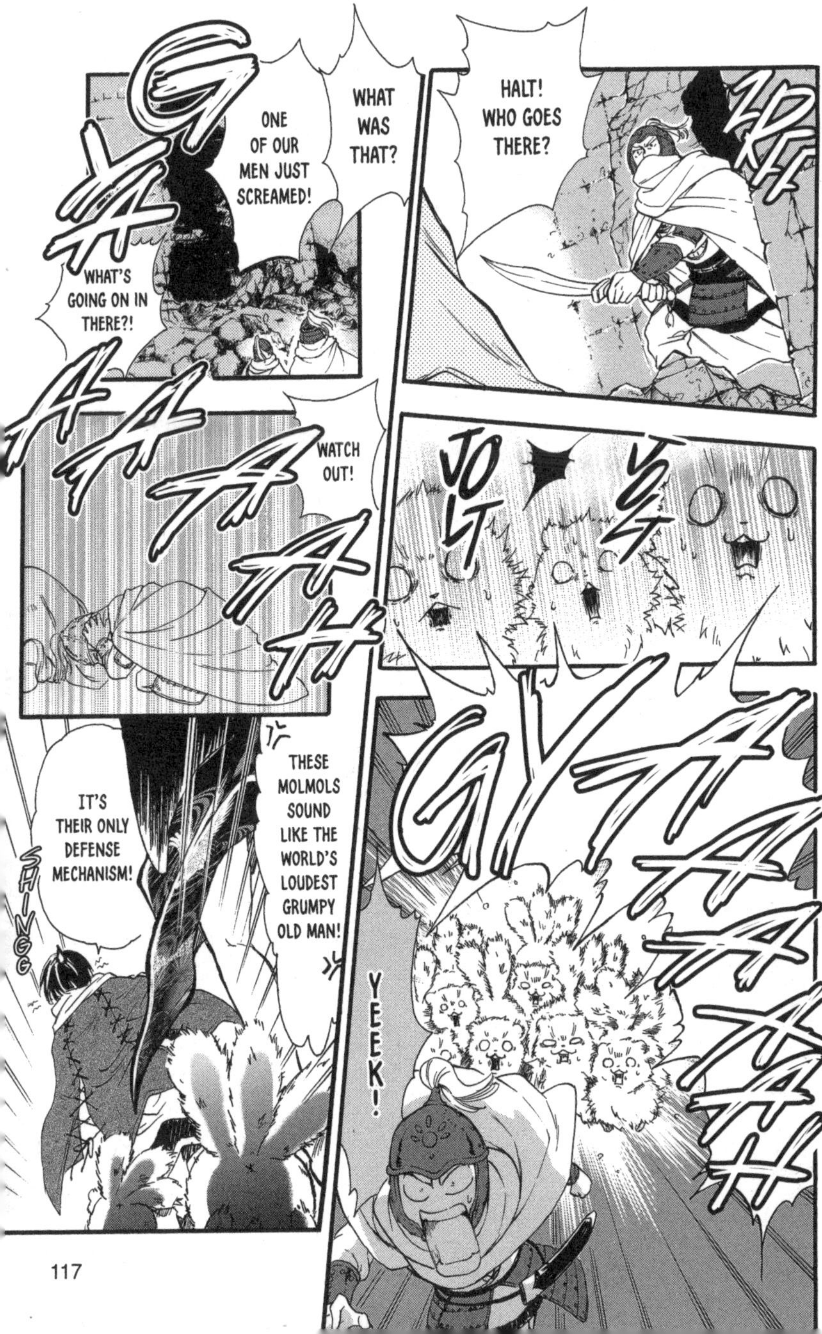
HALT! WHO GOES THERE?
ZRII
WHAT WAS THAT?
ONE OF OUR MEN JUST SCREAMED!
WHAT'S GOING ON IN THERE?!
GYAAAAAH
JOLT
WATCH OUT!
GYAAAAAAAH
YEEEK!
THESE MOLMOLS SOUND LIKE THE WORLD'S LOUDEST GRUMPY OLD MAN!
IT'S THEIR ONLY DEFENSE MECHANISM!
SHINGG

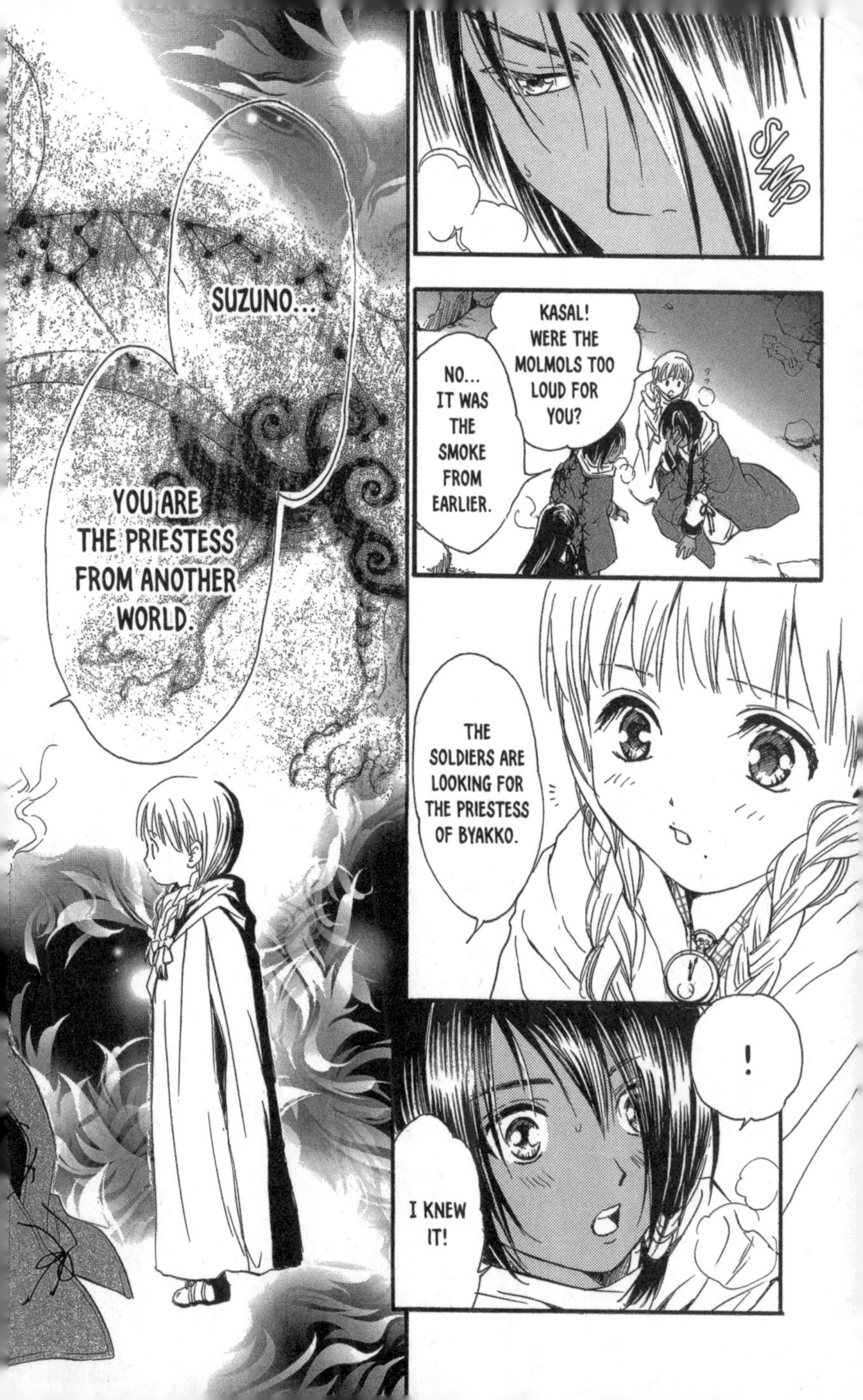
SLMP
KASAL! WERE THE MOLMOLS TOO LOUD FOR YOU?
NO... IT WAS THE SMOKE FROM EARLIER.
THE SOLDIERS ARE LOOKING FOR THE PRIESTESS OF BYAKKO.
!
I KNEW IT!
SUZUNO...
YOU ARE THE PRIESTESS FROM ANOTHER WORLD.

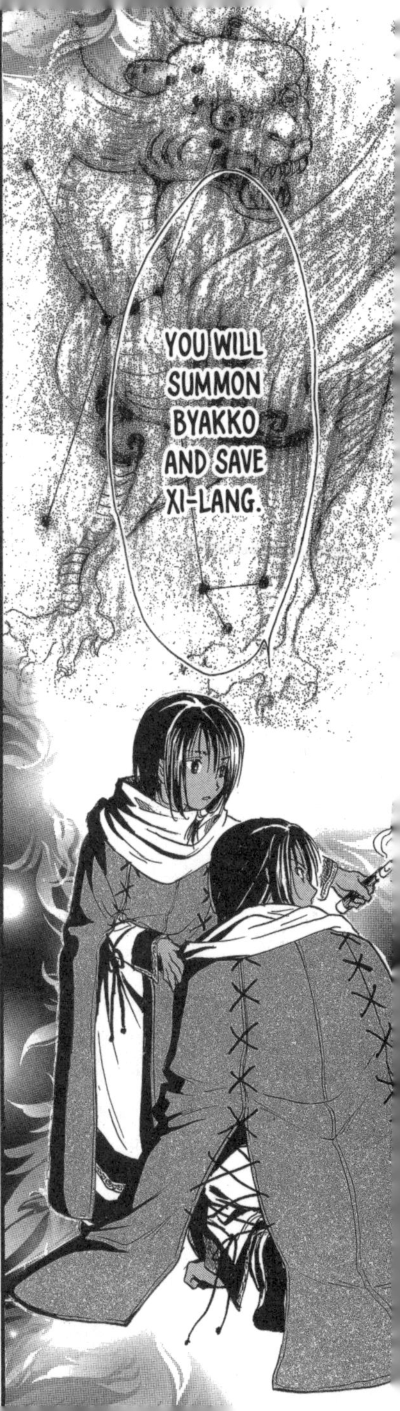
YOU WILL SUMMON BYAKKO AND SAVE XI-LANG.
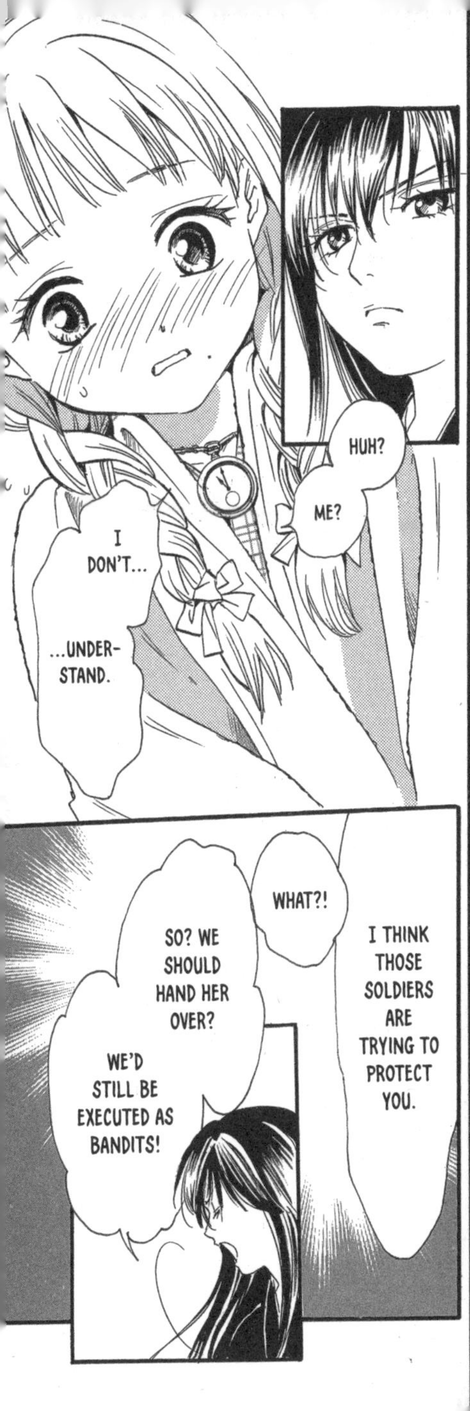
HUH?
ME?
I DON'T...
...UNDER-STAND.
I THINK THOSE SOLDIERS ARE TRYING TO PROTECT YOU.
WHAT?!
SO? WE SHOULD HAND HER OVER?
WE'D STILL BE EXECUTED AS BANDITS!

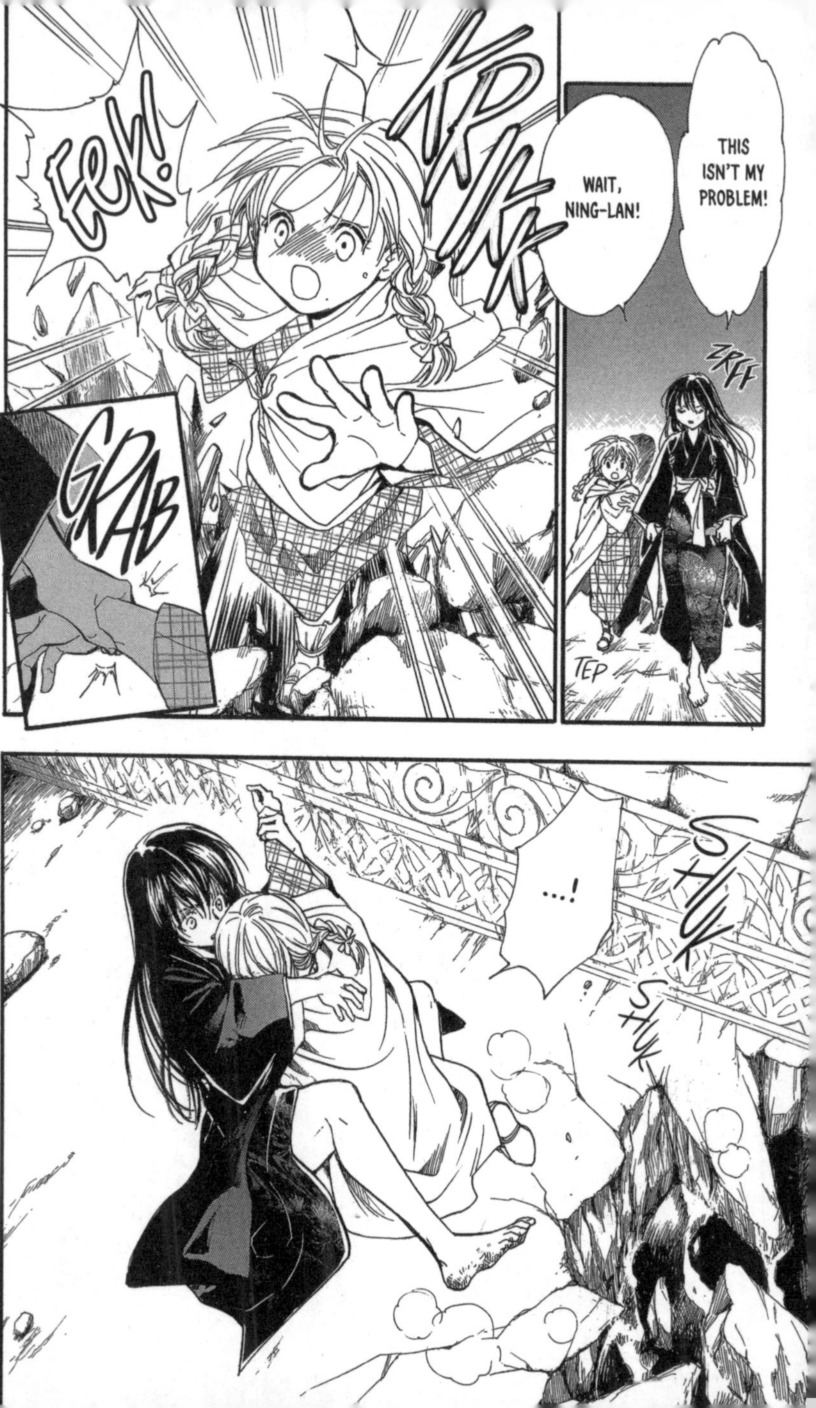
THIS ISN'T MY PROBLEM!
WAIT, NING-LAN!
ZRFF
TEP
KRKKK
EEK!
GRAB
SHUK
SHUK
...!

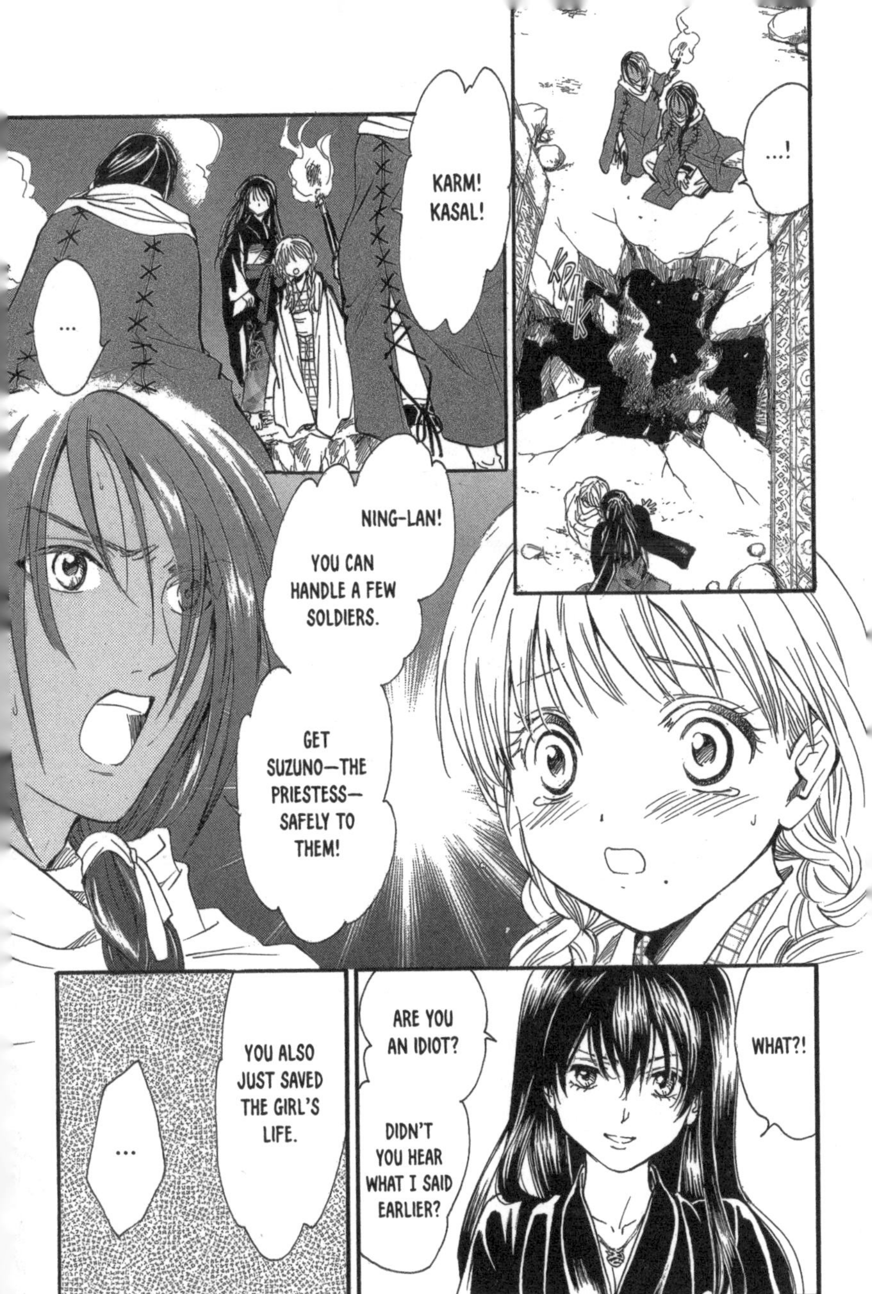
...!
KRAK
KARM! KASAL!
...
NING-LAN!
YOU CAN HANDLE A FEW SOLDIERS.
GET SUZUNO—THE PRIESTESS—SAFELY TO THEM!
WHAT?!
ARE YOU AN IDIOT?
DIDN'T YOU HEAR WHAT I SAID EARLIER?
YOU ALSO JUST SAVED THE GIRL'S LIFE.
...

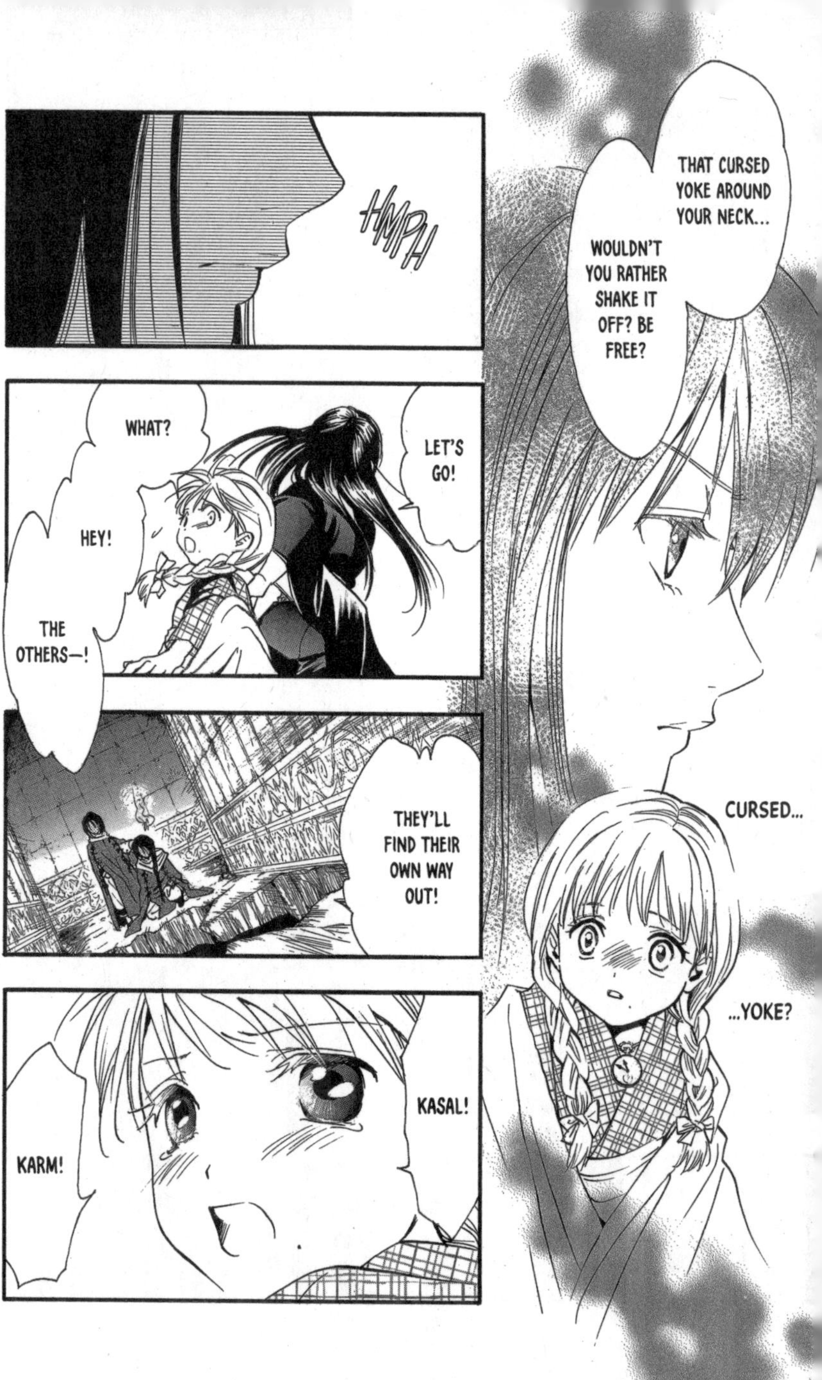
THAT CURSED YOKE AROUND YOUR NECK...
WOULDN'T YOU RATHER SHAKE IT OFF? BE FREE?
CURSED...
...YOKE?
HMPH
LET'S GO!
WHAT?
HEY!
THE OTHERS—!
THEY'LL FIND THEIR OWN WAY OUT!
KASAL!
KARM!

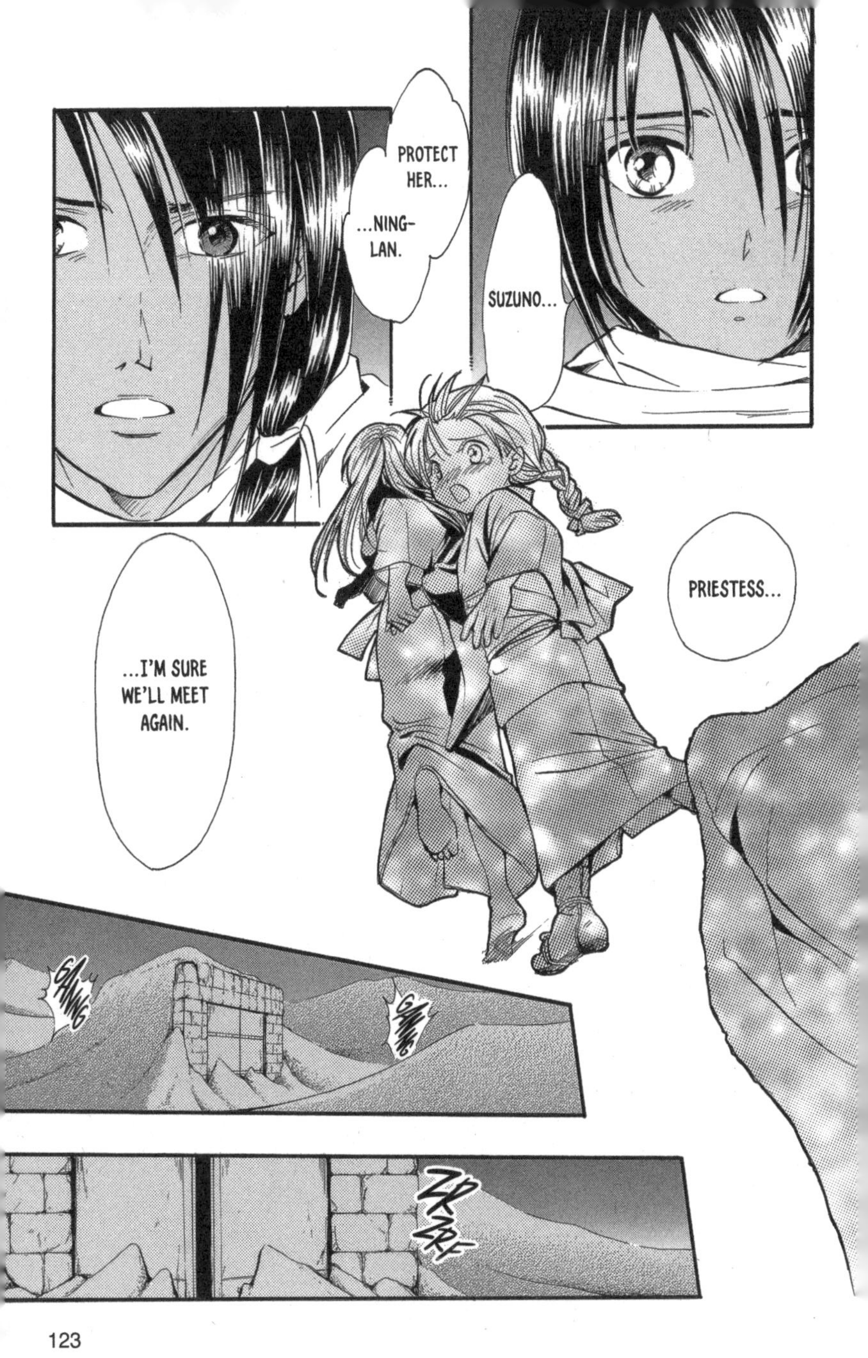
SUZUNO...
PROTECT HER...
...NING-LAN.
PRIESTESS...
...I'M SURE WE'LL MEET AGAIN.
GAANNG
GAANNG
ZR ZRF

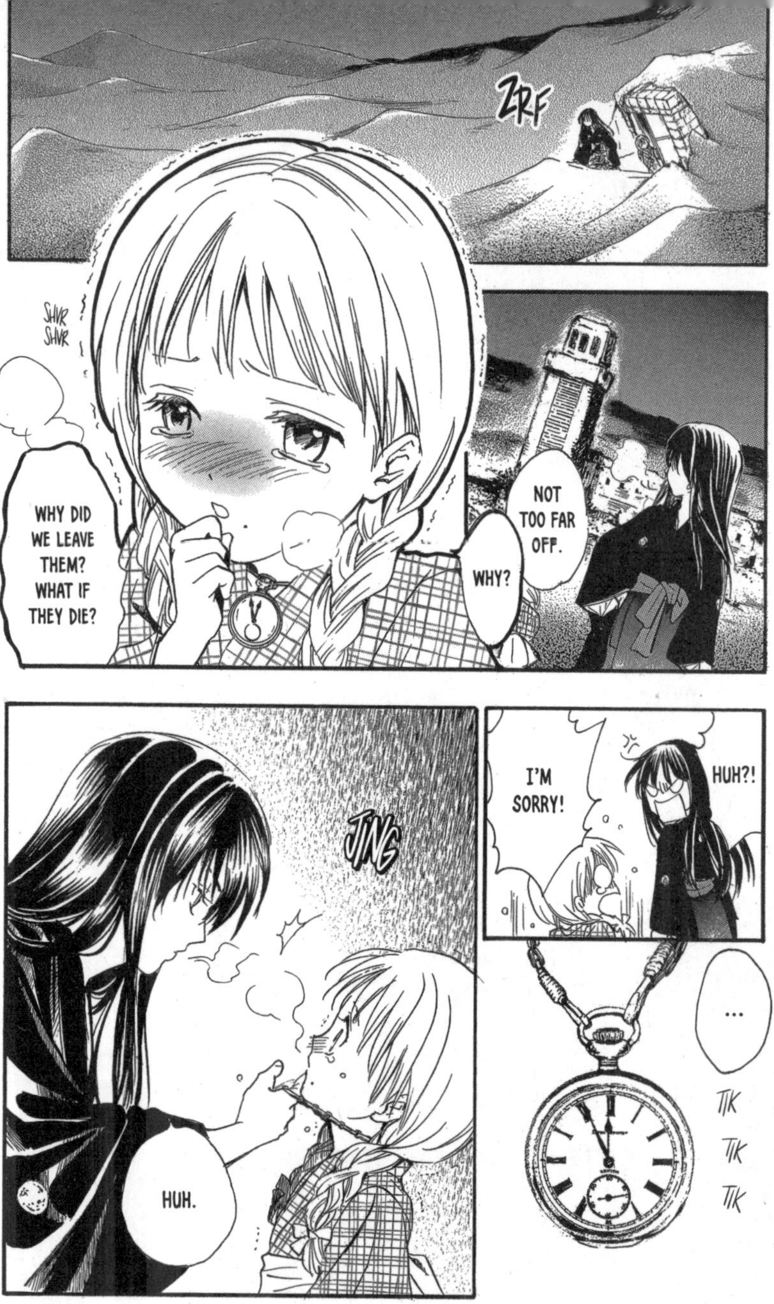
ZRF
NOT TOO FAR OFF.
WHY?
SHVR SHVR
WHY DID WE LEAVE THEM? WHAT IF THEY DIE?
HUH?!
I'M SORRY!
...
TIK
TIK
TIK
JING
HUH.

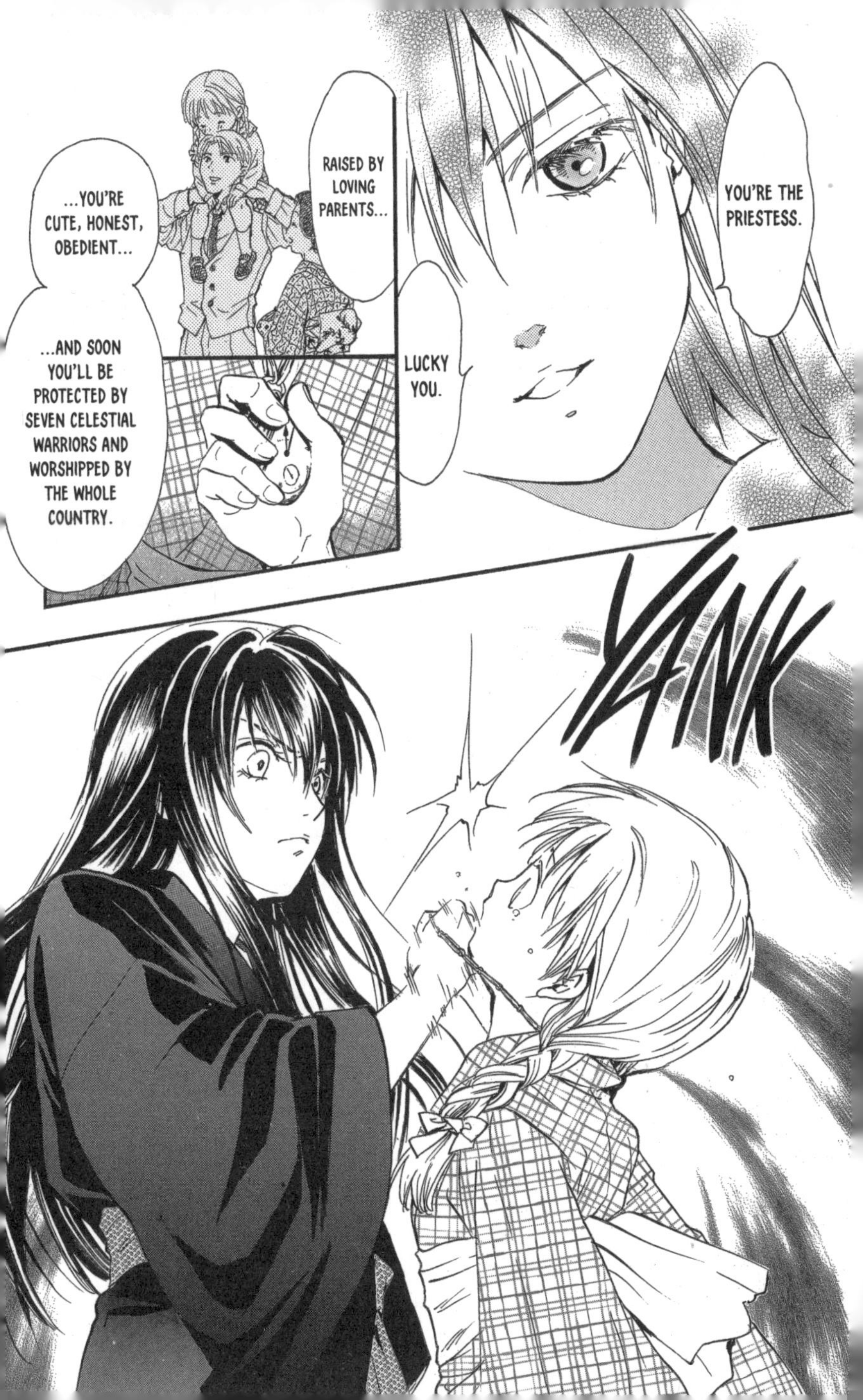
YOU'RE THE PRIESTESS.
LUCKY YOU.
RAISED BY LOVING PARENTS...
...YOU'RE CUTE, HONEST, OBEDIENT...
...AND SOON YOU'LL BE PROTECTED BY SEVEN CELESTIAL WARRIORS AND WORSHIPPED BY THE WHOLE COUNTRY.
YANK

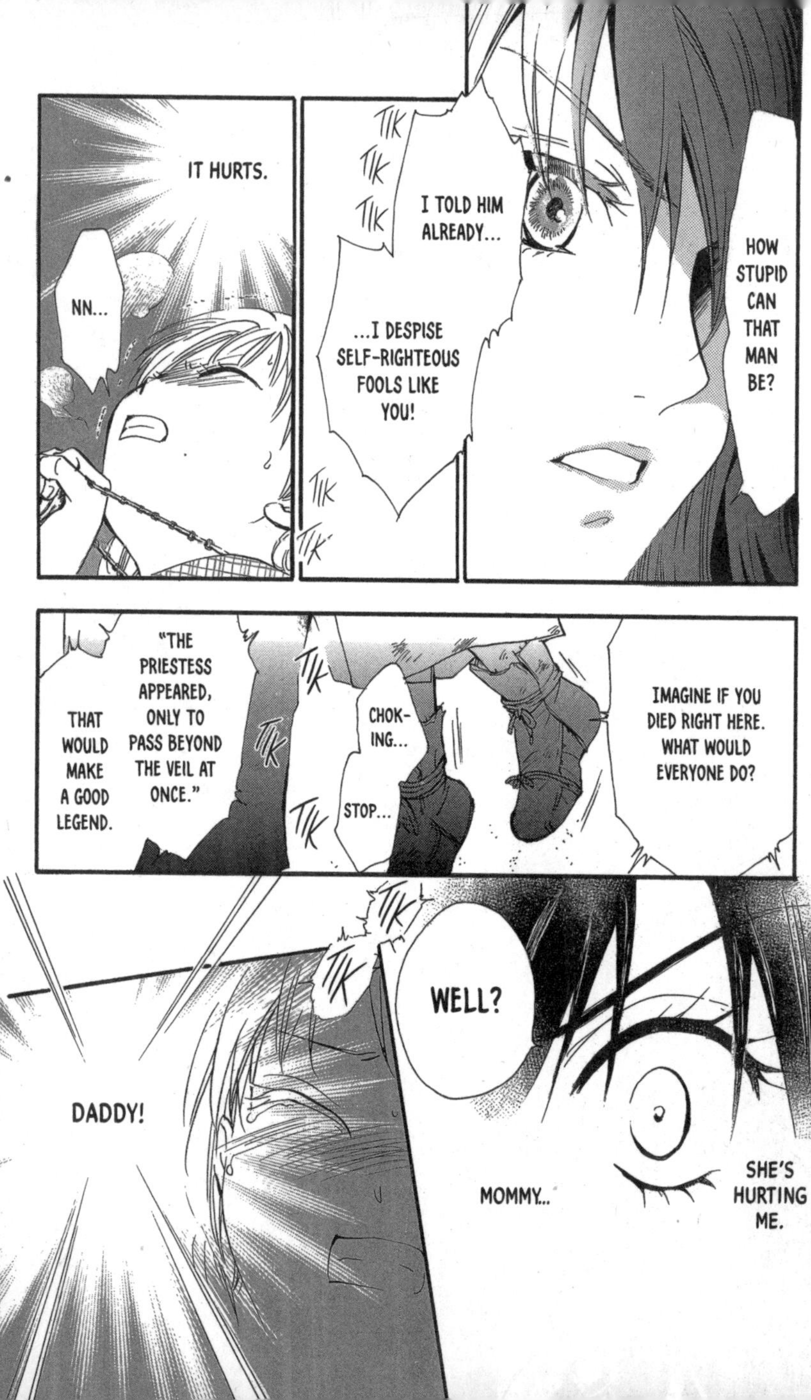
HOW STUPID CAN THAT MAN BE?
TIK
TIK
TIK
I TOLD HIM ALREADY...
...I DESPISE SELF-RIGHTEOUS FOOLS LIKE YOU!
TIK
TIK
IT HURTS.
NN...
IMAGINE IF YOU DIED RIGHT HERE. WHAT WOULD EVERYONE DO?
CHOKING...
STOP...
TIK
TIK
TIK
"THE PRIESTESS APPEARED, ONLY TO PASS BEYOND THE VEIL AT ONCE."
THAT WOULD MAKE A GOOD LEGEND.
SHE'S HURTING ME.
MOMMY...
WELL?
TIK
TIK
DADDY!

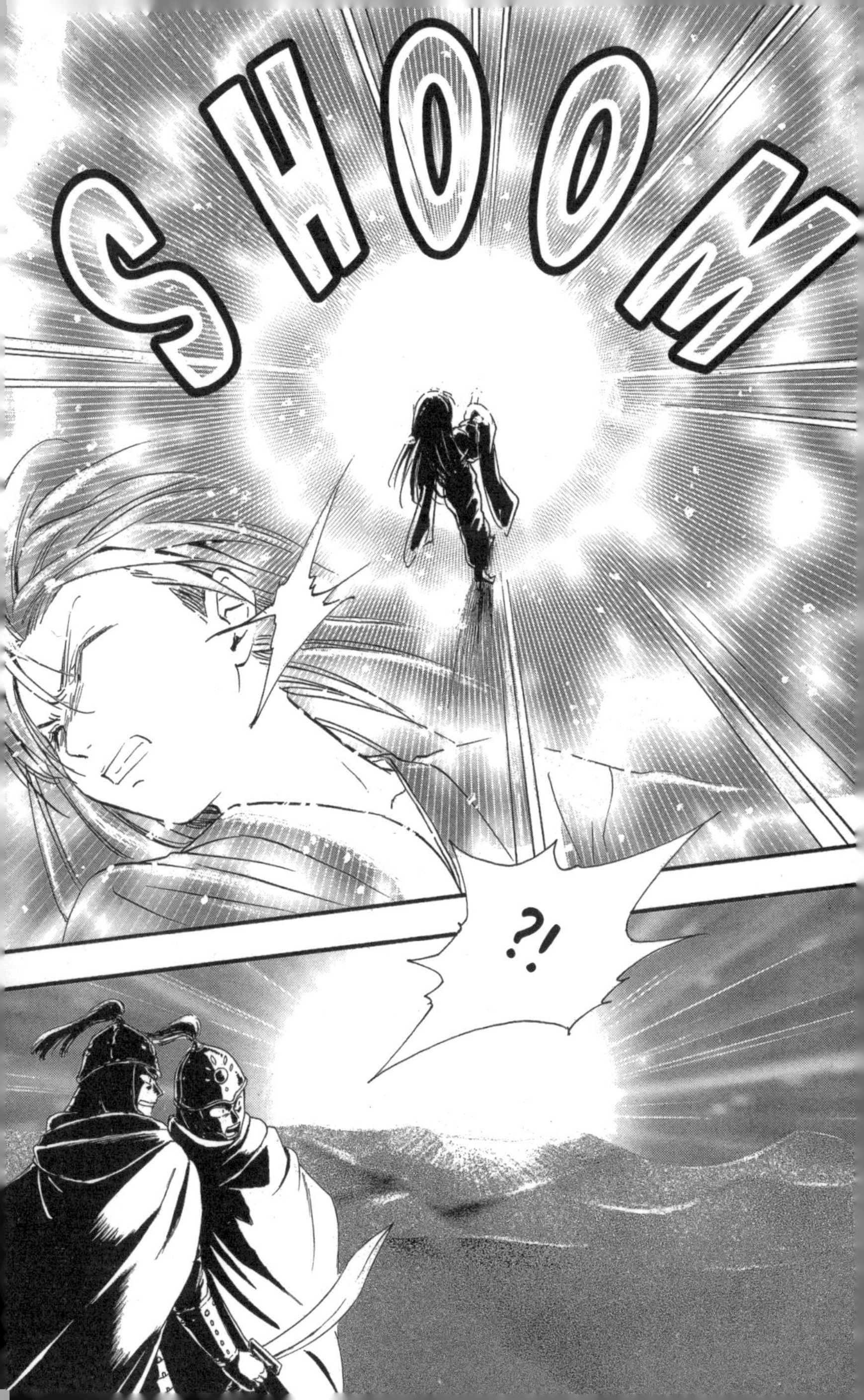
SHOOM
?!

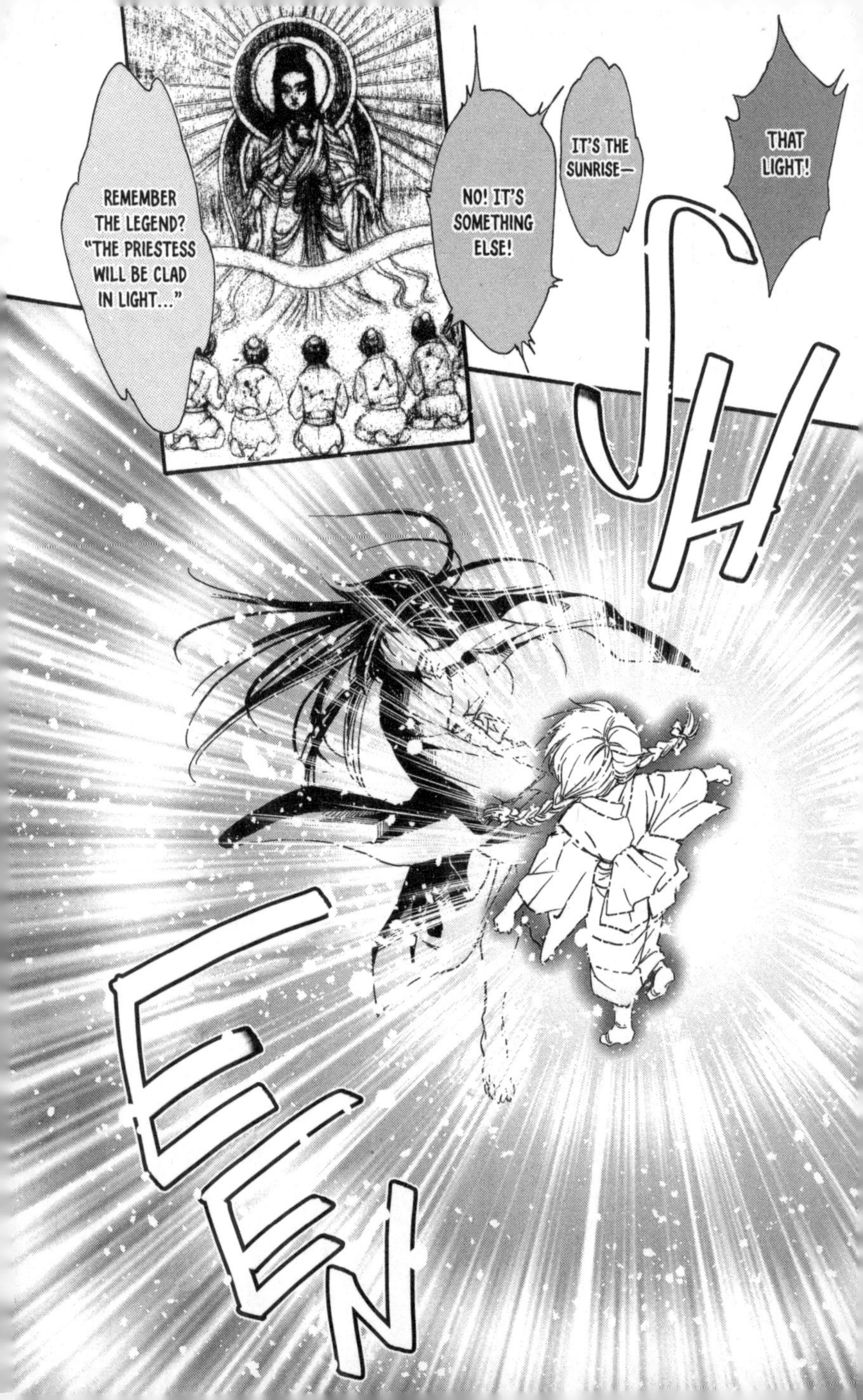
THAT LIGHT!
IT'S THE SUNRISE—
NO! IT'S SOMETHING ELSE!
REMEMBER THE LEGEND? "THE PRIESTESS WILL BE CLAD IN LIGHT..."
SH
EEEN

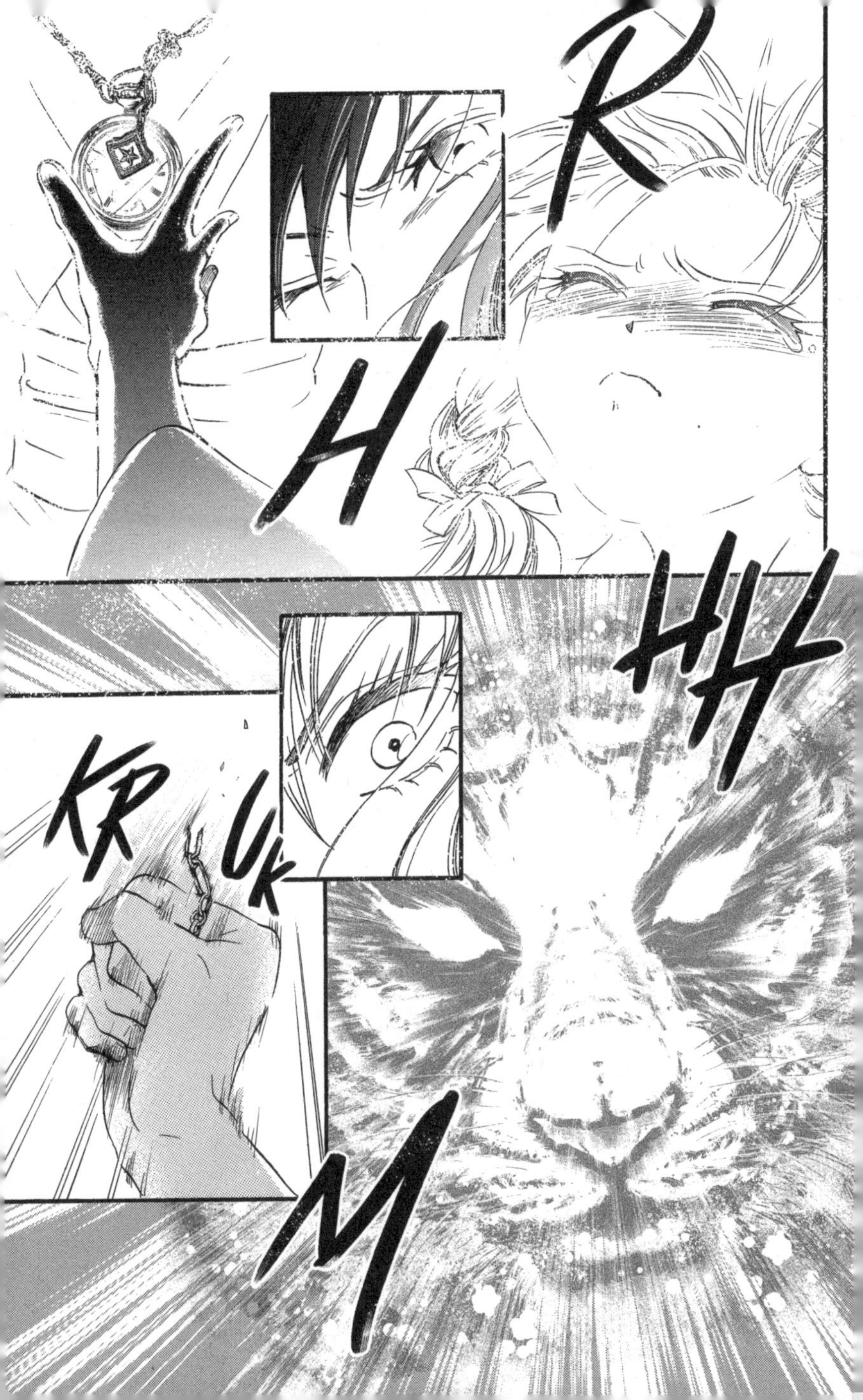
RHHHM
KRUK

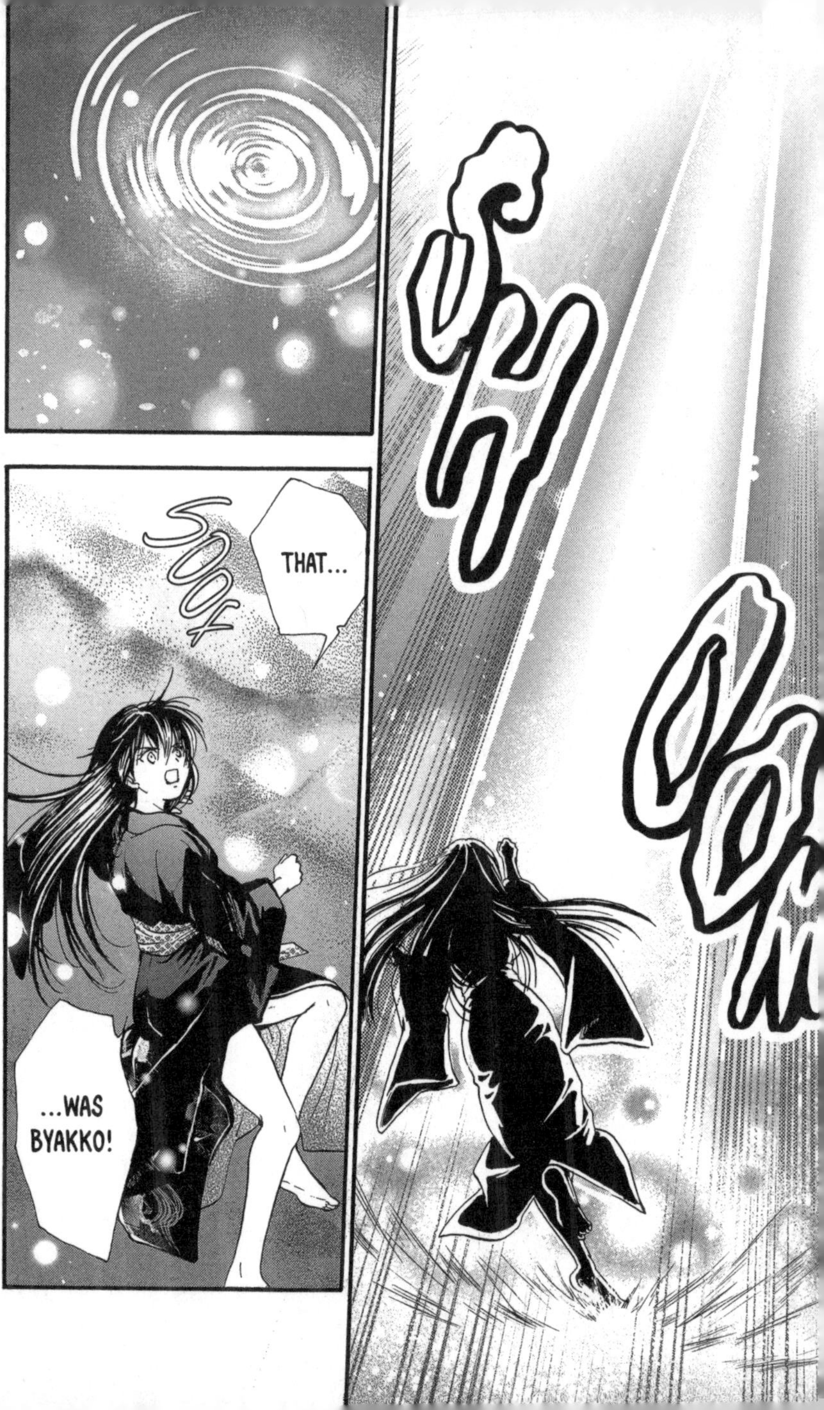
THAT...
...WAS BYAKKO!

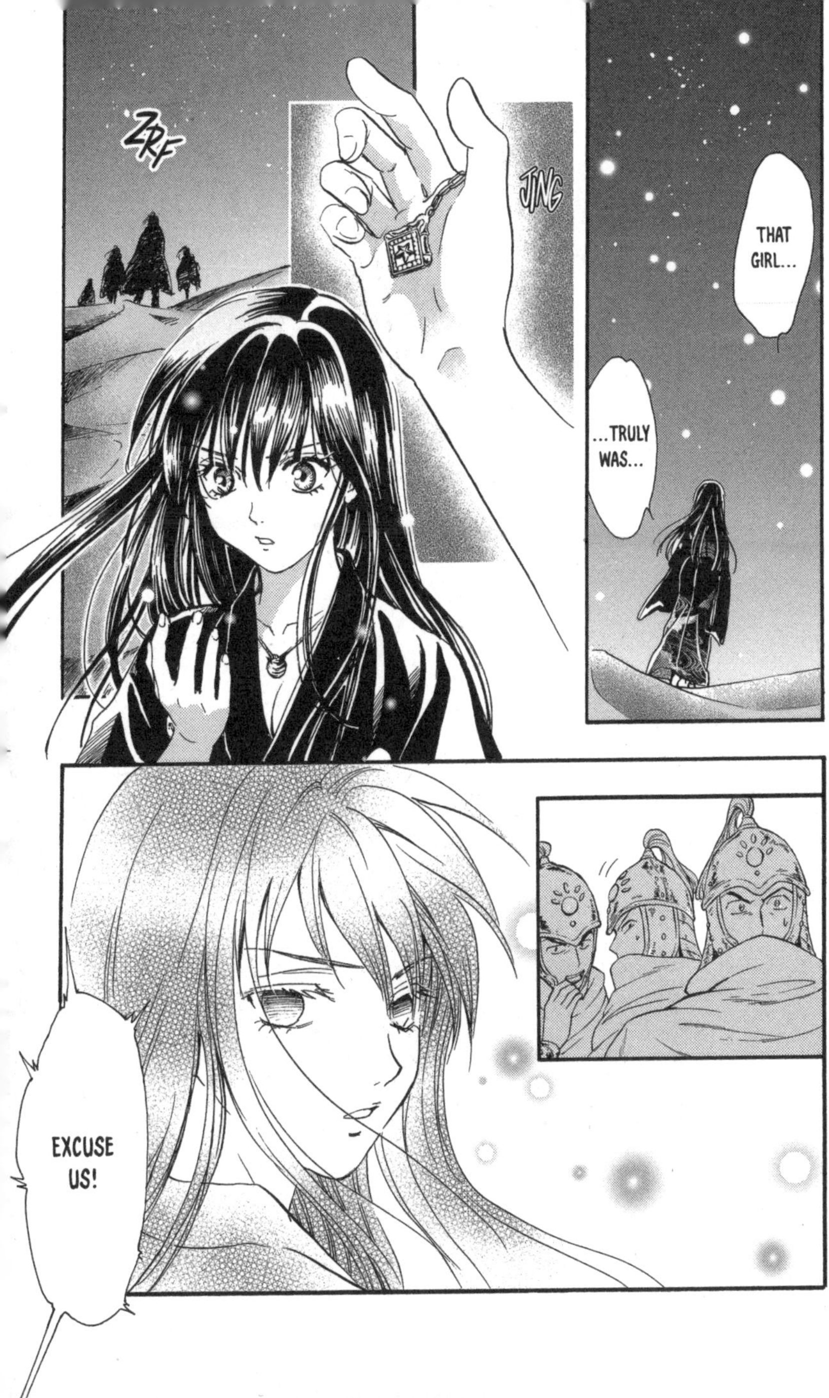
THAT GIRL...
...TRULY WAS...
JING
ZRF
EXCUSE US!

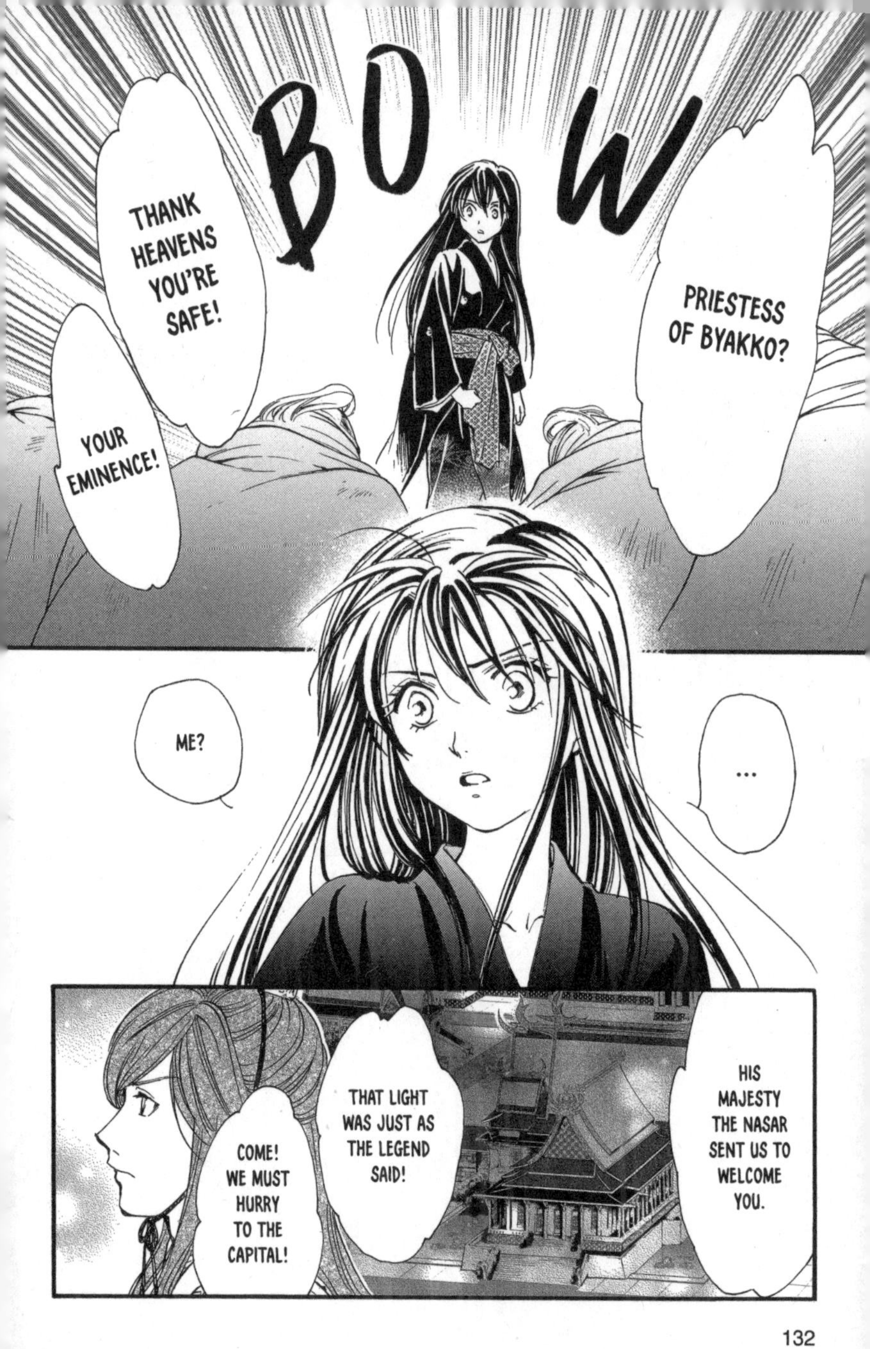
BOW
PRIESTESS OF BYAKKO?
THANK HEAVENS YOU'RE SAFE!
YOUR EMINENCE!
...
ME?
HIS MAJESTY THE NASAR SENT US TO WELCOME YOU.
THAT LIGHT WAS JUST AS THE LEGEND SAID!
COME! WE MUST HURRY TO THE CAPITAL!

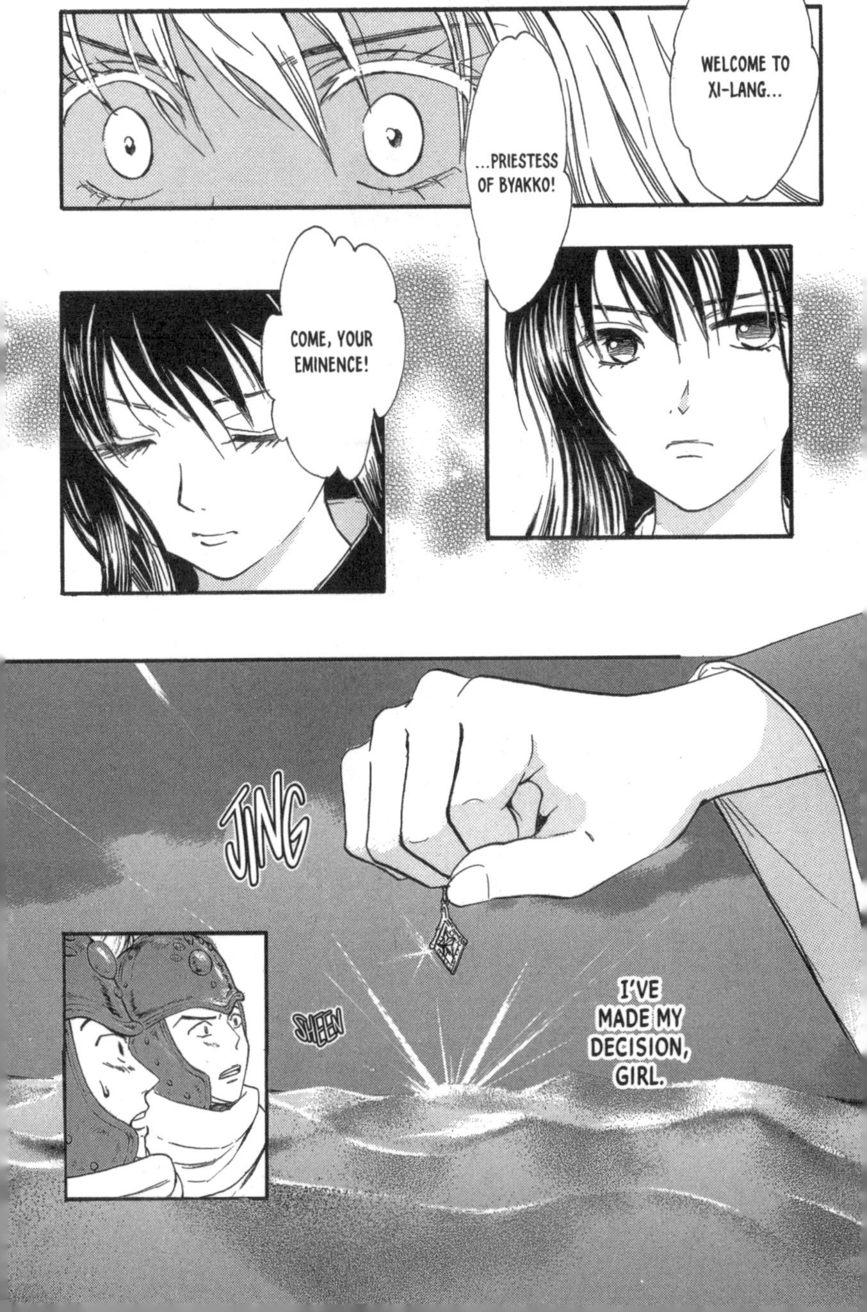
WELCOME TO XI-LANG...
...PRIESTESS OF BYAKKO!
COME, YOUR EMINENCE!
JING
I'VE MADE MY DECISION, GIRL.
SHEEN

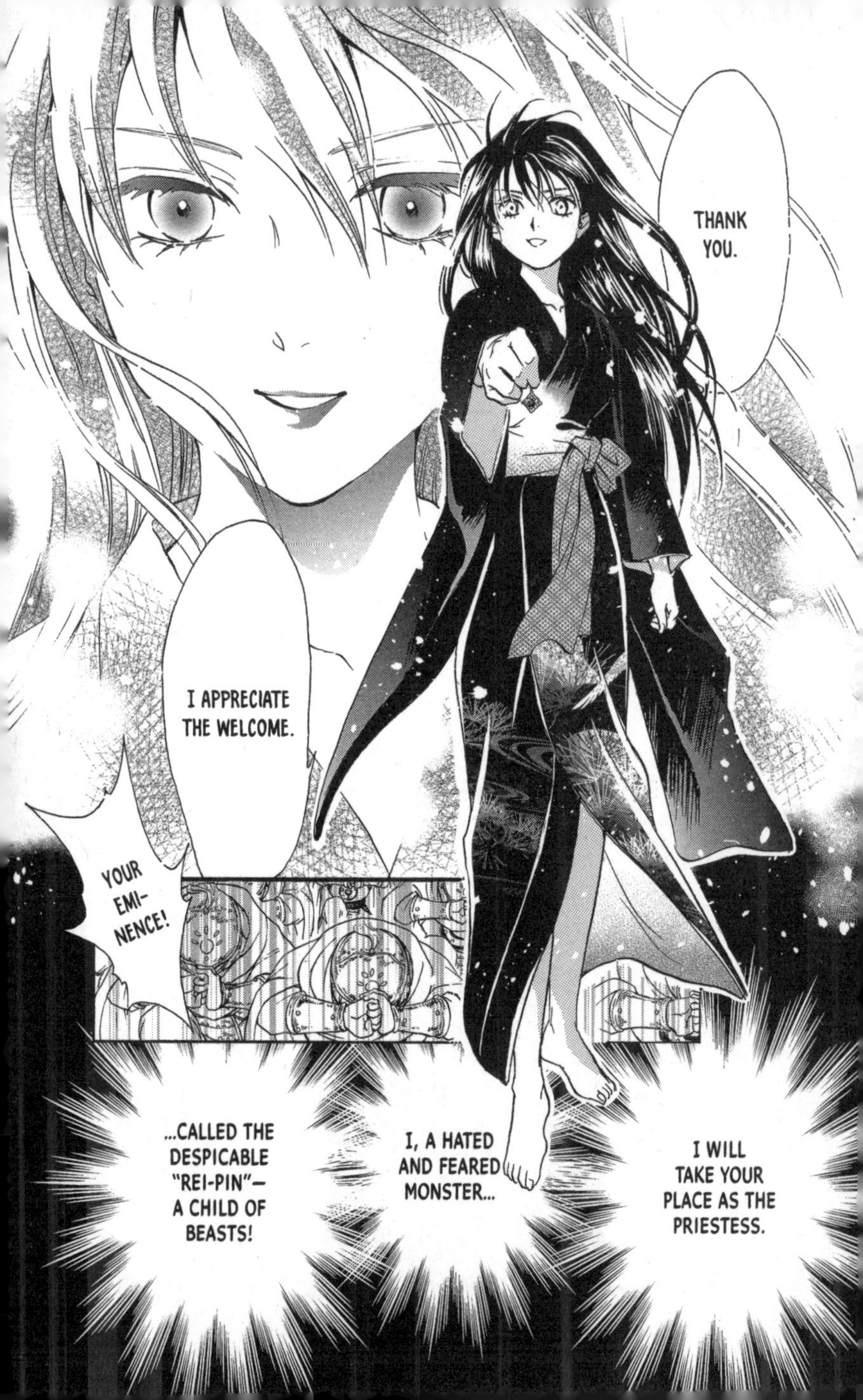
THANK YOU.
I APPRECIATE THE WELCOME.
YOUR EMI-NENCE!
I WILL TAKE YOUR PLACE AS THE PRIESTESS.
I, A HATED AND FEARED MONSTER...
...CALLED THE DESPICABLE "REI-PIN"—A CHILD OF BEASTS!

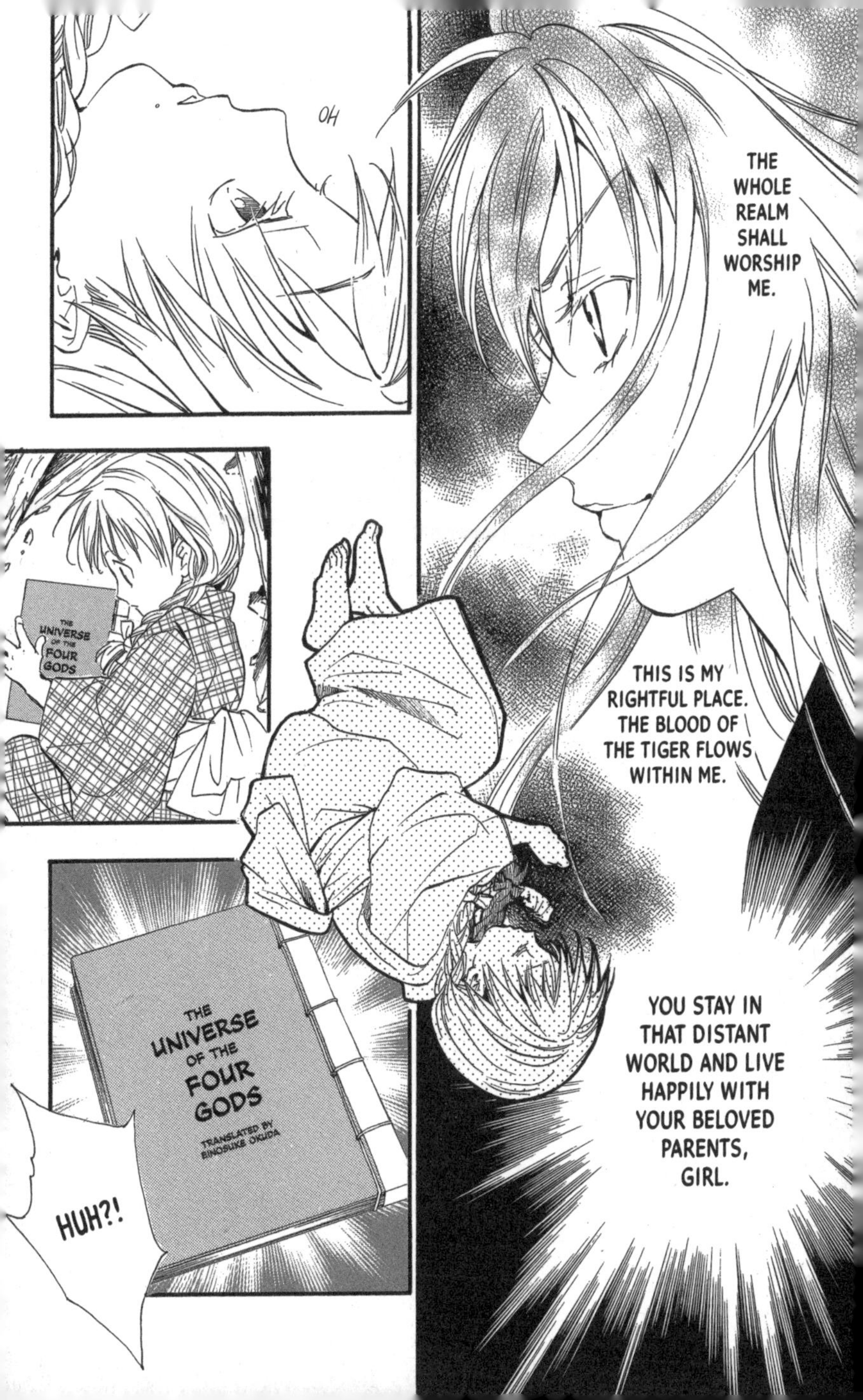
THE WHOLE REALM SHALL WORSHIP ME.
THIS IS MY RIGHTFUL PLACE. THE BLOOD OF THE TIGER FLOWS WITHIN ME.
YOU STAY IN THAT DISTANT WORLD AND LIVE HAPPILY WITH YOUR BELOVED PARENTS, GIRL.
OH
THE UNIVERSE OF THE FOUR GODS
THE UNIVERSE OF THE FOUR GODS
TRANSLATED BY EINOSUKE OKUDA
HUH?!

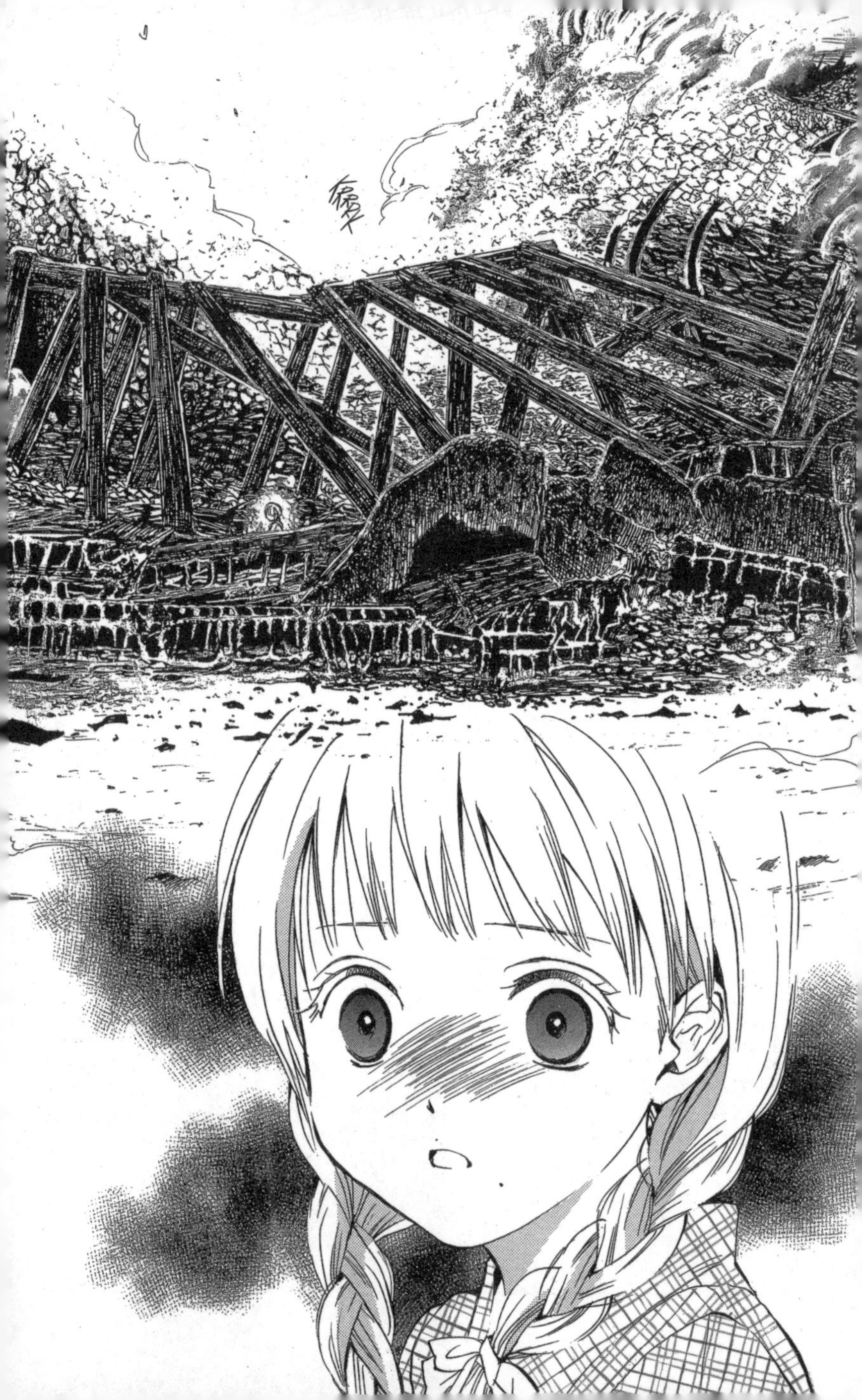

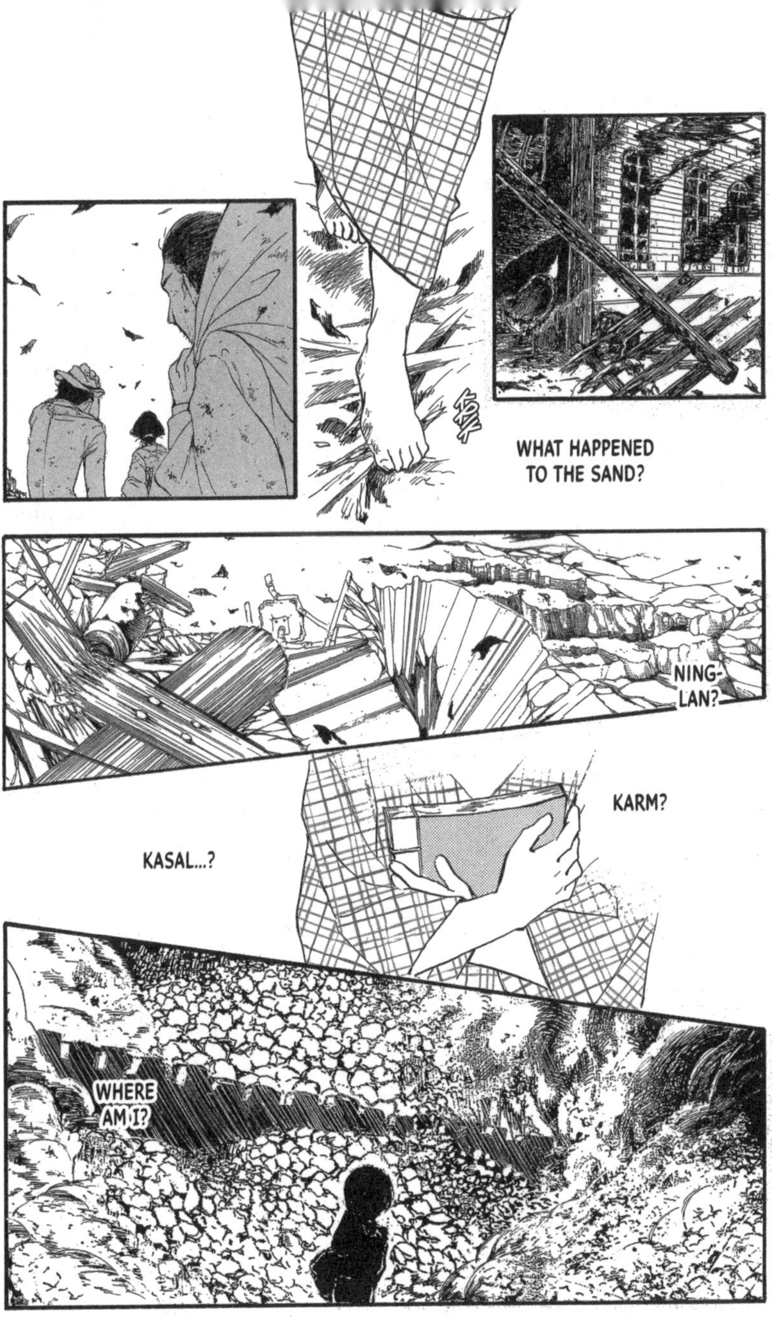
KSK
WHAT HAPPENED TO THE SAND?
NING-LAN?
KARM?
KASAL...?
WHERE AM I?

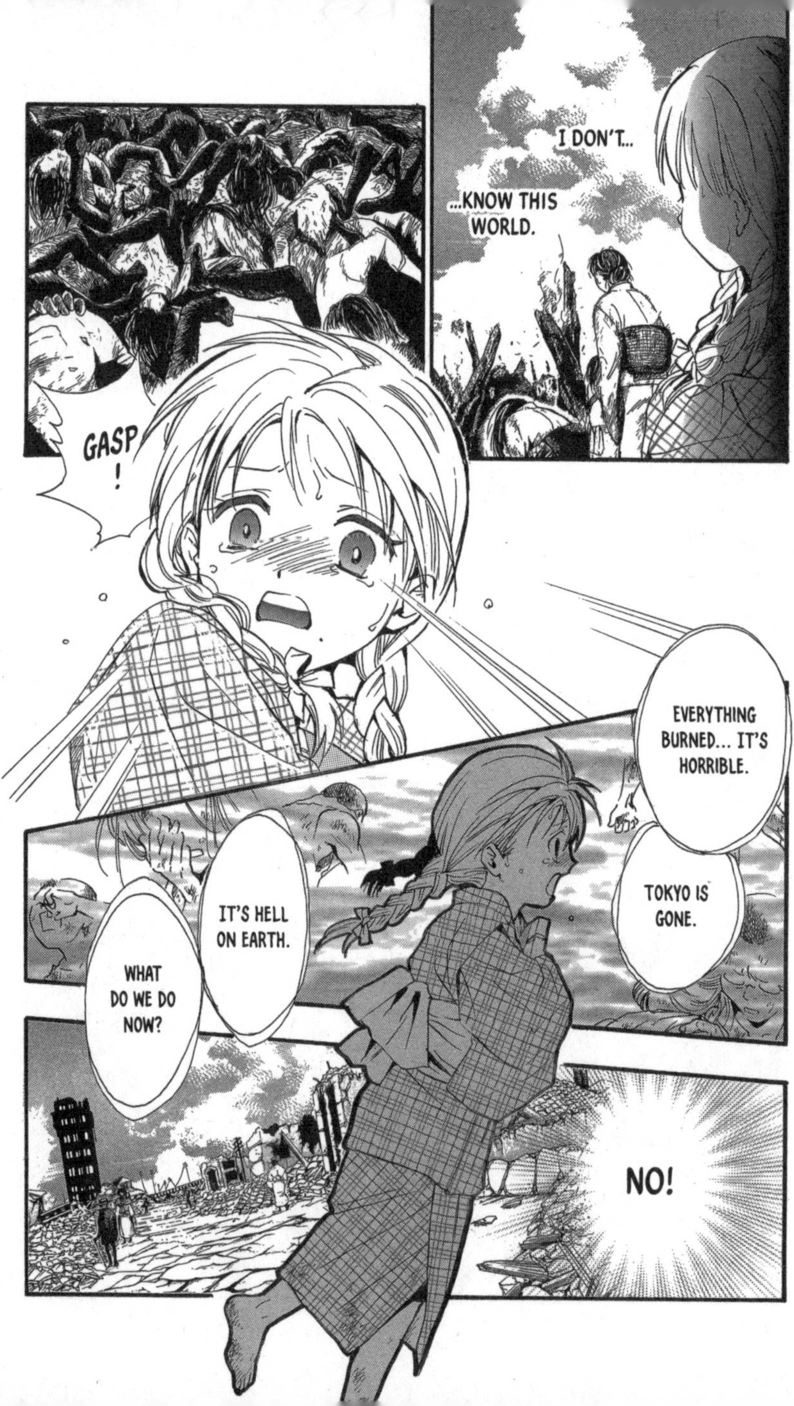
I DON'T...
...KNOW THIS WORLD.
GASP!
EVERYTHING BURNED... IT'S HORRIBLE.
TOKYO IS GONE.
IT'S HELL ON EARTH.
WHAT DO WE DO NOW?
NO!

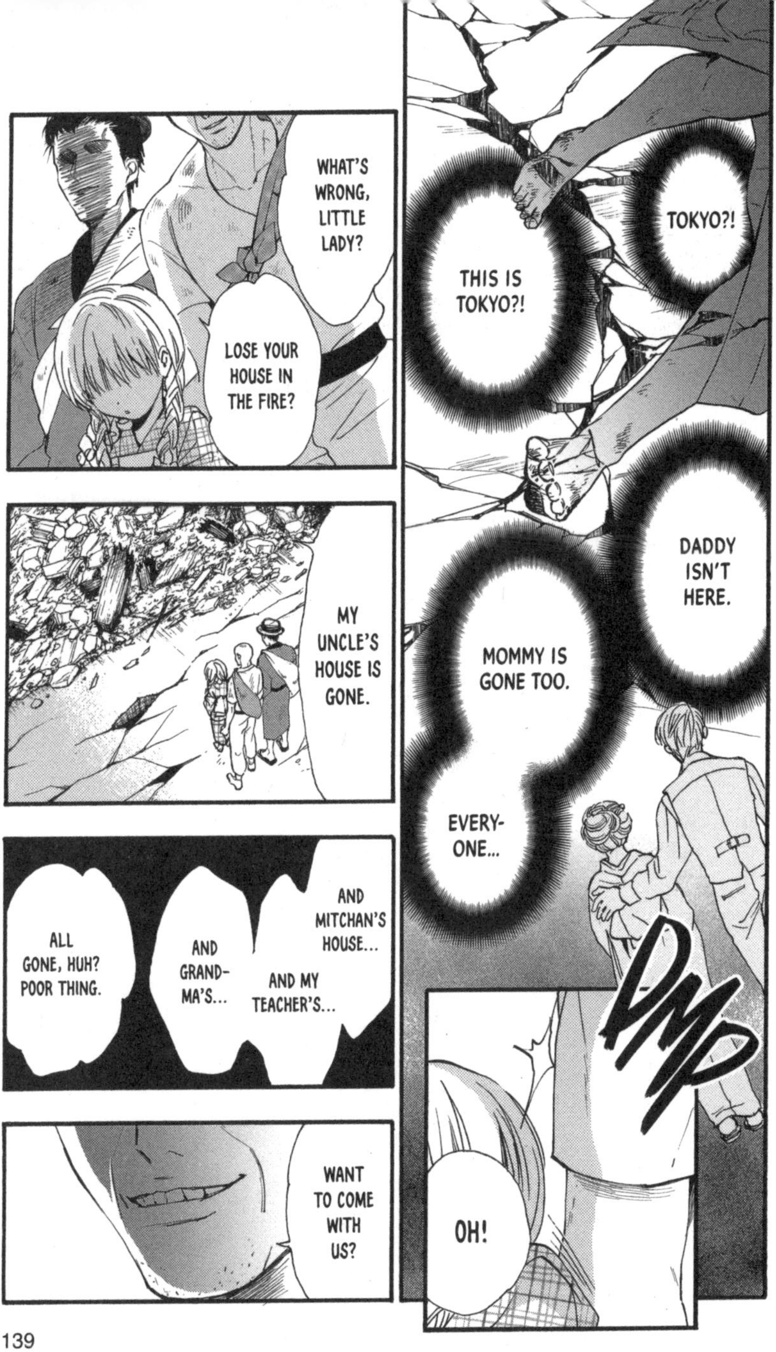
TOKYO?!
THIS IS TOKYO?!
DADDY ISN'T HERE.
MOMMY IS GONE TOO.
EVERY-ONE...
DMP
OH!
WHAT'S WRONG, LITTLE LADY?
LOSE YOUR HOUSE IN THE FIRE?
MY UNCLE'S HOUSE IS GONE.
AND MITCHAN'S HOUSE...
AND MY TEACHER'S...
AND GRAND-MA'S...
ALL GONE, HUH? POOR THING.
WANT TO COME WITH US?

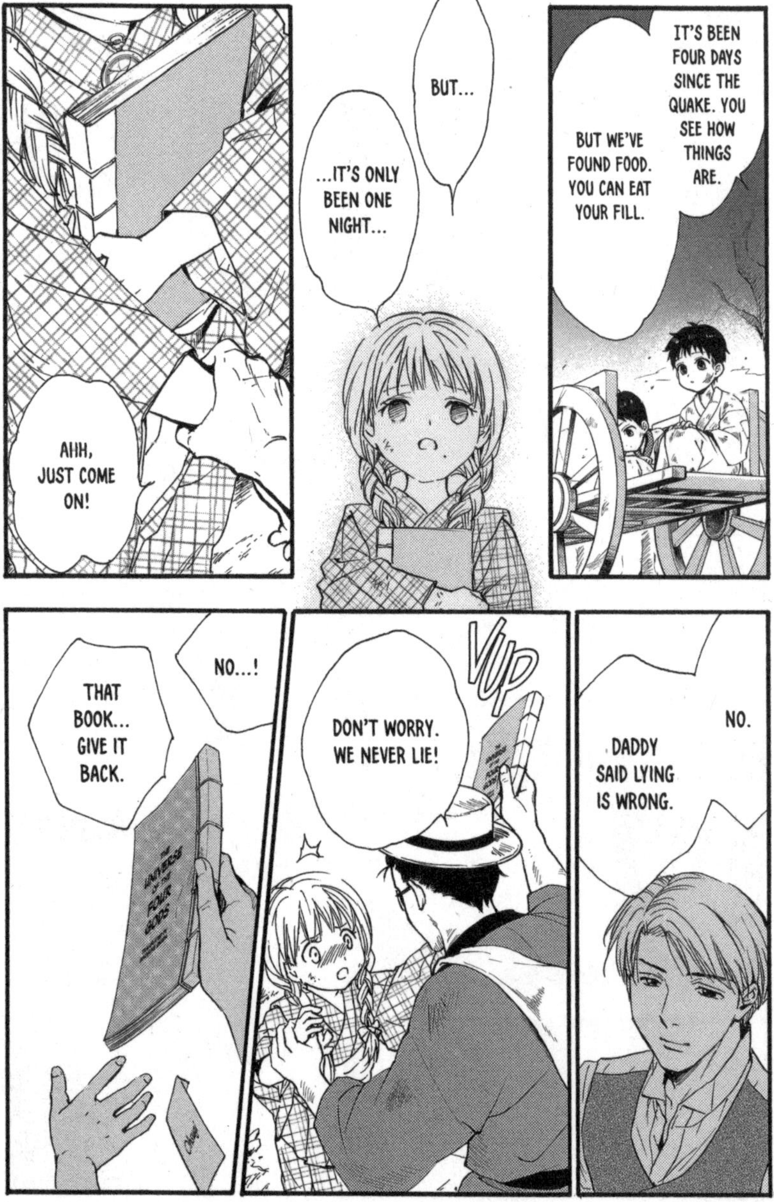
IT'S BEEN FOUR DAYS SINCE THE QUAKE. YOU SEE HOW THINGS ARE.
BUT WE'VE FOUND FOOD. YOU CAN EAT YOUR FILL.
BUT...
...IT'S ONLY BEEN ONE NIGHT...
AHH, JUST COME ON!
NO.
DADDY SAID LYING IS WRONG.
VUP
DON'T WORRY. WE NEVER LIE!
NO...!
THAT BOOK... GIVE IT BACK.
THE UNIVERSE OF THE FOUR GODS

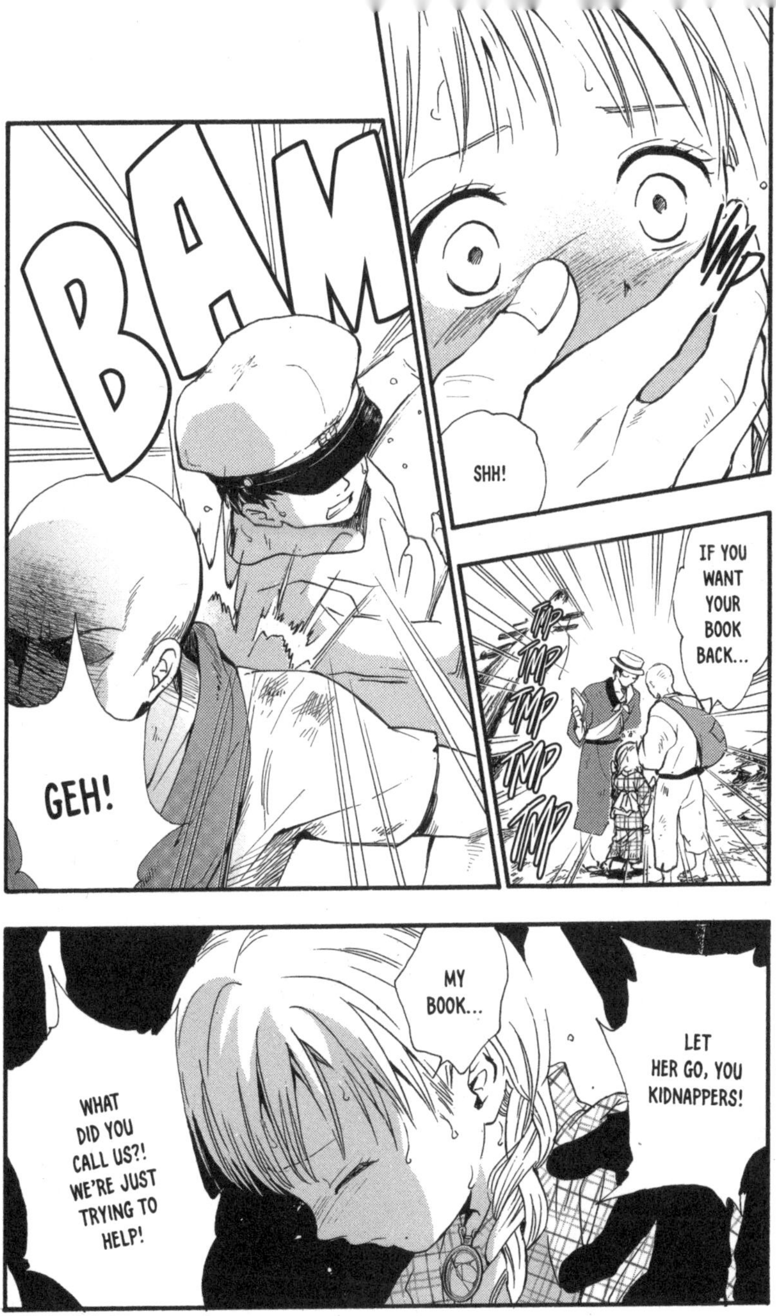
SHH!
IF YOU WANT YOUR BOOK BACK...
TMP TMP TMP TMP
BAM
GEH!
MY BOOK...
LET HER GO, YOU KIDNAPPERS!
WHAT DID YOU CALL US?! WE'RE JUST TRYING TO HELP!

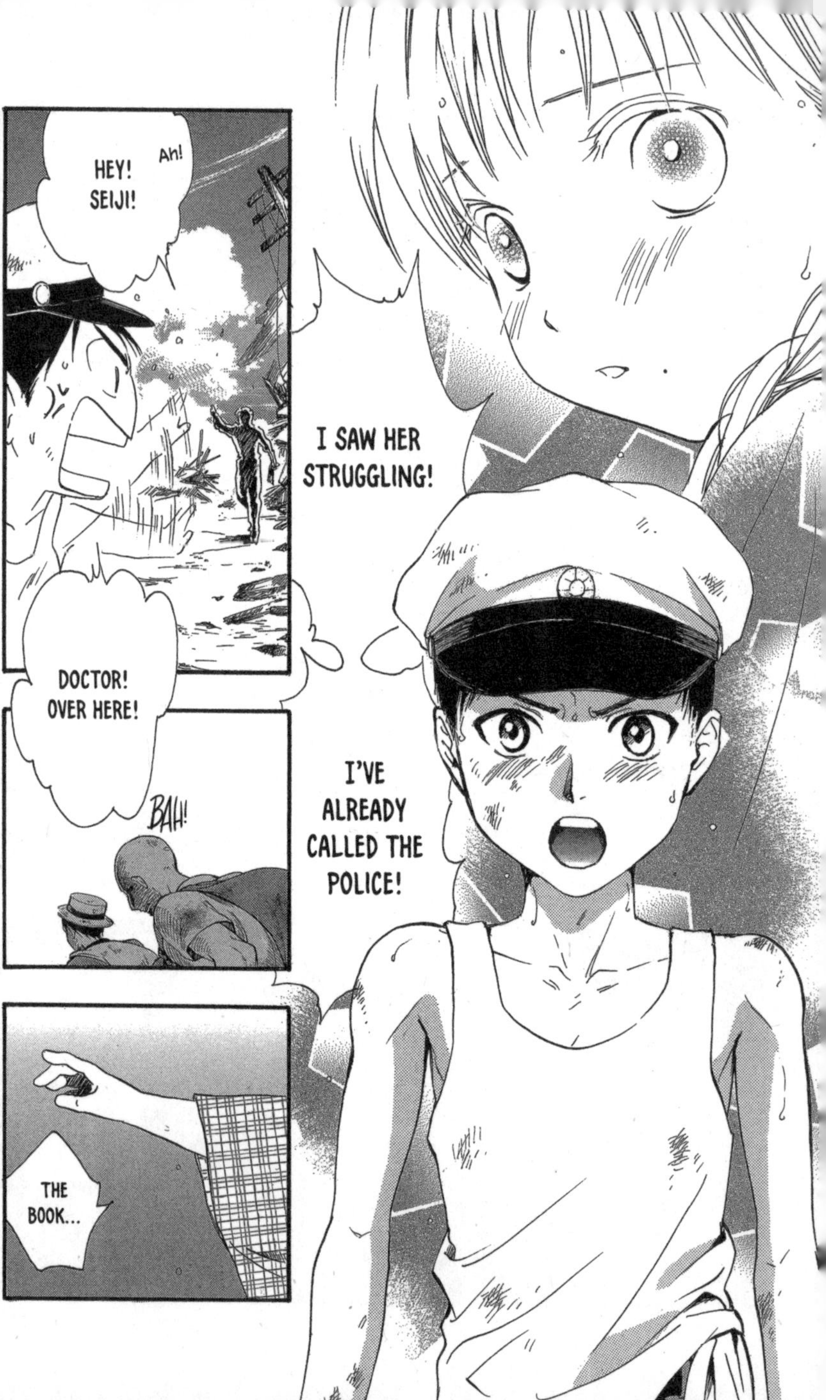
I SAW HER STRUGGLING!
I'VE ALREADY CALLED THE POLICE!
Ah!
HEY! SEIJI!
DOCTOR! OVER HERE!
BAH!
THE BOOK...

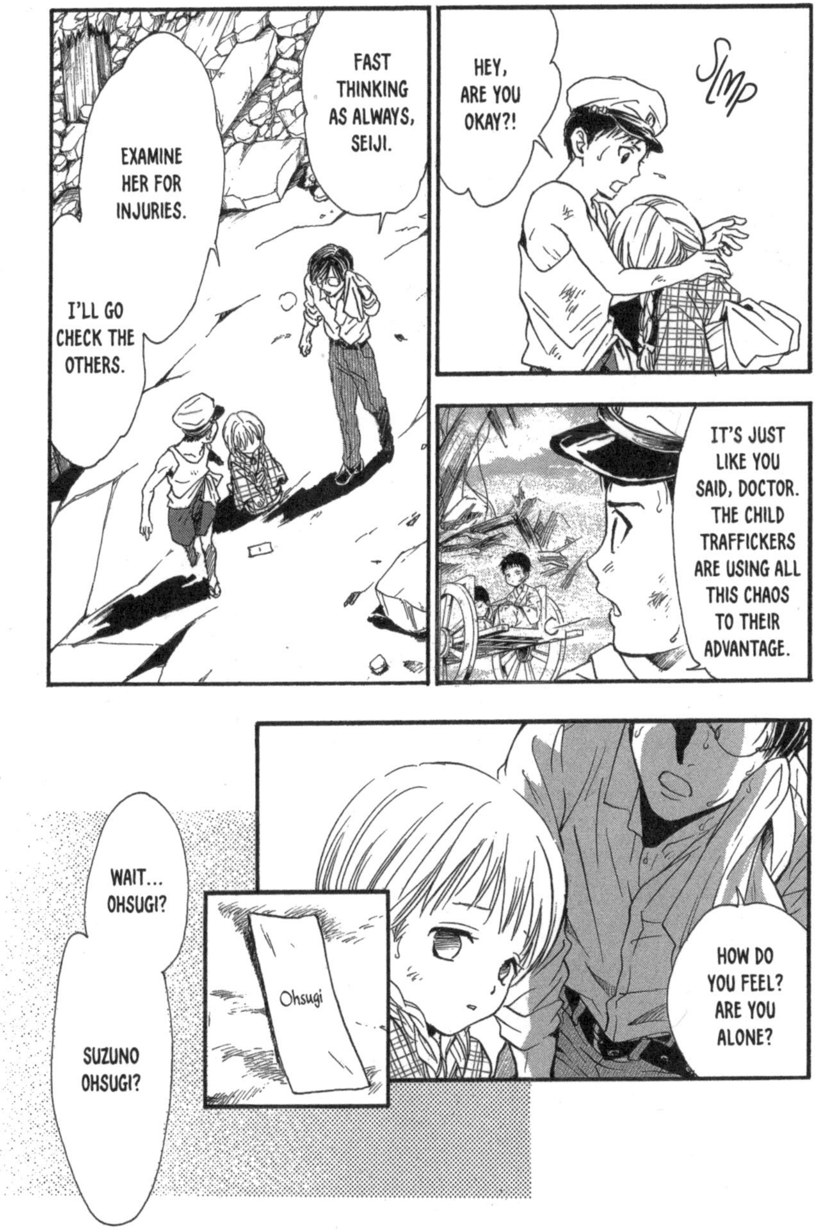
HEY, ARE YOU OKAY?!
SLMP
IT'S JUST LIKE YOU SAID, DOCTOR. THE CHILD TRAFFICKERS ARE USING ALL THIS CHAOS TO THEIR ADVANTAGE.
FAST THINKING AS ALWAYS, SEIJI.
EXAMINE HER FOR INJURIES.
I'LL GO CHECK THE OTHERS.
HOW DO YOU FEEL? ARE YOU ALONE?
Ohsugi
WAIT... OHSUGI?
SUZUNO OHSUGI?

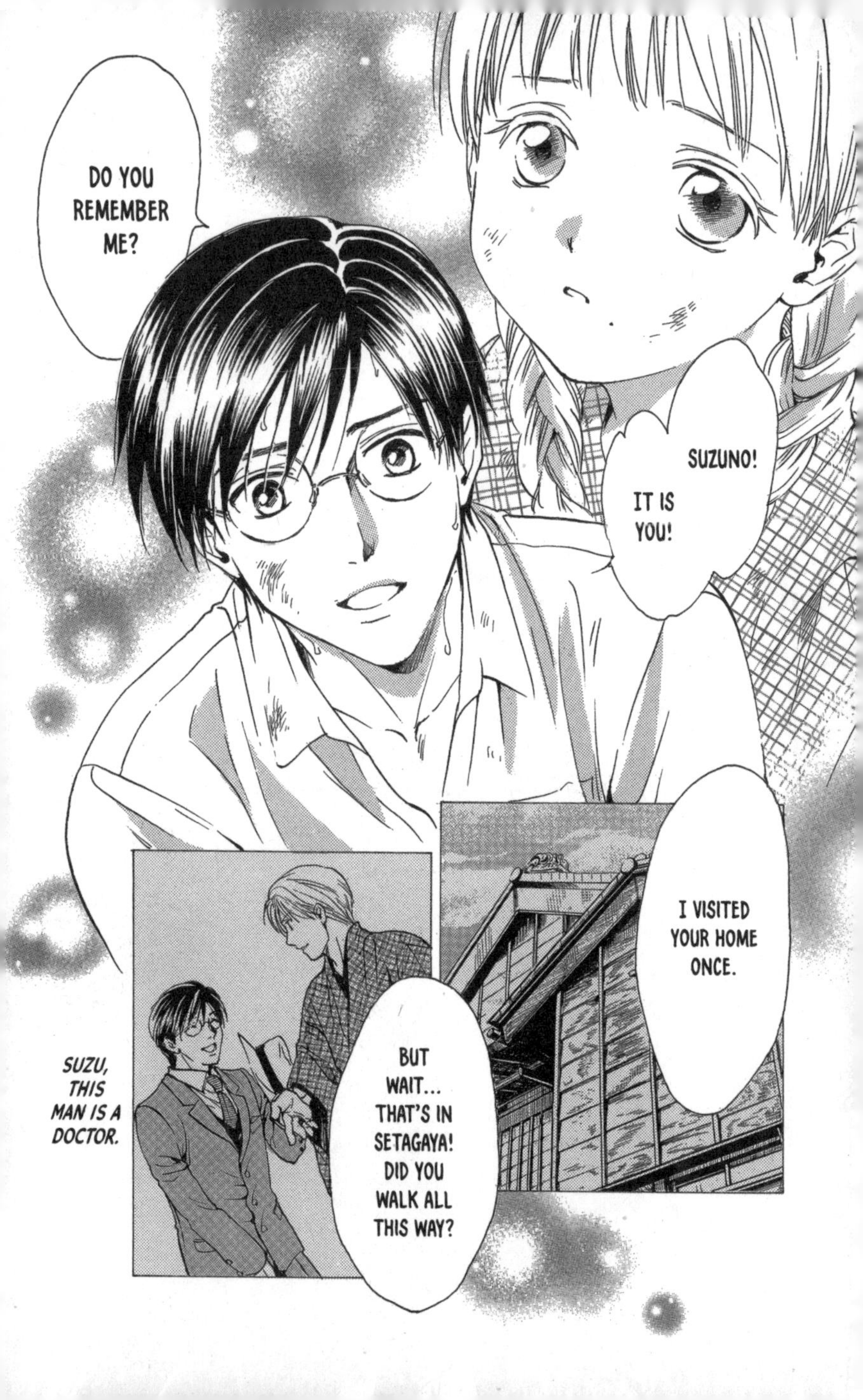
DO YOU REMEMBER ME?
SUZUNO! IT IS YOU!
I VISITED YOUR HOME ONCE.
SUZU, THIS MAN IS A DOCTOR.
BUT WAIT... THAT'S IN SETAGAYA! DID YOU WALK ALL THIS WAY?

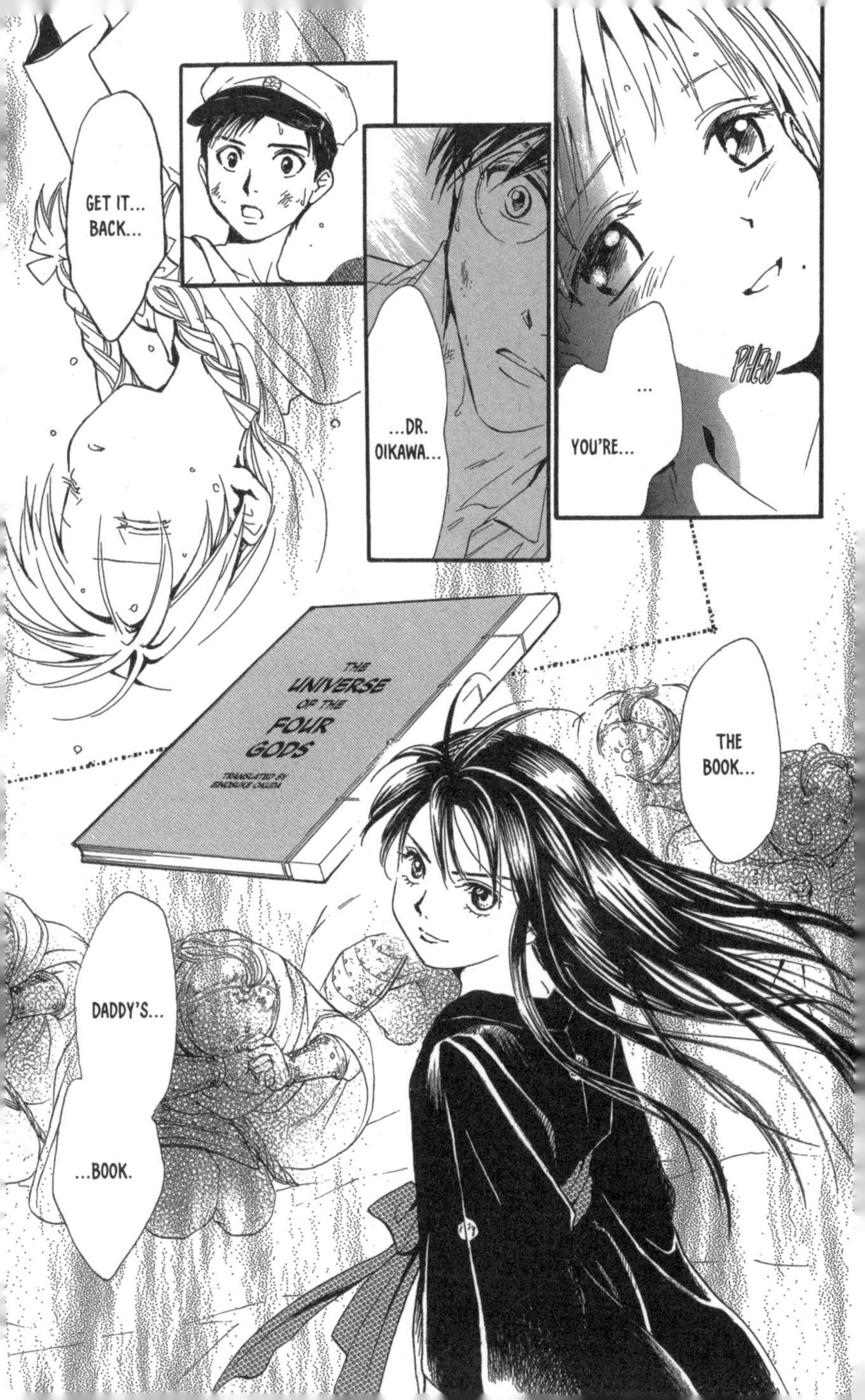

...
YOU'RE...
PHEW
...DR. OIKAWA...
GET IT... BACK...
THE UNIVERSE OF THE FOUR GODS
THE BOOK...
DADDY'S...
...BOOK.

Message from Yuu Watase

Yuu Watase here.

The tale of Byakko has begun at last! It's been a few years (←vague) since *Genbu Kaiden*. To everyone who asked for *Byakko Senki*, everyone who waited without asking and everyone who loves the *Fushigi Yûgi* stories: Thank you!!!

Naturally, first-time *Fushigi Yûgi* readers are welcome too.

I hope you enjoy the story.

So, since this will be the last tale...

Hmm... The first *Fushigi Yûgi* series started in 1991 in a magazine called *Weekly Shojo Comic* (now called *Sho-Comi*). Back then, the Four Gods story was basically the Priestess of Suzaku vs. the Priestess of Seiryu. Thanks to the readers, it became one of my best-known works.

In 2003, *Fushigi Yûgi: Genbu Kaiden* began publication in the special issues of *Shojo Comic* magazine. This tale was about the Priestess of Genbu. I had to take a break for health reasons partway through, and the series eventually finished ten years later in the special issues of *Monthly Flowers* magazine.

After that, I had to deal with a lot of different things. I wasn't sure when I'd be able to draw the final story, but in 2015 *Flowers* published a one-shot about Byakko.

I still remember my mother—always a loyal fan—reading it in the hospital before she passed away. "I just wish I could read the rest," she said with a laugh.

It's been two years since then, but I eventually decided to pull myself out of my grief and draw. In the October 2017 issue of *Flowers*, this new series began at last.

I'm still not fully recovered health-wise for a bimonthly serial, so it may take some time to publish enough chapters to fill a new volume. But please pick up the Japanese magazine to see it published there too. (← Say what?!) You can also read it in digital format!

About my other series in a different magazine—*Weekly Shonen Sunday*... It was on hiatus for a long time, but volume 9 of the "remastered" version of *Arata: The Legend* is out now! It's called a "remaster," but it's more of a remake—a redrawing! This is also an isekai fantasy, but it's different from *FushiYu*. Still, it's a Watase story through and through, so you might enjoy it.

Please give it a try too!

Also, please enjoy my one-shot *Kiri Samurai* and the new edition of *Sakuragari*!

Okay, then! Until volume 2! Maybe in about eight months from now? I intentionally didn't talk about the content of this volume here, but... What will Suzuno do now, do you think?!

See you then.

Yuu Watase
March 2018

CHAPTER 4
Suspicion of Memory

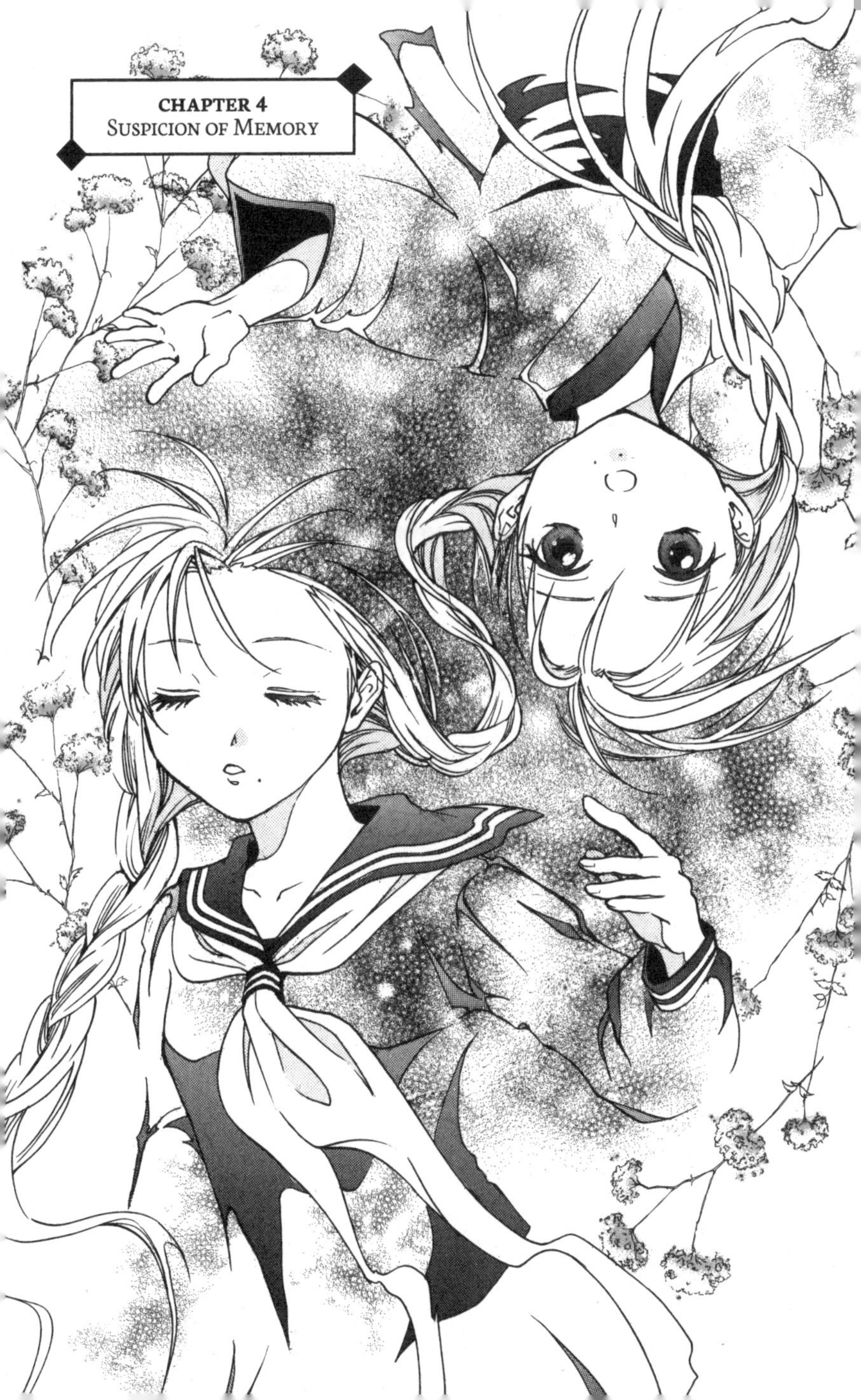

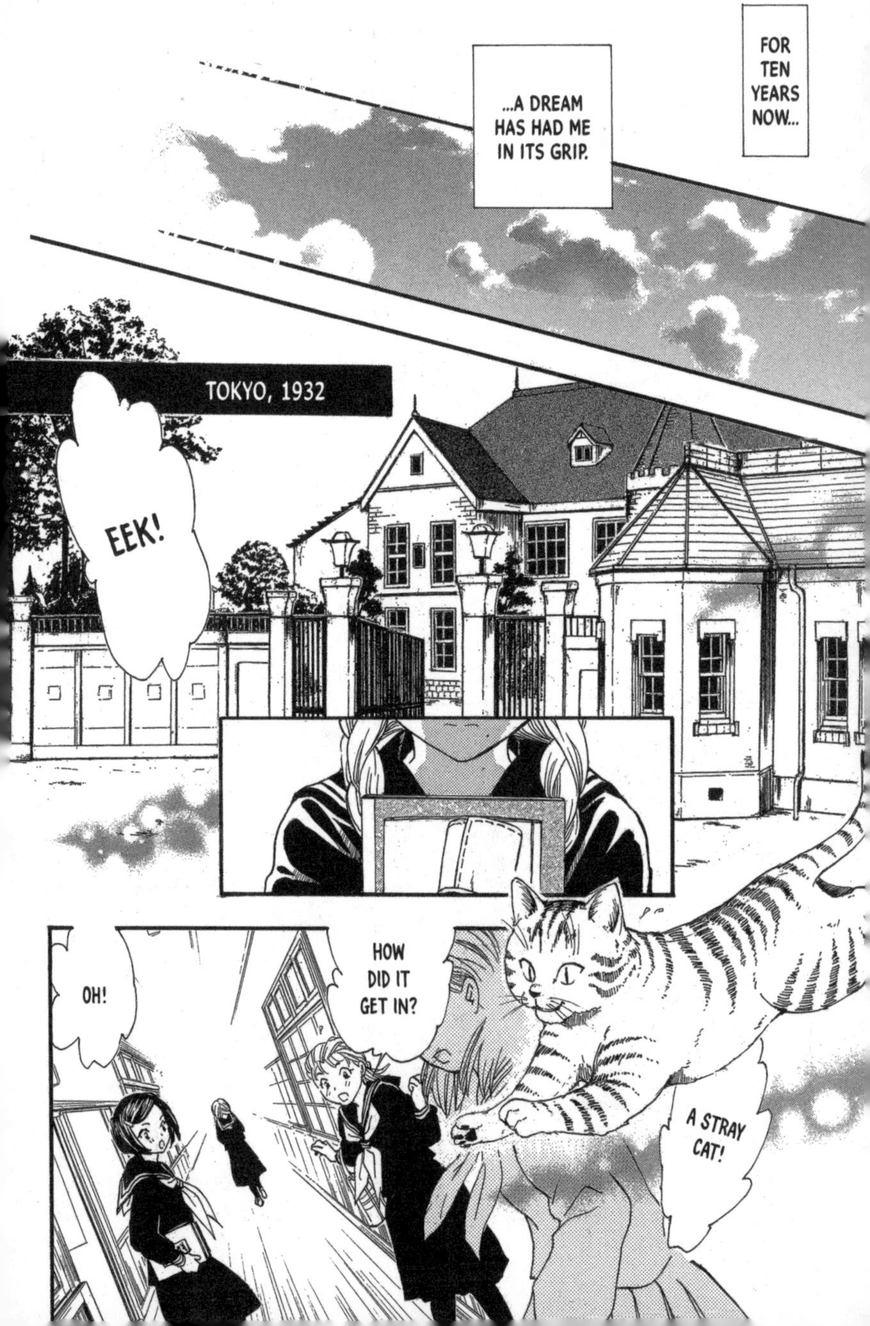
FOR TEN YEARS NOW...
...A DREAM HAS HAD ME IN ITS GRIP.
TOKYO, 1932
EEK!
A STRAY CAT!
HOW DID IT GET IN?
OH!

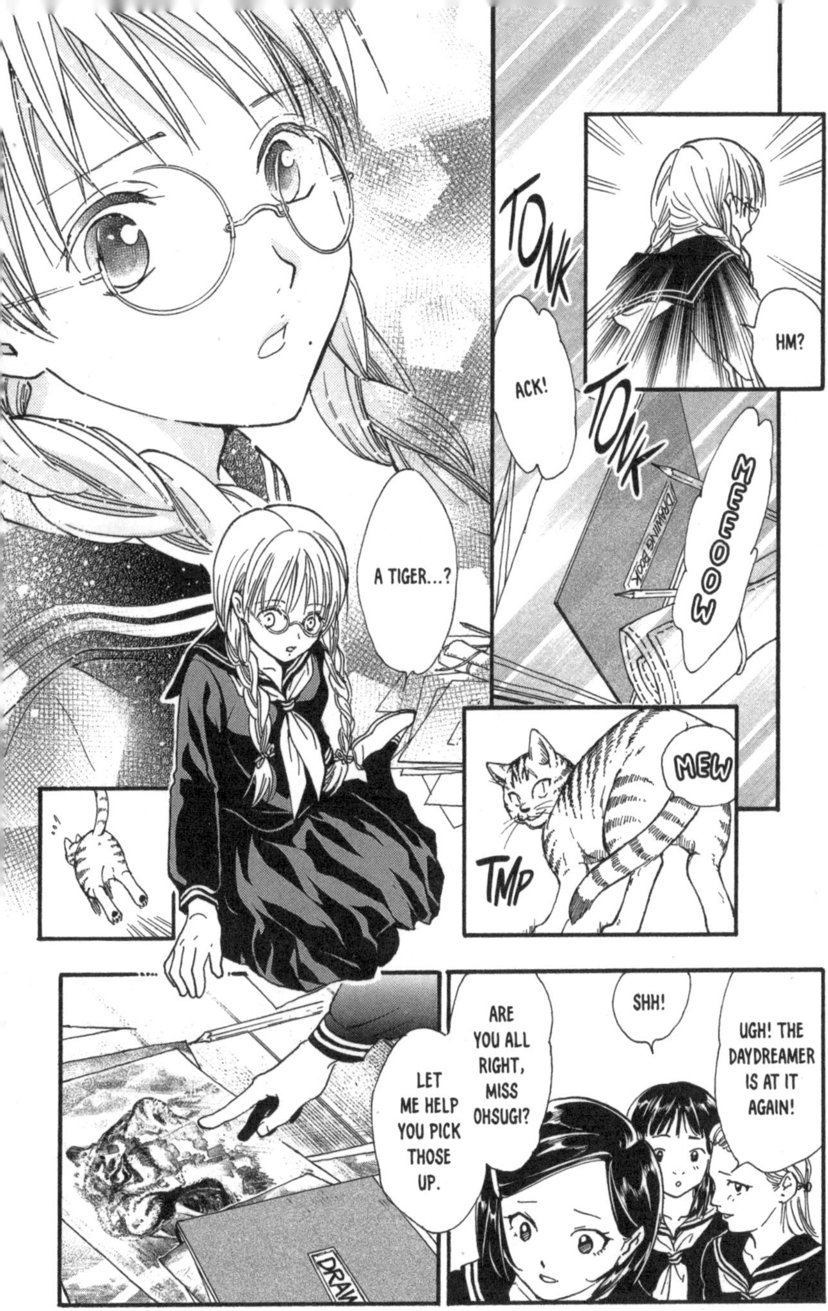
HM?
TONK
TONK
ACK!
DRAWING BOOK
MEEEOOW
MEW
TMP
A TIGER...?
UGH! THE DAYDREAMER IS AT IT AGAIN!
SHH!
ARE YOU ALL RIGHT, MISS OHSUGI?
LET ME HELP YOU PICK THOSE UP.

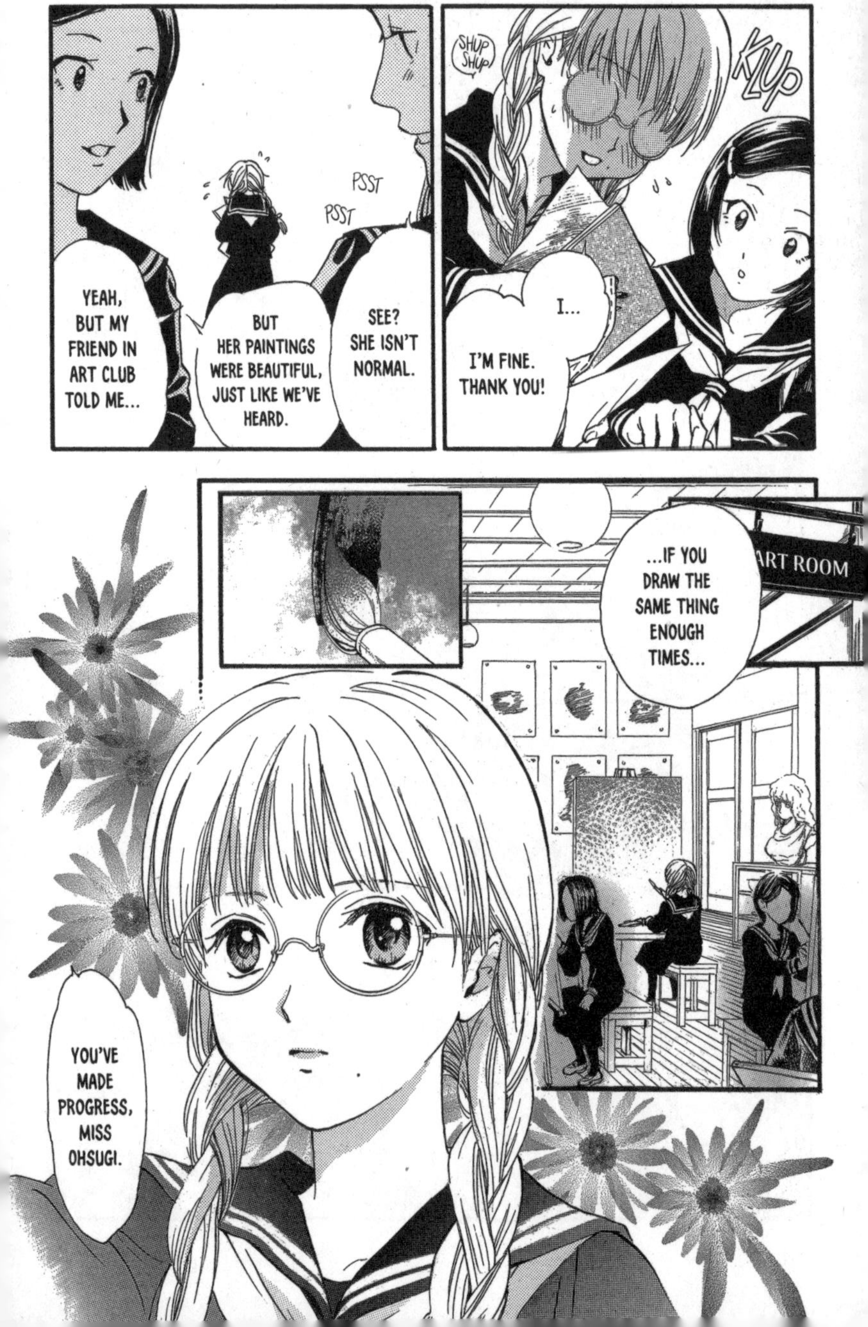
SHUP SHUP
KLUP
I...
I'M FINE. THANK YOU!
PSST
PSST
SEE? SHE ISN'T NORMAL.
BUT HER PAINTINGS WERE BEAUTIFUL, JUST LIKE WE'VE HEARD.
YEAH, BUT MY FRIEND IN ART CLUB TOLD ME...
ART ROOM
...IF YOU DRAW THE SAME THING ENOUGH TIMES...
YOU'VE MADE PROGRESS, MISS OHSUGI.

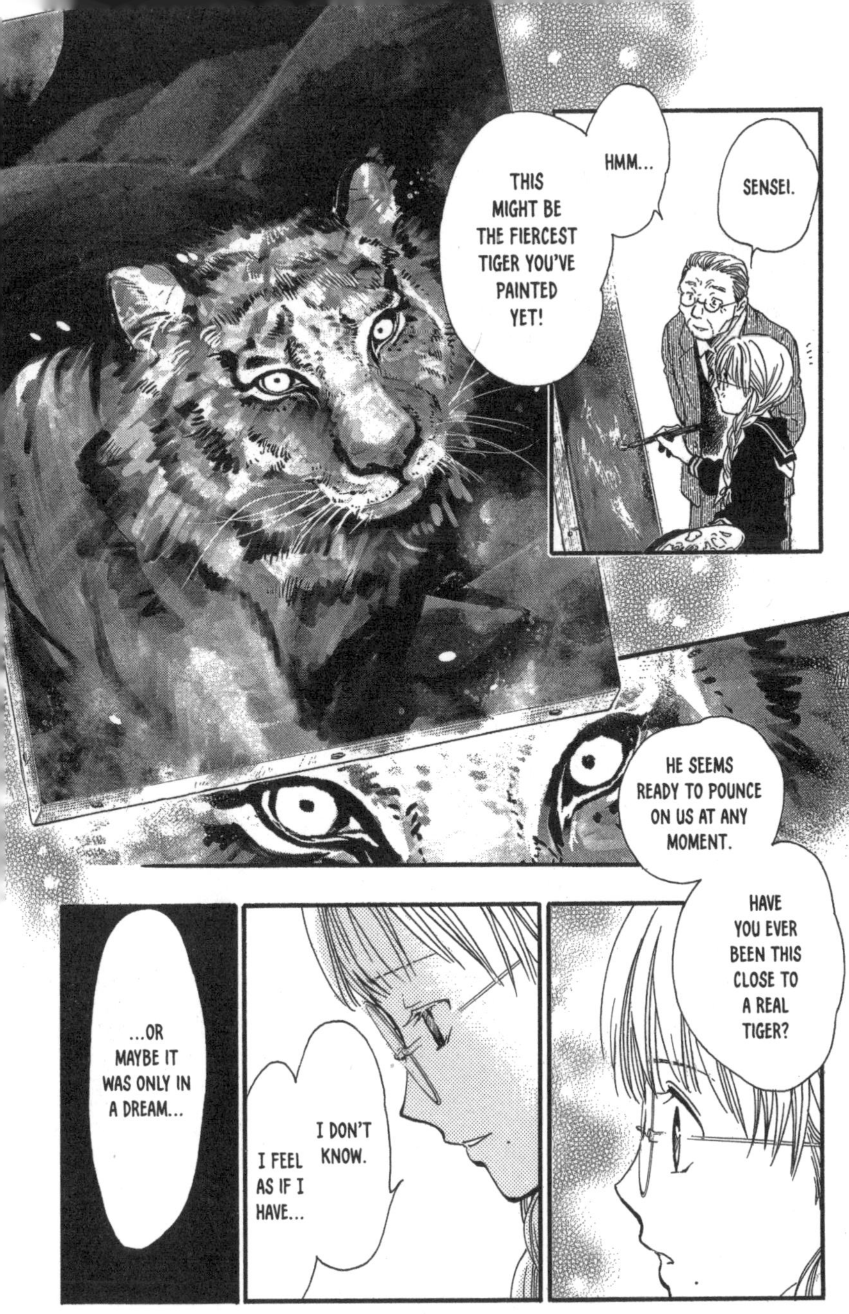
SENSEI.
HMM...
THIS MIGHT BE THE FIERCEST TIGER YOU'VE PAINTED YET!
HE SEEMS READY TO POUNCE ON US AT ANY MOMENT.
HAVE YOU EVER BEEN THIS CLOSE TO A REAL TIGER?
I DON'T KNOW.
I FEEL AS IF I HAVE...
...OR MAYBE IT WAS ONLY IN A DREAM...

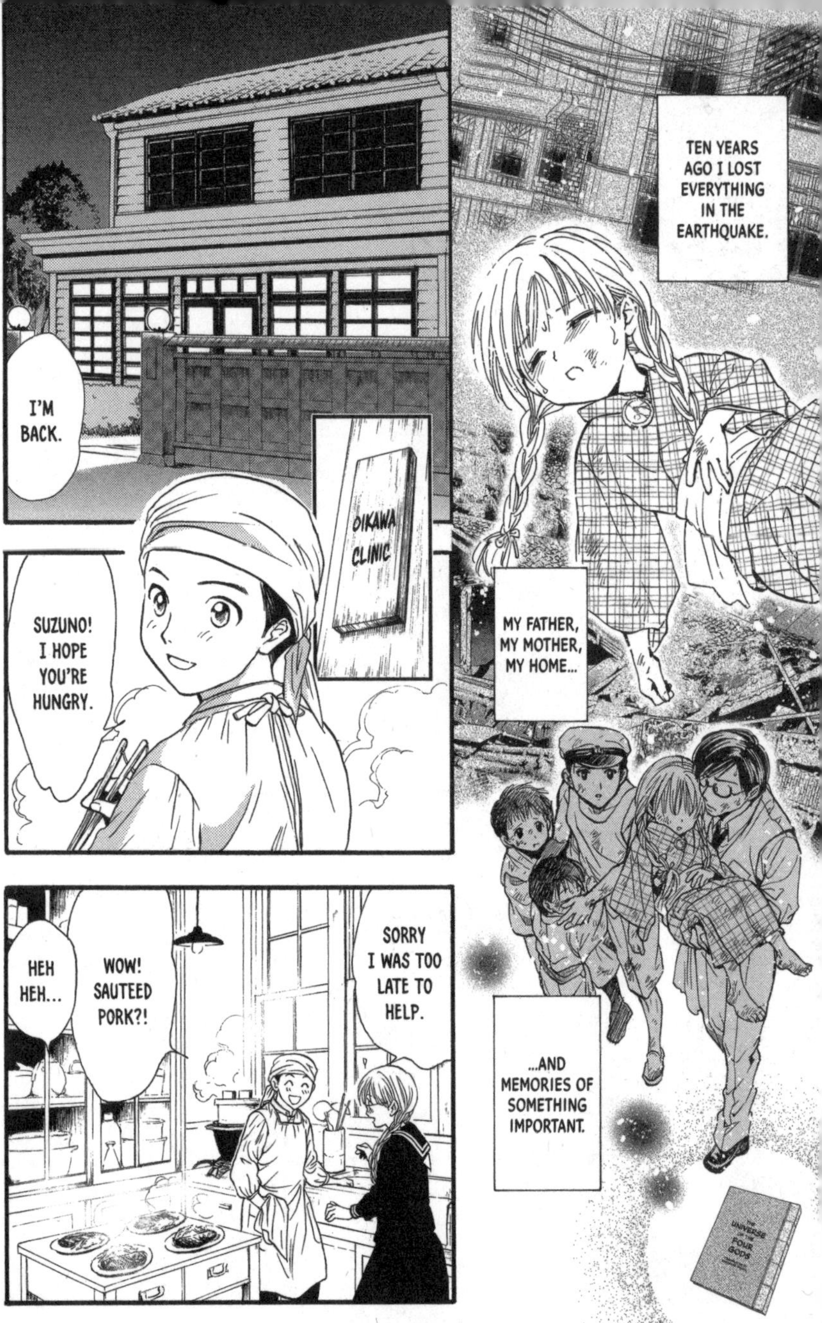
TEN YEARS AGO I LOST EVERYTHING IN THE EARTHQUAKE.
MY FATHER, MY MOTHER, MY HOME...
...AND MEMORIES OF SOMETHING IMPORTANT.
I'M BACK.
OIKAWA CLINIC
SUZUNO! I HOPE YOU'RE HUNGRY.
SORRY I WAS TOO LATE TO HELP.
WOW! SAUTEED PORK?!
HEH HEH...

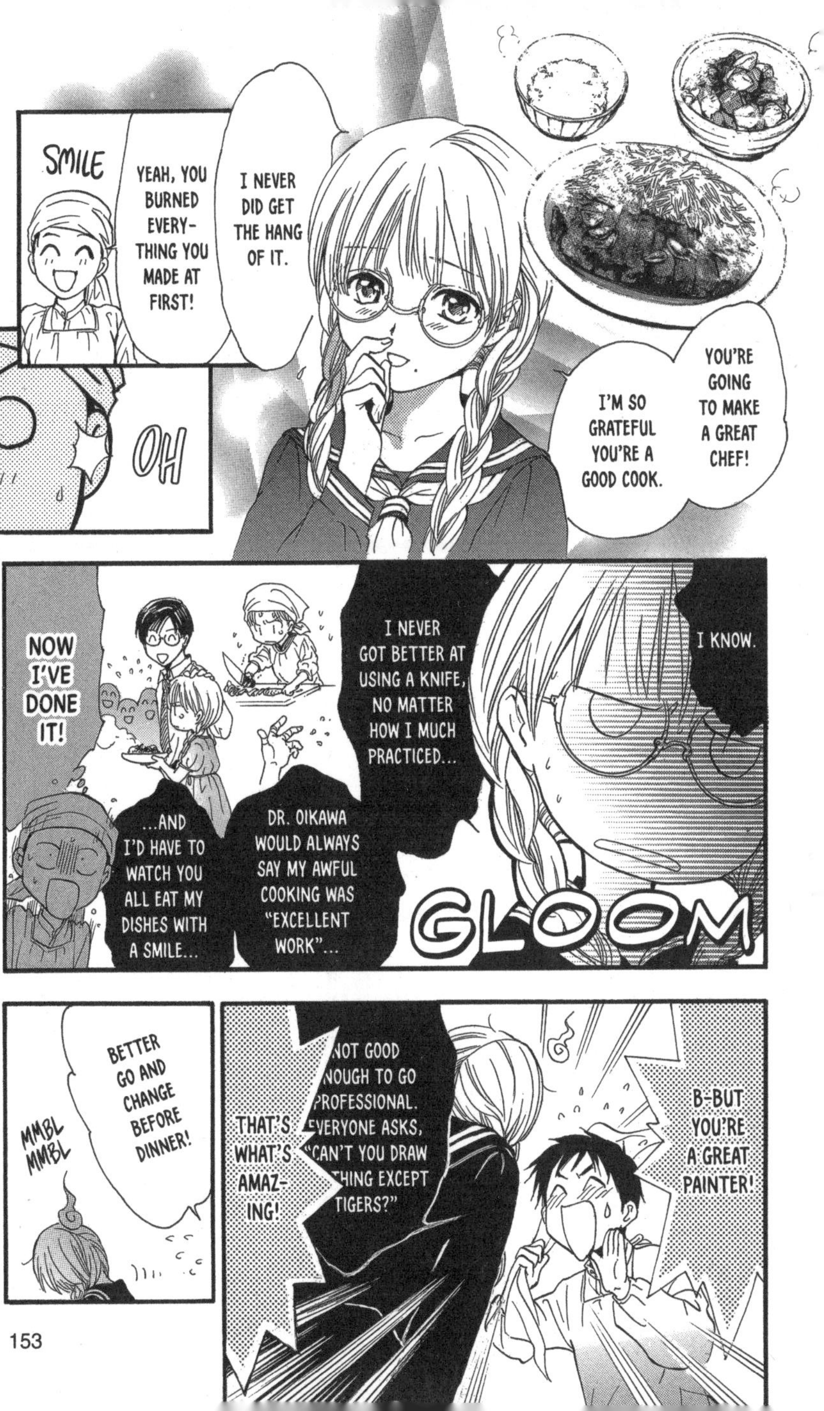

YOU'RE GOING TO MAKE A GREAT CHEF!
I'M SO GRATEFUL YOU'RE A GOOD COOK.
I NEVER DID GET THE HANG OF IT.
YEAH, YOU BURNED EVERY-THING YOU MADE AT FIRST!
SMILE
OH
I KNOW.
GLOOM
I NEVER GOT BETTER AT USING A KNIFE, NO MATTER HOW I MUCH PRACTICED...
DR. OIKAWA WOULD ALWAYS SAY MY AWFUL COOKING WAS "EXCELLENT WORK"...
...AND I'D HAVE TO WATCH YOU ALL EAT MY DISHES WITH A SMILE...
NOW I'VE DONE IT!
B-BUT YOU'RE A GREAT PAINTER!
NOT GOOD NOUGH TO GO PROFESSIONAL. EVERYONE ASKS, "CAN'T YOU DRAW THING EXCEPT TIGERS?"
THAT'S WHAT'S AMAZ-ING!
BETTER GO AND CHANGE BEFORE DINNER!
MMBL MMBL

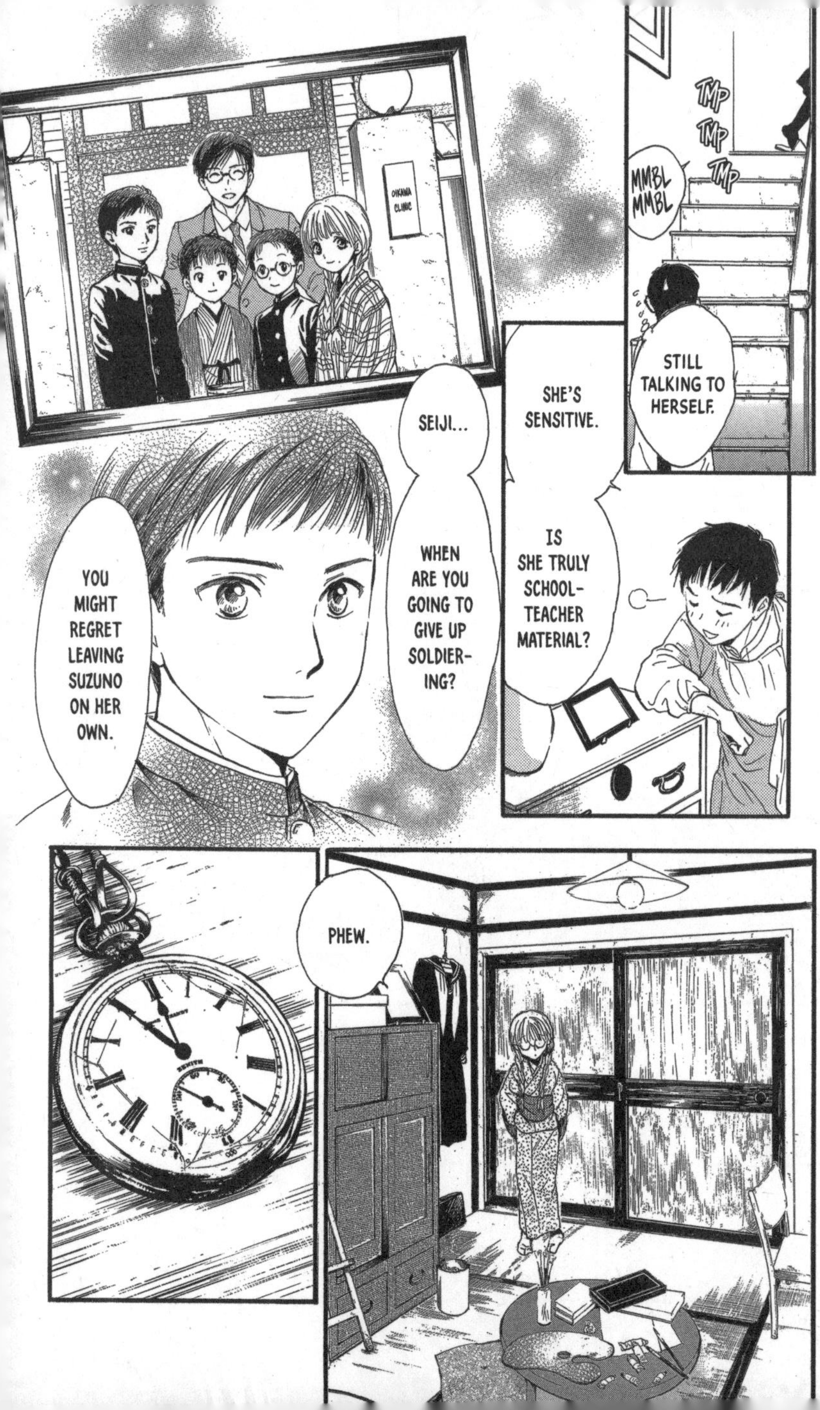
TMP
TMP
TMP
MMBL MMBL
STILL TALKING TO HERSELF.
SHE'S SENSITIVE.
IS SHE TRULY SCHOOL-TEACHER MATERIAL?
OIKAWA CLINIC
SEIJI...
WHEN ARE YOU GOING TO GIVE UP SOLDIER-ING?
YOU MIGHT REGRET LEAVING SUZUNO ON HER OWN.
PHEW.

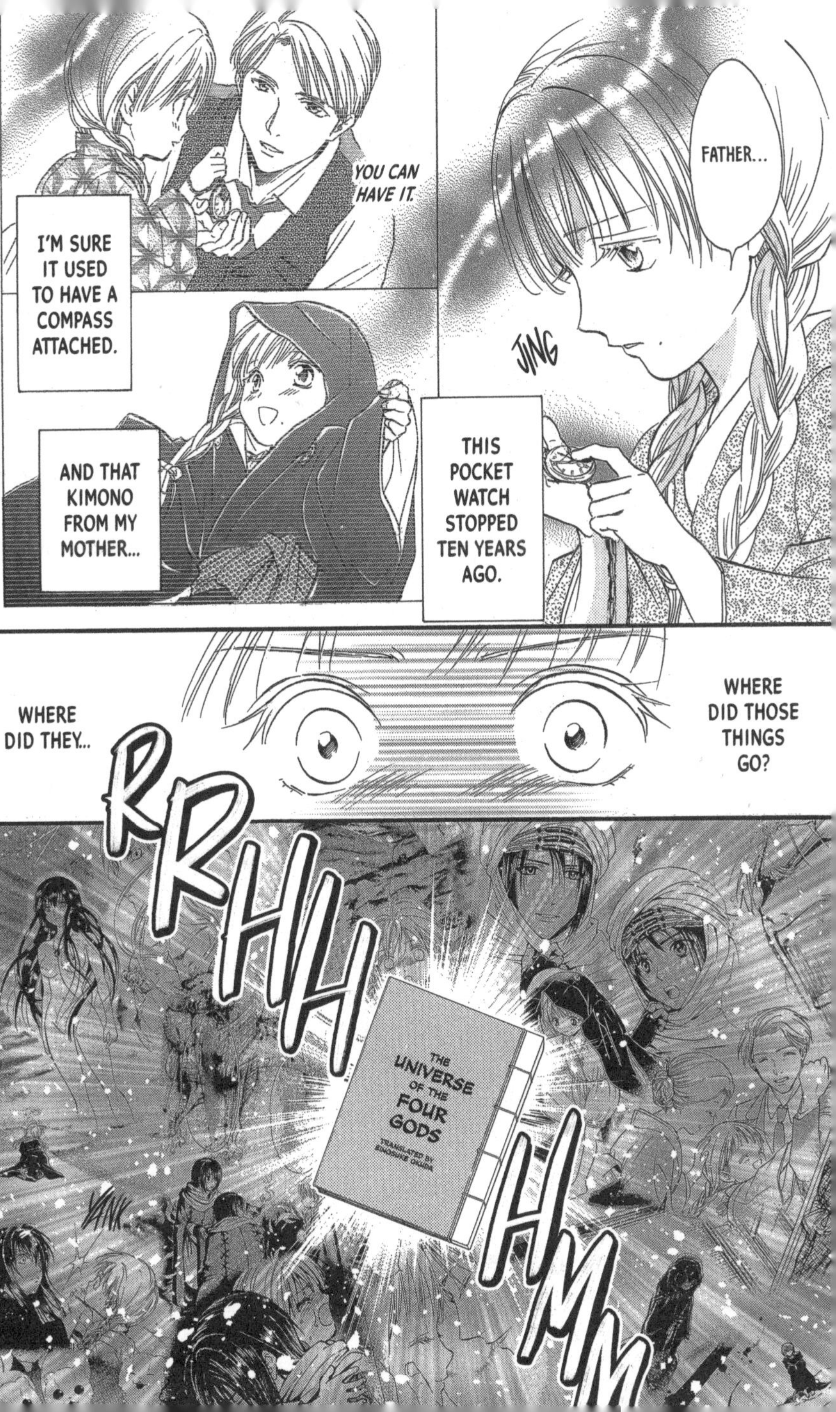
FATHER...
JING
THIS POCKET WATCH STOPPED TEN YEARS AGO.
YOU CAN HAVE IT.
I'M SURE IT USED TO HAVE A COMPASS ATTACHED.
AND THAT KIMONO FROM MY MOTHER...
WHERE DID THOSE THINGS GO?
WHERE DID THEY...
RRHHH
HMMM
THE UNIVERSE OF THE FOUR GODS
YANK

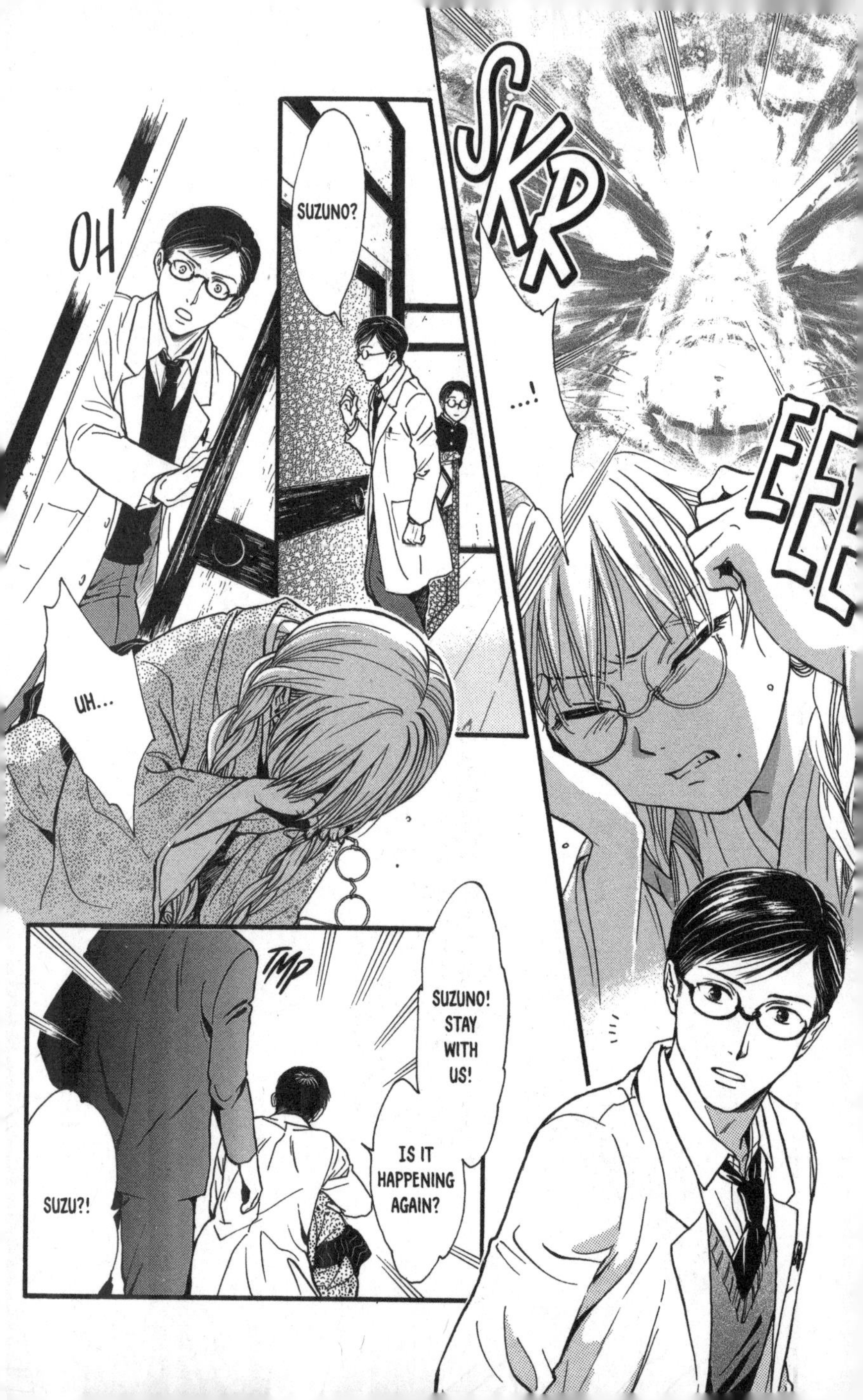
SKR
EEE
...!
SUZUNO?
OH
UH...
TMP
SUZUNO! STAY WITH US!
IS IT HAPPENING AGAIN?
SUZU?!

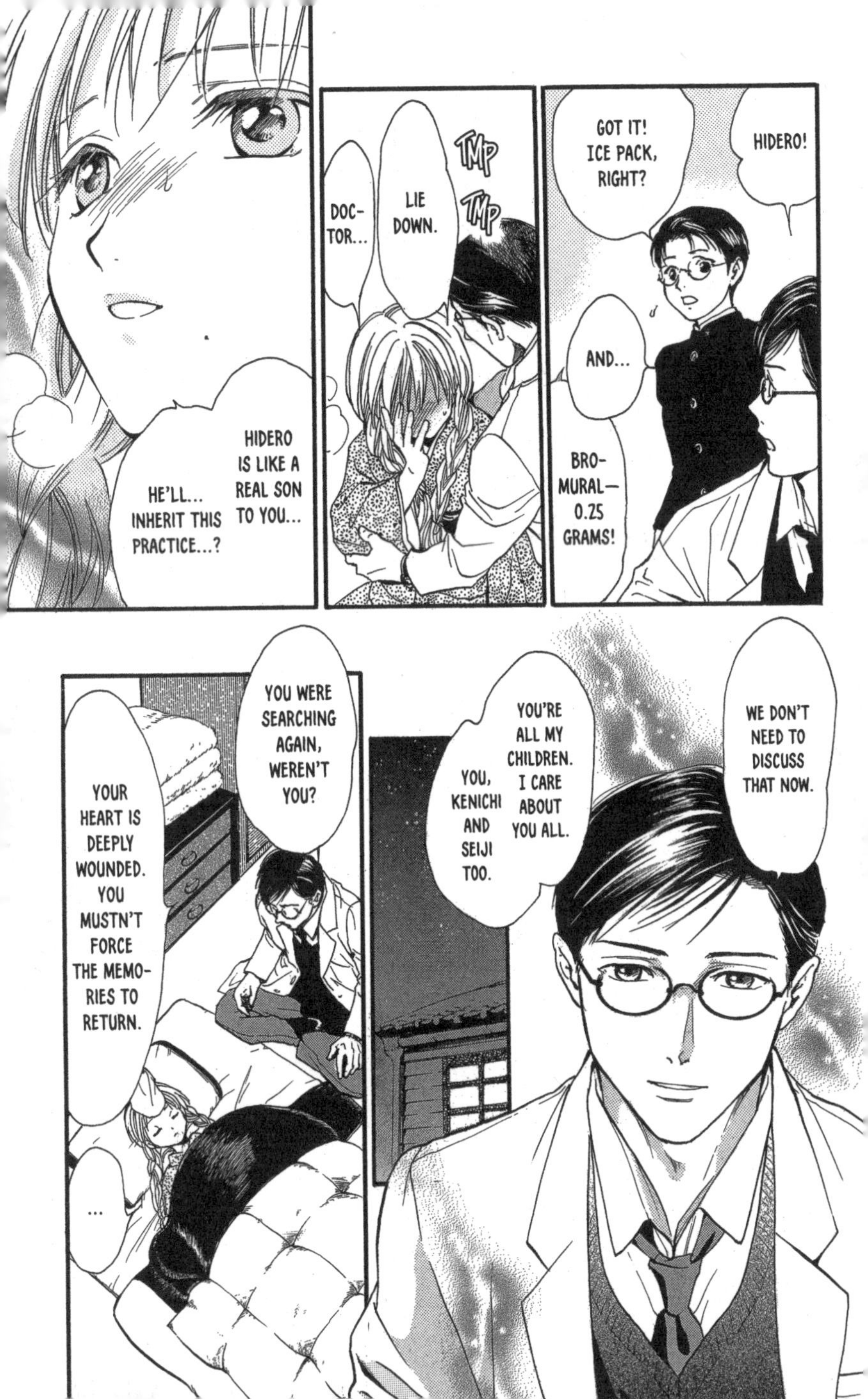
HIDERO!
GOT IT! ICE PACK, RIGHT?
AND...
BRO-MURAL—0.25 GRAMS!
TMP
TMP
LIE DOWN.
DOC-TOR...
HIDERO IS LIKE A REAL SON TO YOU...
HE'LL... INHERIT THIS PRACTICE...?
WE DON'T NEED TO DISCUSS THAT NOW.
YOU'RE ALL MY CHILDREN. I CARE ABOUT YOU ALL.
YOU, KENICHI AND SEIJI TOO.
YOU WERE SEARCHING AGAIN, WEREN'T YOU?
YOUR HEART IS DEEPLY WOUNDED. YOU MUSTN'T FORCE THE MEMO-RIES TO RETURN.
...

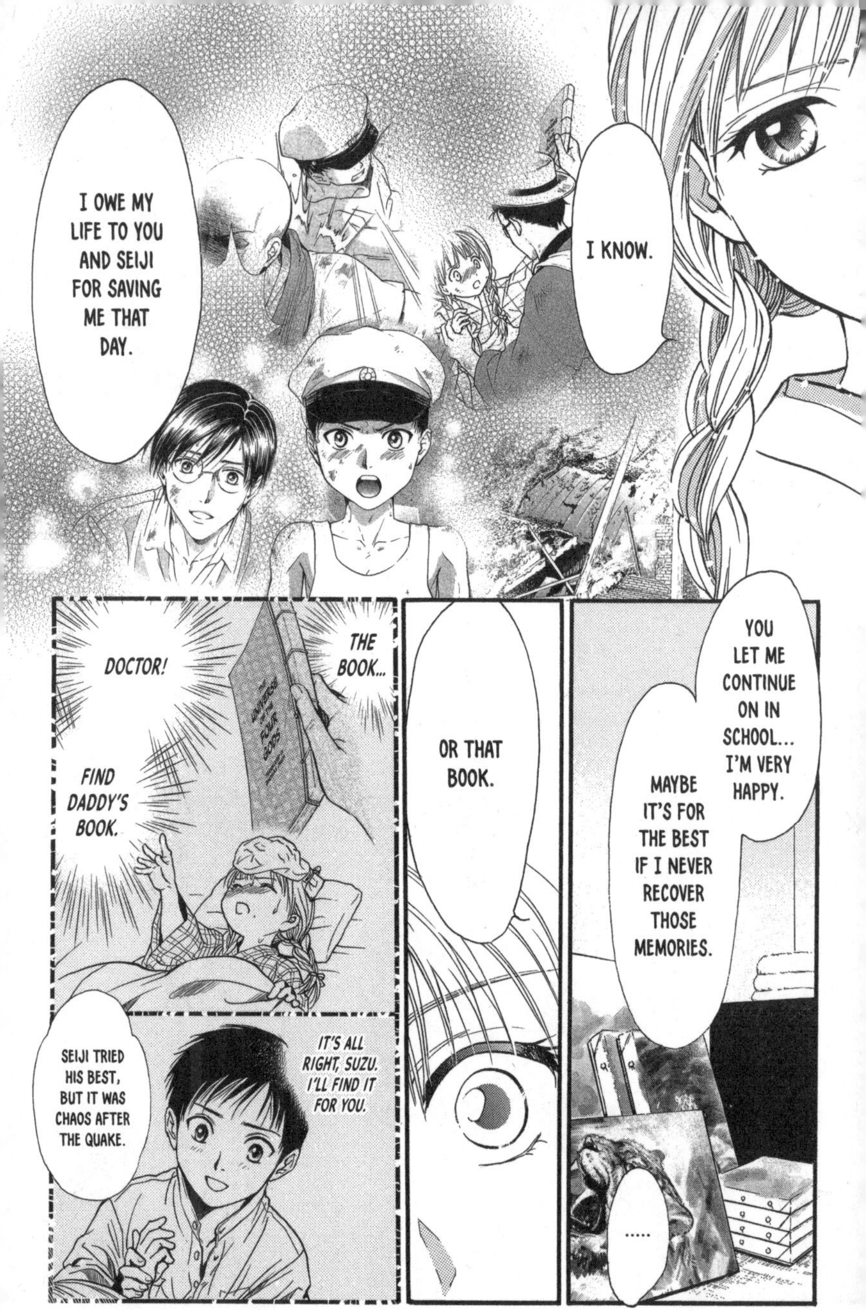
I KNOW.
I OWE MY LIFE TO YOU AND SEIJI FOR SAVING ME THAT DAY.
YOU LET ME CONTINUE ON IN SCHOOL... I'M VERY HAPPY.
MAYBE IT'S FOR THE BEST IF I NEVER RECOVER THOSE MEMORIES.
.....
OR THAT BOOK.
THE BOOK...
DOCTOR!
FIND DADDY'S BOOK.
IT'S ALL RIGHT, SUZU. I'LL FIND IT FOR YOU.
SEIJI TRIED HIS BEST, BUT IT WAS CHAOS AFTER THE QUAKE.

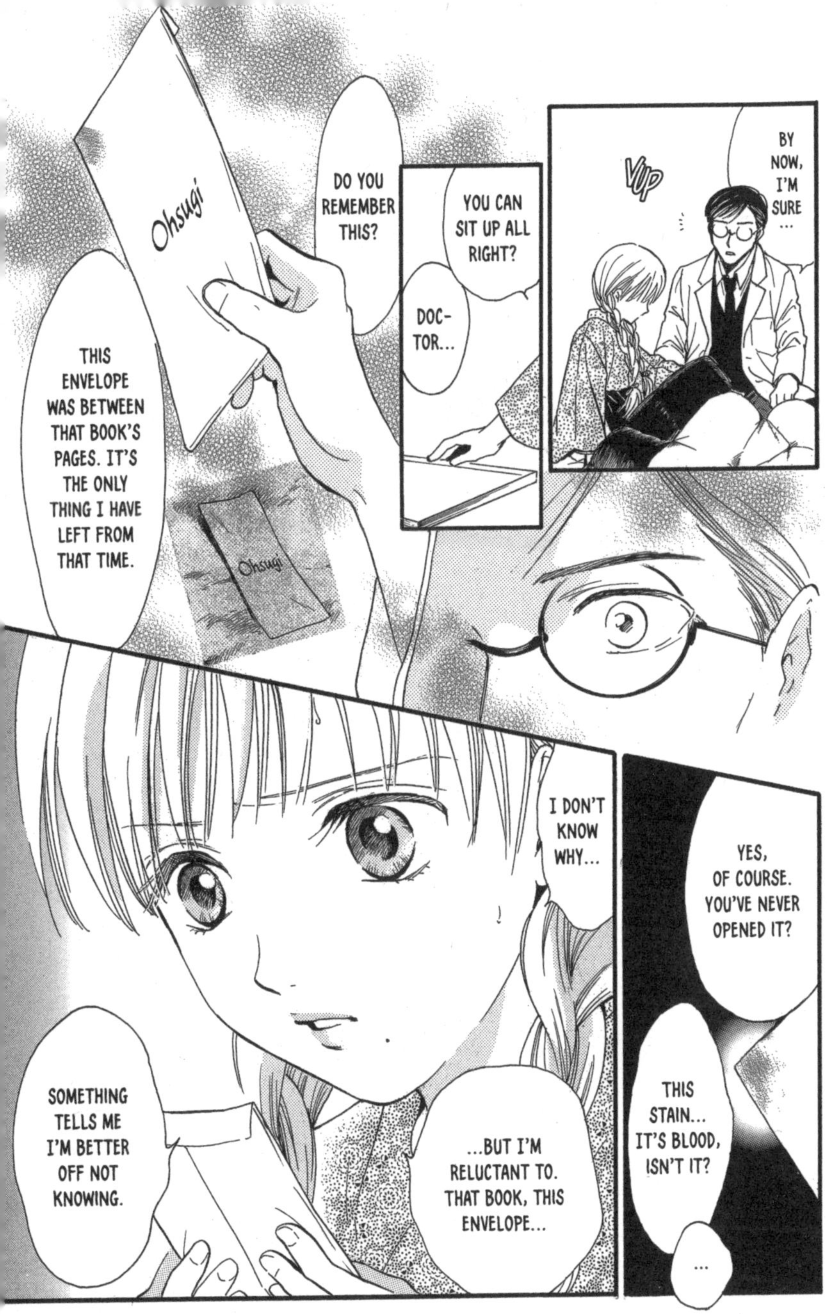
BY NOW, I'M SURE...
VUP
YOU CAN SIT UP ALL RIGHT?
DOCTOR...
DO YOU REMEMBER THIS?
Ohsugi
THIS ENVELOPE WAS BETWEEN THAT BOOK'S PAGES. IT'S THE ONLY THING I HAVE LEFT FROM THAT TIME.
Ohsugi
YES, OF COURSE. YOU'VE NEVER OPENED IT?
THIS STAIN... IT'S BLOOD, ISN'T IT?
...
I DON'T KNOW WHY...
...BUT I'M RELUCTANT TO. THAT BOOK, THIS ENVELOPE...
SOMETHING TELLS ME I'M BETTER OFF NOT KNOWING.

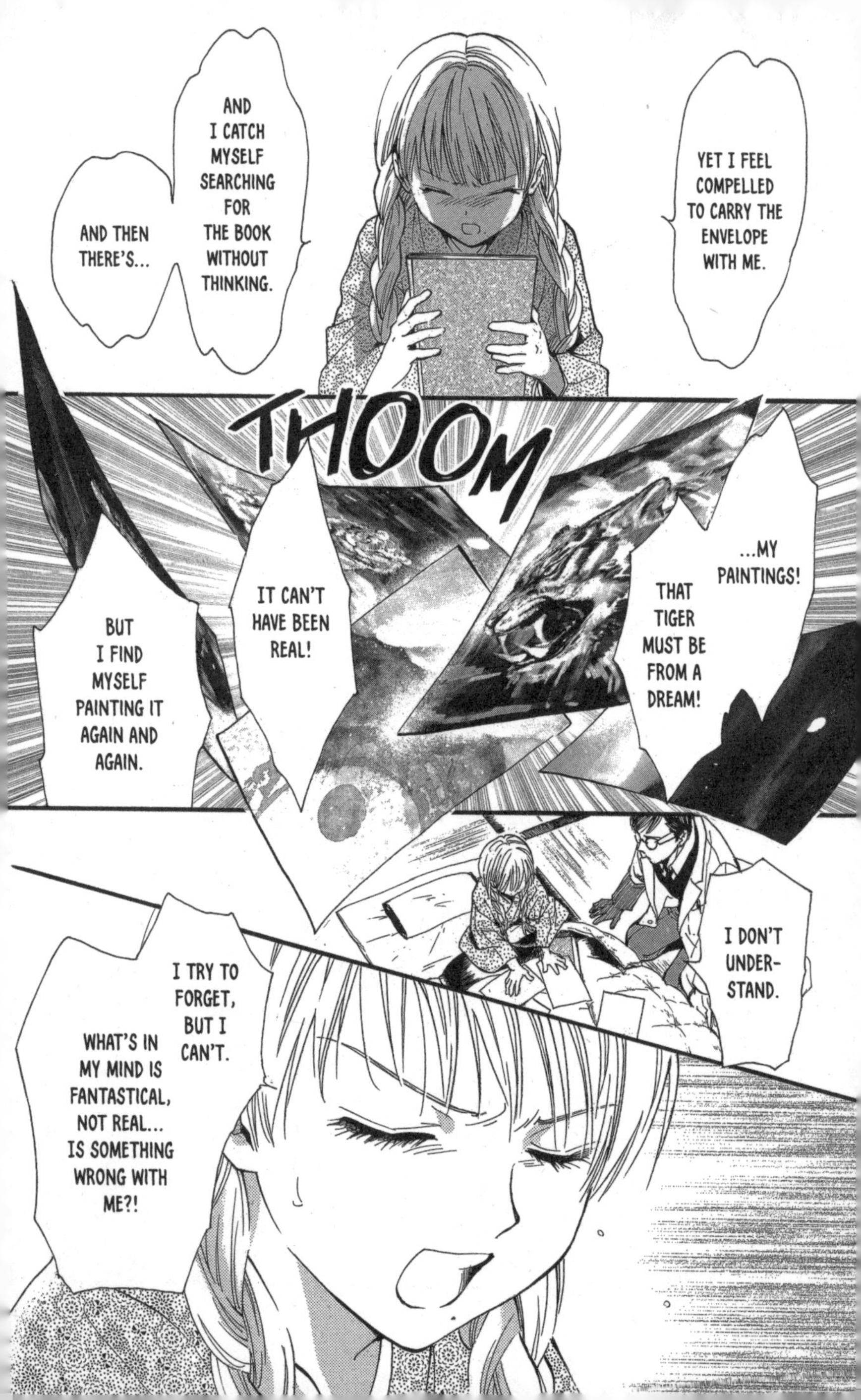
YET I FEEL COMPELLED TO CARRY THE ENVELOPE WITH ME.
AND I CATCH MYSELF SEARCHING FOR THE BOOK WITHOUT THINKING.
AND THEN THERE'S...
THOOM
...MY PAINTINGS!
THAT TIGER MUST BE FROM A DREAM!
IT CAN'T HAVE BEEN REAL!
BUT I FIND MYSELF PAINTING IT AGAIN AND AGAIN.
I DON'T UNDER-STAND.
I TRY TO FORGET, BUT I CAN'T.
WHAT'S IN MY MIND IS FANTASTICAL, NOT REAL... IS SOMETHING WRONG WITH ME?!

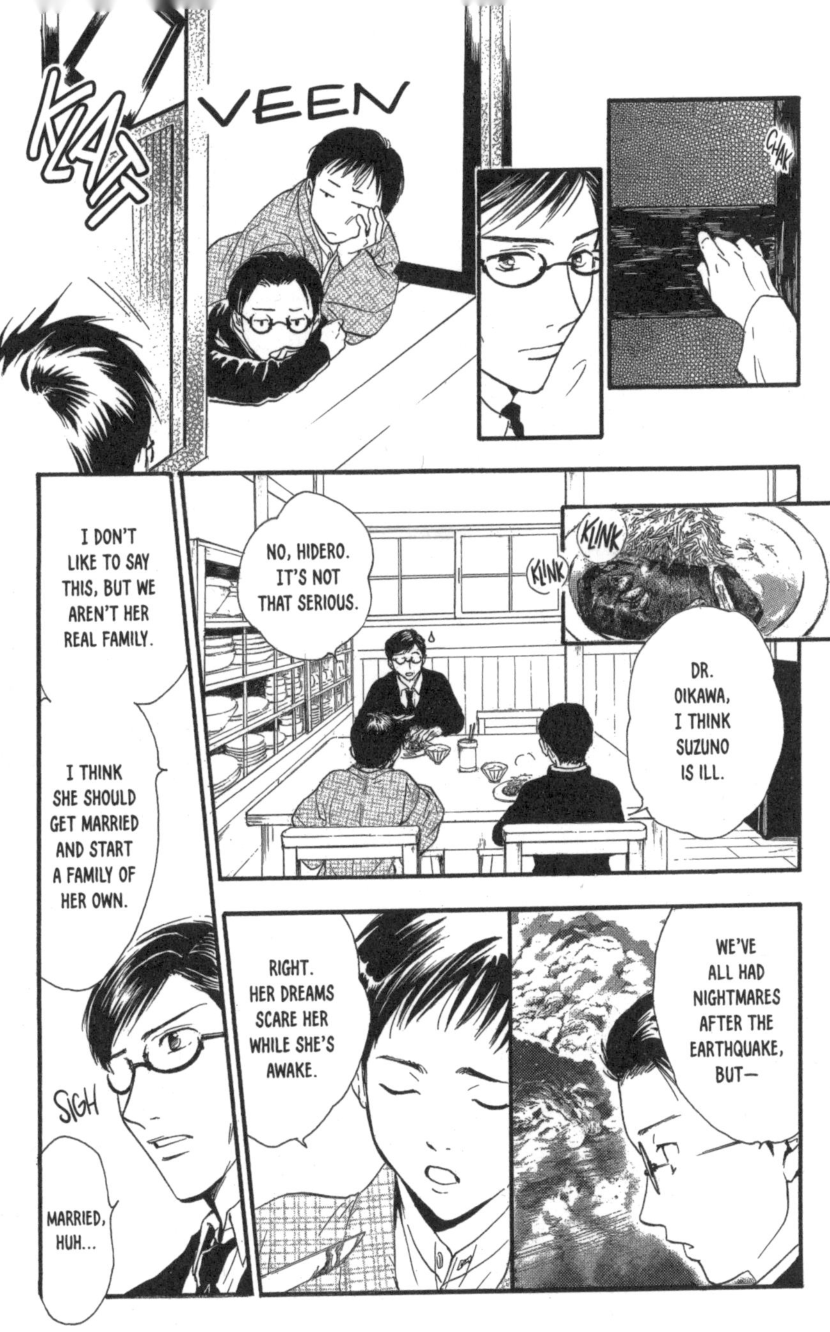
CHAK
VEEN
KLATT
KLINK
KLINK
DR. OIKAWA, I THINK SUZUNO IS ILL.
NO, HIDERO. IT'S NOT THAT SERIOUS.
WE'VE ALL HAD NIGHTMARES AFTER THE EARTHQUAKE, BUT—
RIGHT. HER DREAMS SCARE HER WHILE SHE'S AWAKE.
I DON'T LIKE TO SAY THIS, BUT WE AREN'T HER REAL FAMILY.
I THINK SHE SHOULD GET MARRIED AND START A FAMILY OF HER OWN.
SIGH
MARRIED, HUH...

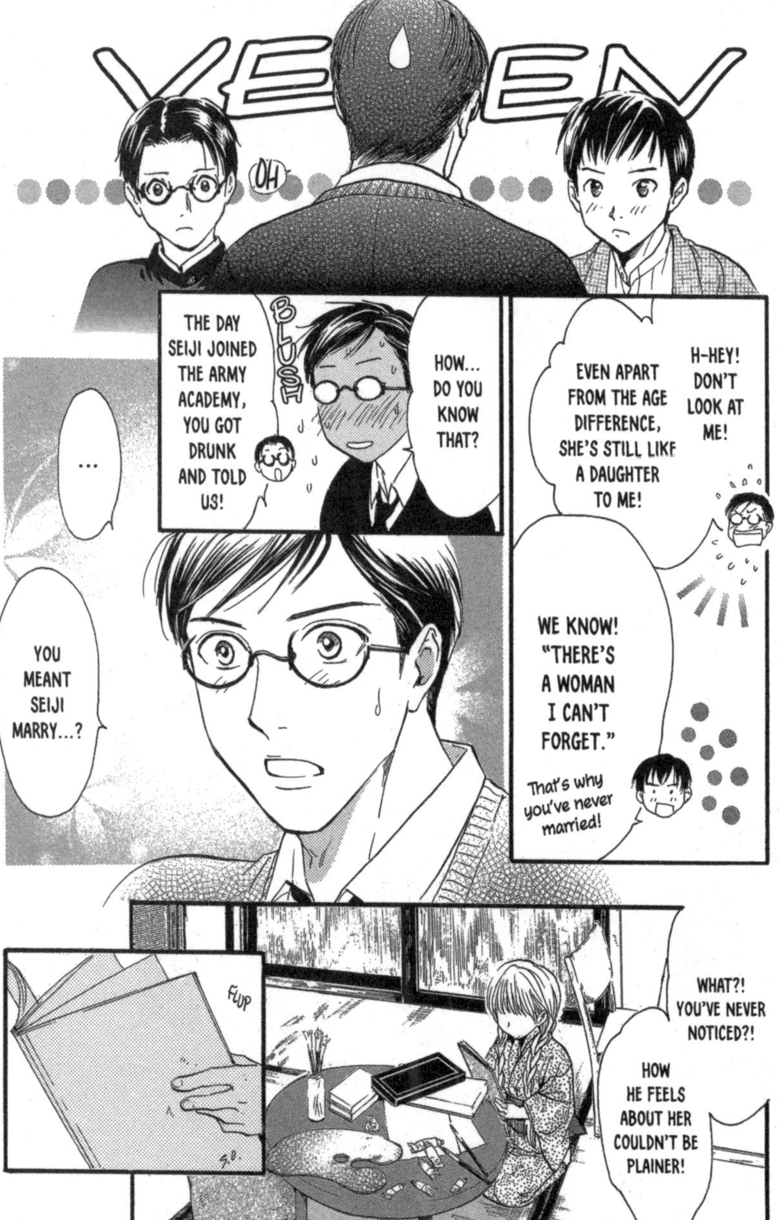
YE EN
OH
H-HEY! DON'T LOOK AT ME!
EVEN APART FROM THE AGE DIFFERENCE, SHE'S STILL LIKE A DAUGHTER TO ME!
WE KNOW! "THERE'S A WOMAN I CAN'T FORGET."
That's why you've never married!
HOW... DO YOU KNOW THAT?
BLUSH
THE DAY SEIJI JOINED THE ARMY ACADEMY, YOU GOT DRUNK AND TOLD US!
...
YOU MEANT SEIJI MARRY...?
WHAT?! YOU'VE NEVER NOTICED?!
HOW HE FEELS ABOUT HER COULDN'T BE PLAINER!
FLUP

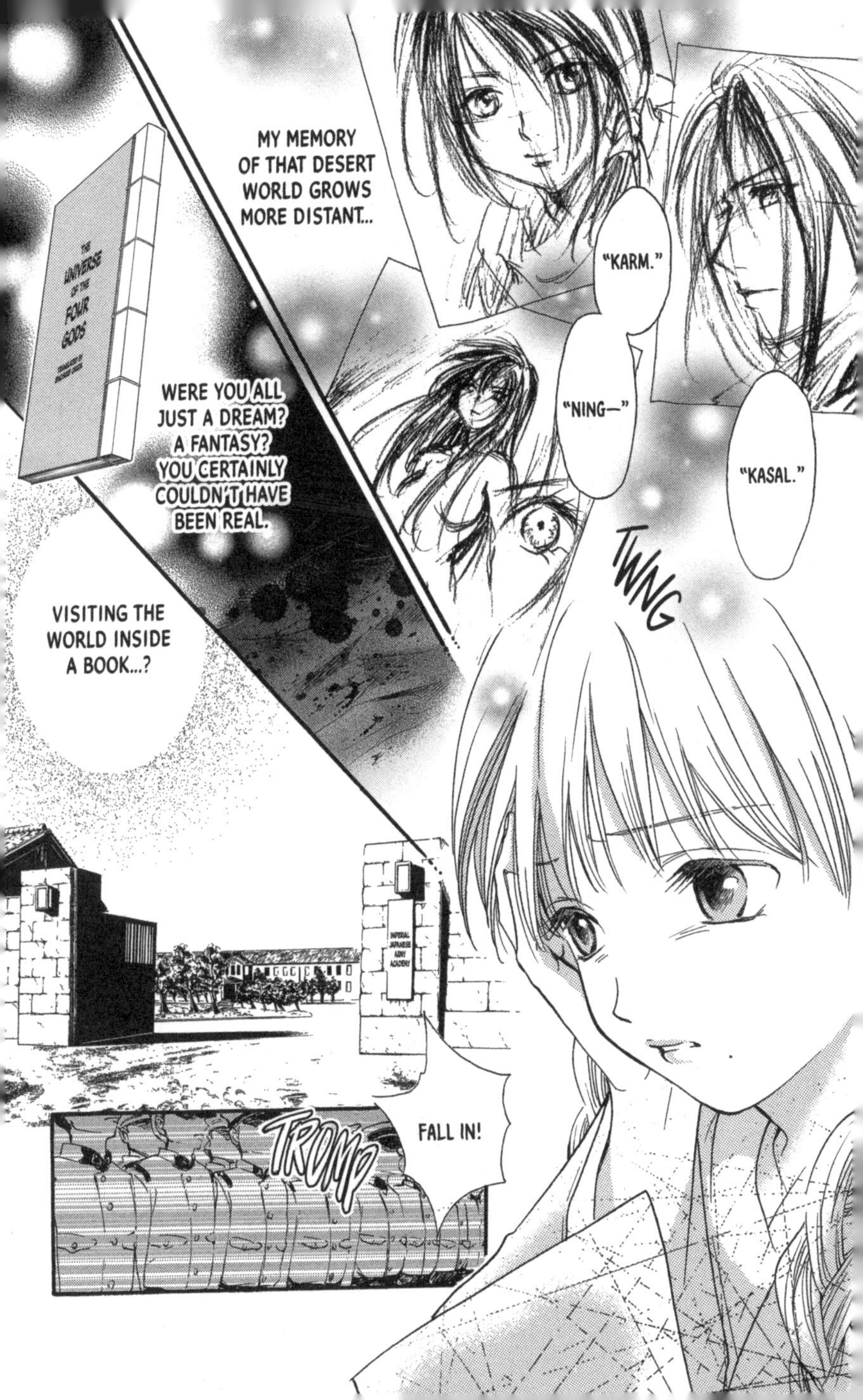
MY MEMORY OF THAT DESERT WORLD GROWS MORE DISTANT...
"KARM."
"KASAL."
"NING—"
TWNG
WERE YOU ALL JUST A DREAM? A FANTASY? YOU CERTAINLY COULDN'T HAVE BEEN REAL.
THE UNIVERSE OF THE FOUR GODS
VISITING THE WORLD INSIDE A BOOK...?
IMPERIAL JAPANESE ARMY ACADEMY
FALL IN!
TROMP

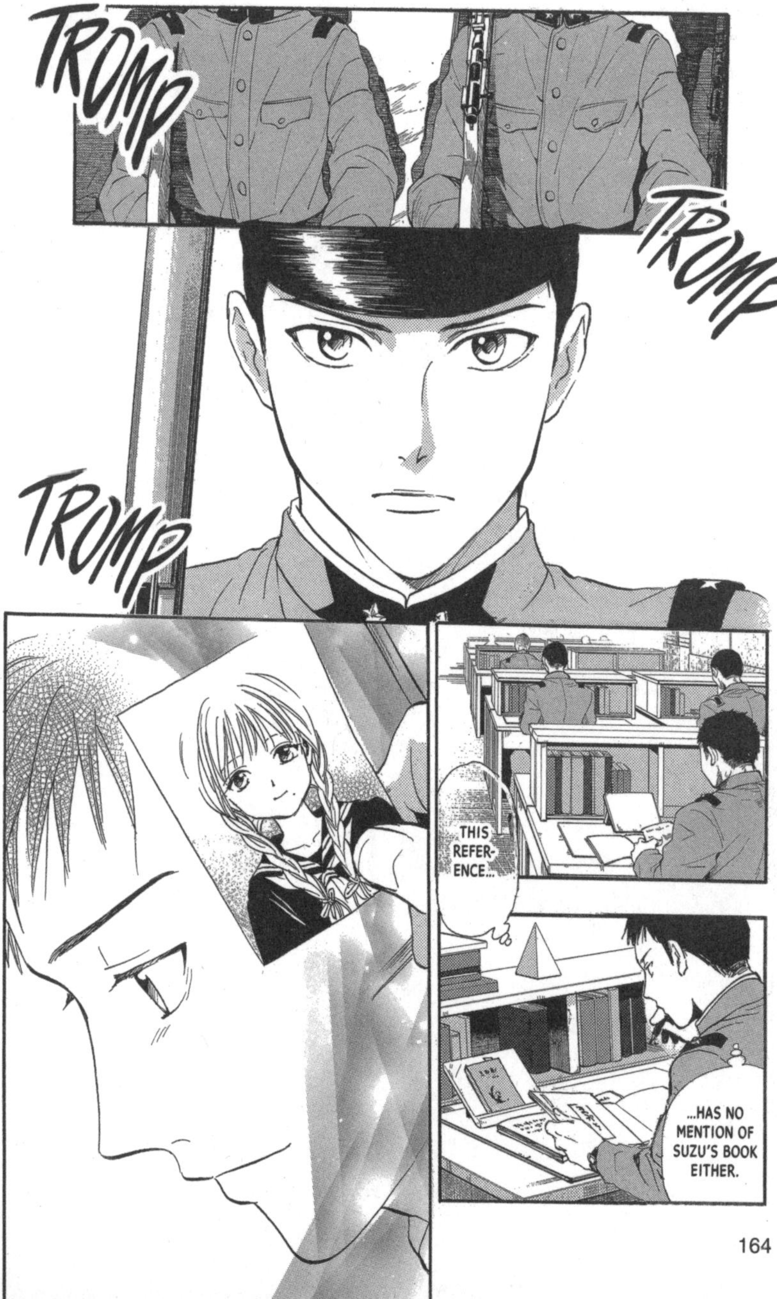
TROMP
TROMP
TROMP
THIS REFERENCE...
...HAS NO MENTION OF SUZU'S BOOK EITHER.

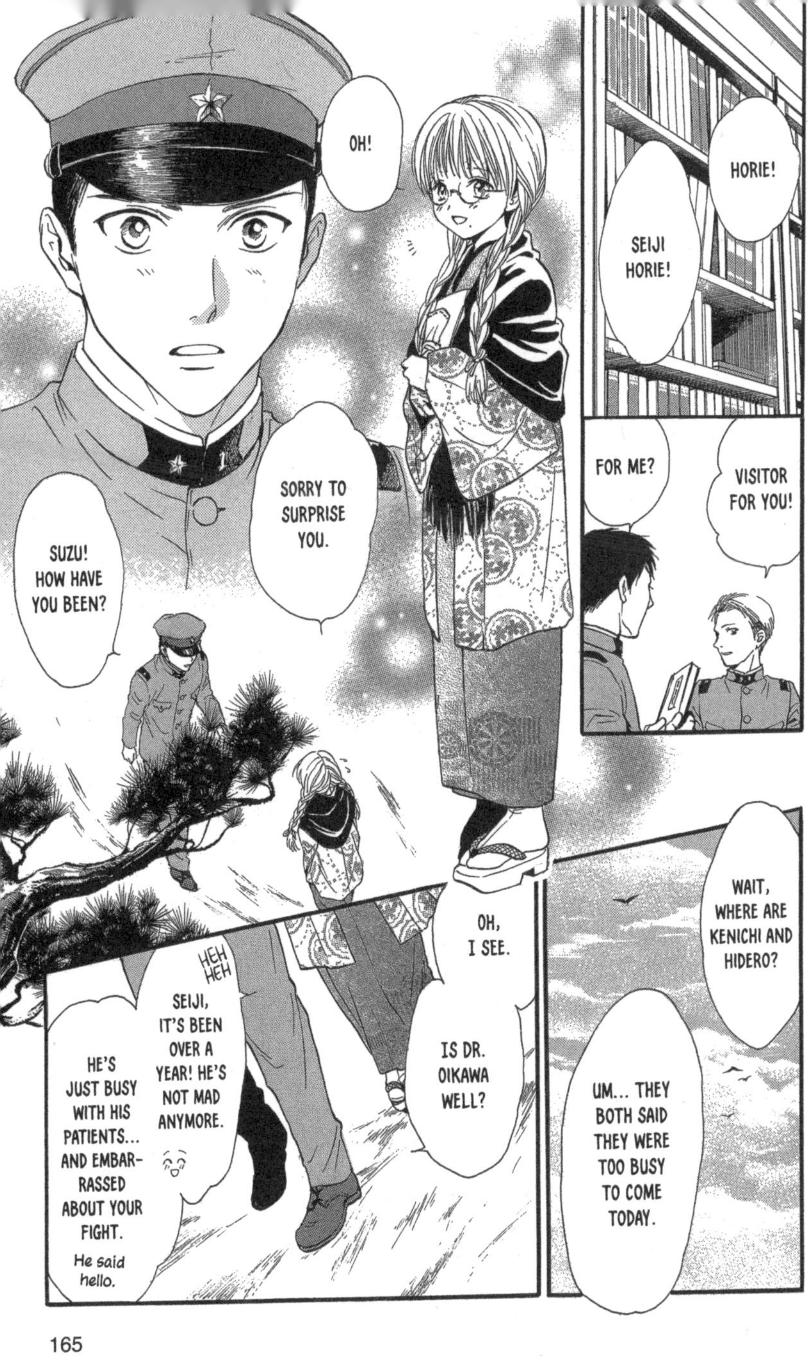
HORIE!
SEIJI HORIE!
VISITOR FOR YOU!
FOR ME?
OH!
SORRY TO SURPRISE YOU.
SUZU! HOW HAVE YOU BEEN?
WAIT, WHERE ARE KENICHI AND HIDERO?
UM... THEY BOTH SAID THEY WERE TOO BUSY TO COME TODAY.
OH, I SEE.
IS DR. OIKAWA WELL?
HEH HEH
SEIJI, IT'S BEEN OVER A YEAR! HE'S NOT MAD ANYMORE.
HE'S JUST BUSY WITH HIS PATIENTS... AND EMBARRASSED ABOUT YOUR FIGHT.
He said hello.

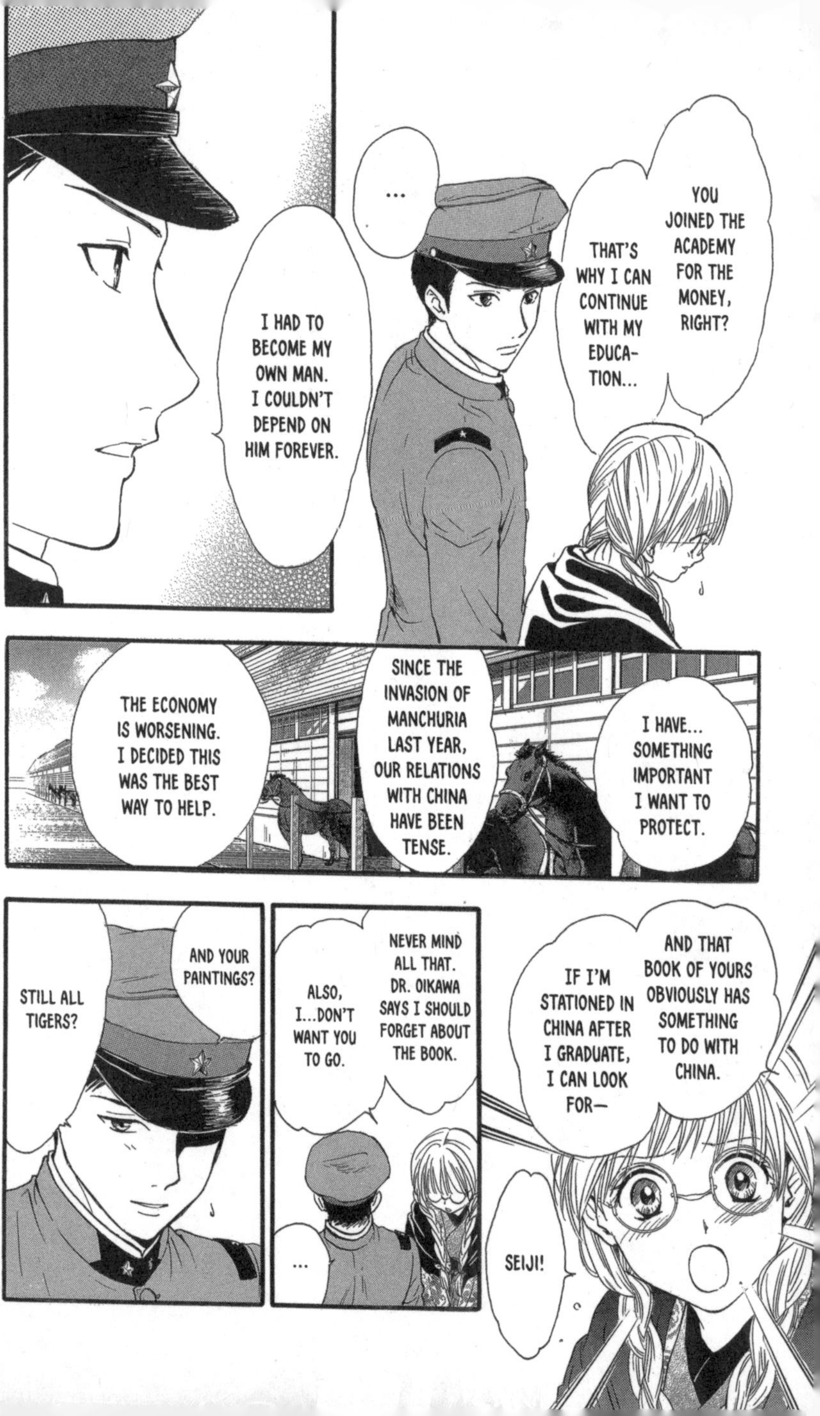
YOU JOINED THE ACADEMY FOR THE MONEY, RIGHT?
THAT'S WHY I CAN CONTINUE WITH MY EDUCATION...
...
I HAD TO BECOME MY OWN MAN. I COULDN'T DEPEND ON HIM FOREVER.
I HAVE... SOMETHING IMPORTANT I WANT TO PROTECT.
SINCE THE INVASION OF MANCHURIA LAST YEAR, OUR RELATIONS WITH CHINA HAVE BEEN TENSE.
THE ECONOMY IS WORSENING. I DECIDED THIS WAS THE BEST WAY TO HELP.
AND THAT BOOK OF YOURS OBVIOUSLY HAS SOMETHING TO DO WITH CHINA.
IF I'M STATIONED IN CHINA AFTER I GRADUATE, I CAN LOOK FOR—
SEIJI!
NEVER MIND ALL THAT. DR. OIKAWA SAYS I SHOULD FORGET ABOUT THE BOOK.
ALSO, I...DON'T WANT YOU TO GO.
...
AND YOUR PAINTINGS?
STILL ALL TIGERS?

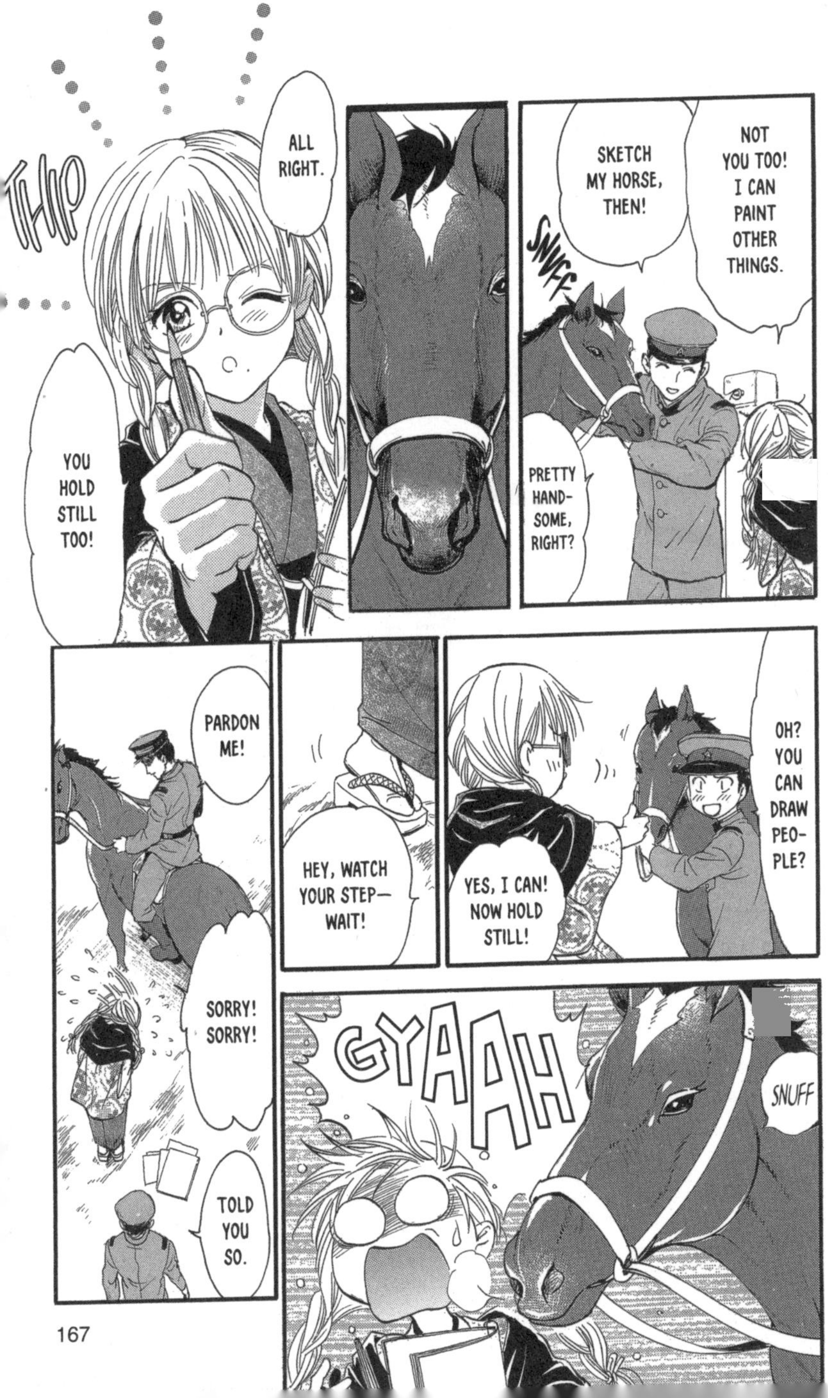
NOT YOU TOO! I CAN PAINT OTHER THINGS.
SKETCH MY HORSE, THEN!
SNUFF
PRETTY HAND-SOME, RIGHT?
ALL RIGHT.
THIP
YOU HOLD STILL TOO!
OH? YOU CAN DRAW PEO-PLE?
YES, I CAN! NOW HOLD STILL!
HEY, WATCH YOUR STEP— WAIT!
SNUFF
GYAAH
PARDON ME!
SORRY! SORRY!
TOLD YOU SO.

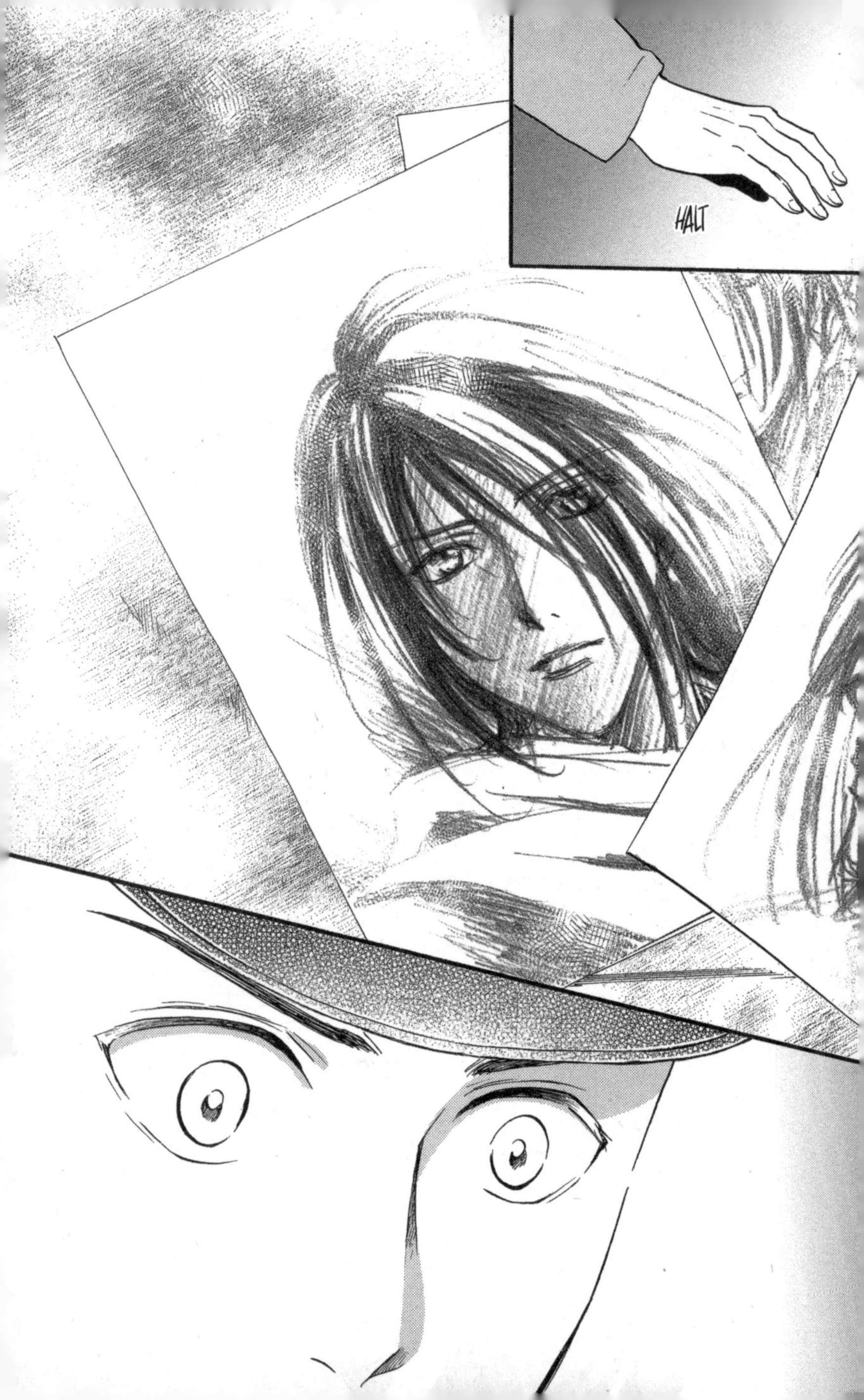
HALT

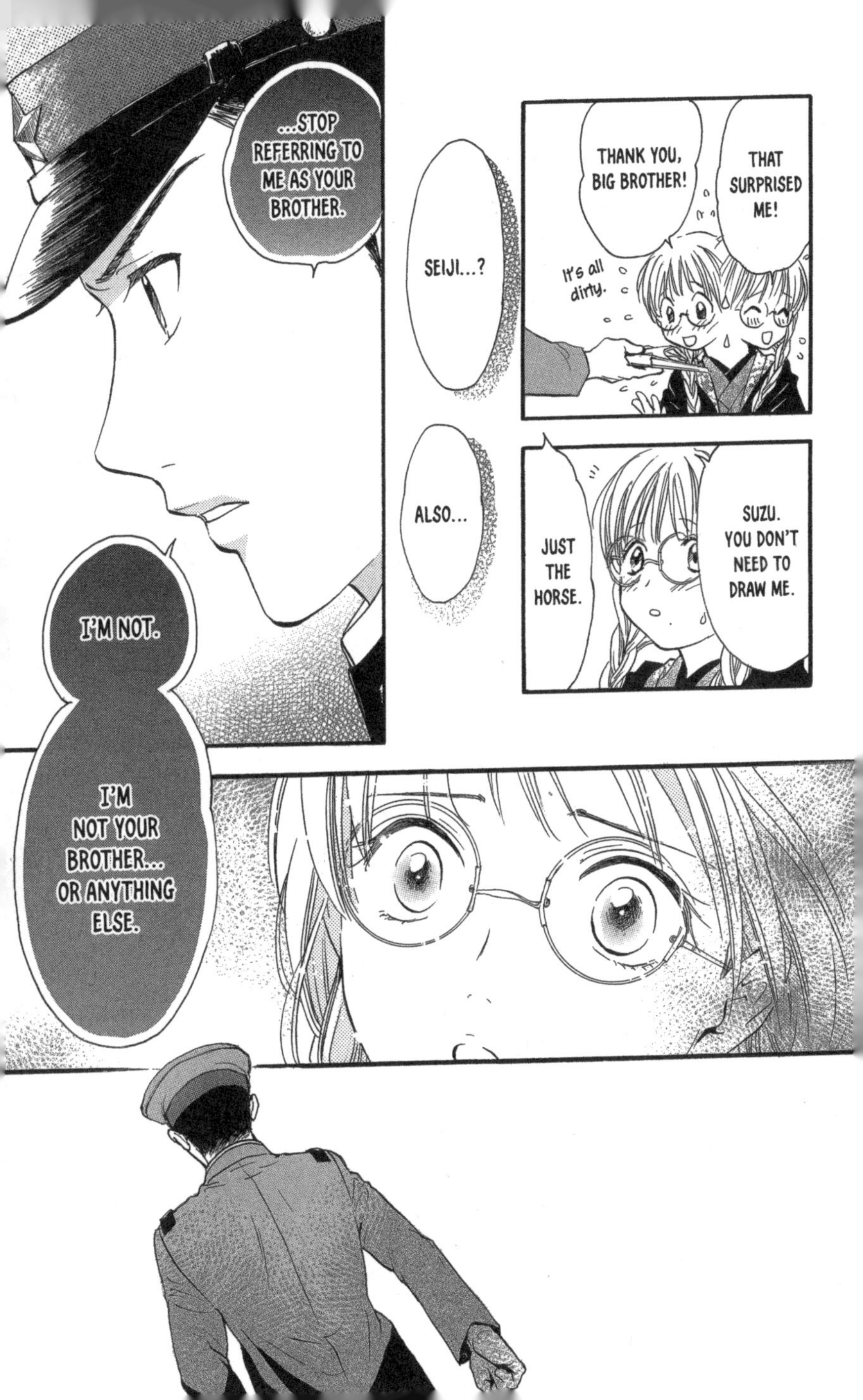
THAT SURPRISED ME!
THANK YOU, BIG BROTHER!
It's all dirty.
SEIJI...?
SUZU. YOU DON'T NEED TO DRAW ME.
JUST THE HORSE.
ALSO...
...STOP REFERRING TO ME AS YOUR BROTHER.
I'M NOT.
I'M NOT YOUR BROTHER... OR ANYTHING ELSE.

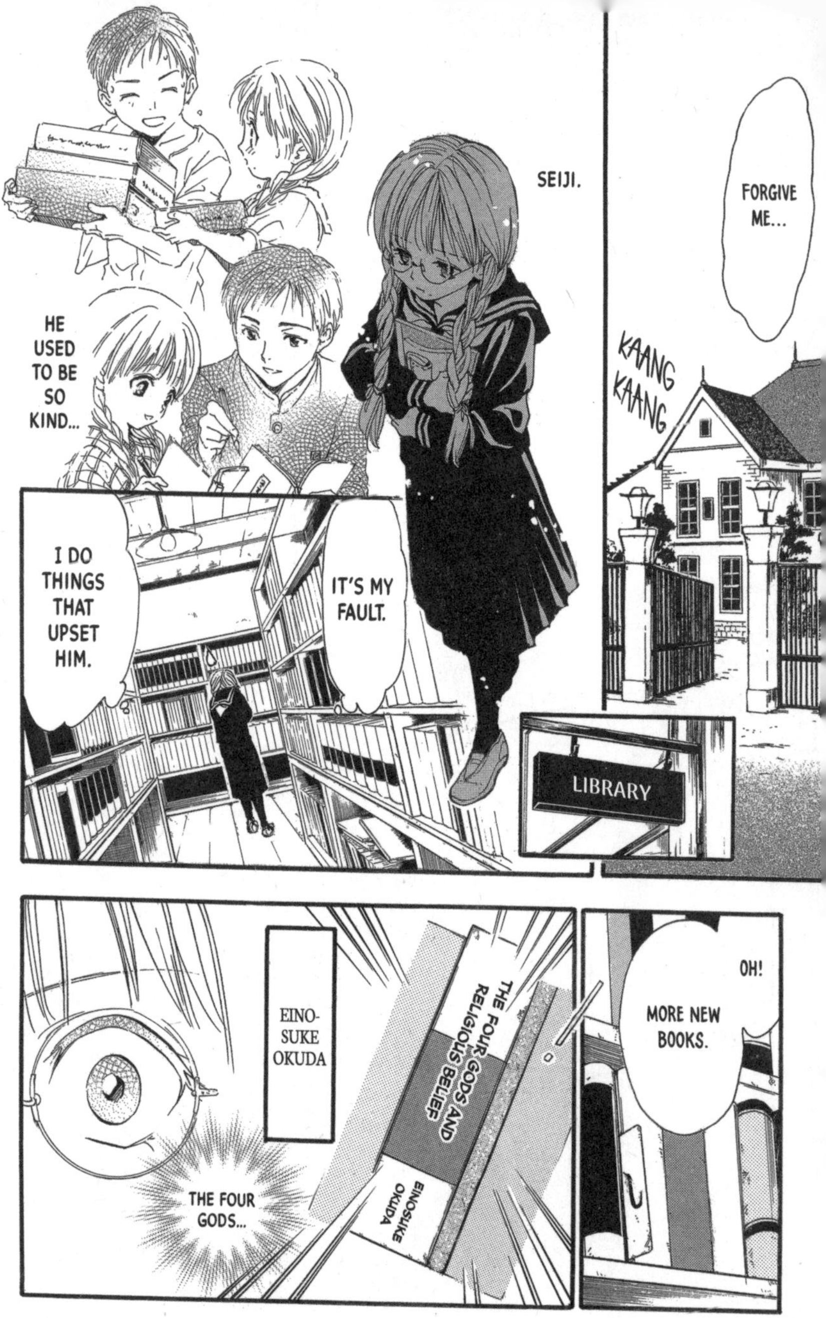
FORGIVE ME...
KAANG KAANG
SEIJI.
HE USED TO BE SO KIND...
LIBRARY
IT'S MY FAULT.
I DO THINGS THAT UPSET HIM.
OH!
MORE NEW BOOKS.
EINO-SUKE OKUDA
THE FOUR GODS AND RELIGIOUS BELIEF
EINOSUKE OKUDA
THE FOUR GODS...

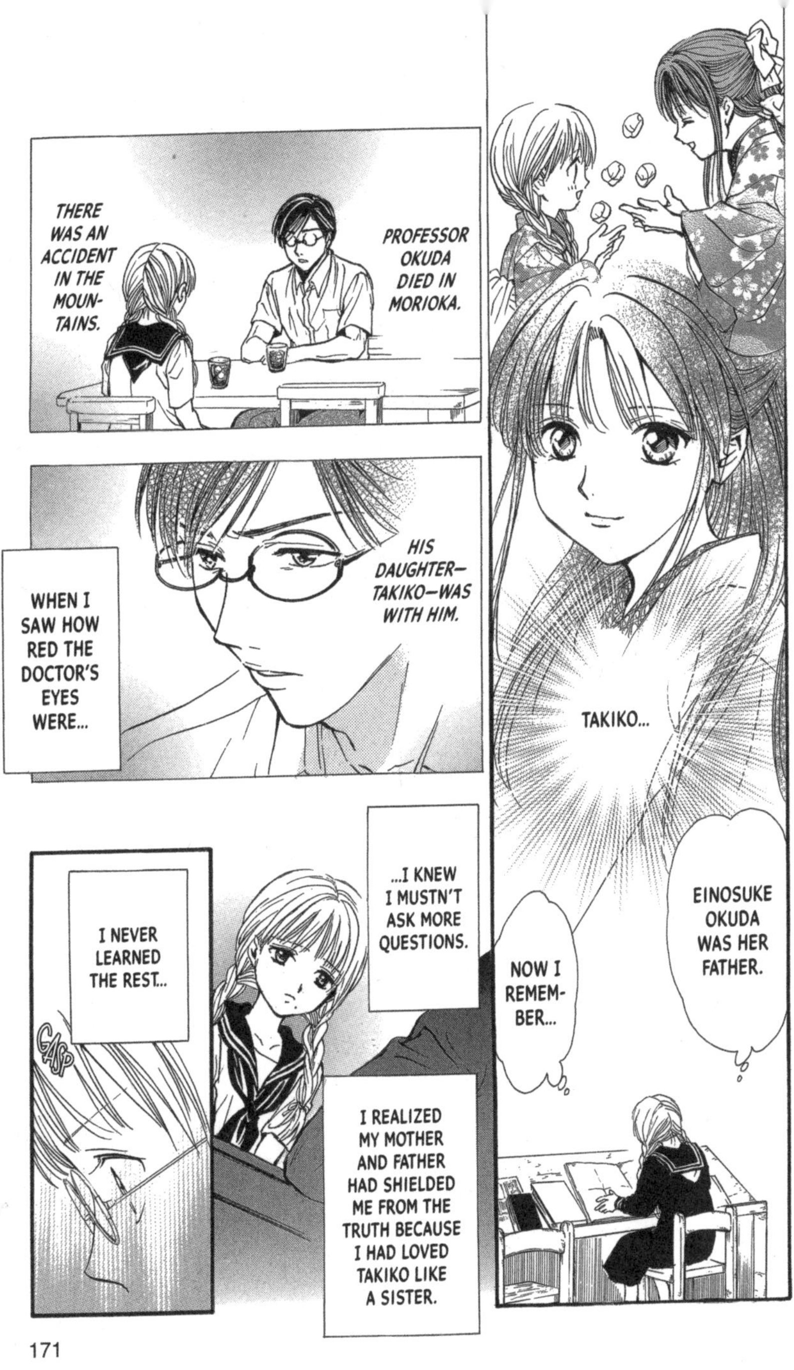
TAKIKO...
EINOSUKE OKUDA WAS HER FATHER.
NOW I REMEMBER...
PROFESSOR OKUDA DIED IN MORIOKA.
THERE WAS AN ACCIDENT IN THE MOUNTAINS.
HIS DAUGHTER—TAKIKO—WAS WITH HIM.
WHEN I SAW HOW RED THE DOCTOR'S EYES WERE...
...I KNEW I MUSTN'T ASK MORE QUESTIONS.
I NEVER LEARNED THE REST...
GASP
I REALIZED MY MOTHER AND FATHER HAD SHIELDED ME FROM THE TRUTH BECAUSE I HAD LOVED TAKIKO LIKE A SISTER.

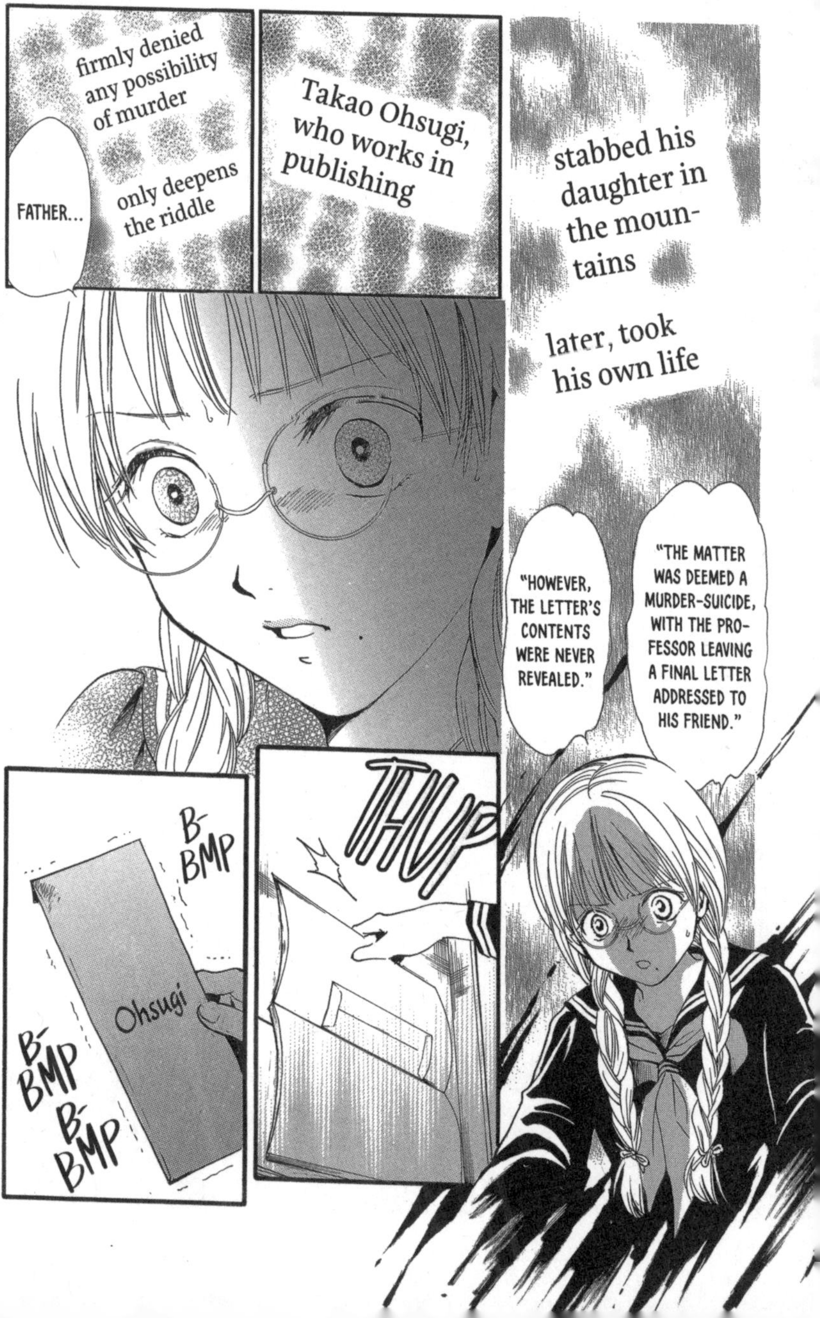
stabbed his daughter in the mountains
later, took his own life
"THE MATTER WAS DEEMED A MURDER-SUICIDE, WITH THE PROFESSOR LEAVING A FINAL LETTER ADDRESSED TO HIS FRIEND."
"HOWEVER, THE LETTER'S CONTENTS WERE NEVER REVEALED."
Takao Ohsugi, who works in publishing
firmly denied any possibility of murder
only deepens the riddle
FATHER...
THUP
B-BMP
Ohsugi
B-BMP B-BMP

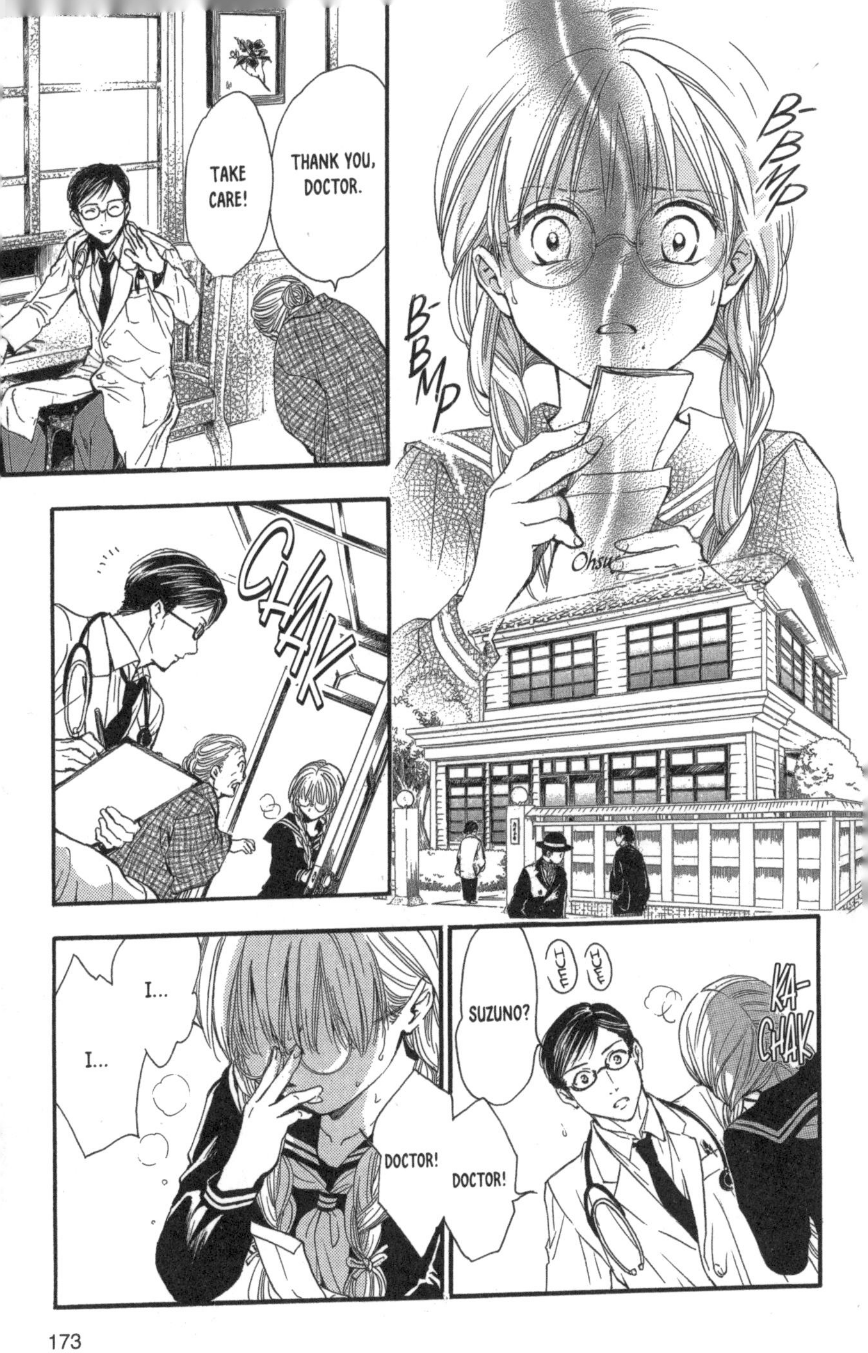
B-BBMP
B-BBMP
Ohsu
THANK YOU, DOCTOR.
TAKE CARE!
CHAK
KA-CHAK
HUFF
HUFF
SUZUNO?
I...
I...
DOCTOR!
DOCTOR!

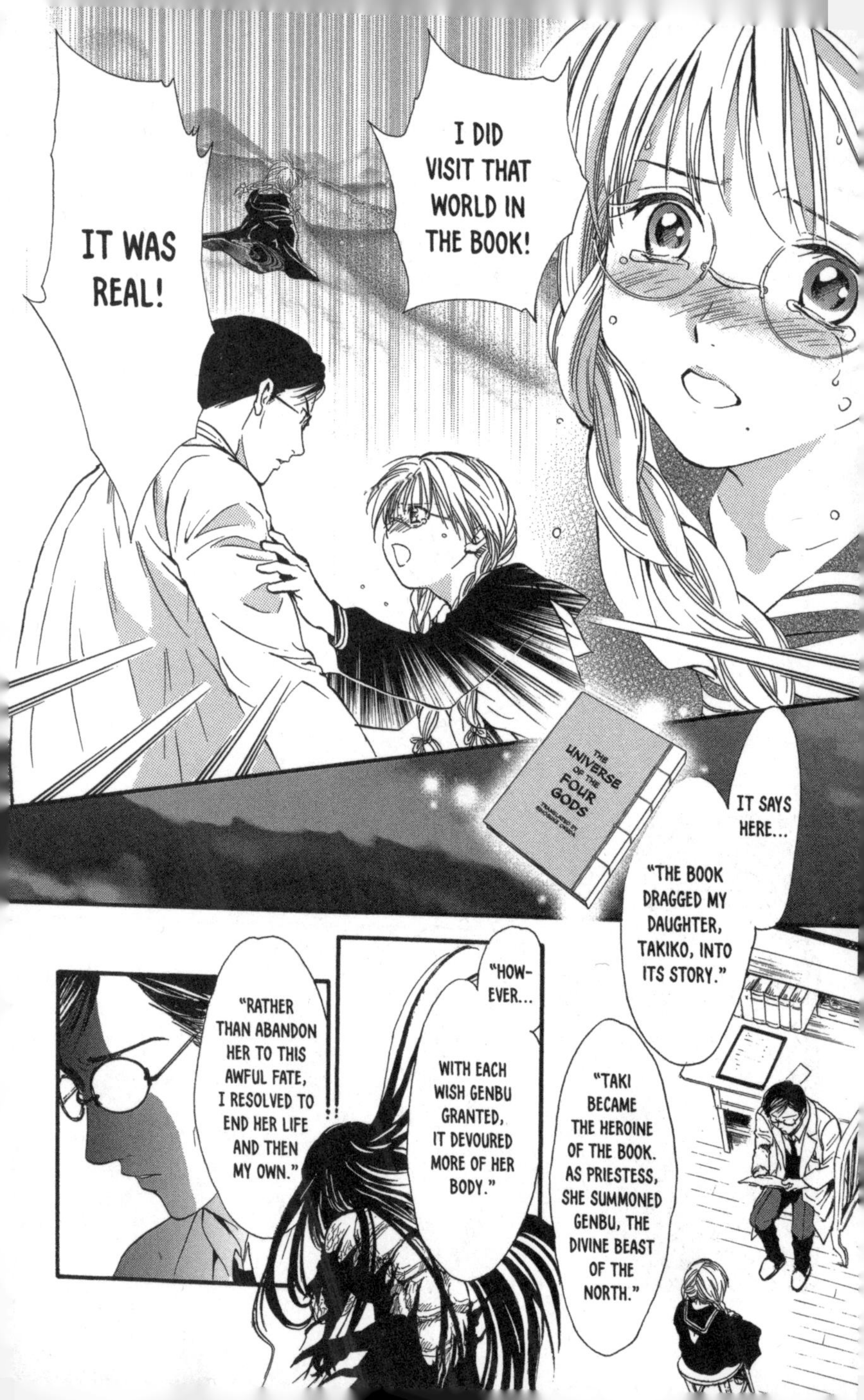
I DID VISIT THAT WORLD IN THE BOOK!
IT WAS REAL!
IT SAYS HERE...
THE UNIVERSE OF THE FOUR GODS
"THE BOOK DRAGGED MY DAUGHTER, TAKIKO, INTO ITS STORY."
"TAKI BECAME THE HEROINE OF THE BOOK. AS PRIESTESS, SHE SUMMONED GENBU, THE DIVINE BEAST OF THE NORTH."
"HOW-EVER...
WITH EACH WISH GENBU GRANTED, IT DEVOURED MORE OF HER BODY."
"RATHER THAN ABANDON HER TO THIS AWFUL FATE, I RESOLVED TO END HER LIFE AND THEN MY OWN."

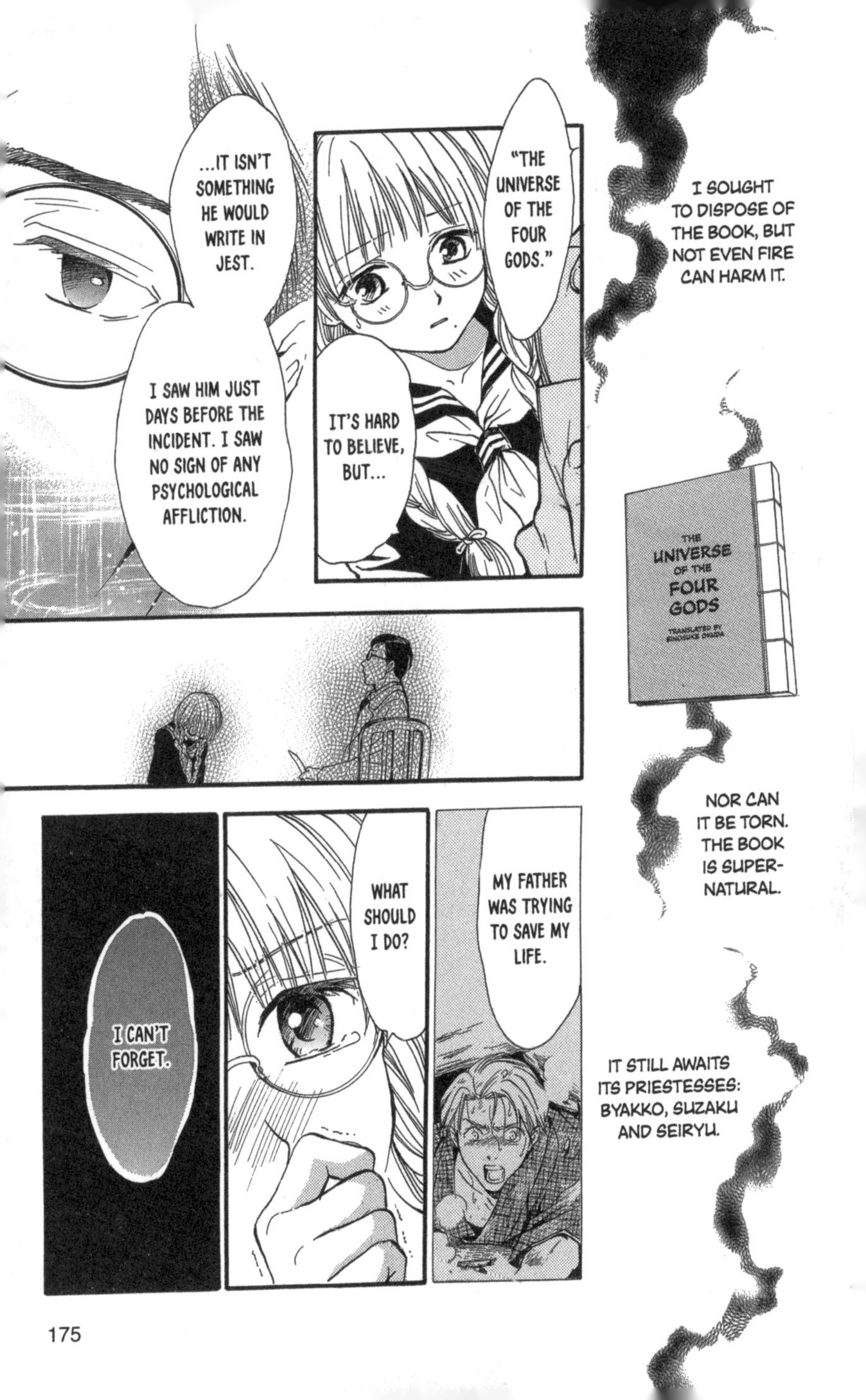
I SOUGHT TO DISPOSE OF THE BOOK, BUT NOT EVEN FIRE CAN HARM IT.
THE UNIVERSE OF THE FOUR GODS
NOR CAN IT BE TORN. THE BOOK IS SUPER-NATURAL.
IT STILL AWAITS ITS PRIESTESSES: BYAKKO, SUZAKU AND SEIRYU.
"THE UNIVERSE OF THE FOUR GODS."
IT'S HARD TO BELIEVE, BUT...
...IT ISN'T SOMETHING HE WOULD WRITE IN JEST.
I SAW HIM JUST DAYS BEFORE THE INCIDENT. I SAW NO SIGN OF ANY PSYCHOLOGICAL AFFLICTION.
MY FATHER WAS TRYING TO SAVE MY LIFE.
WHAT SHOULD I DO?
I CAN'T FORGET.

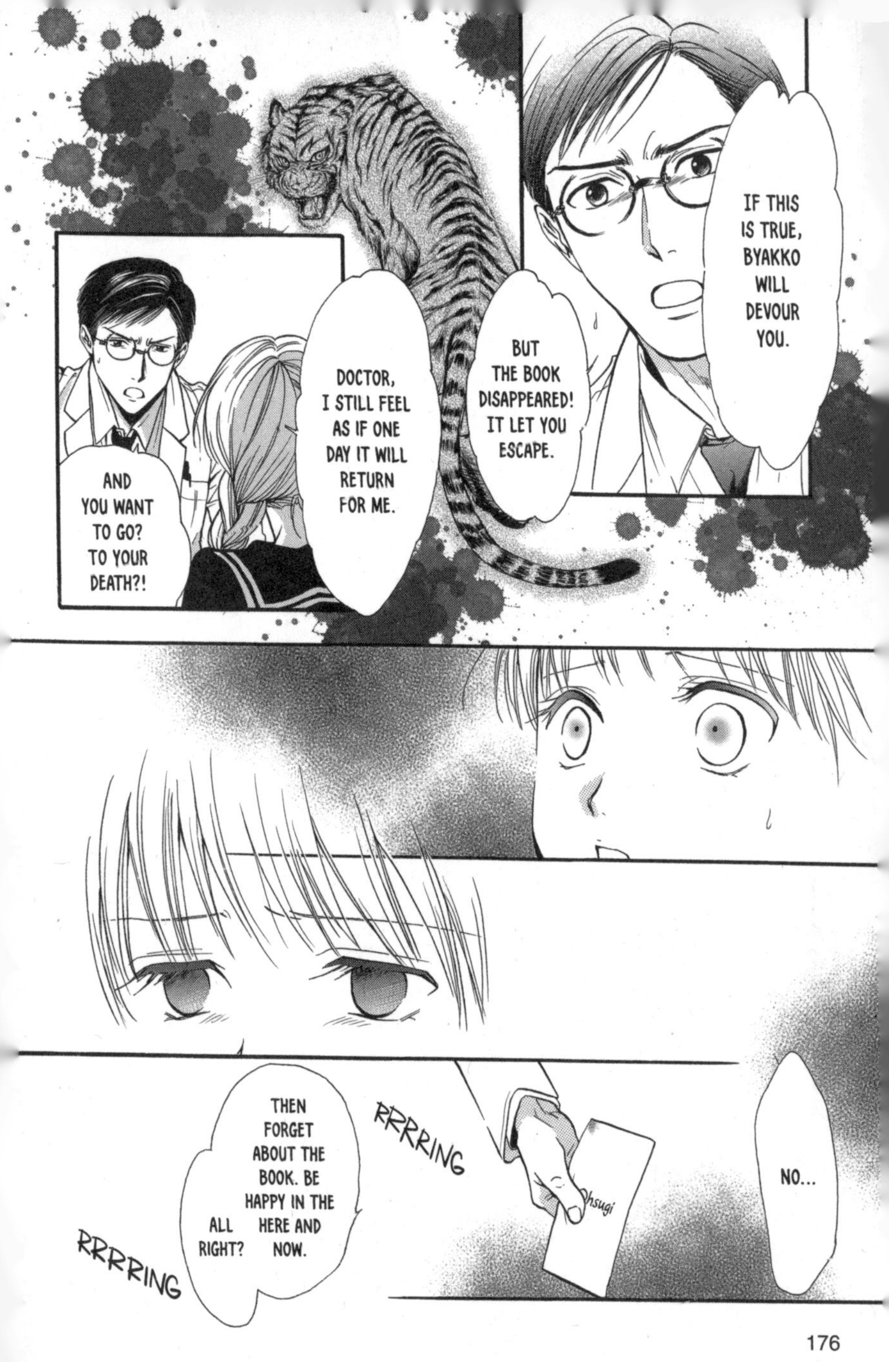
IF THIS IS TRUE, BYAKKO WILL DEVOUR YOU.
BUT THE BOOK DISAPPEARED! IT LET YOU ESCAPE.
DOCTOR, I STILL FEEL AS IF ONE DAY IT WILL RETURN FOR ME.
AND YOU WANT TO GO? TO YOUR DEATH?!
NO...
Ohsugi
RRRRING
THEN FORGET ABOUT THE BOOK. BE HAPPY IN THE HERE AND NOW.
ALL RIGHT?
RRRRING

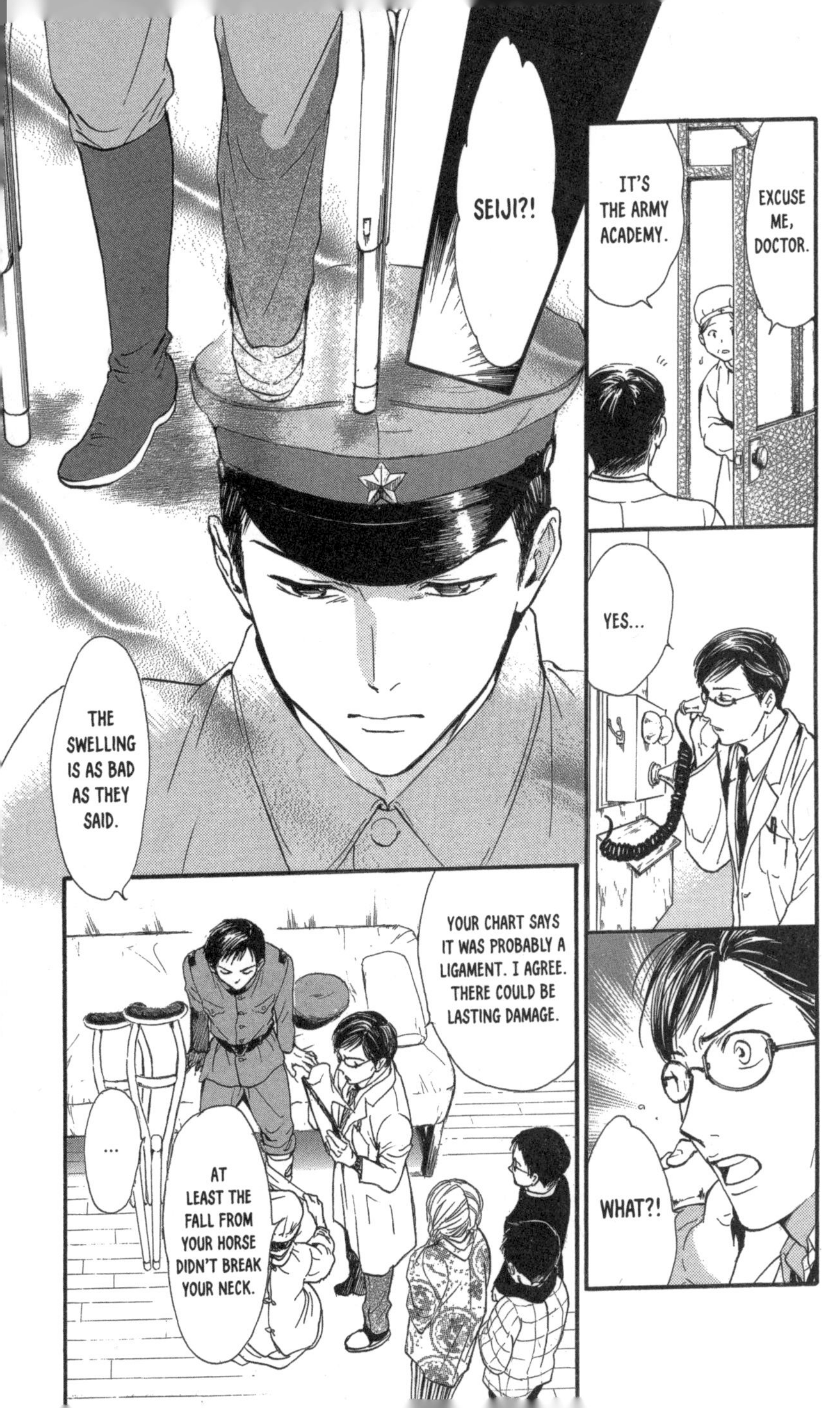
EXCUSE ME, DOCTOR.
IT'S THE ARMY ACADEMY.
YES...
WHAT?!
SEIJI?!
THE SWELLING IS AS BAD AS THEY SAID.
YOUR CHART SAYS IT WAS PROBABLY A LIGAMENT. I AGREE. THERE COULD BE LASTING DAMAGE.
AT LEAST THE FALL FROM YOUR HORSE DIDN'T BREAK YOUR NECK.
...

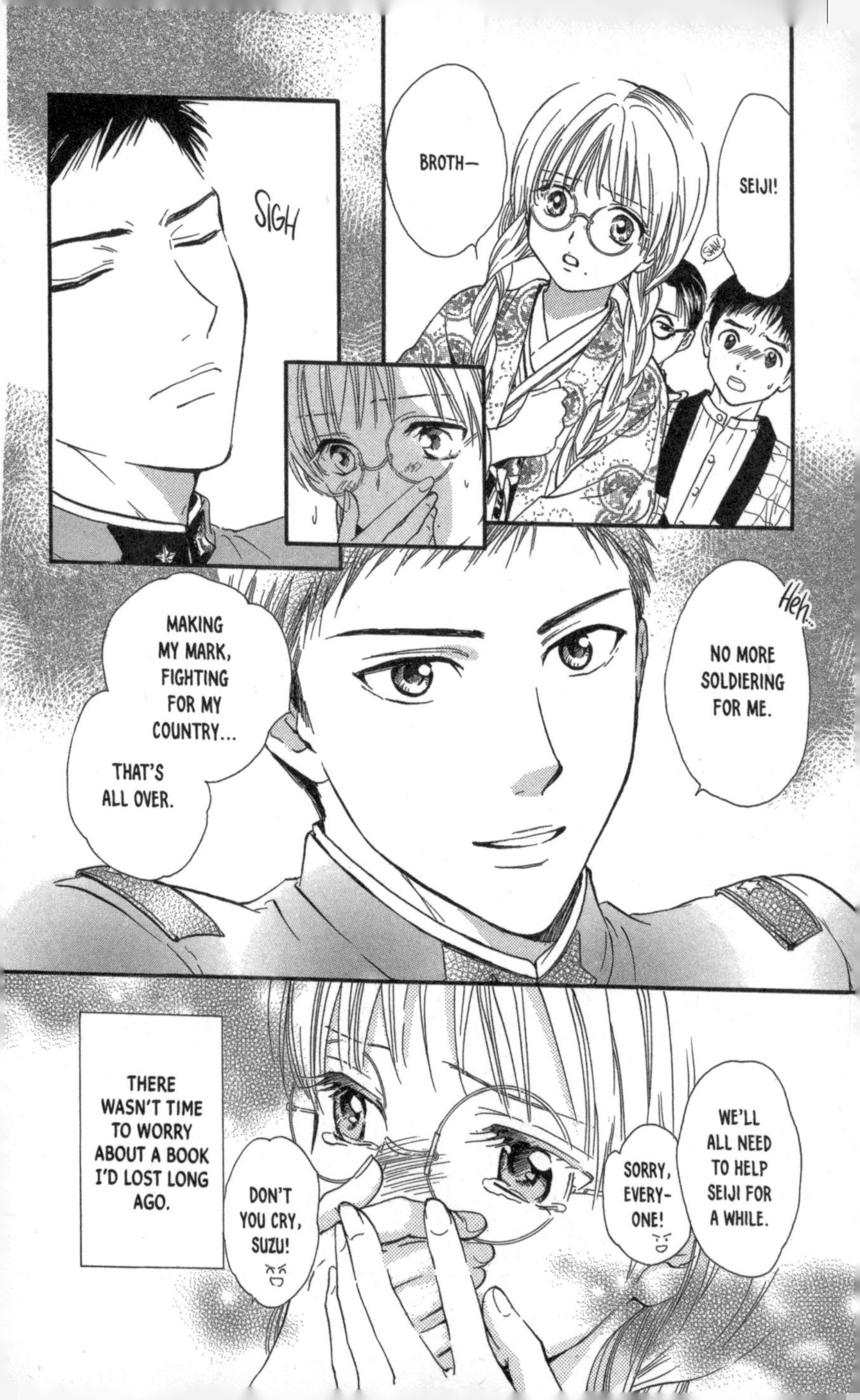
BROTH—
SEIJI!
SHH!
SIGH
Heh..
NO MORE SOLDIERING FOR ME.
MAKING MY MARK, FIGHTING FOR MY COUNTRY...
THAT'S ALL OVER.
WE'LL ALL NEED TO HELP SEIJI FOR A WHILE.
SORRY, EVERY-ONE!
DON'T YOU CRY, SUZU!
THERE WASN'T TIME TO WORRY ABOUT A BOOK I'D LOST LONG AGO.

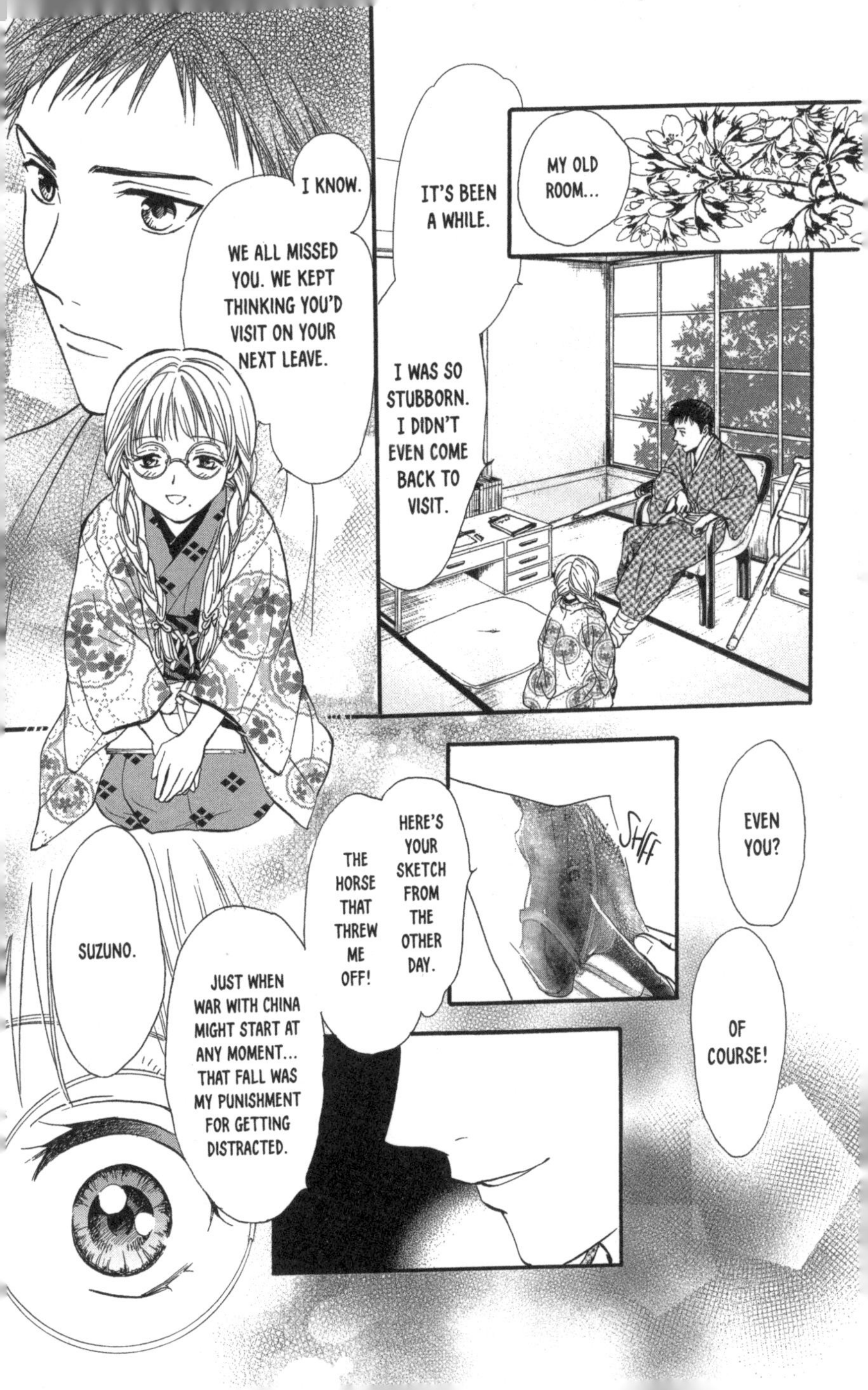
MY OLD ROOM...
IT'S BEEN A WHILE.
I WAS SO STUBBORN. I DIDN'T EVEN COME BACK TO VISIT.
I KNOW.
WE ALL MISSED YOU. WE KEPT THINKING YOU'D VISIT ON YOUR NEXT LEAVE.
EVEN YOU?
OF COURSE!
SHFF
HERE'S YOUR SKETCH FROM THE OTHER DAY.
THE HORSE THAT THREW ME OFF!
JUST WHEN WAR WITH CHINA MIGHT START AT ANY MOMENT... THAT FALL WAS MY PUNISHMENT FOR GETTING DISTRACTED.
SUZUNO.

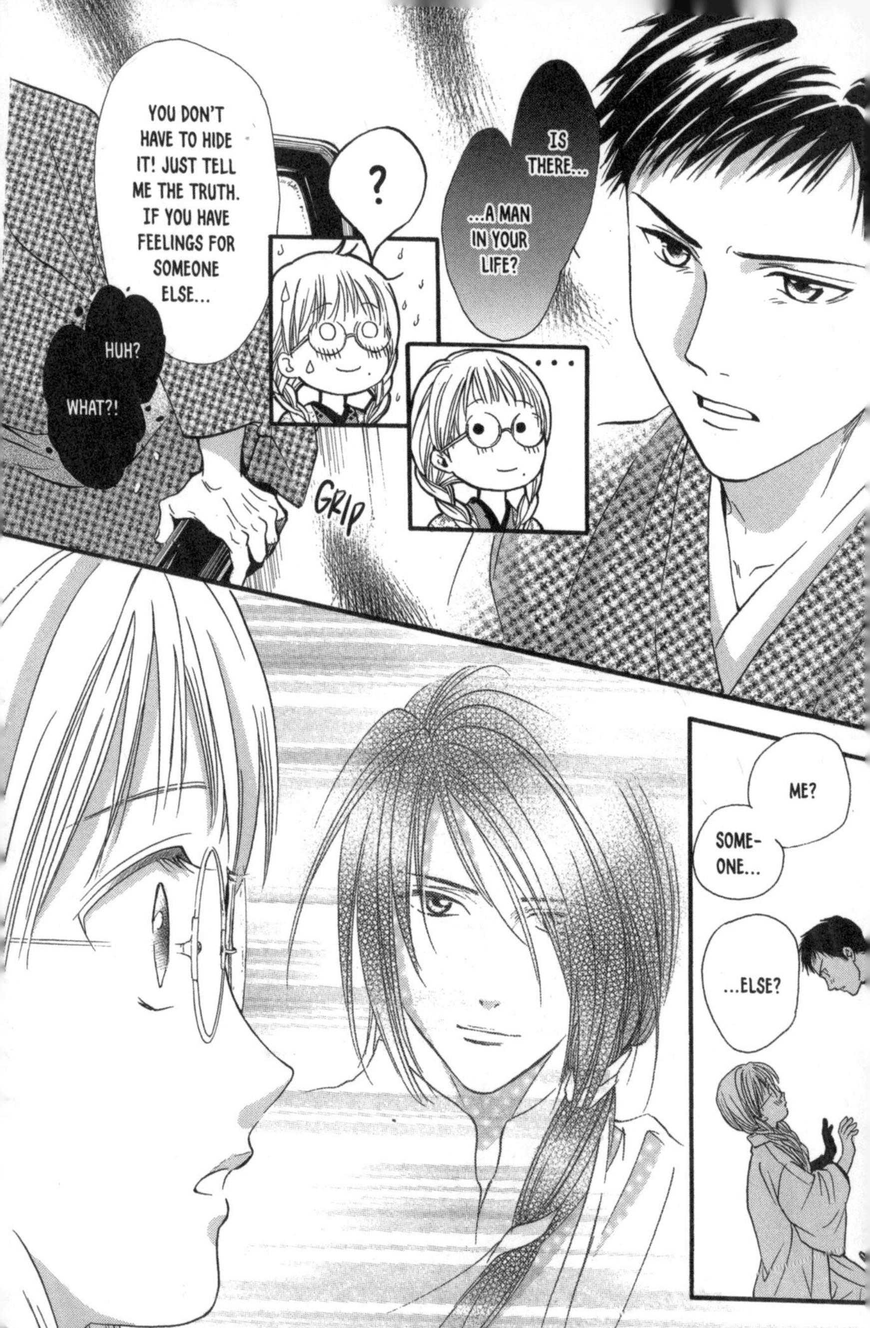
IS THERE...
...A MAN IN YOUR LIFE?
. . .
?
YOU DON'T HAVE TO HIDE IT! JUST TELL ME THE TRUTH. IF YOU HAVE FEELINGS FOR SOMEONE ELSE...
HUH?
WHAT?!
GRIP
ME?
SOME-ONE...
...ELSE?

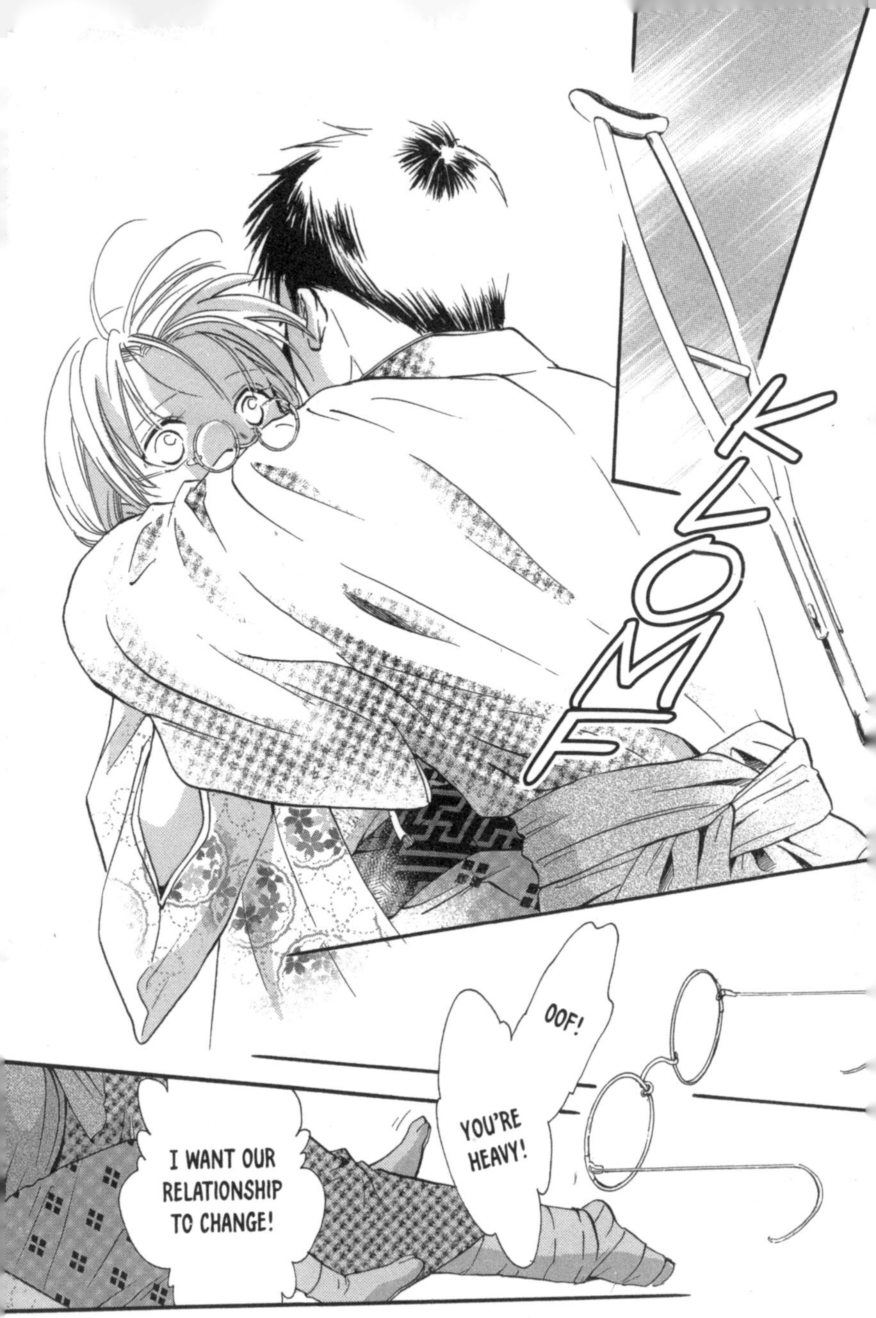
OOF!
YOU'RE HEAVY!
I WANT OUR RELATIONSHIP TO CHANGE!

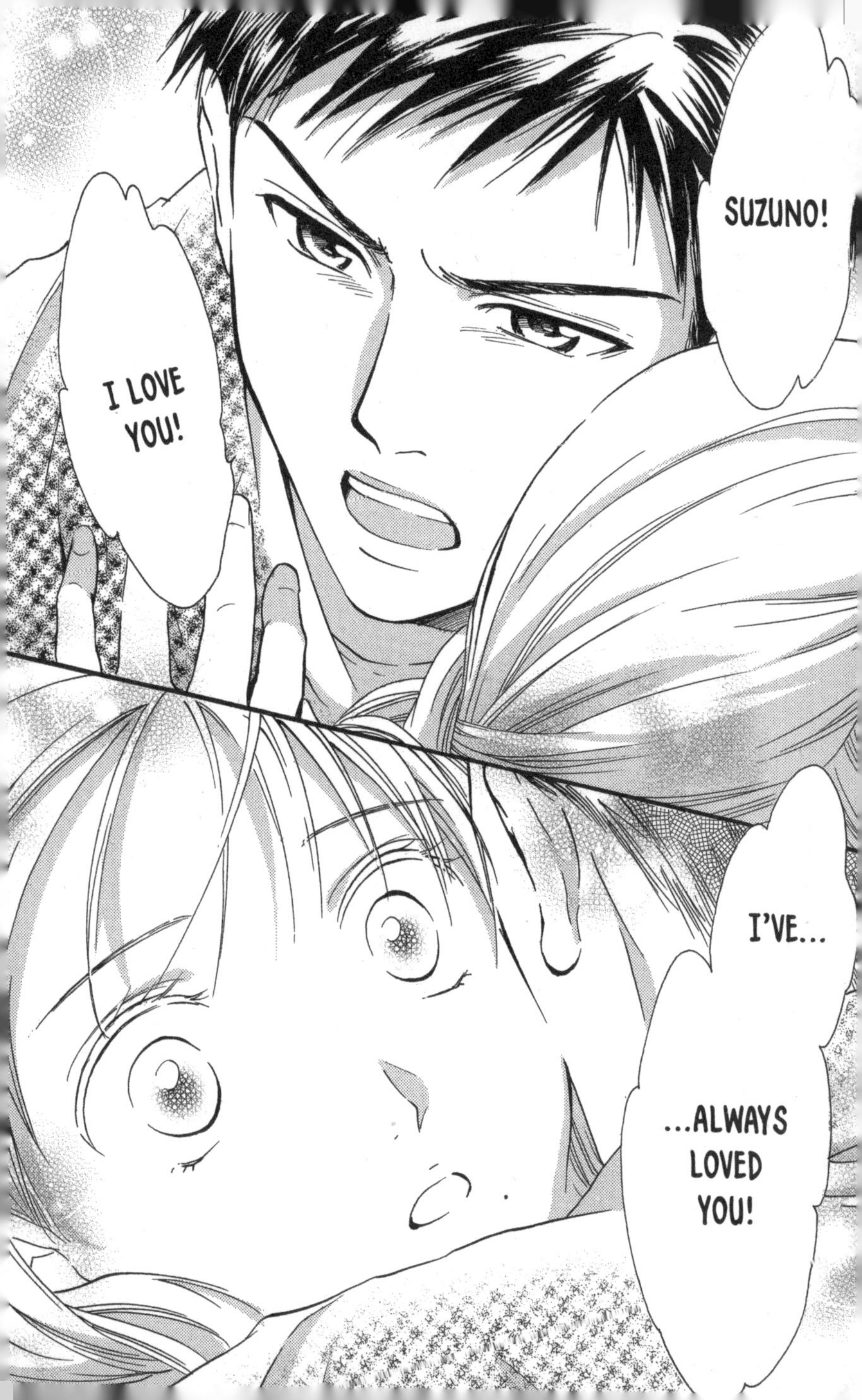
SUZUNO!
I LOVE YOU!
I'VE...
...ALWAYS LOVED YOU!

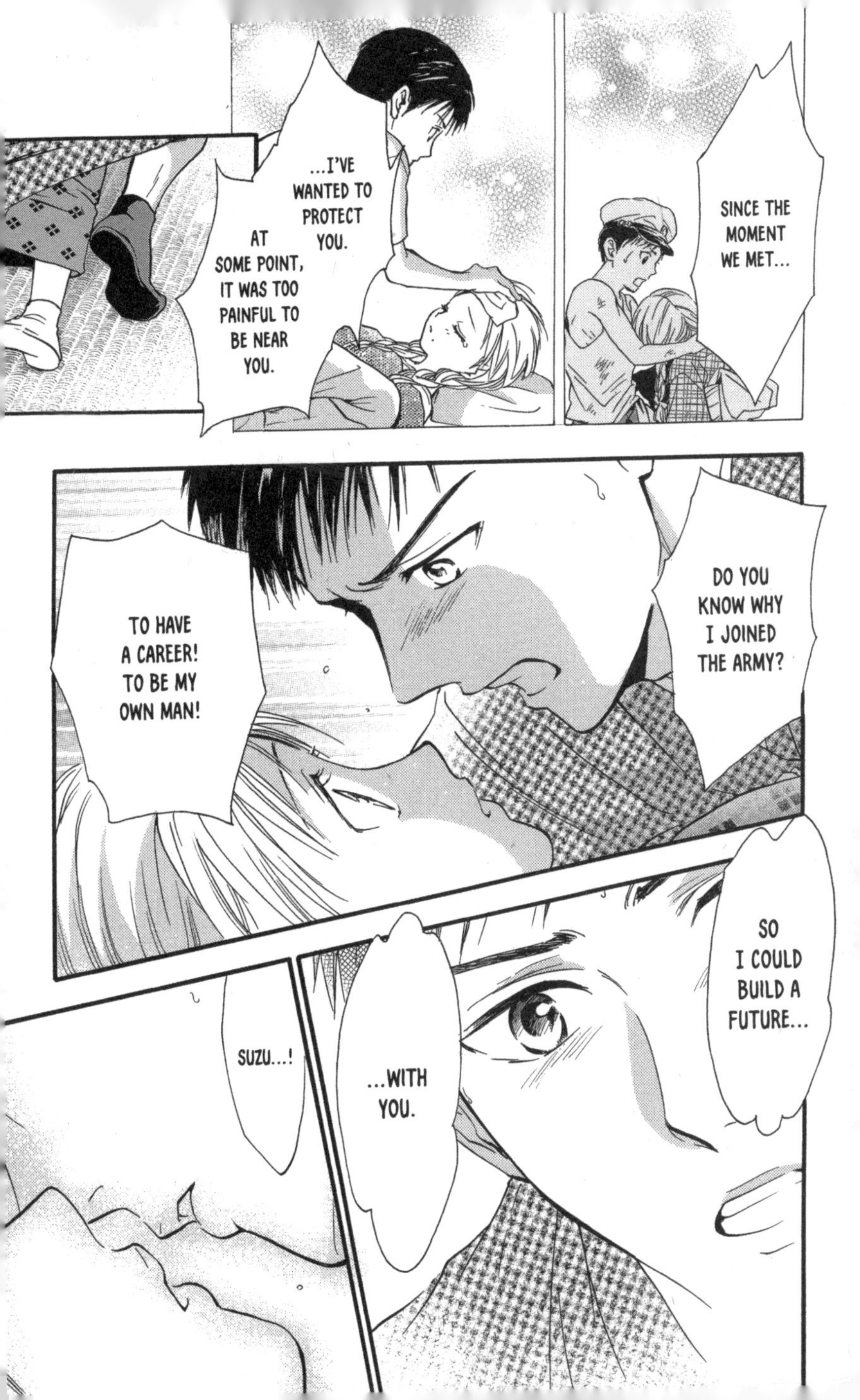
SINCE THE MOMENT WE MET...
...I'VE WANTED TO PROTECT YOU.
AT SOME POINT, IT WAS TOO PAINFUL TO BE NEAR YOU.
DO YOU KNOW WHY I JOINED THE ARMY?
TO HAVE A CAREER! TO BE MY OWN MAN!
SO I COULD BUILD A FUTURE...
...WITH YOU.
SUZU...!

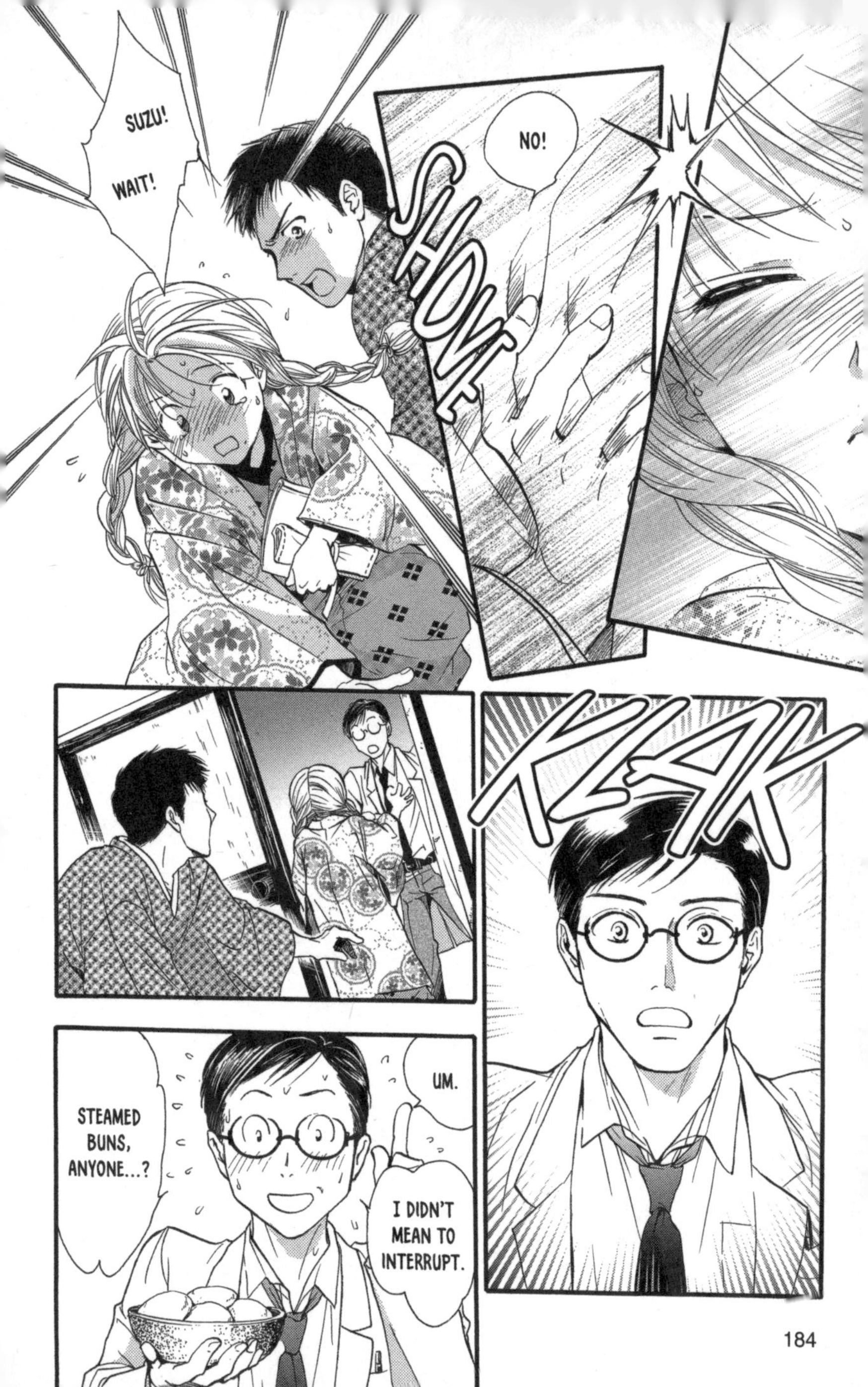
NO!
SHOVE
SUZU!
WAIT!
KLAK
UM.
I DIDN'T MEAN TO INTERRUPT.
STEAMED BUNS, ANYONE...?

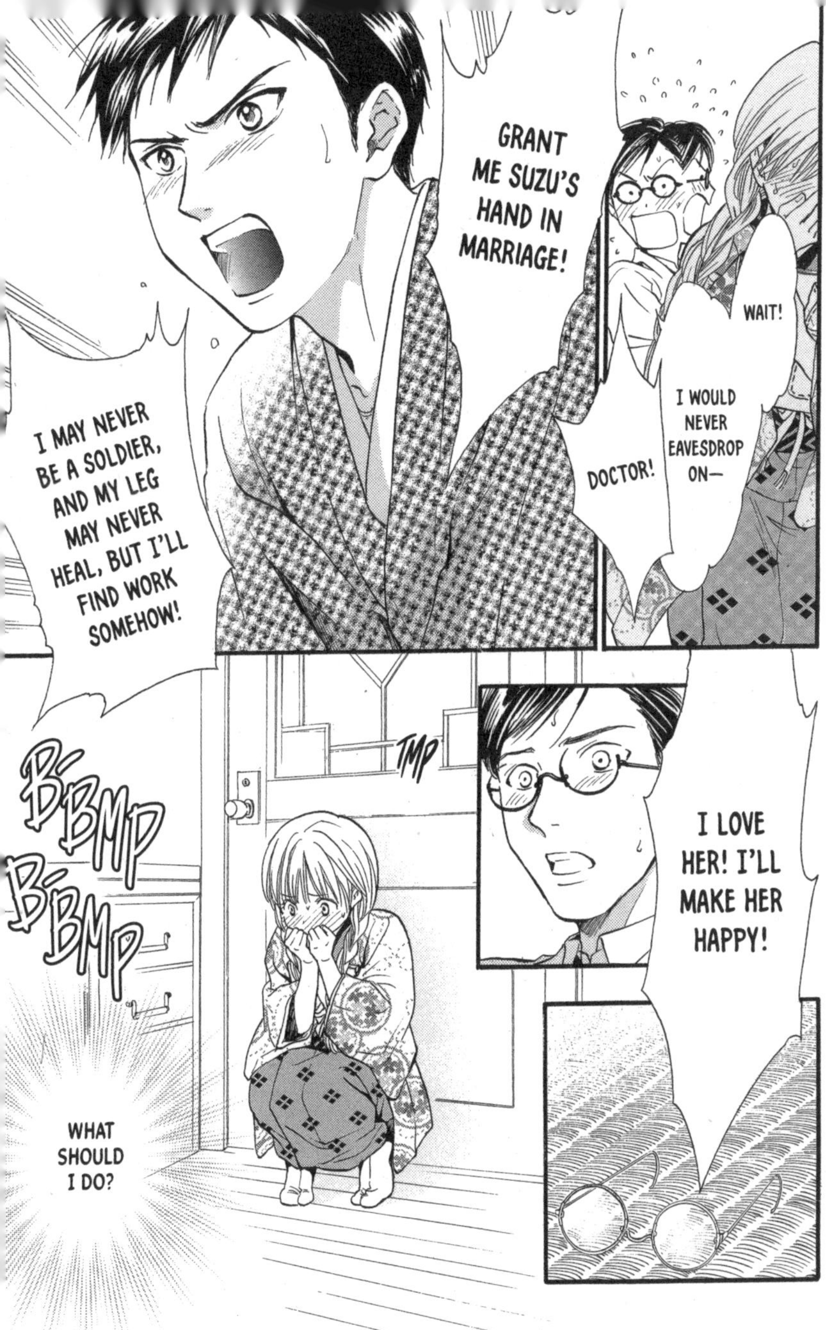
WAIT!
I WOULD NEVER EAVESDROP ON—
DOCTOR!
GRANT ME SUZU'S HAND IN MARRIAGE!
I MAY NEVER BE A SOLDIER, AND MY LEG MAY NEVER HEAL, BUT I'LL FIND WORK SOMEHOW!
I LOVE HER! I'LL MAKE HER HAPPY!
TMP
B-BMP
B-BMP
WHAT SHOULD I DO?

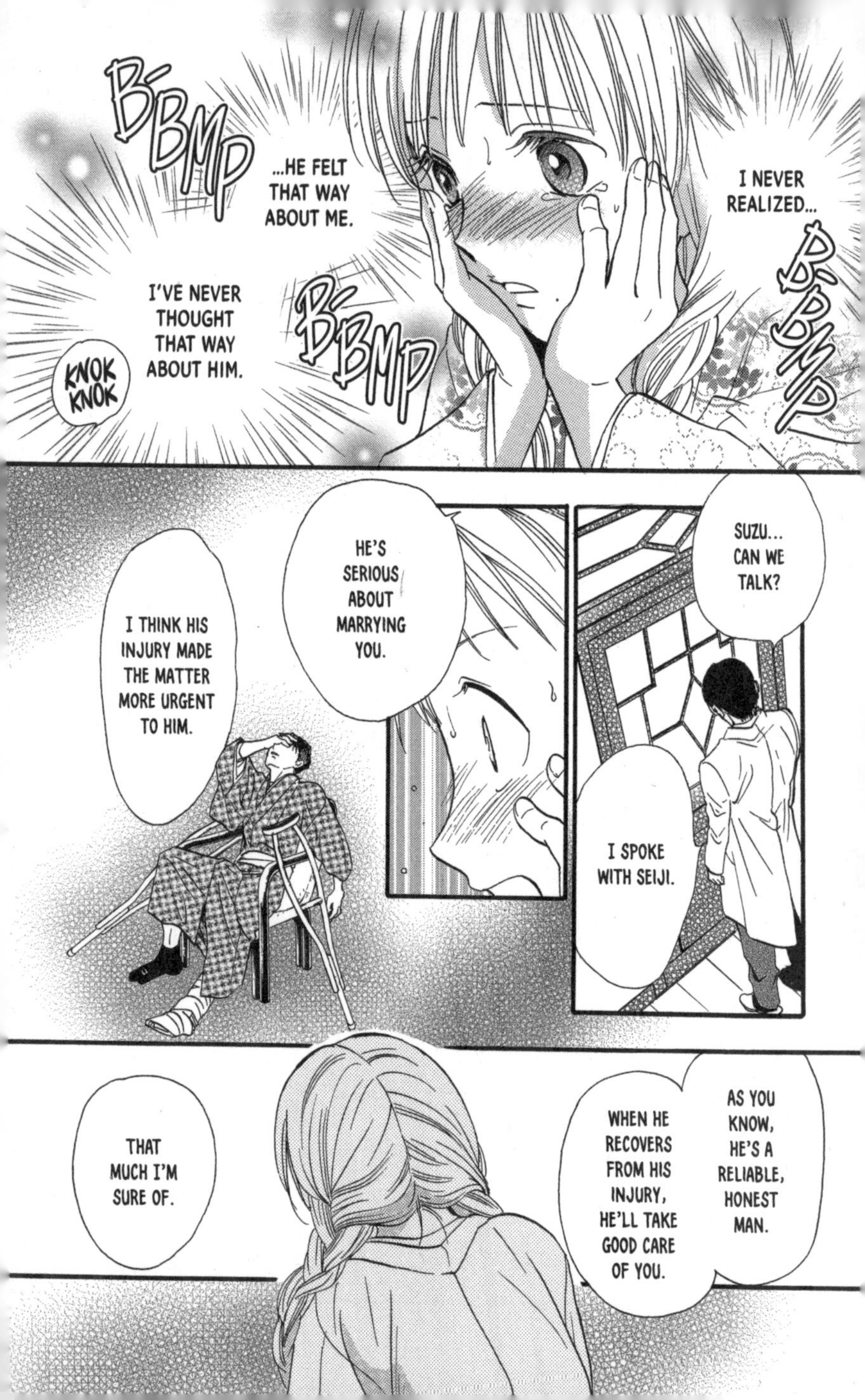
I NEVER REALIZED...
B'-BMP
...HE FELT THAT WAY ABOUT ME.
B'-BMP
B'-BMP
I'VE NEVER THOUGHT THAT WAY ABOUT HIM.
KNOK KNOK
SUZU... CAN WE TALK?
I SPOKE WITH SEIJI.
HE'S SERIOUS ABOUT MARRYING YOU.
I THINK HIS INJURY MADE THE MATTER MORE URGENT TO HIM.
AS YOU KNOW, HE'S A RELIABLE, HONEST MAN.
WHEN HE RECOVERS FROM HIS INJURY, HE'LL TAKE GOOD CARE OF YOU.
THAT MUCH I'M SURE OF.

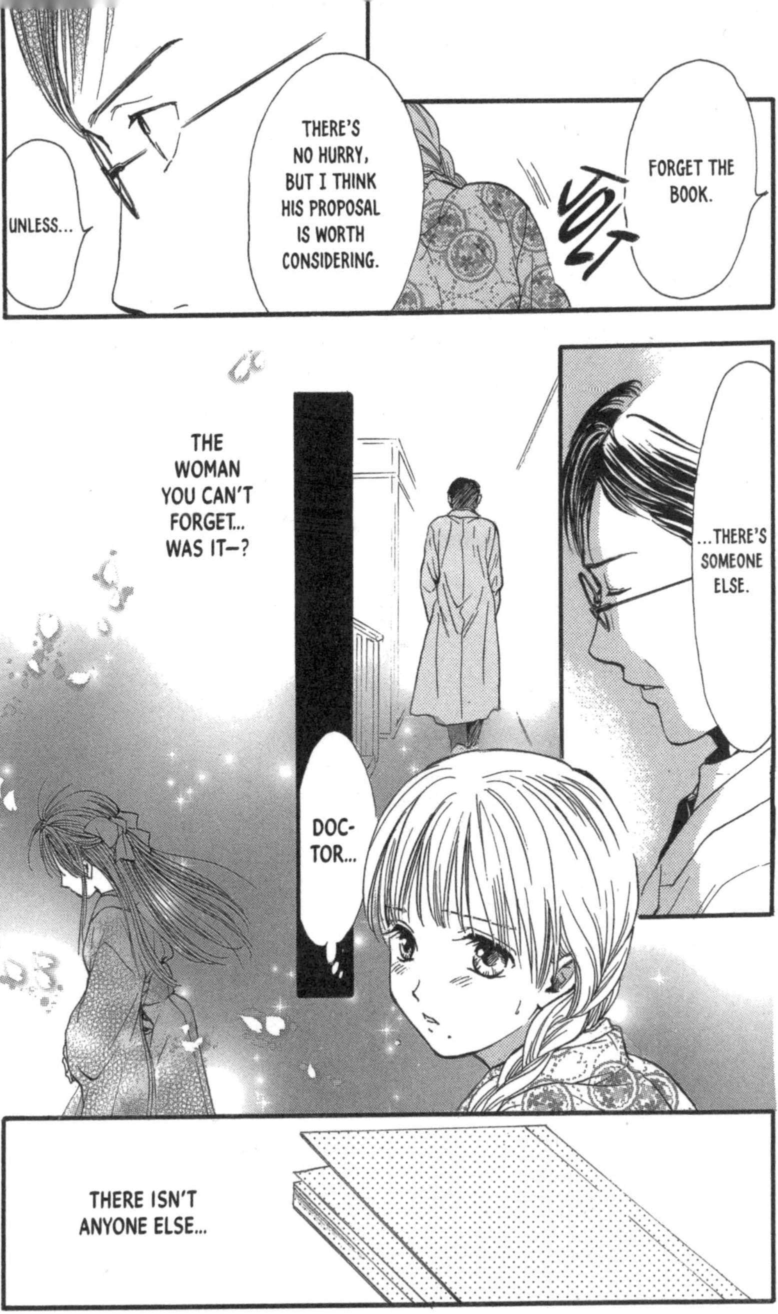
FORGET THE BOOK.
JOLT
THERE'S NO HURRY, BUT I THINK HIS PROPOSAL IS WORTH CONSIDERING.
UNLESS...
...THERE'S SOMEONE ELSE.
THE WOMAN YOU CAN'T FORGET... WAS IT—?
DOC-TOR...
THERE ISN'T ANYONE ELSE...

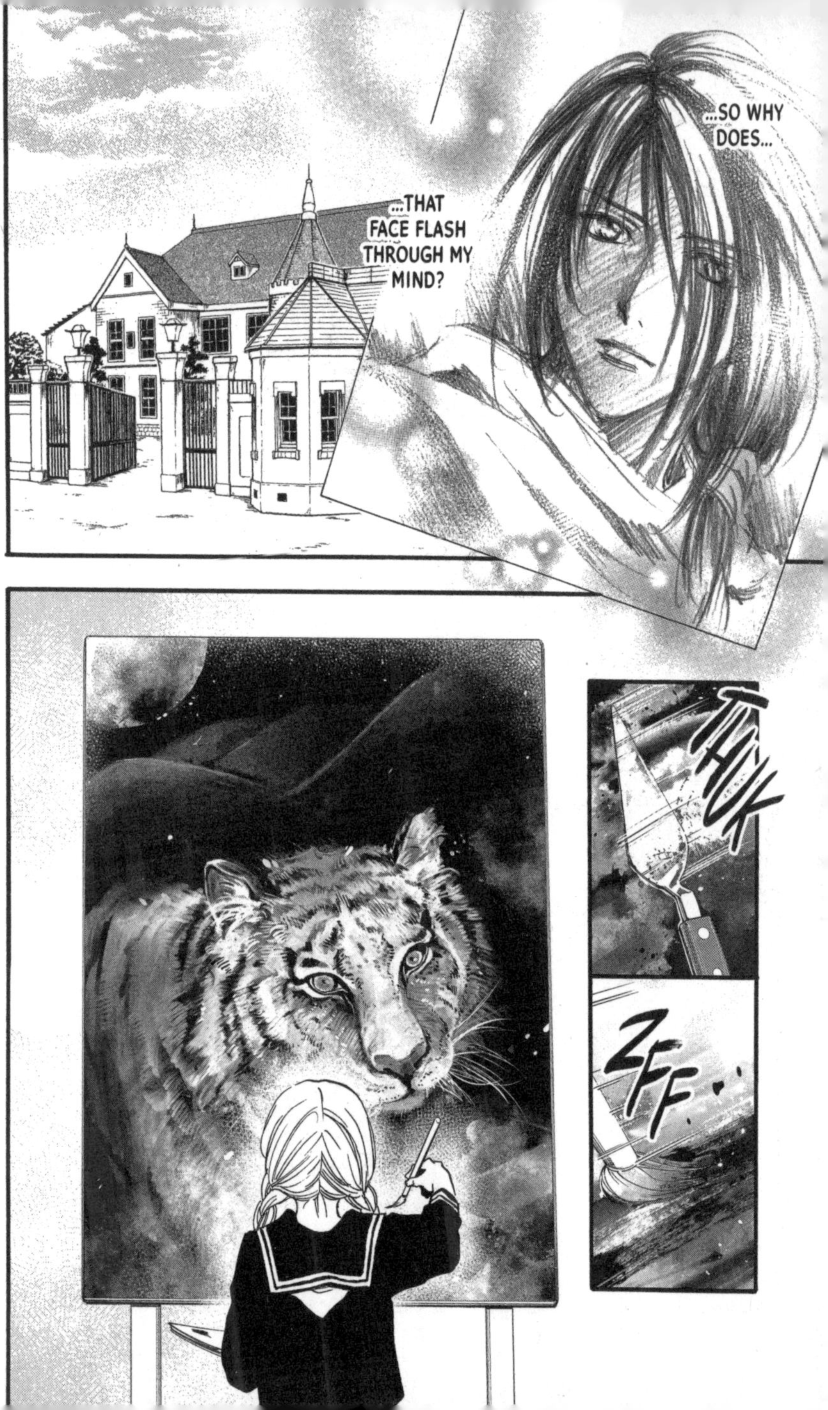
...SO WHY DOES...
...THAT FACE FLASH THROUGH MY MIND?
THUCK
ZFF

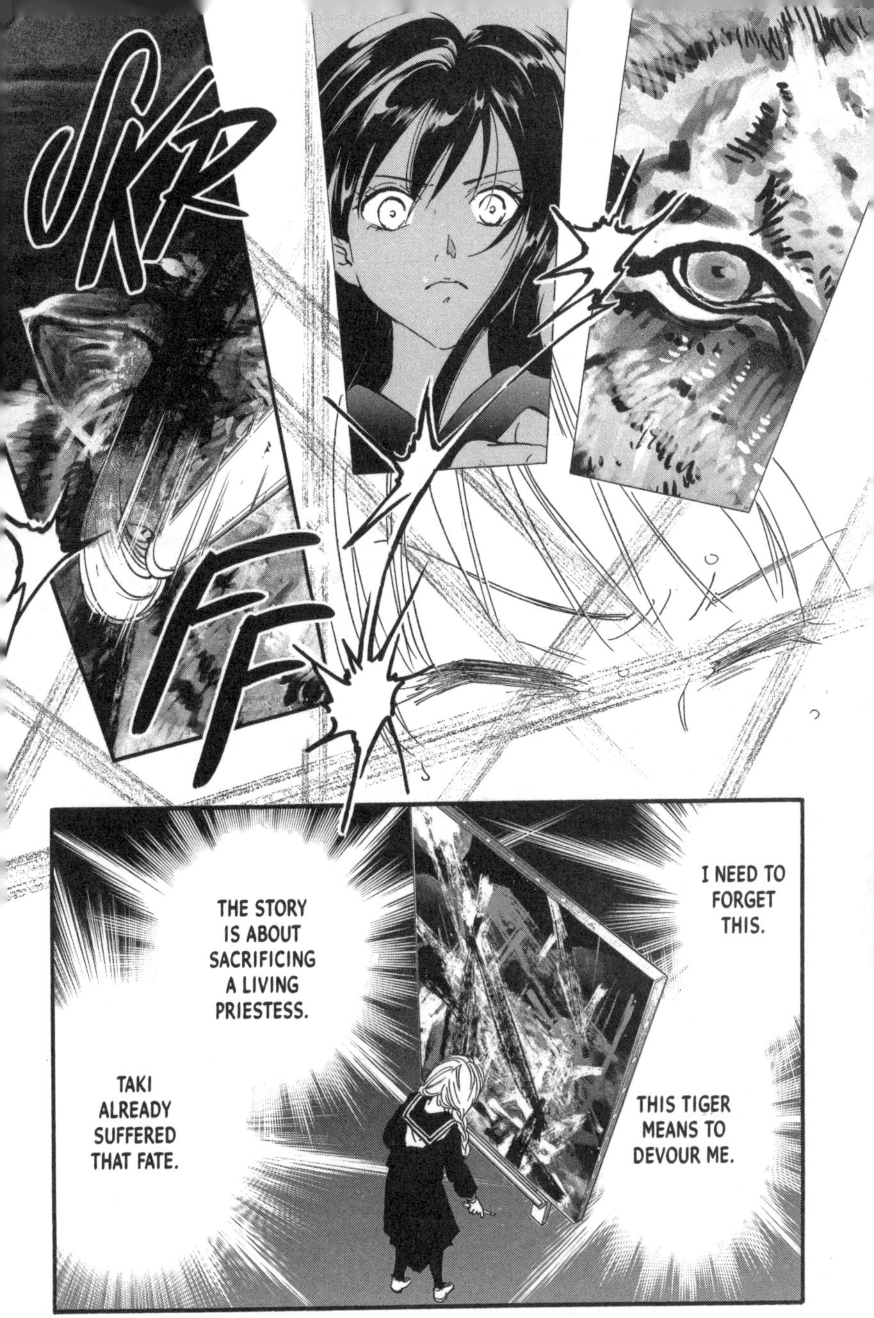
SKR
FF
I NEED TO FORGET THIS.
THE STORY IS ABOUT SACRIFICING A LIVING PRIESTESS.
THIS TIGER MEANS TO DEVOUR ME.
TAKI ALREADY SUFFERED THAT FATE.

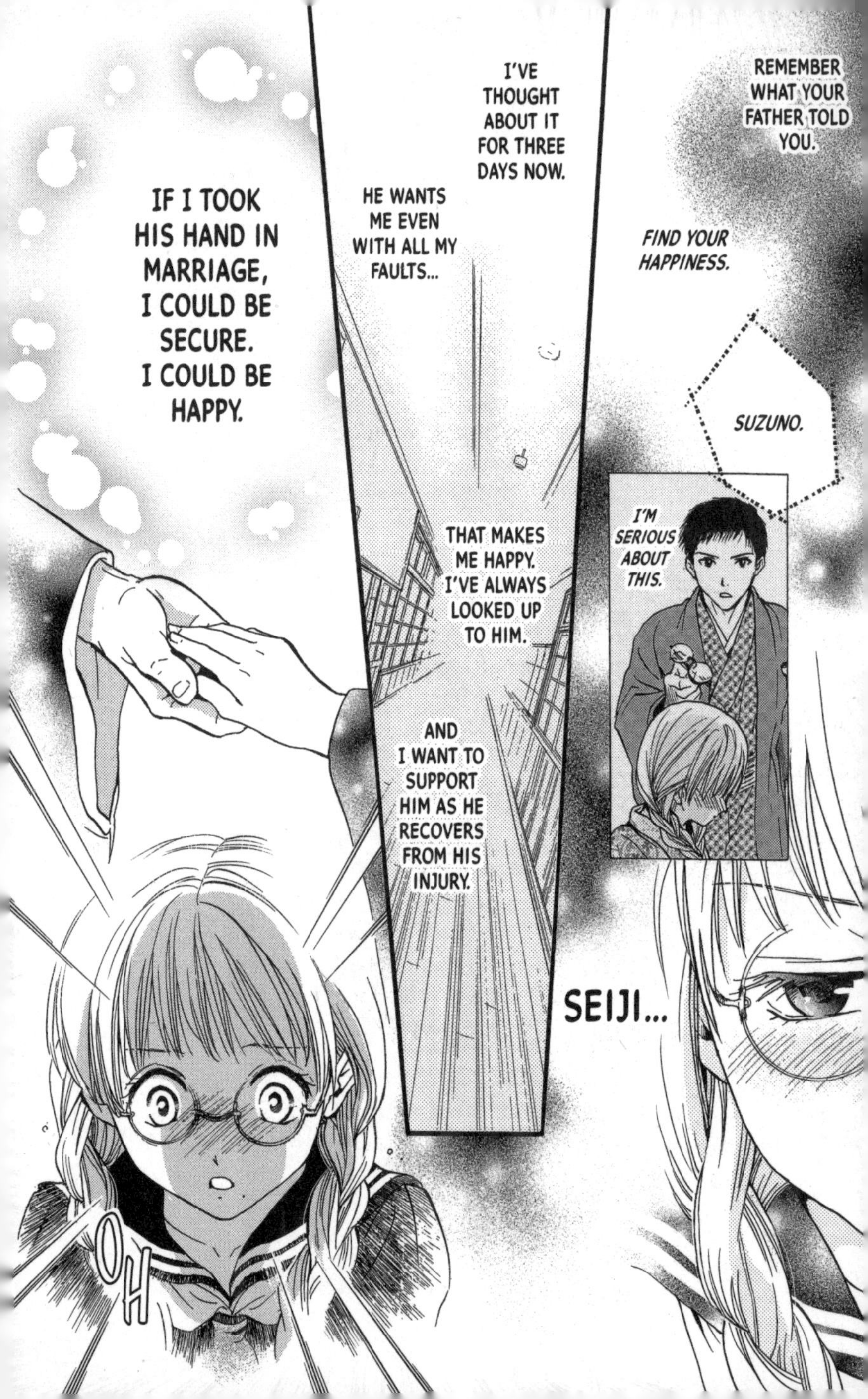
REMEMBER WHAT YOUR FATHER TOLD YOU.
FIND YOUR HAPPINESS.
SUZUNO.
I'M SERIOUS ABOUT THIS.
SEIJI...
I'VE THOUGHT ABOUT IT FOR THREE DAYS NOW.
HE WANTS ME EVEN WITH ALL MY FAULTS...
THAT MAKES ME HAPPY. I'VE ALWAYS LOOKED UP TO HIM.
AND I WANT TO SUPPORT HIM AS HE RECOVERS FROM HIS INJURY.
IF I TOOK HIS HAND IN MARRIAGE, I COULD BE SECURE. I COULD BE HAPPY.
OH

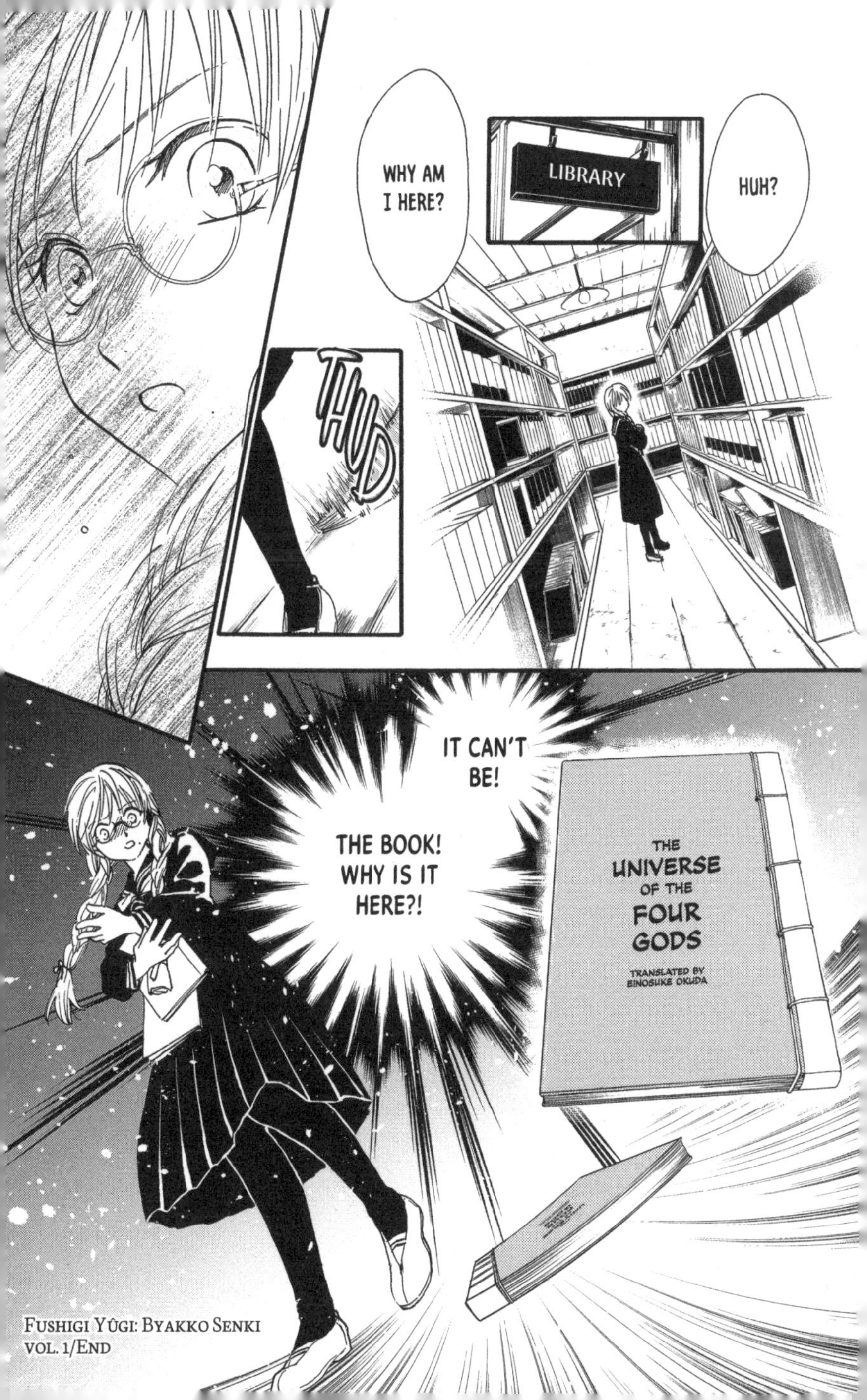
HUH?
LIBRARY
WHY AM I HERE?
THUD
IT CAN'T BE!
THE BOOK! WHY IS IT HERE?!
THE UNIVERSE OF THE FOUR GODS
TRANSLATED BY EINOSUKE OKUDA

Fushigi Yûgi: Byakko Senki
vol. 1/End

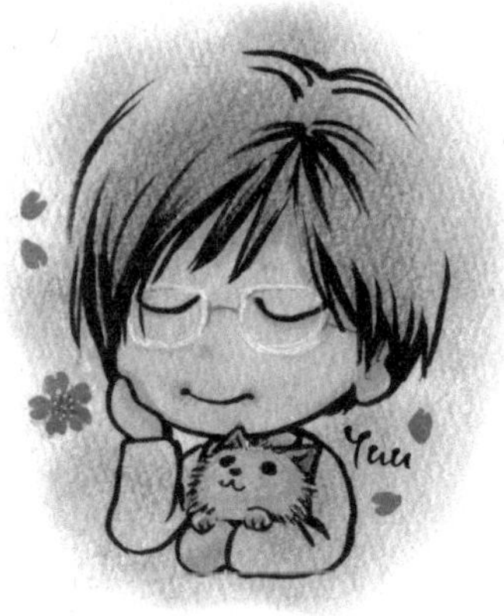
Yuu

On reflection, I've been a manga creator for quite a while now. It's been a long time since I drew the original *Fushigi Yûgi*. Time really does fly...

The Byakko story.
Going from past experience, I expect we still have a long way to go before this story is complete.

I've been thinking of taking up hot yoga lately. I just hope I can stick with it. Oh—the yoga, I mean. I'll do my best to stay fit and healthy and see the final tale of the Four Gods through to the end!

Yuu Watase

Yuu Watase debuted in the *Shôjo Comic* manga anthology in 1989. She won the 43rd Shogakukan Manga Award with *Ceres: Celestial Legend*. One of her most famous works is *Fushigi Yûgi*, a series that inspired the prequel, *Fushigi Yûgi: Genbu Kaiden*. *Byakko Senki* is the final installment in the world of *Fushigi Yûgi*.

Fushigi Yûgi
BYAKKO SENKI

VOLUME 1 · SHOJO BEAT EDITION

STORY + ART *Yuu Watase*

TRANSLATION Matt Treyvaud
TOUCH-UP ART & LETTERING Sara Linsley
DESIGN Shawn Carrico
EDITOR Nancy Thistlethwaite

FUSHIGI YUUGI BYAKKO SENKI Vol. 1
by Yuu WATASE
© 2018 Yuu WATASE
All rights reserved.
Original Japanese edition published by SHOGAKUKAN.
English translation rights in the United States of America,
Canada, the United Kingdom, Ireland, Australia
and New Zealand arranged with SHOGAKUKAN.

ORIGINAL COVER DESIGN Mikiko KOMATSU + Bay Bridge Studio

Printed in Canada

Published by VIZ Media, LLC
P.O. Box 77010
San Francisco, CA 94107

10 9 8 7 6 5 4 3 2 1
First printing, August 2020

PARENTAL ADVISORY
FUSHIGI YŪGI: BYAKKO SENKI is rated T+ for
Older Teen and is recommended for ages 16
and up. This volume contains partial nudity.

 MEDIA

viz.com   shojobeat.com

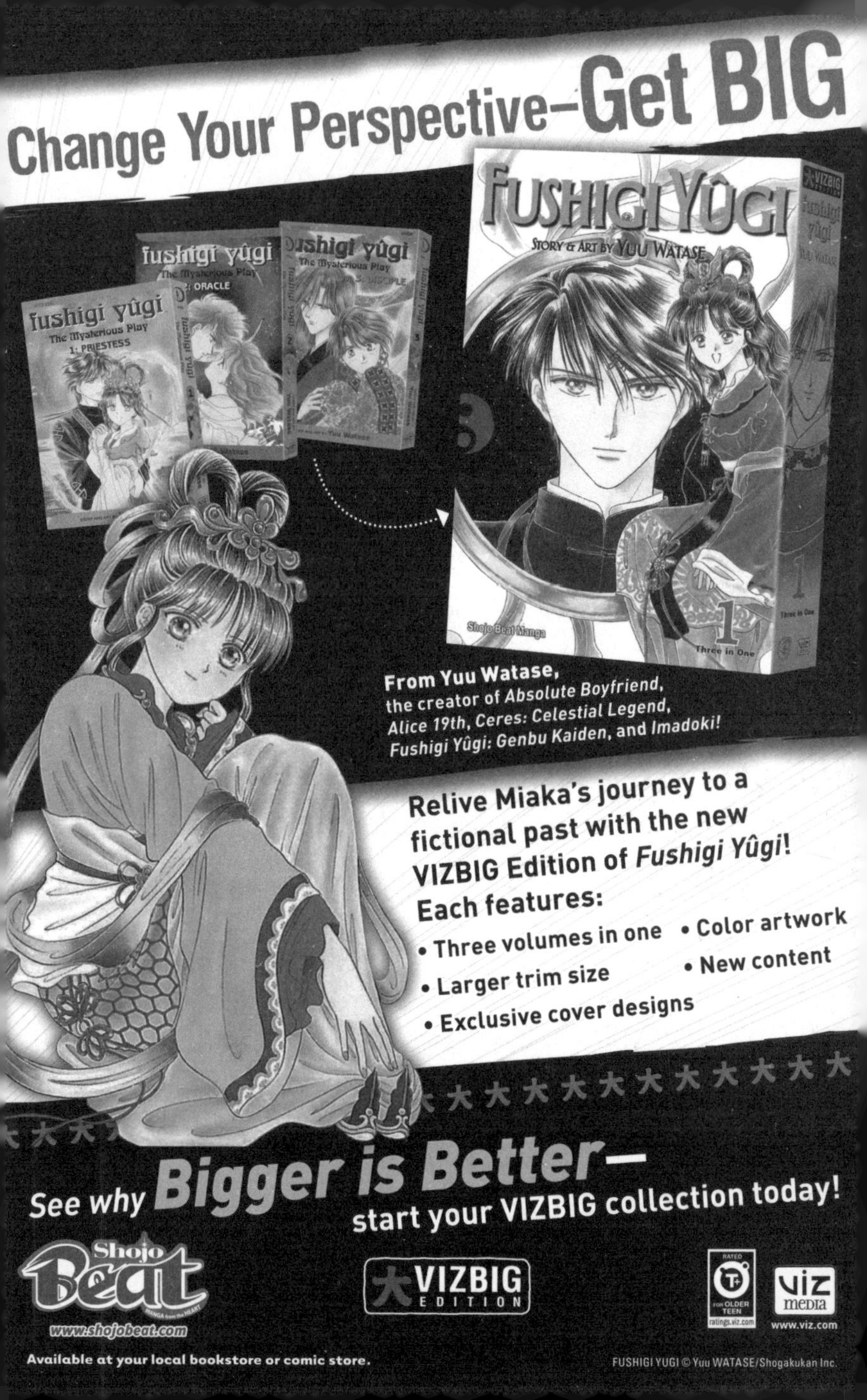
Change Your Perspective–Get BIG
FUSHIGI YÛGI
STORY & ART BY YUU WATASE
Shojo Beat Manga
1
Three in One
fushigi yûgi
The Mysterious Play
1: PRIESTESS
2: ORACLE
3: DISCIPLE
From Yuu Watase,
the creator of Absolute Boyfriend, Alice 19th, Ceres: Celestial Legend, Fushigi Yûgi: Genbu Kaiden, and Imadoki!
Relive Miaka's journey to a fictional past with the new VIZBIG Edition of Fushigi Yûgi!
Each features:
• Three volumes in one
• Larger trim size
• Exclusive cover designs
• Color artwork
• New content
See why Bigger is Better—
start your VIZBIG collection today!
Shojo Beat
MANGA from the HEART
www.shojobeat.com
VIZBIG EDITION
RATED T+ FOR OLDER TEEN
ratings.viz.com
VIZ media
www.viz.com
Available at your local bookstore or comic store.
FUSHIGI YUGI © Yuu WATASE/Shogakukan Inc.

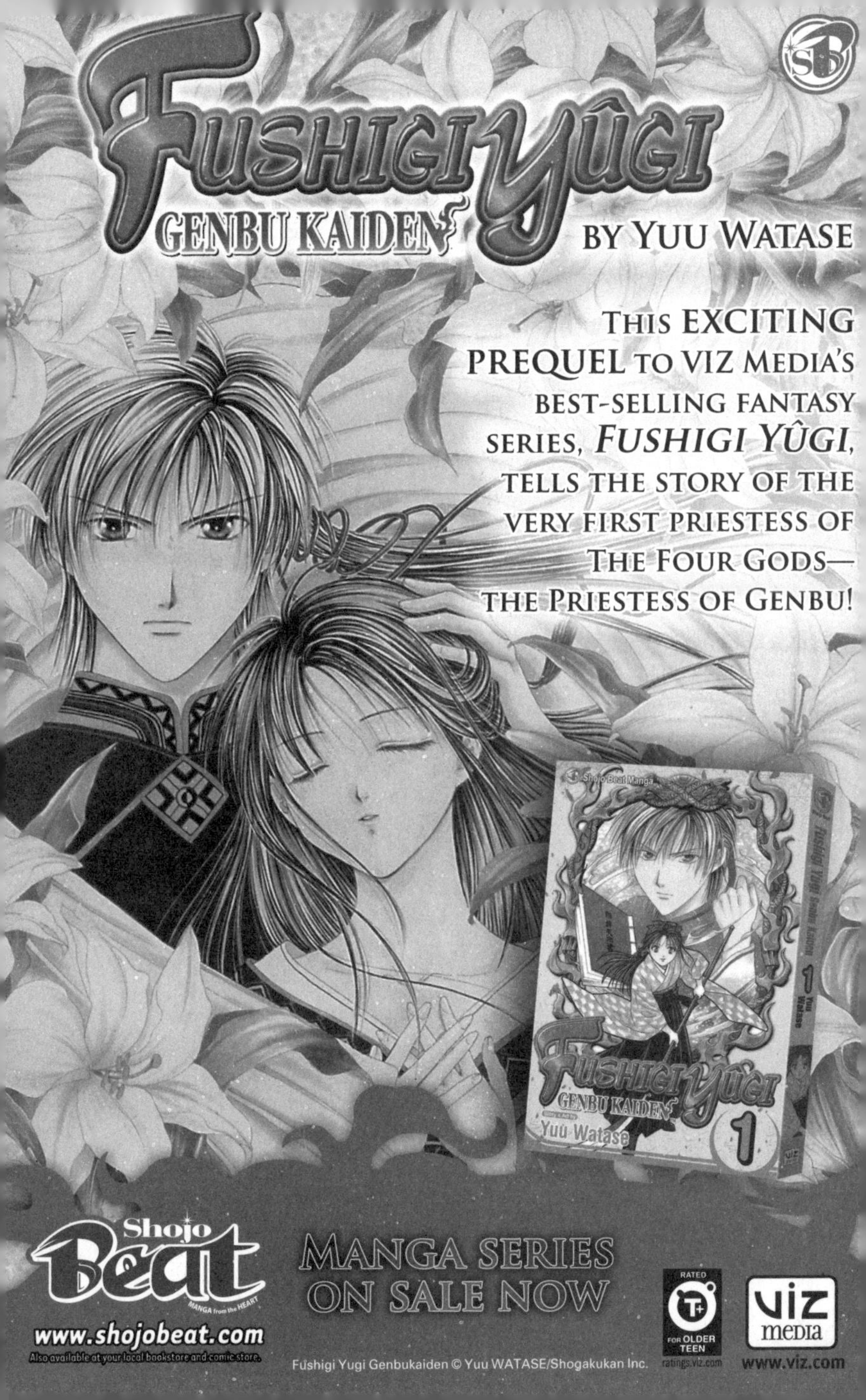
FUSHIGI YÛGI
GENBU KAIDEN
BY YUU WATASE
THIS EXCITING PREQUEL TO VIZ MEDIA'S BEST-SELLING FANTASY SERIES, FUSHIGI YÛGI, TELLS THE STORY OF THE VERY FIRST PRIESTESS OF THE FOUR GODS—THE PRIESTESS OF GENBU!
Shojo Beat Manga
Fushigi Yûgi Genbu Kaiden
1
Yuu Watase
Shojo Beat
MANGA from the HEART
www.shojobeat.com
Also available at your local bookstore and comic store.
MANGA SERIES ON SALE NOW
RATED T+ FOR OLDER TEEN
ratings.viz.com
viz media
www.viz.com
Fushigi Yugi Genbukaiden © Yuu WATASE/Shogakukan Inc.

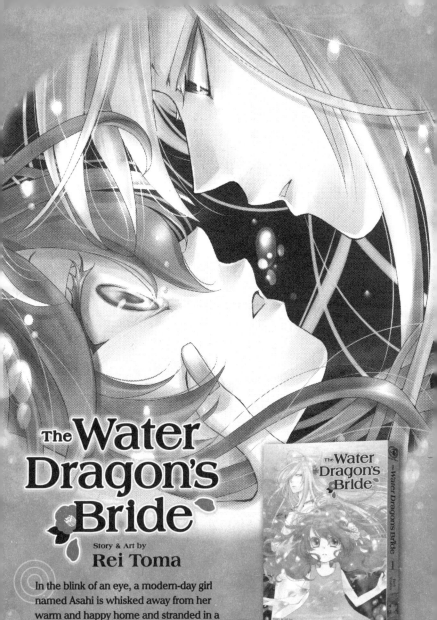

The Water Dragon's Bride

Story & Art by Rei Toma

In the blink of an eye, a modern-day girl named Asahi is whisked away from her warm and happy home and stranded in a strange and mysterious world where she meets a water dragon god!

shojobeat.com

viz media
viz.com

RATED
T
FOR
TEEN

QQ sweeper

Story & Art by
Kyousuke Motomi

By the creator of *Dengeki Daisy* and *Beast Master*!

One day, Kyutaro Horikita, the tall, dark and handsome cleaning expert of Kurokado High, comes across a sleeping maiden named Fumi Nishioka at school... Unfortunately, their meeting is anything but a fairy-tale encounter! It turns out Kyutaro is a "Sweeper" who cleans away negative energy from people's hearts—and Fumi is about to become his apprentice!

THIS IS
THE LAST PAGE.

In keeping with the original Japanese comic format,
this book reads from right to left—so action, sound
effects and word balloons are completely reversed to
preserve the orientation of the original artwork. Check
out the diagram shown here to get the hang of things,
and then turn to the other side of the book to get started.

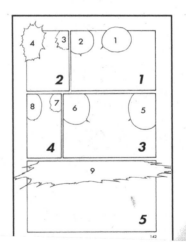